Investigating and Combating Gender–Related Victimization

Gabriela Mesquita Borges
University of Lusiada, Portugal

Ana Guerreiro
University of Maia, Portugal & School of Criminology, Faculty of Law, University of Porto, Portugal

Miriam Pina
School of Criminology, Faculty of Law, University of Porto, Portugal & Faculté de Droit, des Sciences Criminelles et d'administration Publique, Université de Lausanne, Switzerland

A volume in the Advances in
Information Security, Privacy, and
Ethics (AISPE) Book Series

Published in the United States of America by
    IGI Global
    Information Science Reference (an imprint of IGI Global)
    701 E. Chocolate Avenue
    Hershey PA, USA 17033
    Tel: 717-533-8845
    Fax: 717-533-8661
    E-mail: cust@igi-global.com
    Web site: http://www.igi-global.com

Library of Congress Cataloging-in-Publication Data

CIP Pending
ISBN: 979-8-3693-5436-0
EISBN: 979-8-3693-5438-4

British Cataloguing in Publication Data
A Cataloguing in Publication record for this book is available from the British Library.

All work contributed to this book is new, previously-unpublished material.
The views expressed in this book are those of the authors, but not necessarily of the publisher.

For electronic access to this publication, please contact: eresources@igi-global.com.

Advances in Information Security, Privacy, and Ethics (AISPE) Book Series

ISSN:1948-9730
EISSN:1948-9749

Editor-in-Chief: Manish Gupta, State University of New York, USA

MISSION

As digital technologies become more pervasive in everyday life and the Internet is utilized in ever increasing ways by both private and public entities, concern over digital threats becomes more prevalent.

The **Advances in Information Security, Privacy, & Ethics (AISPE) Book Series** provides cutting-edge research on the protection and misuse of information and technology across various industries and settings. Comprised of scholarly research on topics such as identity management, cryptography, system security, authentication, and data protection, this book series is ideal for reference by IT professionals, academicians, and upper-level students.

COVERAGE

- CIA Triad of Information Security
- Computer ethics
- Global Privacy Concerns
- Privacy Issues of Social Networking
- Privacy-Enhancing Technologies
- Telecommunications Regulations
- Internet Governance
- Electronic Mail Security
- IT Risk
- Risk Management

IGI Global is currently accepting manuscripts for publication within this series. To submit a proposal for a volume in this series, please contact our Acquisition Editors at Acquisitions@igi-global.com or visit: http://www.igi-global.com/publish/.

Titles in this Series

For a list of additional titles in this series, please visit:
http://www.igi-global.com/book-series/advances-information-security-privacy-ethics/37157

Navigating Cyber Threats and Cybersecurity in the Logistics Industry
Noor Zaman Jhanjhi (School of Computing Science, Taylor's University, Malaysia) and
Imdad Ali Shah (School of Computing Science, Taylor's University, Malaysia)
Information Science Reference • copyright 2024 • 448pp • H/C (ISBN: 9798369338162)
• US $295.00 (our price)

Analyzing and Mitigating Security Risks in Cloud Computing
Pawan Kumar Goel (Raj Kumar Goel Institute of Technology, India) Hari Mohan Pandey
(Bournemouth University, UK) Amit Singhal (Raj Kumar Goel Institute of Technology,
India) and Sanyam Agarwal (ACE Group of Colleges, India)
Engineering Science Reference • copyright 2024 • 270pp • H/C (ISBN: 9798369332498)
• US $290.00 (our price)

Cybersecurity Issues and Challenges in the Drone Industry
Imdad Ali Shah (School of Computing Science, Taylor's University, Malaysia) and Noor
Zaman Jhanjhi (School of Computing Science, Taylor's University, Malaysia)
Information Science Reference • copyright 2024 • 573pp • H/C (ISBN: 9798369307748)
• US $275.00 (our price)

Emerging Technologies and Security in Cloud Computing
D. Lakshmi (VIT Bhopal University, India) and Amit Kumar Tyagi (National Institute of
Fashion Technology, New Delhi, India)
Information Science Reference • copyright 2024 • 539pp • H/C (ISBN: 9798369320815)
• US $315.00 (our price)

Improving Security, Privacy, and Trust in Cloud Computing
Pawan Kumar Goel (Raj Kumar Goel Institute of Technology, India) Hari Mohan Pandey
(Bournemouth University, UK) Amit Singhal (Raj Kumar Goel Institute of Technology,
India) and Sanyam Agarwal (ACE Group of Colleges, India)

For an entire list of titles in this series, please visit:
http://www.igi-global.com/book-series/advances-information-security-privacy-ethics/37157

701 East Chocolate Avenue, Hershey, PA 17033, USA
Tel: 717-533-8845 x100 • Fax: 717-533-8661
E-Mail: cust@igi-global.com • www.igi-global.com

Table of Contents

Detailed Table of Contents

Chapter 1
Sílvia Ribeiro, Universidade Lusíada do Norte, Portugal

This literature review explores the intricate relationship between substance abuse, sexual dysfunction, and victimization, emphasizing a multifaceted victimological perspective. It delves into research on how expectations regarding sexuality impact and are impacted by sexual dysfunction and drug consumption, affecting mental and emotional well-being. The cycle of initial relief from drugs turning into dependency worsens sexual difficulties and emotional distress. This interplay strains interpersonal relationships, causing communication breakdowns and emotional distance. The comprehensive perspective advocates for empathetic interventions, highlighting the importance of a holistic approach that considers physical and psychological aspects. It stresses open communication and support systems, with trauma-informed approaches crucial for breaking the cycle of victimization and fostering meaningful recovery. Recognizing and addressing these intersections promotes healthier relationships, both with oneself and others.

Chapter 2
*Bárbara Machado, NOVA National School of Public Health, NOVA
    University of Lisboa, Portugal*
*Sónia Maria Martins Caridade, Psychology Research Center, School of
    Psychology, University of Minho, Braga, Portugal*

Cyber interpersonal abuse refers to the detrimental and harmful behaviours that occur within digital communication platforms, encompassing a wide range of negative interactions such as cyber dating abuse, cyberbullying, online harassment, stalking, and various other forms of online aggression. This chapter investigates the nuanced perspectives of adolescents concerning cyber interpersonal abuse, with a particular focus on the profiling of both victims and offenders. Fifteen focus groups were held to collect data, with 108 adolescents, 42 boys and 66 girls, aged between 11 and 15 years (M= 12.87; SD=0.31). The findings unveil adolescents' perceptions of cyber interpersonal abuse, depicting a female victim and a male aggressor profile. The results underscore a nuanced understanding of the dynamics, emphasizing gender complexities. This chapter aims to enhance comprehension of the intricacies of interpersonal cyber interpersonal abuse among adolescents. Additionally, it discusses preventive strategies and outlines future research challenges.

Chapter 3

Gabriela Mesquita Borges, University of Lusíada, Portugal

This chapter explores the complex landscape of asylum-seeking, focusing on the 1951 Refugee Convention and the rights it grants to those seeking refuge, emphasizing principles like non-discrimination and non-refoulement. The chapter highlights the tension between international legal guarantees and state discretion in granting asylum, underscoring the gap between aspirational goals and practical outcomes. It also delves into scholarly literature on migration, border control, and the "deviant migrant" narrative, offering insights into the complexities of asylum practices. It addresses criminological and gendered dimensions, with a specific focus on violence against asylum-seeking women, revealing unique challenges. Overall, the analysis covers historical perspectives, contemporary challenges, and evolving global migration dynamics, providing a comprehensive understanding of the intricate journey asylum seekers undergo for safety and justice.

Chapter 4

Gabriela Mesquita Borges, University of Lusíada, Portugal

Establishing a life in an asylum country presents an exceptionally daunting challenge, particularly for women. In asylum countries, women encounter numerous hurdles like healthcare, language barriers, economic empowerment, childcare, education, cultural adjustment, legal issues, and more. This chapter comprehensively analyzes reception conditions and integration practices in the Portuguese asylum system from a gender perspective, covering seven critical areas: housing, financial support, healthcare, psychological assistance, education, labor market integration, and legal aid. Through 49 interviews (with asylum-seeking women and with professionals working in the Portuguese asylum system), this research unveils deficiencies in support, mainly due to the absence of gender-specific approaches. The chapter aims to promote gender-sensitive policies and practices to aid asylum-seeking women.

Chapter 5

Nathália Castro da Silva, University of Porto, Portugal
Rita Faria, School of Criminology, University of Porto, Portugal

Gender and migration status add to the risk of certain people being victims and have been considered, from an intersectionality perspective, added vulnerabilities to some social groups. Likewise, it can negatively affect the experience that victims have with the police when reporting a crime suffered to the authorities, which can generate secondary victimisation and impact people's lives. This chapter presents the results of empirical research about the experiences of victimised migrant women with the criminal police in Portugal, analysed from a narrative victimology approach under the intersectional lens. Data was collected using semi-structured interviews, and by conducting a narrative analysis, it was found that most migrants suffered secondary victimisation, this situation also being influenced by gender and migrant status. Critical methodological issues will also be dealt with, including the recruitment of participants and the reflexivity of the first author, a migrant herself, researching migrant women.

Chapter 6

Joana Torres, University of Maia, Portugal
Jorge Gracia Ibáñez, Universidad San Jorge, Spain
Sónia Maria Martins Caridade, Psychology Research Center, School of
    Psychology, University of Minho, Braga, Portugal

The Istanbul Convention stands out as a crucial and pioneering tool in addressing gender-based violence (GBV) and violence against women (VAW) within the European context. Recognizing the significance of police responses to such violence, this qualitative study aims to analyze and comprehend the implementation of police officers' responses to intimate partner violence in Portugal, while considering the principles outlined in the Istanbul Convention. Thirteen interviews (M = 46; S.D. = 13.3) were conducted with professionals involved in police response, evenly distributed across Portugal. The objective was to explore their experiences in providing responses to intimate and GBV, which were then scrutinized against the recommendations outlined in the Group of Experts' Report to Combat Violence Against Women and Domestic Violence. The findings revealed a significant gap in knowledge among first-line response personnel regarding the phenomenon. While the establishment of specialized groups within the police force, such as the Investigation and Support Centers for Specific Victims (NIAVE), was viewed as an important and positive resource, it was deemed insufficient due to heavy workloads, resulting in the prioritization of higher-risk cases. Despite the implementation of a risk assessment instrument, there was a notable lack of understanding among professionals regarding its application. The investigation yielded several recommendations for enhancing these responses, including a substantial investment in training for police responses to GBV and bolstering the capacity of NIAVE to ensure effective management of all domestic violence (DV) cases.

Chapter 7
Camila Iglesias, Faculty of Law, University of Porto, Portugal

In recent decades, research on the fear of crime has significantly expanded within the fields of criminology and victimology. Similarly, studies on gender-based violence have also increased, particularly concerning domestic violence and intimate partner violence (IPV) perpetrated against women. Criminological evidence has consistently shown that women report high levels of fear of crime, despite having a lower risk of becoming victims of common (or street) crimes. The disparity between women's fear and risk has given rise to what is known as the "fear-victimization paradox," and several theories have been proposed over time to explain this paradox. However, an apparent dichotomy between public and private spaces still influences empirical evidence, and researchers have often overlooked the effects of domestic violence and IPV on women's fear of crime. This theoretical chapter aims to shed light on a better understanding of this fear-victimization paradox. It seeks to provide an integrated approach to the concepts of women's fear of crime and IPV. Moreover, it will delve into the potential repercussions of this type of victimization and fear on women's quality of life and daily routines, thereby illuminating promising avenues for future research in this crucial area.

Chapter 8
Ariana Correia, University of Maia, Portugal & CIEG (ISCSP-ULisbon), Portugal
Mafalda Ferreira, CIEG (ISCSP-ULisbon), Portugal
Joana Topa, University of Maia, Portugal & CIEG (ISCSP-ULisbon), Portugal
Estefânia Gonçalves Silva, University of Maia, Portugal & CIEG (ISCSP-ULisbon), Portugal
Sofia Neves, University of Maia, Portugal & CIEG (ISCSP-ULisbon), Portugal

This chapter presents the main characteristics of intimate partner violence perpetrated in Portugal, discussing policy, legal, and academic advances in the last three decades. Although relevant steps have been taken concerning victims' rights, with children and women benefiting from policies, legislation, mechanisms, and resources, domestic violence and partner homicide rates are still high, suggesting that measures and strategies to prevent and combat this have not been effective. Future directions are discussed regarding cultural, social, and scientific issues.

Chapter 9

        Cynthia Leite da Silva, University of Porto, Portugal

LGBTI+ people are victims of different forms of violence all over the world, from situations of hate, discrimination, LGBTI+ phobic bullying, domestic violence, and even violence within intimate relationships. A large part of this violence sends a message to the community: a message of intolerance and non-acceptance. These are acts that undermine the dignity and identity of the victims. This chapter therefore aims to specify these forms of violence, outlining and understanding the differential impact that violence has on LGBTI+ victims. At the same time, it seeks to list some measures that can contribute to combating or reducing the occurrence of this violence.

Chapter 10

        Catarina Capucho Conde, Universidade Lusíada, Portugal
        Fabiana Rodrigues Gonçalves, Universidade Lusíada, Portugal
        Beatriz Filipa Andrade, Universidade Lusíada, Portugal

This chapter delves into the intricate intersectionality of transgender identity and involvement in prostitution, shedding light on the heightened vulnerability of transgender prostitutes to sexual and physical violence. The primary focus of this chapter is an exploration of the challenges encountered during a qualitative and criminological study aimed at collecting first-hand accounts through semi-structured interviews with transgender prostitutes. Despite the importance of this research, building a representative sample proved to be notably difficult, highlighting the complexity of engaging this marginalized population in research endeavors. By addressing these challenges, the chapter aims to contribute to the broader discourse on the victimological phenomenon affecting transgender prostitutes and emphasizes the critical importance of overcoming obstacles in conducting empirical research in this field. The ultimate goal is to facilitate future scientific inquiry by raising awareness about the intricacies of researching violence against transgender prostitutes.

Preface

In the ever-evolving landscape of victimology, where the complexities of victimization intersect with the dynamics of justice, our pursuit as editors of *Investigating and Combating Gender-Related Victimization* has been guided by a steadfast commitment to comprehensively unravel the multifaceted dimensions of victim experiences. Rooted in the recognition of victimology as an emerging and dynamic field of study, we embarked on this journey with a resolute determination to provide an invaluable resource that transcends disciplinary boundaries.

As scholars and practitioners hailing from esteemed institutions such as the University of Lusiada, the University of Maia, and the University of Porto, our collaborative effort has been driven by a shared vision to redefine the discourse surrounding victimization. With each page of this handbook, our aim has been to offer not merely a compendium of knowledge, but a beacon of innovation and boldness in understanding and addressing the challenges faced by victims in contemporary society.

The urgency for a modern handbook dedicated to victimology has become increasingly evident in the face of evolving forms of victimization and the corresponding demands placed upon researchers, practitioners, policymakers, and educators. It is within this context that "Modern Insights and Strategies in Victimology" emerges as a pioneering endeavor, seeking to bridge the gap between theory and practice while fostering a deeper, more empathetic understanding of victim experiences.

ORGANIZATION OF THE BOOK

In *Investigating and Combating Gender-Related Victimization*, each chapter offers a unique lens through which to understand the complexities of victimization in contemporary society. Chapter 1 provides a comprehensive literature review, unraveling the intricate relationship between substance abuse, sexual dysfunction, and victimization. It emphasizes a multifaceted victimological perspective, delving into the profound impact of drug consumption on sexual well-being and emotional distress. Through empathetic interventions and trauma-informed approaches, this chapter advocates for holistic support systems to break the cycle of victimization and foster meaningful recovery.

Chapter 2 navigates the realm of cyber interpersonal abuse, shedding light on the detrimental behaviors that occur within digital communication platforms. With a focus on adolescents' perspectives, the chapter examines cyberbullying, online harassment, and other forms of online aggression. By profiling both victims and offenders, it offers nuanced insights into the gender complexities inherent in cyber interpersonal abuse, while also outlining preventive strategies and future research challenges.

In Chapter 3, the focus shifts to the complex landscape of asylum-seeking, exploring the rights and challenges faced by those seeking refuge. It critically analyzes the tension between international legal guarantees and state discretion, highlighting the unique struggles of asylum-seeking women. By addressing historical perspectives and contemporary challenges, this chapter offers a comprehensive understanding of the intricate journey asylum seekers undergo for safety and justice.

Chapter 4 delves into the challenges faced by asylum-seeking women as they establish a life in an asylum country, particularly in Portugal. Through a gender perspective, it examines reception conditions and integration practices, unveiling deficiencies in support and advocating for gender-sensitive policies and practices.

Gender and migration status intersect in Chapter 5, adding layers of vulnerability for victimized migrant women. Through empirical research, this chapter examines their experiences with the criminal police in Portugal, revealing instances of secondary victimization influenced by gender and migrant status. Methodological issues are also addressed, offering insights into narrative victimology under an intersectional lens.

Chapter 6 shifts focus to police responses to intimate partner violence in Portugal. Through qualitative analysis, it uncovers knowledge gaps and challenges in implementing the Istanbul Convention principles. Recommendations include substantial investment in training for police responses to gender-based violence.

The fear-victimization paradox takes center stage in Chapter 7, as the chapter seeks to provide an integrated approach to understanding women's fear of crime and intimate partner violence. By examining the disparities between fear and risk, it aims to shed light on the complex dynamics influencing women's perceptions of safety.

In Chapter 8, the spotlight is on intimate partner violence in Portugal, analyzing policy, legal, and academic advancements. Despite efforts to address victims' rights, domestic violence rates remain high, prompting discussions on future directions for prevention and intervention strategies.

Chapter 9 explores the various forms of violence faced by LGBTI+ individuals worldwide, from hate crimes to domestic violence. By outlining the differential impact of violence on LGBTI+ victims and proposing measures for combatting it, the chapter aims to promote acceptance and reduce occurrences of violence within the community.

Lastly, Chapter 10 delves into the intersectionality of transgender identity and involvement in prostitution. Through a qualitative study, it highlights the heightened vulnerability of transgender prostitutes to sexual and physical violence, while also addressing the challenges of engaging this marginalized population in research endeavors.

Together, these chapters offer a comprehensive exploration of victimology, spanning a wide range of topics and perspectives. It is our hope that this edited reference book will serve as a valuable resource for researchers, practitioners, policymakers, and anyone interested in understanding and addressing the complexities of victimization in our society.

Central to our approach is the recognition that victimology is not a static field, but one that continues to evolve alongside the changing nature of victimization itself. From paradigm shifts in theoretical frameworks to innovative responses such as restorative justice, our handbook traverses the vast terrain of victimology with a keen eye toward both historical perspectives and future possibilities.

Through a unique structure that combines theoretical discourse with empirical research rooted in qualitative methodologies, we invite readers to embark on a journey of exploration into the intricate dimensions of victim experiences. From the historical context of victimology to the special needs of specific populations, from innovative intervention models to strategies for preventing re-victimization, each chapter serves as a testament to our unwavering commitment to advancing the field of victimology.

It is our sincere hope that *Investigating and Combating Gender-Related Victimization* will serve as more than a reference work—it is our aspiration that it will spark conversations, inspire new avenues of research, and ultimately, contribute to the creation of a more just and compassionate society.

CONCLUSION

In conclusion, *Investigating and Combating Gender-Related Victimization* represents a collaborative effort to navigate the complex and evolving landscape of victimization. As editors, our commitment has been to provide a comprehensive resource that transcends disciplinary boundaries and fosters a deeper understanding of victim experiences in contemporary society.

Each chapter of this edited reference book offers a unique perspective, from unraveling the intricate relationship between substance abuse and victimization to exploring the challenges faced by asylum-seeking women. Through empirical research, theoretical discourse, and practical recommendations, these chapters shed light on the multifaceted dimensions of victimology, addressing topics ranging from cyber interpersonal abuse to intimate partner violence.

Central to our approach is the recognition that victimology is not static; it continues to evolve alongside the changing nature of victimization itself. By combining theoretical frameworks with empirical research rooted in qualitative methodologies, we invite readers to explore the intricate dimensions of victim experiences and consider innovative strategies for prevention and intervention.

Ultimately, our hope is that *Investigating and Combating Gender-Related Victimization* will serve as more than just a reference work. It is our aspiration that it will inspire conversations, spark new avenues of research, and contribute to the creation of a more just and compassionate society. We extend our gratitude to the contributors, researchers, practitioners, policymakers, and educators who have joined us in this endeavor.

Gabriela Mesquita Borges
University of Lusiada, Portugal

Ana Guerreiro
University of Maia, Portugal & School of Criminology, Faculty of Law,
University of Porto, Portugal

Miriam Pina
School of Criminology, Faculty of Law, University of Porto, Portugal

Chapter 1
Also, Victims of Expectations:
The Double Bias Complexity
of Drugs and Sexuality

Sílvia Ribeiro
Universidade Lusíada do Norte, Portugal

ABSTRACT

This literature review explores the intricate relationship between substance abuse, sexual dysfunction, and victimization, emphasizing a multifaceted victimological perspective. It delves into research on how expectations regarding sexuality impact and are impacted by sexual dysfunction and drug consumption, affecting mental and emotional well-being. The cycle of initial relief from drugs turning into dependency worsens sexual difficulties and emotional distress. This interplay strains interpersonal relationships, causing communication breakdowns and emotional distance. The comprehensive perspective advocates for empathetic interventions, highlighting the importance of a holistic approach that considers physical and psychological aspects. It stresses open communication and support systems, with trauma-informed approaches crucial for breaking the cycle of victimization and fostering meaningful recovery. Recognizing and addressing these intersections promotes healthier relationships, both with oneself and others.

INTRODUCTION

A recognition of the existence of societies without drugs is inevitable. Consumption patterns vary according to cultural, social, heritage, and economic contexts. Since the 1990s, there has been a notable increase in research focusing on substance

DOI: 10.4018/979-8-3693-5436-0.ch001

dependence (Ferros, 2011). The abuse of alcohol and drugs has emerged as a central issue in Western society, impacting diverse populations (Konvalina-Simas, 2012).

The repercussions of drug consumption manifest directly or indirectly in organic pathologies, such as hepatitis, acquired immunodeficiency syndrome (AIDS), or multidrug-resistant tuberculosis. They also extend to psychosocial pathologies of considerable magnitude, including crime, prostitution, or delinquency. In today's society, the prevailing pursuit of success at all costs, coupled with the shortcomings in civic and health education, exposes citizens increasingly to stimuli for engaging in addictive risk behaviours (Patrício, 2014).

The intricate interplay between substance abuse and societal challenges significantly impacts various aspects of individuals' lives. One pivotal facet affected is sexuality—a central dimension of the human condition. It encompasses issues of sexual relations, gender identity, sexual role and orientation, eroticism, pleasure, intimacy, and reproduction (WHO, 2019). The experience of sexuality is intricately woven into the broader fabric of an individual's well-being.

Furthermore, the experience of sexuality is shaped by a combination of psychological and organic conditions. These include factors such as the nature of the relationship, aspects related to the partner, medical considerations, and individual vulnerability factors. Additionally, family and peer groups wield substantial influence over the sexual behaviour of their members (Matos, 2010). Recognized as a sphere of human behaviour with profound significance, sexuality varies in importance from person to person, emerging as both a challenging and fascinating individual concern.

The impact of drug use on human sexuality is diverse, often manifesting through observable and objective negative effects. This influence on sexual response involves various components and is influenced by multiple factors, including biological, psychological, and sociocultural elements (Gómez & Cartón, 2006).

While the consequences of drug use on sexuality are undeniably significant, researchers like La Pera and his team emphasize the importance of examining the reciprocal influence. In their work, they argue that it is equally, if not more crucial, to assess how sexual dysfunctions influence behaviour, health decisions, and drug consumption (La Pera et al., 2008a).

The potential role of expectations as a cognitive mediator and predictor of behaviour has been studied extensively across various stages of human experience. In the context of psychoactive substance use, expectations refer to individual beliefs that develop before the actual experience. These beliefs are held by an individual regarding the positive and negative effects of consuming the substance in a specific manner (Labbe & Maisto, 2011). What do people anticipate gaining from the consumption of illicit substances? What expectations exist regarding the impact that drug consumption can have on the expression and experience of human sexuality, as well as on individuals and their overall well-being?

We aim to explore the intersection of drug addiction and the anticipated impact of drugs on sexuality as an intensified factor of vulnerability within this demographic. This analysis delves into the complex dynamics that cast substance users as victims, particularly within the context of their sexual lives. This effort aligns with the ongoing pursuit to *"deconstruct normalization, homogenization and classification, increasing more democracy and equality in the complexity of the socio-cultural categories and identities."* (Knudsen, 2006, pp.74).

BACKGROUND

1. Sexuality and Addiction

The historical use of diverse substances with psychoactive properties has been closely linked to human history, adapting to the prevailing norms of different periods and cultures. These substances found application in various contexts, including religious, social, mystical, economic, cultural, medicinal, psychological, and military, primarily driven by the pursuit of pleasure. The Age of Discovery witnessed a notable contribution from the Portuguese, introducing substances with euphoric and stimulating properties to the Old Continent. The Industrial Revolution, the rise of capitalism, urban concentration, and increased interactions with other continents marked a period where the consumption of psychoactive drugs reached concerning levels (Ferreira-Borges & Filho, 2004).

The European Drug Report: Trends and Developments (EMCDDA, 2022) estimates that 83.4 million, or 29% of the European adult population (aged 15-64), have ever experimented with illicit drugs. It emphasizes that the majority of individuals with drug consumption issues use a variety of substances. The report summarizes the identified drug trends with the statement: Everywhere (we can observe the effects of the drug phenomenon everywhere), everything (anything with psychoactive potential risks appearing in the market), everyone (directly or indirectly, we are all affected by drug consumption).

The definition of addiction consistently revolves around a recurring and compelling motivation to engage in an activity that lacks inherent survival value. This motivation is acquired through experience with the activity, even in the face of potential harm or actual harm (West, 2013). Regarding the complex and socially defined construct of drug addiction, the American Psychiatric Association's Manual of Mental Disorders (DSM-V) introduces the term "Substance-Related and Addictive Disorders" (APA, 2013). Some authors critically examine the prevalent emphasis in various conceptual approaches to drug addiction, which tends to highlight vulnerabilities while neglecting an addict's strengths and diligence (e.g., Clark, 2011). This challenges the predominant orientation of addiction models characterizing addiction primarily as a disease. Drawing on extensive experience in the fields of psychiatry and substance abuse, Carqueja (2000) challenges the prevailing perspective by suggesting that certain dependencies, including substance dependencies, may not be illnesses but rather treatments!

Sexual satisfaction is a crucial factor in individuals' sexual health and overall well-being. This dimension is influenced not only by individual and relational factors but also by social and cultural variables. Supported by Bronfenbrenner's Ecological Theory (1994), a review study on the subject in Spain informs us that at the microsystem level, aspects of physical and psychological health are considered, and any sexual dysfunction will have a negative impact on sexual satisfaction. Regarding the mesosystem, relational variables associated with sexual satisfaction include a satisfactory companionship, assertiveness, and sexual communication. Associated with the exosystem, issues such as social support, a good family relationship, and a high socioeconomic level correlate positively with sexual satisfaction. In the macrosystem domain, the studied variables, such as religion, led to contradictory results (Sánchez-Fuentes, Santos-Iglesias, & Sierra, 2014).

Sexual problems encompass a broad range of conditions that affect sexual response in a way that hinders or complicates an individual or couple's ability to enjoy sexual activity. For a clinical diagnosis of sexual dysfunction, it is necessary that the difficulty be recurrent and persistent over time, causing individual or interpersonal distress and significantly disrupting a person's ability to respond sexually or experience sexual pleasure. The same individual may be diagnosed with more than one sexual dysfunction simultaneously (APA, 2013). According to the ICD-11 (WHO, 2019), sexual dysfunction refers to a person's inability to engage in a sexual relationship in the way they desire. Cowen and their working group (2012) highlight the lack of consensus in defining sexual dysfunction, as what may be considered "normal" (e.g., frequency or duration of sexual activity) depends partly on the expectations of the individuals involved.

The exact prevalence of sexual dysfunctions in the general population is not accurately known, as there are significant variations in the results of published studies. Nevertheless, existing data indicate a substantial percentage of men and women experiencing some form of sexual dysfunction throughout their lives. The sexual difficulties most commonly leading to seeking help are hypoactive sexual desire disorder and orgasmic disorder in women, and premature ejaculation and erectile dysfunction in men. It is believed that only a small percentage of individuals with these issues seek specialized consultation, and among them, an even smaller number remains in treatment (Gómez & Cartón, 2006)

Since the 1970s, psychophysiological research on the mechanisms of sexual arousal (inhibition) has particularly focused on the cognitive processes involved in these responses. Master's and Johnson's (1970) innovative proposal established that behaviourally oriented psychotherapy can successfully intervene in various sexual problems. Barlow (1986) presented a model that integrated much of the research up to that point, suggesting that the activation of sexual response depended on relevant tasks in the cognitive processing of sexual stimuli. Barlow proposed that dysfunction arises from the cognitive processing of irrelevant tasks or distraction, as well as an internal shift in self-evaluation of attention. Sexually functional individuals respond to erotic stimuli with positive effects and positive expectations. Sexual response follows a logic of positive feedback: individuals with a history of adequate sexual functioning approach new sexual situations with positive affect and expectations, and vice versa.

Several authors integrated the idea that the interface between psychological processes and sexual genital response occurs through a cognitive window, primarily dependent on the presence of sexual stimuli and the absence of interference with the activation of the response to sexual stimuli. In 1995, Bancroft suggested that a more direct form of neurophysiological inhibition should also be considered (Janssen & Bancroft, 2007).

The relationship between drug consumption and sexuality is a complex and multifaceted field that has intrigued researchers over the years.

The historical quest for substances labelled as aphrodisiacs, believed to enhance male virility and facilitate sexual relations in women, has a longstanding presence. Despite the widespread idea suggesting that alcohol and drug consumption can lead to increased sexual arousal, reduced inhibitions, and promote pleasurable sexual activity, studies indicate that ongoing use of illicit drugs has a detrimental impact on sexual performance. Various substances, including psychotropic medications, have been identified for their potential to induce sexual side effects. Antidepressants, antipsychotics, and anxiolytics, among others, may negatively impact libido, arousal, and overall sexual functioning.

The literature highlights that different drugs affect the central nervous system in distinct ways, which can have direct implications on sexual function. Understanding the pharmacological aspects of these substances is crucial in comprehending the intricate relationship between drug consumption and sexual dysfunction.

Substances such as alcohol, marijuana, cocaine, and opioids have varied effects on libido, sexual response, and sensory perception, contributing to a diverse range of sexual experiences. The impact includes a decrease in orgasmic capacity, arousal, and libido (e.g., Bang-Ping, 2009; Gómez & Cartón, 2006; Greenwood & Bancroft, 1977; Hamilton, Pringle & Hemingway, 2015; James, 2007; Kopetz, Reynolds, Hart, Kruglanski, & Lejuez, 2010; Mintz, O'Hare, O'Brien, & Goldschmidt, 1974; NCASA, 1999).

Additionally, the risk of contracting sexually transmitted infections may increase due to impaired judgment and risk-taking behaviour under the influence. Alcohol and drugs can compromise the ability to assess the risk involved in a particular sexual activity. When considering data suggesting that individuals with substance dependence may have risk-prone personalities, it follows that consumers may engage in a higher number of sexual activities, with more partners, and a lower likelihood of engaging in safe/protected sexual interactions (Bellis & Hughes, 2004; Bellis et al., 2008; Degenhard, 2005; Eaton, Thompson, Hu, Goldstein, Saha, & Hasin, 2015; Goldsamt, Clatts, Le, & Yu, 2015; Graves & Leight, 1995; Kopetz et al., 2010; Mattison, Ross, Wolfson, Franklin, & HNRC Group, 2001; McElrath, 2005; Thompson, Kao & Thomas, 2005).

Research has provided data linking substance abuse to intimate partner violence, regardless of the gender of the aggressor (male or female). This association is particularly heightened when both partners are substance users (El-Bassel et al., 2001; El-Bassel, Gilbert, & Rajah, 2003; Miller, 1990). Alcohol and illicit substance abuse are often considered physiological triggers for aggressive behaviour and deviant sexual arousal, potentially increasing the likelihood of sexual criminality, especially in individuals predisposed to such behaviour (Herman, 1990; Labbe & Maisto, 2011). The interplay between impulsive personality traits and impaired decision-making due to drug consumption may lead to engaging in sexual activity that would be considered inappropriate in other circumstances, with notable implications in contexts discussing consent, such as allegations of sexual assault (Sumnall, Beynon, Conchie, Riley, & Cole, 2007).

The literature underscores the bidirectional relationship between drug consumption and sexual dysfunction. Substance use, including alcohol, illicit drugs, and prescription medications, has been linked to an increased risk of sexual dysfunction. Conversely, the experience of sexual dysfunction may drive individuals towards substance use as a coping mechanism, creating a cyclical pattern. The "La Pera hypothesis" is based on the cause-and-effect relationship between sexual dysfunction and the onset of drug use (La Pera, Carderi, Marianantoni, Lentini, & Taggi, 2006). La Pera and colleagues suggest that a significant percentage of young men initiate drug use as a result of sexual problems. The author and collaborators studied 86 substance abusers, examining dimensions of drug use and sexuality. Approximately 34.1% asserted that their sexual difficulties played a role in the decision to start using drugs: 60% mentioned a minor influence, 26.7% admitted a significant influence, and 13.13% even considered it a decisive factor. The researchers found a higher prevalence of sexual dysfunction before the first drug use among subjects who stated that their sexual problems influenced their initial drug consumption. About half of the subjects used psychotropic drugs to enhance sexual performance

Assuming the close association between sexuality and substance use, this connection will vary depending on the individual's personality and the situation (NCASA, 1999). Individuals often drink or use drugs to gain courage, sedation, or to justify engaging in something embarrassing, irrational, or legally, morally, or religiously prohibited, including sexual activity. In doing so, they seek not only disinhibition but also authorization for specific sexual involvement. Reasons for substance use thus include seeking mood enhancement, sociability, and acceptance, alleviating stress, relieving pressure, addressing low self-esteem or depression, which can also lead to sexual activity (Knibbe, 1998). From a meaning perspective, the realm of sexuality may represent a field of strong social constraints. These constraints may justify the emergence of addictive behaviour to play a role in relieving or avoiding difficulties inherent in sexuality (La Pera et al., 2008b; Lorga, 2001, 2002; Soulignac, Waber, & Khazaal, 2011; Sumnall et al., 2007).

2. Expectations, Drug Addiction, and Sexuality

Cognitive and emotional factors have been consistently assessed as dimensions of great importance for understanding various psychopathological presentations and/ or deviant behaviours.

The Expectancy Theory proposed by Tolman (1932) refers to the notion of internal mental representation of the regularities of the external world or the relationships between the subject's actions and the external world. Although proposing a behavioural theory of learning, Tolman (1932) provides a cognitive approach emphasizing the construct of "expectancy". According to this theory, knowledge is acquired as a result of exposure and attention to environmental events; reward is not necessary, only the contiguity of the experience of events where expectations are strengthened whenever objective events occur in sequence.

The Social Cognitive Theory by Bandura (1986) further solidifies and extends the Expectancy Theory, incorporating various contributions (Fouad & Guillen, 2006). It asserts that behaviour can be partly explained by an individual's belief that a specific outcome will occur as a result of performing a certain behaviour. It is not crucial whether expectations are logical or based on concrete experiences; what matters most is that expectations exist and can have reinforcing effects on an individual's behaviour over time (Jones, Corbin, & Fromme, 2001). It is believed that belief structures influence the formation of expectations (O'Hair, Allman, & Moore, 1996). Expectations are not a static construct; they are malleable (Constantino et al., 2011).

Motivated behaviour is determined by two related expectations: self-efficacy expectations and outcome expectations (Sanna, 1992). Self-efficacy expectations can be defined as the beliefs an individual holds about succeeding in their attempts to perform a particular behaviour competently. These beliefs, in turn, influence the degree of effort and persistence the individual puts into attempting to perform the competent behaviour (Bandura, 1977). Outcome expectations refer to beliefs about the conviction that competent behaviour will or will not lead to desired outcomes; prognostic beliefs about carrying out a specific activity (Allen et al., 1990; Constantino et al., 2011). Outcome expectations arise from observing situations and events in the individual's environment and the tangible results of the actions the individual has taken (Bandura, 1986). In the Expectancy Theory, behaviour is explained by individuals' expectations of obtaining reinforcing outcomes by performing the behaviour in question (Jones et al., 2001).

The Expectancy Theory is a motivation process theory suggesting that individual effort is determined by anticipated outcomes and the value attributed to them. Expectations are robust predictors of behaviour (Driskell & Mullen, 1990; Trautwein et al., 2012), performance, persistence, and task choice (Trautwein et al., 2012). They are motivational forces based on the expectation of social gain, approval or disapproval, and peer decision evaluation (if most others are doing it, it is sensible to do it too) (Fekadu & Kraft, 2002). Behaviour will reflect a multiplicative function (not just a result by summation) of expectations and attributed value (other factors may also be involved in some models) (Trautwein et al., 2012). The individual engages in actions perceived as potentially yielding positive and desirable outcomes, avoiding actions that will produce negative results (Bandura, 2001).

One of the most extensively studied approaches in understanding behavioural problems identifies the intraindividual cognitive representation of anticipations of behavioural consequences as an essential component (e.g., Bandura, 1986). Rooted in the Expectancy Theory proposed by Tolman (1932), various conceptual interpretations of the "expectancy" construct have emerged, particularly in the context of drug use and abuse behaviour (Stacy, Newcomb, & Bentler, 1991). Within this framework, three approaches can be considered: a) Outcome expectancies, were expectations function as causal cognitive mediation in behaviour. They operate autonomously, guiding behaviour even in the presence of contradictory experiential evidence, and act as direct predictors of behaviour. b) Expectations arising as results or effects of behaviours, serving as epiphenomena of previous consumptions and reinforcing effects of behaviour. While these past experiences influence future consumption behaviours and related expectations, expectations do not play a causal role. The predictor of consumption behaviour is the previous behaviour. c) Expectations and drug consumption mutually influencing the determination of future usage behaviour, aligning with the proposal of Social Learning Theory (Bandura, 1977). Expectations determine behaviour, but their definition and strength are moderated by the outcomes of previous behaviours (Stacy et al., 1991). The human quest for drugs is thought to be controlled by the stimulus-drug dyad through representations or expectations of the substance, rather than the direct association between stimulus and response (Hogarth, Dickinson, Wright, Kouvaraki, & Duka, 2007).

The variability in expectations regarding the specific effects of substances may be related to the fact that social learning about the effects begins before the actual onset of use, and these expectations influence the subjective effect of the drug. This variability can also be justified by different consumption contexts and intrinsic differences in the physiological effects of substances (Aarons, Brown, Sticed, & Coe, 2001).

Positive expectations regarding substance use are associated with beliefs, whether conscious or unconscious, that desired/pleasurable effects will occur as a consequence of substance use (Brown, 1980; Patrick et al., 2010). Negative expectations regarding substance use are associated with beliefs that undesired/unpleasant effects or negative consequences will occur as a result of substance use (Brown, 1980; Labbe & Maisto, 2011; Patrick et al., 2010).

Research suggests that expectations may be an important factor during alcohol or drug experimentation (Aarons et al., 2001). The studies conducted seem to indicate that positive expectations regarding alcohol and drugs, particularly expectations of relaxation and tension reduction, are associated with more frequent and severe alcohol and drug consumption (e.g., Kline, 1990; Peters et al., 2012; Schafer & Brown, 1991), especially when coupled with low negative expectations of that behaviour (Katz, Fromme & D'Amico, 2000).

The relationship between expectations and sexuality has primarily been established through the analysis of the impact of expectations on sexuality, although some examples of research in the opposite direction also exist. For instance, Loewenstein, Nagin, and Paternoster (1997) demonstrated that sexual arousal increases expectations of sexual aggression, with this impact not being mediated by perceptions of the cost or benefit of such aggression.

A critical review of recent literature on the psychological, interpersonal, and sociocultural aspects of sexual functioning consistently highlights the importance of childhood experiences, attachment styles, circumstances of sexual activity, personality, cognitive schemas (women with negative sexual self-schemas report less interest in sexual activity, fewer sexual thoughts, and lower sexual arousal than women with more positive sexual self-schemas; men with negative schemas report lower levels of sexual arousal), concerns about infertility, and sexual expectations (e.g., studies manipulating false feedback found a significant impact on subjective arousal in men and women with and without sexual dysfunction, with no observed effect on genital sexual arousal. Thus, the effect of manipulated expectations on sexual arousal appears to be mediated by cognitive processes) in the domain of sexual function and dysfunction (Brotto et al., 2016).

A literature review supports the impact of sexual expectations on dimensions of problematic sexual behaviour (e.g., Leppink et al., 2016), engagement in risky sexual behaviours (e.g., Bermúdez et al., 2016; Newcomb & Mustanski, 2014), sexual function and dysfunction (e.g., Brotto et al., 2016; Nimbi et al., 2018; Peixoto & Nobre, 2017; Tavares et al., 2017), among others. Studies suggest the effective mediation of cognitive factors, particularly sexual expectations, in the experience of sexuality.

Society often shapes expectations around drug consumption and its influence on sexuality. On one hand, some substances are associated with increased sexual liberation, while others are perceived as inhibitors. Individuals may internalize these expectations, shaping their sexual experiences under the influence of psychoactive substances.

Research on drug use and sexuality seems to reach a consensus that the effects of any drug on sexual performance depend on the type of drug, the quantity consumed, the duration of use, and environmental factors, as well as individual expectations (Nobre, Pinto-Gouveia, & Gomes, 2003; Smith, 1982). The authors hypothesize that sexual behaviour and its problems are somehow related to how one thinks about sexuality, beliefs, and/or associated expectations (Nobre et al., 2003). Sexual expectations of substance use are the beliefs that a person holds about the sexual effects of substance use (Starks, Millar, Tuck, & Wells, 2015). The immediate positive pharmacological consequences more strongly influence behaviour than the long-term negative effects (Rohsenow, 1983). Perhaps because positive expectations are more easily accessible in memory than negative expectations (Stacy et al., 1990). It is also true that certain sexual expectations may set the conditions for the activation of cognitive schemas in specific experiences of sexual failure (Nobre et al., 2003).

Calafat and colleagues (2008) clarify that it is common to find each drug associated with a specific effect on sexuality, making the idea of this association particularly precise for young people. The perspective of individuals with substance use disorders suggests that if there is an improvement in mental state with drug use, then sexual performance will also improve, as inhibition and resistance are reduced (Lindesmith, 1980). Consumers communicate how they personally experienced the effects of certain drugs and how they affected their sexuality; this information has implications for the experiences of other consumers. The myth is then created and sustained by the symbolic social expectations of how a particular drug affects sexuality (El-Bassel et al., 2003). These beliefs reinforce the connection between substance use and sex (NCASA, 1999).

We can identify two ways in which substance use expectations impact sexuality: a) Coping Mechanism: Many individuals facing sexual difficulties may resort to substance use as a coping mechanism. The expectation is that drugs can temporarily alleviate stress, anxiety, or performance-related concerns, offering a sense of escape from the challenges of intimacy. b) Enhanced Experience: There is an expectation that certain substances can enhance sexual experiences. Individuals might believe that drugs can heighten pleasure, increase arousal, or prolong performance, contributing to a perceived improvement in their overall sexual satisfaction.

Being an influential force behind behaviour (Fekadu & Kraft, 2002), expectations about the effects of drugs and alcohol can influence sexual experience and behaviour (Romo, 2004; Romo et al., 2009; Wilson & Lawson, 1976, 1978). Consumers who anticipate that the use of alcohol or drugs will reduce social anxiety during sexual encounters or increase sexual pleasure are more likely to use substances in both general and intimate situations. Even when confronted with evidence contradicting these assumptions, the same expectations may persist (McKee, Hinson, Wall, & Spriel, 1998; O'Hare, 1998; Schafer & Brown, 1991).

The research supports sexual expectations as a conceptual framework for understanding motivations for drug use. It suggests a significant relationship between sexual expectations of substance use and actual drug consumption (e.g., Kuiper et al., 2019; Starks et al., 2015).

We investigated with a representative sample of Portuguese heroin users undergoing opioid substitution treatment (N = 488), aiming to assess expectations regarding the impact of heroin consumption on sexual functioning and obtain a detailed characterization of the sexual activity of this group (Ribeiro, 2019). The Substance Use and Sexual Behaviour Survey (SUSB), adapted for the Portuguese population of substance users, proved to be a valuable tool. Exploratory factor analysis unveiled a comprehensive four-component structure, designated as follows: 1) Inhibitor Impact of Substance Abuse on Sexuality, 2) Indissociability of Sexuality and Substance Use, 3) Enhancer Impact of Substance on Sexuality, and 4) Substance Use Favouring Risky Sexual Behaviours. These components collectively elucidated around 65% of the total variance, providing a nuanced understanding of the intricate interplay between substance abuse and sexuality.

The confirmatory factor analysis exhibited overall fits (Rawson et al., 2002; Ribeiro et al., 2015). This instrument is very useful for identifying patients at greater risk of abandoning treatment and engaging in sexual risk behaviour, those with positive expectations about the impact of drug use on sexuality, allowing for targeted interventions and prevention programs.

The obtained results underscore, with statistical significance, the pivotal role of expectations as mediators in the impact of heroin consumption on sexual life. For heroin users, sexuality and substance use seem to intertwine sexual thoughts and feelings often trigger craving, and the quality of sexual thoughts experienced under the influence of heroin is a source of concern. Upon analysing the results, regardless of expectations of a favourable impact and even during an initial phase of improved sexual performance, opioid use is associated with negative consequences in most aspects of sexual experience. These negative effects are more pronounced in heroin consumption, comparatively less detrimental in methadone substitution treatment, with individuals medicated with buprenorphine exhibiting the least compromise in sexual experience (Ribeiro, 2019).

Studies consistently demonstrate that individuals hold diverse expectations about sexual experiences. These expectations, shaped by cultural, social, and personal factors, including drug use, play a pivotal role in influencing an individual's sexual well-being. Unrealistic expectations or apprehensions about sexual dysfunction can lead to performance anxiety, adversely impacting sexual satisfaction. Therefore, we can consider these expectations as factors contributing to vulnerability for both sexual dissatisfaction and psychotropic substance use.

3. Victimhood, Substance Users, and Sexuality

Victimology traditionally examines individuals who have experienced harm or victimization. In the context of substance use, individuals grappling with addiction often face a myriad of challenges, including societal stigmatization, marginalization, and the consequences of their own harmful behaviours.

Intersectionality appeared in 1989, by professor Kimberlé Crenshaw, acknowledging that everyone has their own unique experiences of discrimination, and we must considerer everything: gender, nationality, ethnicity, sexuality, (dis) ability, illness, class, ... Intersectionality tries to catch the relationships between socio-cultural categories and identities (Knudsen, 2006).

Substance users can be perceived as victims of diverse societal, psychological, or environmental factors, from a multidimensional standpoint. They may undergo victimization through societal judgment, discrimination, and the inherent health risks linked to addiction. Moreover, the cyclical nature of addiction, characterized by relapses and challenges in overcoming it, sustains a prevailing sense of victimhood. Elements like socioeconomic disparities, trauma, and mental health challenges contribute to the vulnerability that may drive individuals toward substance abuse as a coping mechanism. Trauma, often an antecedent to substance abuse, introduces a layer of victimization. Individuals may turn to substances as maladaptive coping mechanisms, inadvertently subjecting themselves to a cycle of victimization (e.g., Aarons et al., 2001; Brown, 1980; Katz et al., 2000; Labbe & Maisto, 2011; Patrick et al., 2010; Peters et al., 2012).

The impact of substance use on sexuality introduces a unique layer of vulnerability. As victims of their addiction, individuals may engage in risky sexual behaviours, exposing themselves to health risks and potential victimization. This vulnerability is compounded by the societal stigma surrounding substance use, further exacerbating feelings of victimhood in the sexual sphere (e.g., Bermúdez et al., 2016; Brotto et al., 2016; Leppink et al., 2016; Loewenstein et al., 1997; Newcomb & Mustanski, 2014; Nimbi et al., 2018).

Toxic dependence often leads to internalized stigma and self-blame, where individuals view themselves as responsible for their addiction and its consequences. This self-perception can extend to the sexual domain, fostering a sense of victimhood as users grapple with the repercussions of their actions on their sexual health and relationships. Individuals experiencing sexual dysfunction may undergo emotional distress, relational strain, and a sense of powerlessness, echoing the themes inherent in victimological perspectives (e.g., Brotto et al., 2016; Nimbi et al., 2018; Peixoto & Nobre, 2017; Tavares et al., 2017).

The victimization narrative gains complexity as the cyclical relationship between substance abuse, sexual dysfunction, and psychological distress unfolds. Individuals resort to substance use as a means to cope with the victimization inherent in sexual dysfunction, perpetuating a cycle that further entrenches them in a victimized state. Societal attitudes towards substance abuse and sexual dysfunction play a pivotal role in the victimization experienced by individuals. Stigmatization and judgmental perspectives can exacerbate feelings of victimhood, hindering individuals from seeking help and perpetuating a cycle of substance abuse and sexual dysfunction.

DISCUSSION

Therapeutic and Preventive Considerations

Exploring the intricate interplay between expectations and the profound impact of drug consumption on sexuality is imperative for the nuanced development of effective therapeutic and preventive approaches. In the realm of mental health, it is incumbent upon professionals, including both mental health practitioners and addiction specialists, to delve beyond the neurochemical aspects and consider the intricate web of psychosocial influences that intricately shape individual experiences.

An essential component of this comprehensive understanding involves recognizing the underlying beliefs associated with specific behaviors, such as drug consumption. This recognition not only sheds light on the intricacies of substance uses but also serves as a pivotal foundation for formulating targeted intervention strategies. This approach gains particular relevance when exploring the intersection of substance abuse with other psychopathologies, such as schizophrenia (Asher & Gask, 2010). Regularly assessing patients' expectations becomes paramount, with a keen awareness of the malleable and non-static nature of these expectations. Such assessments emerge as a strategic imperative to enhance the adaptive outcomes of psychotherapeutic interventions (Constantino et al., 2011).

Furthermore, a crucial recommendation emerges for the integration of sexological consultation into substance abuse treatment programs. This integration emphasizes the importance of consistently and comprehensively addressing sexual issues and concerns within the broader context of substance abuse treatment. Overlooking, underestimating, or leaving these issues untreated might inadvertently contribute to relapse and hinder the overall recovery process (Bartholomew et al., 2000; Carroll et al., 2001; James, 2007; Katz et al., 2000; Palha & Esteves, 2002).

To fortify these efforts, it is strongly advocated to design and implement specific programs that challenge positive expectations regarding the impact of substance use on sexuality. Moreover, such programs should be tailored, considering the division of target groups by gender, as empirical evidence suggests that this approach enhances effectiveness (James, 2007; Labbe & Maisto, 2011). This multifaceted approach not only addresses the complexities of substance abuse but also aims to foster a more comprehensive and gender-specific understanding, thereby contributing to more tailored and successful therapeutic outcomes.

CONCLUSION

Seeking insight into an individual's attitudes, beliefs, expectations, or ideologies regarding substance use and addiction is crucial for a comprehensive understanding of treatment objectives. Recognizing expectations as a pivotal cognitive factor in mediating drug-seeking behaviour and acknowledging the potential for modifying these expectations through intervention, we can foresee that diminishing positive expectations and fostering negative expectations related to drug use will contribute to a reduction in consumption.

A comprehensive understanding of the reciprocal impact of sexual dysfunction on drug consumption dynamics is essential for developing targeted prevention and intervention strategies that consider the multifaceted nature of this relationship. Further research is warranted to explore specific substance-related effects on sexual function and the effectiveness of integrated treatment modalities.

From a victimological standpoint, treatment strategies should extend beyond addressing substance abuse and sexual dysfunction in isolation. Therapeutic interventions should encompass trauma-informed care, empowerment models, and stigma reduction initiatives to effectively address the victimization experienced by individuals caught in this intricate web.

This comprehensive review integrates the victimological perspective into the nuanced relationship between substance abuse, sexual dysfunction, and victimization. Recognizing individuals within this framework allows for more empathetic and targeted interventions, emphasizing the need for holistic approach that considers both the physical and psychological aspects, fostering open communication, and providing support systems to individuals navigating these complex challenges; trauma-informed approaches to break the cycle of victimization and foster meaningful recovery. By acknowledging and addressing these intersections, we can work towards promoting healthier relationships, both with oneself and with others.

Further research is encouraged to explore the intersectionality of victimization and develop interventions that address the intricate dynamics involved.

REFERENCES

Aarons, G., Brown, S., Sticed, E., & Coe, M. (2001). Psychometric evaluation of the marijuana and stimulant effect expectancy questionnaires for adolescents. *Addictive Behaviors*, *26*(2), 219–236. doi:10.1016/S0306-4603(00)00103-9 PMID:11316378

Allen, J., Leadbeater, B., & Aber, J. (1990). The relationship of adolescents' expectations and values to delinquency, hard drug use, and unprotected sexual intercourse. *Development and Psychopathology*, *2*(1), 85–98. doi:10.1017/S0954579400000614

American Psychiatric Association. (2013). *Diagnostic and Statistical Manual of Mental Disorder* (5th ed.). APA.

Asher, C., & Gask, L. (2010). Reasons for illicit drug use in people with schizophrenia: Qualitative study. *Psychiatry*, *10*, 94–109. doi:10.116/1471-244X-10-94 PMID:21092168

Bandura, A. (1977). Self-efficacy: Toward a unifying theory of behavioral change. *Psychological Review*, *84*(2), 191–215. doi:10.1037/0033-295X.84.2.191 PMID:847061

Bandura, A. (1986). *Social foundations of thought and action: A social cognitive theory*. Prentice Hall.

Bandura, A. (2001). Social cognitive theory: An agentic perspective. *Annual Review of Psychology*, *52*(1), 1–26. doi:10.1146/annurev.psych.52.1.1 PMID:11148297

Bang-Ping, J. (2009). Sexual dysfunction in men who abuse illicit drugs: A preliminary report. *Journal of Sexual Medicine*, *6*(4), 1072–1080. doi:10.1111/j.1743-6109.2007.00707.x PMID:18093094

Barlow, D. (1986). Causes of sexual dysfunction: The role of anxiety and cognitive interference. *Journal of Consulting and Clinical Psychology*, *54*(2), 140–157. doi:10.1037/0022-006X.54.2.140 PMID:3700800

Bartholomew, N., Hiller, M., Knight, K., Nucatola, D., & Simpson, D. (2000). Effectiveness of communication and relationship skills training for men in substance abuse treatment. *Journal of Substance Abuse Treatment, 18*(3), 217–225. doi:10.1016/S0740-5472(99)00051-3 PMID:10742634

Bellis, M., & Hughes, K. (2004). Sex potions. Relationships between alcohol, drugs and sex. *Adicciones, 16*(4), 249–258. doi:10.20882/adicciones.390

Bellis, M., Hughes, K., Calafat, A., Juan, M., Ramon, A., Rodriguez, J., Mendes, F., Schnitzer, S., & Phillips-Howard, P. (2008). Sexual uses of alcohol and drugs and the associated health risks: A cross sectional study of young people in nine European cities. *BMC Public Health, 8*(1), 155–165. doi:10.1186/1471-2458-8-155 PMID:18471281

Bermúdez, L., Araújo, L., Reyes, A., Hernández-Quero, J., & Teva, I. (2016). Analysis of cognitive variables and sexual risk behaviors among infected and HIV-uninfected people from Spain. *AIDS Care, 28*(7), 890–897. doi:10.1080/09540121.2016.1161163 PMID:26981840

Bronfenbrenner, U. (1994). Ecological models of human development. In T. Husen & T. Postlethwaite (Eds.), *The International Encyclopedia of Education* (2nd ed., Vol. 3, pp. 1643–1647). Elsevier.

Brotto, L., Atallah, S., Johnson-Agbakwu, C., Rosenbaum, T., Abdo, C., Byers, E., Graham, C., Nobre, P., & Wylie, K. (2016). Psychological and interpersonal dimensions of sexual function and dysfunction. *Journal of Sexual Medicine, 13*(4), 538–571. doi:10.1016/j.jsxm.2016.01.019 PMID:27045257

Brown, S., Goldman, M., Inn, A., & Anderson, L. (1980). Expectations of reinforcement from alcohol: Their domain and relation to drinking patterns. *Journal of Consulting and Clinical Psychology, 48*(4), 419–426. doi:10.1037/0022-006X.48.4.419 PMID:7400427

Calafat, A., Juan, M., Becoña, E., & Montecón, A. (2008). Qué drogas se prefieren para las relaciones sexuales en contextos recreativos. *Adicciones, 20*(1), 37–48. doi:10.20882/adicciones.287 PMID:18299780

Carqueja, H. (2000). Doença e toxicodependências. *Toxicodependências (Lisboa), 6*(3), 83–85.

Carroll, J., McGinley, J., & Macck, S. (2001). Exploring the self-reported sexual problems and concerns of drug-dependent males and females in modified, therapeutic community treatment. *Journal of Substance Abuse Treatment, 20*, 245–250. doi:10.1016/S0740-5472(01)00164-7 PMID:11516595

Clark, M. (2011). Conceptualizing addiction: How useful is the construct? *International Journal of Humanities and Social Science*, *1*(13), 55–64.

Constantino, M., Arnkoff, D., Glass, C., Ametrano, R., & Smith, J. (2011). Expectations. *Journal of Clinical Psychology*, *67*(2), 184–192. doi:10.1002/jclp.20754 PMID:21128304

Cowen, P., Harrison, P., & Burns, T. (2012). *Shorter Oxford textbook of psychiatry* (6th ed., Vol. 1 & 2). University Press. doi:10.1093/med/9780199605613.001.0001

Crenshaw, K. (1989). Demarginalizing the intersection of race and sex: a black feminist critique of antidiscrimination doctri, feminist theory and antiracist politics. *University of Chicago Legal Forum*, (1), 139-167. https://chicagounbound.uchicago.edu/uclf/vol1989/iss1/8

Degenhardt, L. (2005). Drug use and risk behaviour among regular ecstasy users: Does sexuality make a difference? *Culture, Health & Sexuality*, *7*(6), 599–614. doi:10.1080/13691050500349875 PMID:16864225

Driskell, J., & Mullen, B. (1990). Status, expectations, and behavior: A meta-analytic review and test of the theory. *Personality and Social Psychology Bulletin*, *16*(3), 541–553. doi:10.1177/0146167290163012

Eaton, N., Thompson, R. Jr, Hu, M., Goldstein, R., Saha, T., & Hasin, D. (2015). Regularly drinking alcohol before sexual activity in a national representative sample: Prevalence, sociodemographics, and associations with psychiatric and substance use disorders. *American Journal of Public Health*, *105*(7), 1387–1393. doi:10.2105/AJPH.2015.302556 PMID:25973812

El-Bassel, N., Fontdevila, J., Gilbert, L., Voisin, D., Richman, B., & Pitchell, P. (2001). HIV risks of men in methadone maintenance tretment programs who abuse their intimate partners: A forgotten issue. *Journal of Substance Abuse*, *13*(1-2), 1–15. doi:10.1016/S0899-3289(01)00068-2 PMID:11547622

El-Bassel, N., Gilbert, L., & Rajah, V. (2003). The relationship between drug abuse and sexual performance among women on methadone. Heightening the risk of sexual intimate violence and HIV. *Addictive Behaviors*, *28*(8), 1385–1403. doi:10.1016/S0306-4603(02)00266-6 PMID:14512062

Fekadu, Z., & Kraft, P. (2002). Expanding the theory of planned behavior: The role of social norms and group identification. *Journal of Health Psychology*, *7*(1), 33–43. doi:10.1177/1359105302007001650 PMID:22114225

Ferreira-Borges, C., & Filho, H. (2004). *Uso, abusos e dependências: alcoolismo e toxicodependência.* Climepsi Editores.

Ferros, L. (2011). *Toxicodependência: afectos e psicopatologia.* Livpsic.

Fouad, N., & Guillen, A. (2006). Outcome expectations: Looking to the past and potential future. *Journal of Career Assessment, 14*(1), 130–142. doi:10.1177/1069072705281370

Goldsamt, L., Clatts, M., Le, G., & Yu, G. (2015). Injection and sexual risk practices among young heroin users in Hanoi, Vietnam. *Drugs: Education Prevention & Policy, 22*(2), 166–172. doi:10.3109/09687637.2014.979765 PMID:25995608

Gómez, C., & Cartón, M. (2006). Drogas y disfunción sexual. *Adicciones, 18*(1), 231–243.

Graves, K., & Leight, B. (1995). The relationship of substance use to sexual activity among young adults in the United States. *Family Planning Perspectives, 27*(1), 18–22. doi:10.2307/2135972 PMID:7720848

Greenwood, J., & Bancroft, J. (1977). Notas de aconselhamento para problemas sexuais. *A Sexologia Clínica,* 363-364.

Hamilton, I., Pringle, R., & Hemingway, S. (2015). Psychotropic induced sexual dysfunction for people with a dual diagnosis. *Advances in Dual Diagnosis, 8*(4), 167–178. doi:10.1108/ADD-09-2015-0021

Herman, J. (1990). Sex offenders: a feminist perspective. In W. Marshall, D. Laws, & H. Barbaree (Eds.), *Handbook of sexual assault: issues, theories, and treatment of the offender* (pp. 177–198). Plenum Press. doi:10.1007/978-1-4899-0915-2_11

Hogarth, L., Dickinson, A., Wright, A., Kouvaraki, M., & Duka, T. (2007). The role of drug expectancy in the control of human drug seeking. *Journal of Experimental Psychology. Animal Behavior Processes, 33*(4), 484–496. doi:10.1037/0097-7403.33.4.484 PMID:17924795

James, R. (2007). Strategies for incorporating women-specific sexuality education into addiction treatment models. *American Journal of Sexuality Education, 2*(3), 3–25. doi:10.1300/J455v02n03_02

Janssen, E., & Bancroft, J. (2007). The Dual Control Model: The role of sexual inhibition and excitation in sexual arousal and behavior. In E. Janssen (Ed.), *The psychophysiology of sex* (pp. 197–222). Indiana University Press.

Jones, B., Corbin, W., & Fromme, K. (2001). A review of expectancy theory and alcohol consumption. *Addiction (Abingdon, England)*, *96*(1), 57–72. doi:10.1046/j.1360-0443.2001.961575.x PMID:11177520

Katz, E., Fromme, K., & D'Amico, E. (2000). Effects of outcome expectancies and personality on young adults' illicit drug use, heavy drnking, and risky sexual behavior. *Cognitive Therapy and Research*, *24*(1), 1–22. doi:10.1023/A:1005460107337

Kline, R. (1990). The relation of alcohol expectancies to drinking patterns among alcoholics: Generalization across gender and race. *Journal of Studies on Alcohol*, *51*(2), 175–182. doi:10.15288/jsa.1990.51.175 PMID:2308356

Knibbe, R. (1998). Measuring drinking context. *Alcohol, Clinical and Experimental Research*, *22*(2), 15s–20s. doi:10.1111/j.1530-0277.1998.tb04369.x PMID:9603302

Knudsen, S. (2006). Intersectionality – a theoretical inspiration in the analysis of minority cultures and identities in textbooks. In Caught in the web or lost in the textbook, 8th (pp. 61–76). Academic Press.

Konvalina-Simas, T. (2012). *Introdução à biopsicossociologia do comportamento desviante*. Maia: Reis dos Livros.

Kopetz, C., Reynolds, E., Hart, C., Kruglanski, A., & Lejuez, C. (2010). Social context and perceived effects of drugs on sexual behavior among individuals who use both heroin and cocaine. *Experimental and Clinical Psychopharmacology*, *18*(3), 214–220. doi:10.1037/a0019635 PMID:20545385

Kuiper, L., Beloate, L., Dupuy, B., & Coolen, L. (2019). Drug-taking in a social-sexual context enhances vulnerability for addiction in male rats. *Neuropsychopharmacology*, *44*(3), 503–513. doi:10.1038/s41386-018-0235-1 PMID:30337639

La Pera, G., Carderi, A., Marianantoni, Z., Lentini, M., & Taggi, F. (2006). The role of sexual dysfunctions in inducing the use of drug in young males. *Archivio Italiano di Urologia, Andrologia*, *78*(3), 101–106. PMID:17137024

La Pera, G., Carderi, A., Marianantoni, Z., Peris, F., Lentini, M., & Taggi, F. (2008a). Sexual dysfunction prior to first drug use among former drug addicts and its possible causal meaning on drug addiction: Preliminary results. *Journal of Sexual Medicine*, *5*(1), 164–172. doi:10.1111/j.1743-6109.2007.00571.x PMID:17666038

La Pera, G., Carderi, A., Marianantoni, Z., Sette, D., Gallo, G., Livi, S., & Macchia, T. (2008b). Can sexual dysfunctions lead to substance abuse disorders? *Sexologies*, *17*(S1), 134–135. doi:10.1016/S1158-1360(08)72889-5

Labbe, A., & Maisto, S. (2011). Alcohol expectancy challenges for college students: A narrative review. *Clinical Psychology Review, 31*(4), 673–683. doi:10.1016/j.cpr.2011.02.007 PMID:21482325

Leppink, E., Chamberlain, S., Redden, S., & Grant, J. (2016). Problematic sexual behavior in young adults: Associations across clinical, behavioral, and neurocognitive variables. *Psychiatry Research, 246,* 230-235. doi: , 2016.09.044 doi:10.1016/j.psychres

Lindsmith, A. (1980). A general theory of addiction to opiate-type drugs. *NIDA Research Monograph, 30,* 34–37. PMID:6779192

Loewenstein, G., Nagin, D., & Paternoster, R. (1997). The effect of sexual arousal on expectations of sexual forcefulness. *Journal of Research in Crime and Delinquency, 34*(4), 443–473. doi:10.1177/0022427897034004003

Lorga, P. (2001). Toxicodependência e sexualidade: Revisão bibliográfica a propósito das suas possíveis interacções (ParteI). *Toxicodependências (Lisboa), 7*(3), 41–52.

Lorga, P. (2002). Toxicodependência e sexualidade: Revisão bibliográfica a propósito das suas possíveis interacções (ParteII). *Toxicodependências (Lisboa), 8*(1), 53–64.

Masters, W., & Johnson, V. (1970). *Human sexual inadequacy.* Little, Brown and Co.

Matos, M. (2010). *Sexualidade, afectos e cultura. Gestão de problemas de saúde em meio escolar.* Coisas de Ler.

Mattison, A., Ross, M., Wolfson, T., & Franklin, D.HNRC Group. (2001). Circuit party attendance, club drug use, and unsafe sex in gay men. *Journal of Substance Abuse, 13*(1-2), 119–126. doi:10.1016/S0899-3289(01)00060-8 PMID:11547613

McElrath, K. (2005). MDMA and sexual behavior: Ecstasy users' perceptions about sexuality and sexual risk. *Substance Use & Misuse, 40*(9), 1461–1477. doi:10.1081/JA-200066814 PMID:16048828

McKee, S., Hinson, R., Wall, A., & Spriel, P. (1998). Alcohol outcome expectancies and coping styles as predictors of alcohol use in young adults. *Addictive Behaviors, 23*(1), 17–22. doi:10.1016/S0306-4603(97)00008-7 PMID:9468737

Miller, B. (1990). The interrelationships between alcohol and drugs and family violence. *NIDA Research Monograph, 103,* 177–207. PMID:2096287

Mintz, J., O'Hare, K., O'Brien, C., & Goldschmidt, J. (1974). Sexual problems of heroin addicts. *Archives of General Psychiatry, 31*(5), 700–703. doi:10.1001/archpsyc.1974.01760170088014 PMID:4474860

National Center on Addiction and Substance Abuse. (1999). *Dangerous Liaisons: substance abuse and sex*. NCASA.

Newcomb, M., & Mustanski, B. (2014). Cognitive influences on sexual risk and risk appraisals in men who have sex with men. *Health Psychology*, *33*(7), 690–698. doi:10.1037/hea0000010 PMID:23977876

Nimbi, F., Tripodi, F., Rossi, R., & Simonelli, C. (2018). Expanding the analysis of psychosocial factors of sexual desire in men. *Journal of Sexual Medicine*, *15*(2), 230–244. doi:10.1016/j.jsxm.2017.11.227 PMID:29292060

Nobre, P., Pinto-Gouveia, J., & Gomes, F. (2003). Sexual dysfunctional beliefs questionnaire: An instrument to assess sexual dysfunctional beliefs as vulnerability factors to sexual problems. *Sexual and Relationship Therapy*, *18*(2), 171–204. doi:10.1080/1468199031000061281

O'Hair, D., Allman, J., & Moore, S. (1996). A cognitive-affective model of relational expectations in the provider-patient context. *Journal of Health Psychology*, *1*(3), 307–322. doi:10.1177/135910539600100305 PMID:22011994

O'Hare, T. (1998). Alcohol expectancies and excessive drinking contexts in young adults. *Social Work Research*, *22*(1), 44–50. doi:10.1093/swr/22.1.44

Observatório Europeu da Droga e da Toxicodependência. (2022). *Relatório Europeu sobre drogas. Tendências e evoluções*. Serviço das Publicações da União Europeia. doi:10.2810/21871

Palha, A., & Esteves, M. (2002). A study of the sexuality of opiate addicts. *Journal of Sex & Marital Therapy*, *28*(5), 427–437. doi:10.1080/00926230290001547 PMID:12378844

Patrício, L. (2014). *Políticas e dependências. Álcool e (de) mais drogas em Portugal 30 anos depois*. Vega.

Patrick, M., Wray-Lake, L., Finlay, A., & Maggs, J. (2010). Cognitive effects. The long arm of expectancies: Adolescent alcohol expectancies predict adult alcohol use. *Alcohol and Alcoholism (Oxford, Oxfordshire)*, *45*(1), 17–24. doi:10.1093/alcalc/agp066 PMID:19808940

Peixoto, M., & Nobre, P. (2017). The activation of incompetence schemas in response to negative sexual events in heterosexual and lesbian women: The moderator role of personality traits and dysfunctional sexual beliefs. *Journal of Sex Research*, *54*(9), 1188–1196. doi:10.1080/00224499.2016.1267103 PMID:28059574

Peters, E., Khondkaryan, E., & Sullivan, T. (2012). Associations between expectancies of alcohol and drug use, severity of partner violence, and posttraumatic stress among women. *Journal of Interpersonal Violence*, *27*(11), 2108–2127. doi:10.1177/0886260511432151 PMID:22258078

Rawson, R., Washton, A., Domier, C., & Reiber, C. (2002). Drugs and sexual effects: Role of drug type and gender. *Journal of Substance Abuse Treatment*, *22*(2), 103–108. doi:10.1016/S0740-5472(01)00215-X PMID:11932136

Ribeiro, S. (2019). *Droga e Exectativas Sexuais: Impacto das expectativas acerca do efeito do consume de opiáceos na sexualidade*. Dissertação de doutoramento. FPCE-Universidade do Porto.

Ribeiro, S., Negreiros, J., Oliveira, J., & Teixeira, P. (2015). Substance Use and Sexual Behavior Survey: A validation study. *Psicologia, Saúde & Doenças*, *16*(2), 207–216. doi:10.15309/15psd160207

Rohsenow, D. (1983). Drinking habits and expectancies about alcohol's effects for self versus others. *Journal of Consulting and Clinical Psychology*, *51*(5), 752–756. doi:10.1037/0022-006X.51.5.752 PMID:6630690

Romo, N. (2004). *Género y uso de droga: la invisibilidade de las mujeres*. Fundación Medicina y Humanidades Médicas.

Romo, N., Marcos, J., Rodríguez, A., Cabrera, A., & Hernán, M. (2009). Girl power: Risky sexual behaviour and gender identity amongst young Spanish recreational drug users. *Sexualities*, *12*(3), 3355–3377. doi:10.1177/1363460709103895

Sánchez-Fuentes, M., Santos-Iglesias, P., & Sierra, J. (2014). A systematic review of sexual satisfaction. *International Journal of Clinical and Health Psychology*, *14*(1), 67–75. doi:10.1016/S1697-2600(14)70038-9

Sanna, L. (1992). Self-efficacy theory: Implications for social facilitation and social loafing. *Journal of Personality and Social Psychology*, *62*(5), 774–786. doi:10.1037/0022-3514.62.5.774

Schafer, J., & Brown, S. (1991). Marijuana and cocaine effect expectancies and drug use patterns. *Journal of Consulting and Clinical Psychology*, *59*(4), 558–565. doi:10.1037/0022-006X.59.4.558 PMID:1918560

Smith, D. (1982). Sexological aspects of substance use and abuse. *Journal of Psychoactive Drugs*, *14*(1-2), 1–3. doi:10.1080/02791072.1982.10471906 PMID:7119933

Soulignac, R., Waber, L., & Khazaal, Y. (2011). Sexuality and addictions: Narrations for links and meanings. *Sexologies*, *20*(2), 100–101. doi:10.1016/j.sexol.2010.06.003

Stacy, A., Newcomb, M., & Bentler, P. (1991). Cognitive motivation and drug use: A 9-year longitudinal study. *Journal of Abnormal Psychology*, *100*(4), 502–515. doi:10.1037/0021-843X.100.4.502 PMID:1757664

Stacy, A., Widaman, K., & Marlatt, G. (1990). Expectancy models of alcohol use. *Journal of Personality and Social Psychology*, *58*(5), 918–928. doi:10.1037/0022-3514.58.5.918 PMID:2348377

Starks, T., Millar, B., Tuck, A., & Wells, B. (2015). The role of sexual expectancies of substance use as a mediator between adult attachment and drug use among gay and bisexual men. *Drug and Alcohol Dependence*, *153*, 187–193. doi:10.1016/j.drugalcdep.2015.05.028 PMID:26051159

Sumnall, H., Beynon, C., Conchie, S., Riley, S., & Cole, J. (2007). An investigation of subjective experiences of sex after alcohol or drug intoxication. *Journal of Psychopharmacology (Oxford, England)*, *21*(5), 525–537. doi:10.1177/0269881106075590 PMID:17446200

Tavares, I., Laan, E., & Nobre, P. (2017). Cognitive-affective dimensions of female orgasm: The role of automatic thoughts and affect during sexual activity. *Journal of Sexual Medicine*, *14*(6), 818–828. doi:10.1016/j.jsxm.2017.04.004 PMID:28479134

Thompson, J., Kao, T., & Thomas, R. (2005). The relationship between alcohol use and risk-taking sexual behaviors in a large behavioral study. *Preventive Medicine*, *41*(1), 247–252. doi:10.1016/j.ypmed.2004.11.008 PMID:15917018

Tolman, E. (1932). *Purposive Behavior in Animal and Men*. Appleton – Century – Crofts.

Trautwein, U., Marsh, H., Nagengast, B., Lüdtke, O., Nagy, G., & Jonkmann, K. (2012). Probing for multiplicative term in modern expectancy-value theory: A latent interaction modeling study. *Journal of Educational Psychology*, *104*(3), 763–777. doi:10.1037/a0027470

West, R. (2013). *EMCDDA Insights, 14. Models of addiction*. Publications Office of the European Union., doi:10.2810/99994

Wilson, G., & Lawson, D. (1976). Expectancies, alcohol, and sexual arousal in male social drinkers. *Journal of Abnormal Psychology*, *85*(6), 587–594. doi:10.1037/0021-843X.85.6.587 PMID:993455

Wilson, G., & Lawson, D. (1978). Expectancies, alcohol, and sexual arousal in women. *Journal of Abnormal Psychology*, *87*(3), 358–367. doi:10.1037/0021-843X.87.8.358 PMID:681606

World Health Organization. (2019). *The International Classification of Diseases – 11*th *revision*. WHO.

Chapter 2
Unravelling Adolescent Perceptions:
Profiles of Victims and Offenders in Cyber Interpersonal Abuse

Bárbara Machado
NOVA National School of Public Health, NOVA University of Lisboa, Portugal

Sónia Maria Martins Caridade
ⓘ https://orcid.org/0000-0003-0387-7900
Psychology Research Center, School of Psychology, University of Minho, Braga, Portugal

ABSTRACT

Cyber interpersonal abuse refers to the detrimental and harmful behaviours that occur within digital communication platforms, encompassing a wide range of negative interactions such as cyber dating abuse, cyberbullying, online harassment, stalking, and various other forms of online aggression. This chapter investigates the nuanced perspectives of adolescents concerning cyber interpersonal abuse, with a particular focus on the profiling of both victims and offenders. Fifteen focus groups were held to collect data, with 108 adolescents, 42 boys and 66 girls, aged between 11 and 15 years (M= 12.87; SD=0.31). The findings unveil adolescents' perceptions of cyber interpersonal abuse, depicting a female victim and a male aggressor profile. The results underscore a nuanced understanding of the dynamics, emphasizing gender complexities. This chapter aims to enhance comprehension of the intricacies of interpersonal cyber interpersonal abuse among adolescents. Additionally, it discusses preventive strategies and outlines future research challenges.

DOI: 10.4018/979-8-3693-5436-0.ch002

INTRODUCTION

The widespread dissemination of mobile technology and the ubiquitous accessibility of the internet have significantly contributed to the exponential growth of online connectivity and communication, surpassing any previous era in human history (Aslan & Karakus Yilmaz, 2021). Vogels et al. (2022) confirmed that 35% of teens use at least one of the top five online platforms "almost constantly." When faced with the prospect of giving up social media, 54% of teenagers express difficulty in doing so, particularly girls (58%). According to the same study, most adolescents own digital devices, including smartphones (95%), desktop or laptop computers (90%), and gaming consoles (80%). Meanwhile, teens' internet use stands at 97%.

Currently, "digital skills" are widely recognized as technical and operational communication capabilities influenced by individual, social, and national factors, and are unevenly distributed. Given their potential for professional advancement, personal development, and civic participation, digital skills are essential. The absence of digital literacy or the inability to enhance one's digital literacy significantly limits opportunities for career advancement, personal development, and social engagement. Despite their importance, there is still much to be understood about how these skills develop and how best to support them. Furthermore, little is known about the potential benefits of digital skills for the well-being, social engagement, or resilience of children and teenagers in virtual environments. Currently, formal education plays a crucial role in determining the quality of digital education provided, largely influenced by individual instructors and schools. However, to better support digital skills in formal education, increased collaboration and coordinated efforts with stakeholders outside of the education sector are needed. Establishing a standardized definition of digital skills, appropriate conceptual frameworks, and reliable metrics for assessing them is essential. Only with this shared understanding can evidence-based interventions be developed and policies effectively guided. In 2022, the second Youth Skills (ySkills) longitudinal study, a project on digital skills in adolescence, was conducted. This project investigates how digital skills mitigate the potential hazards of ICT use among European youth, specifically those between 12 and 17. Portugal was one of the six European countries where the study took place. Portuguese teens recognize the importance of working with office tools, such as sending an email. This conclusion reinforces the project's main goal and reflects the benefits of digital abilities in teens' lives (Donoso, 2022). In Portugal, 956 students from eight different schools participated in the surveys. The results show that, on average, Portuguese teenagers believe they excel in 70% of digital activities related to communication and interaction. These activities include using appropriate means, reporting harmful content about themselves or groups they belong to, and identifying if someone is a target of cyberbullying (Safer Internet Center,

2022). Despite these positive findings, it is crucial to recognize that adolescents are highly susceptible to cyber interpersonal abuse (CIA), often emerging as primary participants. Investigating the underlying factors contributing to this phenomenon is imperative for a comprehensive understanding of its dynamics.

Adolescence, recognized as a pivotal developmental stage, is characterized by an increase in peer influence and a diminished impact of parental influence. This transitional phase, situated between childhood and adulthood, spans from approximately 10 to 22 years of age, though specific age ranges may vary across diverse cultural contexts (Blakemore & Mills, 2014). Attaining acceptance among peers holds significant importance in the lives of adolescents, as the sense of connection with a broad social network becomes integral to this influential social experience. Adolescents often prioritize the need for inclusivity and interconnectedness with diverse individuals, contributing to the complexity and richness of their social interactions (Crone & Konijn, 2018). Positive experiences of social acceptance online are reinforced through various forms of reward, including likes, popularity, positive comments, and hashtags (Burrow & Rainone, 2017). Effectively, neuropsychological research has demonstrated that acceptance activates brain regions associated with receiving other rewards, such as money or pleasant tastes. Notably, this area shows increased activity when individuals are socially accepted through likes in online environments, as observed in children, adolescents, and adults. This response is diminished in adolescents with depression or a history of maternal negative affect. Previous social experiences, such as parental relations, play a crucial role in understanding which adolescents are more sensitive to the impact of social media. Research in this context indicates that popularity moderates depression, and attachment styles and loneliness increase the likelihood of seeking socio-affective bonding with media figures (Crone & Konijn, 2018; Rössler, 2017).

During adolescence, gender differences become evident in the varied interests and activities of girls and boys. Notably, studies, such as the one conducted by Leonhardt & Overå (2021), indicate a clear distinction in daily habits. A significant percentage of boys, approximately 40%, are daily players of console or computer games, while the corresponding figure for girls is notably lower at 10%. Despite these distinct preferences, it's important to recognize that both genders actively participate in digital practices, and social media plays a pivotal role in shaping their lives. The prevalence of digital engagement highlights the evolving landscape of adolescent interests, with technology serving as a common thread that transcends gender boundaries. Understanding these nuances is crucial for recognizing the diverse ways in which adolescents, irrespective of gender, incorporate technology and social media into their daily lives.

This chapter aims to understand and analyze students' subjective experiences regarding various types of cyber interpersonal abuse (CIA), in order to access their perspectives and experiences. First, we conduct a literature review on the social challenges associated with CIA. Subsequently, we describe the methodological approach employed in the empirical study, its results, and the discussion thereof. Finally, the main conclusions and practical implications of the study are presented and discussed.

BACKGROUND

Cyber Interpersonal Abuse: A Societal Challenge

Participating in digital practices significantly heightens the probability of encountering instances of CIA, as the dynamics of digital conversations make them increasingly accessible to a wide range of individuals across diverse locations and contexts.

In various regions worldwide, the issue of cyber abuse is gaining prominence as a substantial concern, affecting an increasing number of individuals, with a particular emphasis on its impact on women and young people (Council of Europe, 2020). Moreover, it has been emphasized that cyber abuse is not an isolated occurrence, often mirroring the patterns observed in offline violence (European Institute for Gender Equality, 2020). The Council of Europe (CE) defines cyber abuse as the utilization of computer systems to cause, enable, or threaten violence against individuals, leading to, or likely to result in, physical, sexual, psychological, or economic harm or suffering. This may also encompass the exploitation of an individual's circumstances, characteristics, or vulnerabilities (Council of Europe, 2020).

While the use of digital tools brings numerous advantages to the social interactions of adolescents, these practices also heighten their vulnerability to interpersonal intrusiveness, increasing the risk of experiencing cyber dating abuse (CDA), cyberstalking, cyberbullying, and sexting (Jun, 2020; Machado et al., 2022). Interactions on the internet possess distinct characteristics that facilitate and incentivize behaviours aimed at intimidation, such as control and monitoring (Stephenson et al., 2018). This makes aggression possible at any time, and the physical proximity to the victim becomes less relevant in the online environment. Furthermore, the offender is unable to witness the immediate reaction of the victim, creating a temptation to downplay the consequences of their actions (Muñoz-Fernández & Sánchez-Jiménez, 2020). Lastly, the online context provides a cloak of anonymity for the offender, potentially making them feel immune, while the victim may endure heightened humiliation due to the potentially larger audience (Stonard, 2020). In younger communities, experiencing victimization from interpersonal violence always represents an adverse childhood experience with potentially long-lasting effects on one's lifetime well-being (Kowalski et al., 2019).

The analysis of the CIA has led to outcomes that are not only highly diverse but also intricate, encompassing a substantial range of content and multifaceted consequences. Understanding the CIA involves navigating a complex landscape of diverse elements, contributing to the intricate nature of its outcomes (Caridade et al., 2019). The literature on CIA, as explored by researchers such as Cava et al (2020), Caridade & Braga (2019), Galende et al. (2020), and Gkiomisi et al. (2017) has predominantly concentrated on cyberbullying and CDA. A study by Jun (2020) demonstrated that 34% of adolescents were implicated in cyberbullying, assuming roles as offenders (6.3%), victims (14.6%), or both offenders and victims (13.1%). Regarding CDA, empirical evidence indicates that 56% of adolescents involved in dating relationships have encountered CDA (Cava et al., 2020). It is noteworthy that prevalence rates exhibit fluctuations concerning patterns of victimization or perpetration. For instance, in the realm of cyber control behaviour, Borrajo et al. (2015) discovered that 10.6% of adolescents admitted to engaging in direct cyber abuse against their partners; this rate surged to 82% for direct cyber aggression against their partners. Victimization rates demonstrate similar patterns, depending on whether direct cyber aggression (14%) or cyber control (75%) was measured.

While prevalence rates may exhibit variations, the data on cyber violence raise substantial concerns, particularly among adolescents who find themselves in a vulnerable stage of life. The discrepancies in prevalence rates emphasize the need for heightened awareness and intervention strategies to address the specific challenges faced by adolescents in the digital realm. Understanding this variability, it is imperative to delve into the inherent characteristics of the online environment where cyber violence occurs. This space is in a constant state of evolution. By acknowledging the dynamic nature of the digital landscape, we can gain insights into the intricate interplay of factors influencing the occurrence and manifestation of cyber violence across diverse contexts and platforms. The digital realm unfolds many possibilities, embracing state-of-the-art innovations in internet access, technological progress, and the evolution of sophisticated devices like advanced computers, smartphones, and other gadgets. This dynamic landscape continues to shape how individuals interact with the digital sphere, influencing various aspects of daily life and societal dynamics (Machado et al., 2022). CIA poses a significant challenge for our society, with elevated rates of perpetration and victimization standing at 63.2% and 58.8%, respectively, in this case in Portugal (Caridade & Braga, 2019). CIA can be conceptualized as a multidimensional construct that encapsulates a diverse range of sexual and nonsexual behaviours, systematically categorized into distinct dimensions across various fields. This intricate framework reflects the complexity of cyber interpersonal interactions, highlighting the multifaceted nature of behaviours exhibited in the digital landscape. A scoping review conducted by Machado et al. (2022), highlighted cyber violence as an extension of face-to-face violence, introducing new behaviours like control and monitoring, cyber-sexual violence, or public aggression. The study emphasizes the importance of authors defining terms such as aggression, abuse, and violence for a consistent theoretical framework. Achieving conceptual and methodological uniformity is crucial for enhancing the generalizability of research findings in this field and for effective prevention and intervention. Additionally, there is a need to establish clear criteria for measuring aggression, abuse, or violence among young people (Machado et al., 2022). Understanding the profiles of both victims and offenders could represent a crucial step in gaining deeper insights into this complex issue, leading to the development of more effective solutions and interventions.

METHODOLOGY

Present Study

CIA is a field of study that relies on the subjective experiences of those involved, and it is a domain of self-report measurement (Machado et al., 2022). Conducting qualitative research in this field would provide a comprehensive insight into the experiences and perceptions of key stakeholders in the CIA (Tracy, 2019). With this in mind, some studies analysing cyberbullying have focused on the youth's perceptions and experiences (Hendry et al., 2023; Wang et al., 2019). The same principle guided our research, but we aimed to understand and analyse students' subjective experiences in all types of CIA, encompassing their perspectives and experiences. The primary purpose of this research was to investigate the diverse aspects of adolescents' perspectives on CIA and integrate participants' perspectives on the profiles of victims and offenders in CIA. The exploration of the multifaceted aspects of both victims and perpetrators aims to advance our understanding of the intricacies surrounding CIA among the adolescent population. Exploring the multifaceted aspects of victims and offenders is intended to enhance our understanding of the complexities CIA among the adolescent population. Moreover, it will facilitate the extraction of crucial evidence to better support the identification of preventive strategies for this type of abuse, as well as to support the development of intervention programs in this field.

Participants

This study comprised fifteen focus groups of 108 adolescents, 42 boys and 66 girls, according to the following inclusion criteria: being adolescents between 6th grade and 9th grade. The age of participants ranged from 11 and 15 years of age ($M = 12.87$; $SD = 0.31$).

Instruments

A semi-structured interview script, comprising six sections, was developed for data collection. The first section explores interviewees' perceptions of the CIA and the meanings attributed to the abuse. The second section is designed to identify and characterize participants' knowledge regarding the impact of the CIA on the victim and their reactions. The third section aims to understand the progression of abusive behaviour. In the fourth section, the participants were asked about gender issues related to the CIA. The fifth section delves into the motivations inherent in abusive behaviour. Finally, the sixth section comprises personalized questions, wherein participants were queried about situations in which they could be victims, aggressors, or bystanders. Only sections first, second, and fourth were considered for the present study. Additionally, participants were requested to complete a sociodemographic questionnaire to characterize them in terms of sex, age, and grade.

Procedures

The study initially obtained approval from the institutional ethics committee. Participants had the voluntary right to withdraw from the focus group at any time, and confidentiality was emphasized, with a request to avoid using names when discussing incidents involving others. This chapter represents a segment of a more extensive study. Ethical procedures included obtaining consent from all involved entities and obtaining consent from parents or guardians in the case of participants under 18 years of age. All schools included in the study were public, and the recruitment process involved reaching out to the headmaster to assess the school's interest. After securing parental consent, participants also provided their consent, and interview dates were scheduled. Focus groups were conducted in May 2022, with durations ranging from 45 minutes to 1 hour, depending on participant willingness and readiness. These sessions were facilitated by researchers experienced in interviewing victims and possessing specific training in the scope of domestic violence.

Given the potential to discuss distressing experiences, participants were also informed about the potential psychological consequences of the interview. Additionally, where necessary and in the interest of the participant, further specialized support was made available. The interviews were recorded using digital audio and were verbatim transcribed to preserve the integrity of the reports for subsequent analysis.

Data Analysis

This study incorporated meticulous recording and transcription of focus group discussions to ensure accuracy. Thematic analysis of the data, grounded in a constructionist perspective, was conducted following Bardin's approach (Bardin, 2013). This method allowed for a deep understanding of the analysed phenomenon, its meaning, and the way it is socially constructed and reproduced (Braun & Clarke, 2006).

The researcher systematically reviewed transcripts, initially establishing codes. These codes underwent refinement through additional readings, reflexive journaling, and organizational techniques like mind mapping and memo writing. This iterative process led to the creation of meaningful code groupings and the identification of overarching themes. The identified themes and sub-themes were discussed and achieved consensus within the research team. The coding process involved generating semantic and open codes through multiple readings until data saturation was attained.

For data validation, a detailed description and codification aimed for inclusivity to preserve potentially significant extracts within the themes. Nvivo 14.0 software facilitated the organization, coding, and interpretation of the data. To ensure reliability and credibility, two independent researchers, unfamiliar with the participants and experienced in qualitative data analysis, coded the transcribed interviews. One researcher coded the entire sample independently, while the other coded 20% (four focus group interviews), resulting in an 89% agreement for the identified themes. A senior researcher audited the entire coding process.

Reflexivity

During the study, the researchers immersed themselves in a digital world characteristic of the new generations. Their proficiency in Information Communication Technology was remarkable, and it was evident that for all of them, a world without digital tools was unimaginable. Digital tools serve as the foundation of their communication; they are how they perceive the world and experience the initiation of most relationships, whether friendships or dating. It was fascinating to observe how they seamlessly integrate digital practices into their daily lives, as if it were part of their DNA.

However, on the other side, it was concerning to understand their reliance on digital devices and their lack of proficiency in face-to-face communication. While they are adept at communicating in real-time digitally, they struggle with in person interactions. They are inundated with information, yet they often feel overwhelmed by it. They may have extensive knowledge about violence but have difficulty recognizing when they perpetrate it themselves. We have a generation that emerged and is raised in digital practices. However, we also have a generation that requires support in navigating the abundance of information and risks that these digital practices constantly present.

This fieldwork provided the researchers with the opportunity to explore various perspectives and gain personal insights. It instils hope that equipping our children with the necessary tools to either escape from or, at the very least, cope with the digital violence they frequently encounter should be a priority for their future.

Results

Based on the multiple perspectives of teenagers on CIA, with a special focus on defining profiles of both victims and aggressors, two major themes emerged, each encompassing different categories and subcategories (cf. Table 1).

Table 1. Themes, categories, and sub-categories resulting from data analysis

Themes	Categories	Subcategories
Cyber Interpersonal Abuse	Abusive behaviours	Telling lies
		Spreading rumours
		Frame
		Uploading and sharing photos, videos, and explicit content
		Hacking
		Show off private life
		Image manipulation
		Threats
		Insult
		Take photos
	Aggressor profile	Gender (male)
		Social status
		Personal characteristics
	Victim profile	Sociodemographic characteristics (female, sexual orientation, ethnicity)
		Physical characteristics
		Psychological characteristics
		Social functioning
Cyber Interpersonal Abuse and Gender	Gender roles	Stereotypic female roles
		Stereotypic male roles
	Social values	Male
		Female
	Impact of CIA	Male
		Female

Participants described two themes distributed in six categories (cf. table 1). In the abusive behaviour category, emerged a subcategory abusive behaviours, were the participants identified telling lies ("Telling lies is serious" – P27), spreading rumours ("Spreading rumours or fake news about us is very serious and very bad" – P28), frame colleges ("Framing a person for cyber-attacks" – P29), post photos or videos ("Posting photos of other people without permission is very serious" – P5; "Sharing videos and photos is also serious, not just publishing. And if they are nudes, it is even more serious" – P11; "I think publishing and sharing photos and videos is serious" – P30), hacking ("Hacking social networks, as we mentioned in that case, is very serious" – P31), show off private life ("Showing things from someone's private life is serious" – P32), image manipulation ("It is also very serious when there are people who make photo montages and then publish them" – P15), threats ("Threatening the person or the family is very serious" – P22), insults ("Insults are less severe because it's easier to ignore the person" – P33) and take photos ("Taking pictures of the person is less serious as long as they don't post them" – P34).

The victim and the aggressor profiles were also mentioned by the participants. The aggressor and the victim profile were related to the gender ("It happens more than girls are the victim and boys are the aggressors" – P36; "When the aggressor is a girl, it is usually girl against girl" – P37; "It happens more than girls are the victim and boys are the aggressors" – P32). The aggressor profile is also related to social status ("Bullies are sometimes not just the popular ones. Sometimes they have the same characteristics as the victims, and they do this to feel superior" – P38) and personal characteristics ("Bullies, most of the time, are confident individuals with no self-esteem problems" – P3). Concerning the victim profile also included physical characteristics ("They also make mean comments to people who wear glasses or who have a disability" – P39; "Those young people who have acne also make fun of them" – P40; "If we are too short, they make fun of our photos on social networks, but if we are too tall, too" – P41), psychological characteristics ("Very shy people are also easy targets because they don't complain or tell anyone, they usually suffer in silence" – P27), sociodemographic characteristics ("People who are victims are also victims because they assume on social networks that they are, for example, homosexuals, that they are not Christians and sometimes have ethnicities that are different from ours" – P42; "Being a foreigner can also lead to cyber violence, with mean comments because people don't express themselves so well in our language" – P43) and social functioning ("The fact that they always take pictures with the same clothes, because they are poor, can already make the person a possible cyber victim" – P11).

CIA and gender included three categories: gender roles, social values, and the impact of CIA. On the gender roles, participants identify stereotypic female and male roles, respectively ("Girls have to play with dolls; otherwise, they may be the victims of teasing" – P55; "Boys have to know how to play ball or at least have to play sports, like basketball and so on; otherwise, they can be teased" – P56). Regarding the social values we have, male and female, respectively ("Boys also have standards of beauty that society creates, such as being tall, muscular, blond and blue-eyed" – P58; "Girls suffer a lot from beauty standards because there is the issue of appearance, like being thin, tall, blonde, but also being smart and not having acne. Furthermore, there is more societal pressure for girls to meet these standards" – P59). At last, students considered that the impact of CIA is different in males and females, respectively ("Boys do not suffer so much, I think, because they do not care so much about insults or bad jokes, especially if they are related to appearance" – P3; "Girls suffer a lot from cyberbullying, especially if it is related to appearance. Moreover, because they are very mean to each other and offend each other about her physically aspect" – P68).

DISCUSSION

The main objective of this study was to explore various aspects of adolescents' perspectives on CIA and synthesize their viewpoints regarding the profiles of victims and offenders in CIA. The aim was to achieve a nuanced understanding of this phenomenon, making a significant contribution to the existing literature. Notably, the prevailing research in this field has primarily favored quantitative approaches to studying CIA. By adopting a qualitative lens, this study sought to enrich the literature by providing in-depth insights into the subjective experiences and perceptions of adolescents involved in or affected by CIA.

Additionally, the study aimed to contribute to the development of targeted intervention strategies and preventive measures. Understanding the subjective experiences of those involved in CIA is crucial for formulating effective policies, educational programs, and support systems to mitigate the impact of cyber abuse among adolescents. Ultimately, the study endeavors to bridge the gap between quantitative dominance and the need for a richer, qualitative understanding in the realm of CIA.

Participants in the study reported various forms of CIA, encompassing behaviors such as telling lies, spreading rumors, framing, uploading and sharing explicit content, hacking, exposing private lives, manipulating images, making threats, insulting, and taking photos. Identifying these manifestations of CIA is a fundamental step in adolescents' efforts to tackle this issue. Therefore, this type of study is significant as it aids in understanding adolescents' perspectives on CIA, offering valuable insights to empower them with tools to combat this social and developmental challenge.

While this approach is crucial, the literature also delves into alternative solutions to comprehensively address the issue.

Adolescents' widespread use of social media has prompted the exploration of alternative responses to CIA. One such approach involves content moderators who can identify abusive text and remove cyberbullies from online communities. However, the immense volume of daily social media data makes manual human moderation impractical. Consequently, social media platforms are increasingly turning to machine learning classifiers for automated cyberbullying detection (Van Hee et al., 2018). Despite notable advancements in recent years, existing models must undergo continuous refinement for real-world applications. This need for improvement is attributed, in part, to deficiencies in the training and testing data (Rosa et al., 2019; Salawu et al., 2017). As technology evolves, ongoing enhancements to these models are crucial for effectively addressing the challenges posed by cyberbullying in online environments.

A study conducted on the Twitter platform aimed to comprehend the characteristics of abusive behavior (Chatzakou et al., 2019). Initial measures, such as preventing suspended users from creating new accounts (Pham, 2017) or temporarily restricting users for abusive behavior (Sulleyman, 2017), could enhance social media's response to CIA. These actions represent the first stages in addressing the ongoing conflict involving abusers, victims, online bystanders, and the hosting of online platforms (Chatzakou et al., 2019). Another study (Ziems et al., 2020) conducted on the Twitter platform generated an original dataset for cyberbullying detection research, introducing an approach to enhance the accuracy of cyberbullying detection. The labelling scheme was explicitly crafted to align with cyberbullying definitions, with classes differentiating cyberbullying from other related behaviors like isolated aggression or crude joking. The researchers introduced a new set of features to quantify the criteria associated with cyberbullying, leading to improved performance of standard text-based models. Despite these positive results, they emphasized the importance of social networks and language-based measurements in capturing the nuanced social characteristics of cyberbullying. This is crucial for the classifiers' ability to achieve the high levels of precision and recall anticipated in real-world detection systems (Ziems et al., 2020). Keeping this study in mind helps us comprehend the challenging task of cyberbullying detection and underscores the significance of the initial solution we approach to the CIA problem, which involves adolescents being able to identify the main types of abusive behavior to combat this problem.

From the perspective of the participants in the present study, peers exert a significant influence on almost all aspects of adolescents' lives. Participant reports suggest that teenagers tend to report more cases of cyberbullying, with girls appearing to be more susceptible than boys. This perspective from participants is in line with existing scientific evidence, which consistently suggests that women are victims of cyberbullying more often than men. Consequently, girls report experiencing more cyberbullying, including threats, harassment and intimidation (Chocarro & Garaigordobil, 2019). Indeed, the study developed by Garaigordobil et al. (2019) reveals that women are 3.3% more likely to be victims than men, with 4.2% of the samples experiencing gender-based cyberbullying. Other study, conducted Álvarez Lara & Castillo Mauricio (2022) by also determined that in 78% of cases, males mostly take on the role of cyber-aggressor rather than cyber victim, which is the opposite for females. Additionally, 20% of the studies indicate victimization predominantly towards males (Ching Espinosa, 2021). Men are more involved in cyberbullying, and with minority participation, women tend to take on the role of the victim. Hence, most studies agree on examining causality in factors such as gender, age, and roles involved in this type of bullying, leading to opposite findings (Chocarro & Garaigordobil, 2019). So, our result followed the literature tendency, with girls being more victimized that boys.

In the current study, participants illuminate a critical facet of CIA by underscoring the influence of societal gender roles and its potential impact on the occurrence of CIA. According to their perspectives, societal expectations, as well as our own, as citizens, often prescribe specific behaviours based on one's assigned gender at birth. This dynamic could potentially lead to CIA if an individual's behaviour deviates from societal expectations. For instance, as perceived by the participants, societal norms dictate that boys should not engage in activities like ballet. Consequently, if a boy decides to pursue ballet, he might become a victim of CIA, as his peers may subject him to ridicule. Another recurring example involves the societal expectation that girls should play with dolls; failure to adhere to this norm could also make them susceptible to mockery.

A study developed by Mishna et al. (2020) contends that boys' roles and behaviours were frequently overlooked, while girls were consistently brought into focus, often being held accountable and criticized. The experiences of girls were frequently downplayed and normalized by their peers, and these experiences were connected to gender norms and stereotypes that went unnoticed by the participants. The study found that gendered and sexualized bullying and cyberbullying are part of a socialization process in which girls anticipate experiencing gender-based aggression, violence, and inequality in their lives. Hence, bullying and cyberbullying are linked to societal norms that place girls at risk of harassment, violence, abuse, and discrimination.

Digital media present new opportunities for adolescents to navigate gender and sexual identity formation and exploration (Freeman & Wohn, 2020; Scarcelli et al., 2021). Consensual and intentional online sexual practices, particularly the sharing of self-determined intimate body images, are already a reality among young people and are likely to persist in the future (Mahlknecht & Bork-Hüffer, 2023). From the same perspective, these authors highlight that the enduring and intricate "sexual double standard" is particularly detrimental to young females. This standard legitimizes the unwarranted hyper-sexualization of their bodies online while simultaneously restricting their right to self-determined sexual practices in the online realm. Therefore, it is crucial to deconstruct girls' perspectives of themselves to minimize the impact of CIA on their lives.

In recent years, much has been discussed about how Information and Communication Technologies (ICT) also contribute to indirect violence, including bullying, discrimination, harassment, identity theft, and attacks through electronic means (Kula, 2022; Mishra et al., 2023). Many authors (Li et al., 2022; Machado et al., 2022; Telzer et al., 2018) concur that preventing such situations requires a thorough investigation of this social problem and an understanding of the predisposing factors influencing the mental health of children and adolescents. Therefore, an analysis of various factors such as biological aspects, lifestyle, physical and economic environment, social dynamics, people's roles in society, and access to fundamental resources and services like housing, education, and healthcare is essential (García-Carrión et al., 2019).

Keeping that in mind, it is essential to consider that adolescents' ability to make more informed decisions will be more successful if we tailor interventions to match their developmental capabilities. We can also pinpoint these capabilities by connecting adolescents' neuronal and cognitive development with their behaviour in various social contexts (Ciranka & Van den Bos, 2019).

According to Ciranka & Van den Bos (2019), participants across all age groups tended to make riskier decisions in the presence of risky social information. They opted for safer choices when presented with safe social information. Hence, when peers value risk aversion, social information can encourage adolescent safety-promoting behaviours. Leveraging the discovery that social information can promote safe decision-making could result in improved interventions, potentially reducing real-world risks (Ciranka & Van den Bos, 2019). The literature presents an optimistic view of adolescent decision-making, further endorsing the use of adolescent social motivation for favourable outcomes, including the prevention of cyber-interpersonal abuse on social media (Ciranka & Van den Bos, 2019; Telzer et al., 2018; Van Hoorn et al., 2018).

Given the association of CIA with adverse outcomes during adolescence, educators and other professionals must comprehend how children's diverse roles in cyber abuse correlate with psychosocial well-being outcomes and which factors may influence this relationship (Hellfeldt et al., 2020). So, as a multidimensional problem, prevention and intervention programs targeting cyber abuse could be enhanced by incorporating specific strategies that foster increased seeking and perceiving functional social support from family and school during adolescence.

Despite the significant contributions made by this study to enhance our understanding of the CIA phenomenon, it is crucial to acknowledge certain limitations for a more nuanced interpretation. While the utilization of participant reports offers valuable insights into the CIA phenomenon, specifically capturing the participants' unique understanding, it simultaneously introduces a limitation by narrowing the focus to the experiences and perspectives of this particular group. The setting of data collection, within a school context, might have influenced responses due to social desirability bias. It is essential to recognize this potential limitation and consider the implications for the generalizability of findings beyond the school environment. Another limitation arises from the sample's characteristics, as the study exclusively involved public schools in the northern region of Portugal. This regional specificity may restrict the generalizability of findings to other cultural and regional contexts. Future research should strive for a more comprehensive approach, encompassing diverse regional and cultural backgrounds to capture the full spectrum of influences on this form of abuse.

In light of these limitations, it is recommended that future studies in this field adopt a more inclusive approach, encompassing a broader range of educational institutions and cultural settings. This would enable a more thorough exploration of the social and cultural factors that might influence the occurrence and manifestation of CIA, thereby enriching the overall understanding of this complex phenomenon.

CONCLUSION

Adolescents are often characterized by their propensity for engaging in what is commonly perceived as excessive risk-taking, particularly within social contexts. Considering that the decisions made by adolescents in these risky situations can have substantial health implications and potentially lead to long-term consequences, there have been numerous endeavours to gain insights into the multifaceted factors that influence social risk-taking among adolescents, both as potential victims and aggressors in the context of CIA.

Gender remains a scientific determinant, as observed from the perspective of violence in young and adolescent partner relationships. Girls remain mostly victims; hence, boys are the perpetrators. Our study highlights a new student's perspective, considering the social pressure to achieve social standardization attributed to societal gender roles. This viewpoint is a recent addition to the CIA study, with few studies contemplating this problem and the students claiming that this is a phenomenon that contributes to CIA victimization or aggression. More studies should analyse this variable to consider the actual impact on CIA.

Considering CIA as a multidimensional problem and its impact on gender, it is crucial to consider a concerted approach between several entities to minimize the problem and reduce the impact on adolescents' development, with the school as the main centre of change. Considering viable approaches to the problem, a study (Ciranka & Van den Bos, 2019) show us that safe social information has a more decisive influence on adolescents' decisions than risky information. These results add further evidence that adolescent social sensitivity can result in safe, health-promoting behaviour and could be a way to combat CIA in adolescence. Including parents, schools, and the community in solving the problem reduces the problem and helps adolescents have a healthier childhood.

We emphasize the immediate necessity of persisting in addressing problematic gender inequality and raising awareness, particularly among young people, to dismantle traditional gendered discourses and sexual and moral hierarchies that disproportionately affect females. This can only happen through a combination of educational efforts and extracurricular programs addressing the problematic nature of traditional gender concepts. Collaborative efforts should involve educational and awareness initiatives targeting young adults, parents, and teachers. Intensive collaborative work is essential to empowering young girls and boys, extending beyond issues of gender and sexuality. Future research should integrate students' perspectives into programmes combating the CIA during adolescence.

REFERENCES

Álvarez Lara, M. C., & Castillo Mauricio, M. S. (2022). *Ciberbullying en niños y adolescentes desde la perspectiva de género: Una revisión sistemática.* https://hdl.handle.net/20.500.12692/86862

Aslan, A., & Karakus Yilmaz, T. (2021). Changes in Safer Internet Use of Children in Turkey between 2010-2015 and Impact of Contextual Issues. *Malaysian Online Journal of Educational Technology, 9*(1), 1–18. doi:10.17220/mojet.2021.9.1.238

Bardin, L. (2013). *Análise de Conteúdo* [Content analysis]. Edições 70.

Blakemore, S. J., & Mills, K. L. (2014). Is adolescence a sensitive period for sociocultural processing? *Annual Review of Psychology, 65*(1), 187–207. doi:10.1146/annurev-psych-010213-115202 PMID:24016274

Borrajo, E., Gámez-Guadix, M., Pereda, N., & Calvete, E. (2015). The development and validation of the cyber dating abuse questionnaire among young couples. *Computers in Human Behavior, 48*, 358–365. doi:10.1016/j.chb.2015.01.063

Braun, V., & Clarke, V. (2006). Using thematic analysis in psychology. *Qualitative Research in Psychology*, *3*(2), 77–101. doi:10.1191/1478088706qp063oa

Burrow, A. L., & Rainone, N. (2017). How many likes did I get?: Purpose moderates links between positive social media feedback and self-esteem. *Journal of Experimental Social Psychology*, *69*, 232–236. doi:10.1016/j.jesp.2016.09.005

Caridade, S., & Braga, T. (2019). Versão portuguesa do Cyber Dating Abuse Questionaire (CDAQ)–Questionário sobre Ciberabuso no Namoro (CibAN): Adaptação e propriedades psicométricas [Portuguese version of the Cyber Dating Abuse Questionnaire (CDAQ)–Cyber Abuse in Dating Questionnaire (CibAN): Adaptation and psychometric properties]. *Análise Psicológica*, *105*(1), 93–105. doi:10.14417/ap.1543

Caridade, S., Braga, T., & Borrajo, E. (2019). Cyber dating abuse (CDA): Evidence from a systematic review. *Aggression and Violent Behavior*, *48*, 152–168. doi:10.1016/j.avb.2019.08.018

Cava, M. J., Martínez-Ferrer, B., Buelga, S., & Carrascosa, L. (2020). Sexist attitudes, romantic myths, and offline dating violence as predictors of cyber dating violence perpetration in adolescents. *Computers in Human Behavior*, *111*, 106449. doi:10.1016/j.chb.2020.106449

Chatzakou, D., Leontiadis, I., Blackburn, J., De Cristofaro, E., Stringhini, G., Vakali, A., & Kourtellis, N. (2019). Detecting cyberbullying and cyberaggression in social media. *ACM Transactions on the Web*, *13*(3), 1–51. doi:10.1145/3343484

Ching Espinosa, E. G. P. (2021). *Cyberbullying en niños y adolescentes: una revisión sistemática*. https://hdl.handle.net/20.500.12692/66060

Chocarro, E., & Garaigordobil, M. (2019). Bullying and cyberbullying: Sex differences in victims, aggressors and observers. *Pensamiento Psicológico*, *17*(2), 57–71. doi:10.11144/Javerianacali.PPSI17-2.bcds

Ciranka, S., & Van den Bos, W. (2019). Social influence in adolescent decision-making: A formal framework. *Frontiers in Psychology*, *10*, 1915. doi:10.3389/fpsyg.2019.01915 PMID:31555164

Council of Europe. (2020). *Cyberviolence*. https://www.coe.int/en/web/cyberviolence/home#%7B%2250020850%22:[0]%7D

Crone, E. A., & Konijn, E. A. (2018). Media use and brain development during adolescence. *Nature Communications*, *9*(1), 588. doi:10.1038/s41467-018-03126-x PMID:29467362

Donoso V. (2022). *Youth digital skills: Insights from the ySKILLS project.* Hamburg: Leibniz-Institut für Medienforschung | Hans-Bredow-Institut (HBI); CO:RE - Children Online: Research and Evidence. doi:10.21241/ssoar.78951

European Institute for Gender Equality. (2020). *Violence at a glance.* https://eige.europa.eu/gender-equality-index/2020/domain/violence

Freeman, G., & Wohn, D. Y. (2020). Streaming your identity: Navigating the presentation of gender and sexuality through live streaming. *Computer Supported Cooperative Work, 29*(6), 795–825. doi:10.1007/s10606-020-09386-w

Galende, N., Ozamiz-Etxebarria, N., Jaureguizar, J., & Redondo, I. (2020). Cyber dating violence prevention programs in universal populations: A systematic review. *Psychology Research and Behavior Management, 13*, 1089–1099. doi:10.2147/PRBM.S275414 PMID:33299362

Garaigordobil, M., Mollo-Torrico, J. P., & Larrain, E. (2019). Prevalencia de Bullying y Cyberbullying en Latinoamérica: una revisión. *Revista Iberoamericana de psicología, 11*(3), 1–18. doi:10.33881/2027-1786.rip.11301

García-Carrión, R., Villarejo-Carballido, B., & Villardón-Gallego, L. (2019). Children and adolescents mental health: A systematic review of interaction-based interventions in schools and communities. *Frontiers in Psychology, 10*, 918. doi:10.3389/fpsyg.2019.00918 PMID:31068881

Gkiomisi, A., Gkrizioti, M., Gkiomisi, A., Anastasilakis, D. A., & Kardaras, P. (2017). Cyberbullying among Greek high school adolescents. *Indian Journal of Pediatrics, 84*(5), 364–368. doi:10.1007/s12098-016-2256-2 PMID:27957645

Hellfeldt, K., López-Romero, L., & Andershed, H. (2020). Cyberbullying and psychological well-being in young adolescence: The potential protective mediation effects of social support from family, friends, and teachers. *International Journal of Environmental Research and Public Health, 17*(1), 45. doi:10.3390/ijerph17010045 PMID:31861641

Hendry, B. P., Hellsten, L.-A. M., McIntyre, L. J., & Smith, B. R. R. (2023). Recommendations for cyberbullying prevention and intervention: A Western Canadian perspective from key stakeholders. *Frontiers in Psychology, 14*, 1067484. doi:10.3389/fpsyg.2023.1067484 PMID:36960003

Jun, W. (2020). A study on the cause analysis of cyberbullying in Korean adolescents. *International Journal of Environmental Research and Public Health, 17*(13), 4648. doi:10.3390/ijerph17134648 PMID:32605227

Kowalski, R. M., Limber, S. P., & McCord, A. (2019). A developmental approach to cyberbullying: Prevalence and protective factors. *Aggression and Violent Behavior*, *45*, 20–32. https://psycnet.apa.org/doi/10.1016/j.avb.2018.02.009. doi:10.1016/j. avb.2018.02.009

Kula, M. E. (2022). Cyberbullying: A Literature Review on Cross-Cultural Research in the Last Quarter. In M. Kula (Ed.), *Handbook of Research on Digital Violence and Discrimination Studies* (pp. 610–630). IGI Global. doi:10.4018/978-1-7998-9187-1.ch027

Leonhardt, M., & Overå, S. (2021). Are there differences in video gaming and use of social media among boys and girls?—A mixed methods approach. *International Journal of Environmental Research and Public Health*, *18*(11), 6085. doi:10.3390/ ijerph18116085 PMID:34200039

Li, C., Wang, P., Martin-Moratinos, M., Bella-Fernández, M., & Blasco-Fontecilla, H. (2022). Traditional bullying and cyberbullying in the digital age and its associated mental health problems in children and adolescents: A meta-analysis. *European Child & Adolescent Psychiatry*, 1–15. doi:10.1007/s00787-021-01763-0 PMID:36585978

Machado, B., Caridade, S., Araújo, I., & Faria, P. L. (2022). Mapping the cyber interpersonal violence among young populations: A scoping review. *Social Sciences (Basel, Switzerland)*, *11*(5), 207. doi:10.3390/socsci11050207

Mahlknecht, B., & Bork-Hüffer, T. (2023). 'She felt incredibly ashamed': Gendered (cyber-) bullying and the hypersexualized female body. *Gender, Place and Culture*, *30*(7), 989–1011. doi:10.1080/0966369X.2022.2115981

Mishna, F., Schwan, K. J., Birze, A., Van Wert, M., Lacombe-Duncan, A., McInroy, L., & Attar-Schwartz, S. (2020). Gendered and sexualized bullying and cyber bullying: Spotlighting girls and making boys invisible. *Youth & Society*, *52*(3), 403–426. doi:10.1177/0044118X18757150

Mishra, D., Le, A. N., & McDowell, Z. (2023). *Communication Technology and Gender Violence*. Springer Nature.

Muñoz-Fernández, N., & Sánchez-Jiménez, V. (2020). Cyber-aggression and psychological aggression in adolescent couples: A short-term longitudinal study on prevalence and common and differential predictors. *Computers in Human Behavior*, *104*, 106191. doi:10.1016/j.chb.2019.106191

Pham, S. (2017). Twitter tries new measures in crackdown on harassment. *CN-Ntech*.

Rosa, H., Pereira, N., Ribeiro, R., Ferreira, P. C., Carvalho, J. P., Oliveira, S., Coheur, L., Paulino, P., Simão, A. M. V., & Trancoso, I. (2019). Automatic cyberbullying detection: A systematic review. *Computers in Human Behavior*, *93*, 333–345. doi:10.1016/j.chb.2018.12.021

Rössler, P. (2017). *The international encyclopedia of media effects, 4 volume set*. John Wiley & Sons. doi:10.1002/9781118783764

Safer Internet Center. (2022). *Estudo sobre competências digitais de adolescentes portugueses indica maior à-vontade em comunicação e interação* [Study on digital skills of Portuguese teenagers indicates greater ease in communication and interaction]. https://www.internetsegura.pt/noticias/estudo-sobre-competencias-digitais-de-adolescentes-portugueses-indica-maior-vontade-em

Salawu, S., He, Y., & Lumsden, J. (2017). Approaches to automated detection of cyberbullying: A survey. *IEEE Transactions on Affective Computing*, *11*(1), 3–24. doi:10.1109/TAFFC.2017.2761757

Scarcelli, C. M., Krijnen, T., & Nixon, P. (2021). Sexuality, gender, media. Identity articulations in the contemporary media landscape. *Information Communication and Society*, *24*(8), 1063–1072. doi:10.1080/1369118X.2020.1804603

Stephenson, V. L., Wickham, B. M., & Capezza, N. M. (2018). Psychological abuse in the context of social media. *Violence and Gender*, *5*(3), 129–134. doi:10.1089/vio.2017.0061

Stonard, K. E. (2020). "Technology was designed for this": Adolescents' perceptions of the role and impact of the use of technology in cyber dating violence. *Computers in Human Behavior*, *105*, 106211. doi:10.1016/j.chb.2019.106211

Sulleyman, A. (2017). Twitter temporarily limiting users for abusive behaviour. *Independent*.

Telzer, E. H., Van Hoorn, J., Rogers, C. R., & Do, K. T. (2018). Social influence on positive youth development: A developmental neuroscience perspective. *Advances in Child Development and Behavior*, *54*, 215–258. doi:10.1016/bs.acdb.2017.10.003 PMID:29455864

Tracy, S. J. (2019). *Qualitative research methods: Collecting evidence, crafting analysis, communicating impact*. John Wiley & Sons.

Van Hee, C., Jacobs, G., Emmery, C., Desmet, B., Lefever, E., Verhoeven, B., De Pauw, G., Daelemans, W., & Hoste, V. (2018). Automatic detection of cyberbullying in social media text. *PLoS One*, *13*(10), e0203794. doi:10.1371/journal.pone.0203794 PMID:30296299

Van Hoorn, J., McCormick, E. M., & Telzer, E. H. (2018). Moderate social sensitivity in a risky context supports adaptive decision making in adolescence: Evidence from brain and behavior. *Social Cognitive and Affective Neuroscience*, *13*(5), 546–556. doi:10.1093/scan/nsy016 PMID:29529318

Vogels, E. A., Gelles-Watnick, R., & Massarat, N. (2022). *Teens, social media and technology*. Pew Research Center. https://www.pewresearch.org/internet/2018/05/31/teens-social-media-technology-2018/

Wang, C.-W., Musumari, P. M., Techasrivichien, T., Suguimoto, S. P., Chan, C.-C., Ono-Kihara, M., Kihara, M., & Nakayama, T. (2019). "I felt angry, but I couldn't do anything about it": A qualitative study of cyberbullying among Taiwanese high school students. *BMC Public Health*, *19*(1), 1–11. doi:10.1186/s12889-019-7005-9 PMID:31138175

Ziems, C., Vigfusson, Y., & Morstatter, F. (2020). Aggressive, repetitive, intentional, visible, and imbalanced: Refining representations for cyberbullying classification. *Proceedings of the International AAAI Conference on Web and Social Media, 14*, 808–819. https://github.com/cjziems/cyberbullying-representations808

Chapter 3

In Quest of Sanctuary:
The Gendered Challenges Within the Complex Landscape of Asylum–Seeking

Gabriela Mesquita Borges
University of Lusíada, Portugal

ABSTRACT

This chapter explores the complex landscape of asylum-seeking, focusing on the 1951 Refugee Convention and the rights it grants to those seeking refuge, emphasizing principles like non-discrimination and non-refoulement. The chapter highlights the tension between international legal guarantees and state discretion in granting asylum, underscoring the gap between aspirational goals and practical outcomes. It also delves into scholarly literature on migration, border control, and the "deviant migrant" narrative, offering insights into the complexities of asylum practices. It addresses criminological and gendered dimensions, with a specific focus on violence against asylum-seeking women, revealing unique challenges. Overall, the analysis covers historical perspectives, contemporary challenges, and evolving global migration dynamics, providing a comprehensive understanding of the intricate journey asylum seekers undergo for safety and justice.

INTRODUCTION

Contemporary societies are marked by discernible trends toward protectionism and exclusion, vividly exemplified in media portrayals casting asylum seekers as menacing and prone to violence. This narrative often extends, unjustly, to encompass diverse groups such as Muslim terrorists and undocumented Mexicans posing as refugees (Zedner, 2020).

DOI: 10.4018/979-8-3693-5436-0.ch003

In the current discourse on migration, global and national dialogues prominently feature keywords like "protection" and "security", responding to perceived foreign threats. This conversation, however, is entangled with traditional dichotomies between criminals and law-abiding citizens, reinforcing a stark division between the foreign and the national (Aas, 2019; 2013).

The surge in xenophobic sentiments, characterized by intolerance and suspicion toward those seeking protection and asylum, has given rise to pervasive depictions of asylum seekers and refugees as "false", "opportunists", "bogus", "outsiders", "folk devils", and "crimmigrant others" (Melossi, 2015; Cohen, 2011).

Against the backdrop of the European refugee crisis, criminology's examination of displacement has bifurcated into two primary branches: Crimmigration and Border Criminologies.

Crimmigration scrutinizes social control over specific migrant categories, aiming to preserve European Union cohesion from perceived threats posed by undocumented and criminally involved displacement (Guia & Pedroso, 2015; Aas & Bosworth, 2013; Guia, 2015). This has resulted in heightened migration control efforts to secure EU borders, fostering a divisive narrative of "us versus them" fueled by xenophobia and mistrust (Zedner, 2020; Aas, 2019; Vilmer et al., 2018; Bauman, 2016).

On the other hand, Border Criminologies delves into the transformative effects of migration on penal power, examining its implications for punishment, law, justice, and citizenship (Aas, 2019; Barker, 2018; Fassin, 2018; Bosworth, 2011). The disoriented, unwelcome, and apprehensive displacement of groups of people has prompted numerous inquiries into the detrimental impacts of armed conflict, social and economic inequalities, and violence, often serving as catalysts for international forced migration rooted in human rights concerns (Aliverti, 2020).

This insightful exploration into the transformative dynamics of migration within the realm of Border Criminologies lays a critical foundation for understanding the broader implications of displacement. Pursuing sanctuary as an asylum seeker involves navigating a complex landscape that is often fraught with challenges, and these challenges are not gender-neutral. Gender plays a significant role in shaping the experiences of individuals seeking asylum, influencing their vulnerabilities, access to resources, and the nature of the obstacles they face.

In recent years, the intersection of criminology, victimology, and feminist studies has significantly contributed to a nuanced understanding of the multifaceted challenges faced by women seeking asylum. This interdisciplinary approach offers a more comprehensive and contemporary perspective, delving into the intricate social, political, and personal contexts that shape the experiences of these women throughout their displacement journey and in their country of asylum. Scholars in this burgeoning field have proved beyond conventional analyses, shedding light on the vulnerabilities these women face, encompassing physical, psychological, sexual, and emotional dimensions of violence (Cochrane, 2018; Canning, 2020; Sapia, 2018; Baczynska & Ledwith, 2016; Freedman, 2016; 2015; Hathaway & Foster, 2014; Hathaway, 2005; Atlani & Rousseau, 2000).

Criminological insights, as articulated by Cochrane (2018), Canning (2017), and Sapia (2018), among others, provide a valuable lens through which to examine the criminalization of displacement, the challenges women encounter within the asylum-seeking process, and the impact of border control policies on their well-being. Studies such as Baczynska and Ledwith (2016), Freedman (2019; 2016a), and Hathaway and Foster (2014), delve into the victimization experienced by these women, shedding light on the specific forms of harm they endure, such as exploitation, abuse, and violence. This lens underscores how women seeking asylum navigate unique challenges shaped by gender roles, power dynamics, and cultural norms.

The evolving body of literature in this realm not only captures the vulnerabilities but also advocates for policy changes, shedding light on the need for gender-sensitive approaches to asylum-seeking and refugee protection. Together, these interdisciplinary perspectives contribute to a more nuanced, empathetic, and actionable understanding of the complex experiences of women seeking asylum in contemporary societies.

This chapter unfolds in three parts, meticulously navigating the legal frameworks, societal frameworks, and gender-specific challenges that shape the complex terrain traversed by asylum seekers in their quest for safety and justice. As an invaluable resource, this comprehensive exploration contributes not only to the scholarly understanding of the multifaceted issues surrounding asylum but also serves as a critical reference for researchers seeking nuanced insights into the intersection of criminology, migration, and gender studies.

Additionally, it offers an enlightening perspective for the general public, fostering a more informed discourse on the experiences of asylum seekers and the broader implications of border control policies, ultimately promoting empathy, awareness, and informed decision-making in our interconnected global society.

PART I

Insights Into the 1951 Refugee Convention and Non-Discrimination, Non-Penalization, and Non-Refoulement Rights

The 1951 Refugee Convention, consolidating earlier international instruments, comprehensively codifies refugee rights globally. As per the UK Public General Act, specifically the 1999 Immigration and Asylum Act, Section 94(1), an asylum seeker refers to an individual who has sought asylum under the 1951 Refugee Convention but awaits evaluation by the legal authorities of the country where the request was made. Consequently, an individual maintains asylum seeker status for the duration of the pending asylum application. It's noteworthy that not every asylum seeker will receive international protection and be acknowledged as a refugee; however, every refugee starts their journey as an asylum seeker.

Today, it is unequivocal that asylum seekers and refugees, as per international law, deserve a legal framework ensuring the protection and realization of their rights (Goodwin-Gill & McAdam, 2007). Granting asylum aligns with a historical norm and is integral to the Universal Declaration of Human Rights (UDHR, 1948). The 1951 Refugee Convention, its 1967 Protocol, and the UNHCR establish specific rights, freedoms, and minimum treatment standards for foreigners in asylum countries, covering areas like movement, religion, association, welfare, employment, administrative assistance, and property rights.

States adhering to the 1951 Refugee Convention, or its Protocol must cooperate with the UNHCR, fulfil assigned duties, and respect the refugee's status (Edwards, 2005). While states aren't obligated to grant asylum, they are prohibited from sending individuals to a place jeopardizing life, security, or welfare.

Despite these legal provisions, an exploration of the 1951 Refugee Convention's aspirations and practicalities reveals significant distinctions, as elaborated in the subsequent analysis.

The 1951 Convention defines a refugee as an individual or group compelled to leave their country due to violence, torture, or external pressures resulting from ongoing wars, political, religious, or social motives. The Convention, in Article 1(2), specifies inclusion criteria, emphasizing a "well-founded fear of persecution" based on race, religion, nationality, membership in a social group, or political opinion. However, the definition faces challenges at three levels: inclusion, exclusion, and cessation.

In terms of inclusion, refugee status requires fulfillment of four cumulative conditions: being outside the home country, unable or unwilling to avail oneself of home country protection due to a well-founded fear of persecution on limiting grounds. The primary aim of the 1951 Refugee Convention is to provide an alternative protection source when the home state fails (Edwards, 2005). However, the "nexus" condition limits the scope, excluding various causes of forced migration.

Concerning exclusion, even if meeting inclusion criteria, recognition depends on authorities in the asylum country. The 1951 Refugee Convention excludes those suspected of war crimes, crimes against humanity, serious non-political crimes, or acts contrary to its principles. The burden is on the asylum seeker to prove eligibility, such as life or security threats.

In terms of cessation, refugee status is temporary and ceases when no longer justified. Article 1(C) outlines cessation clauses for interpretative guidance. Despite the 1951 Refugee Convention's attempt to define refugees distinctly, uncertainty persists due to varying state and organizational criteria. While the Convention addresses traditional causes of forced migration, there is ongoing debate on including those displaced by climate change (Fawzy et al., 2020; Scott, 2020). The evolving nature of displacement necessitates a broader understanding of refugee status beyond conventional definitions.

The principles of nondiscrimination, non-penalization, and non-refoulement are critical safeguards in international human rights, refugee, humanitarian, and customary law. Non-discrimination, as outlined in the UDHR Article 2 and echoed in the 1951 Refugee Convention Article 3, ensures equal treatment for asylum-seekers and refugees without discrimination based on race, religion, country of origin, sex, age, disability, or other prohibited grounds (Dowd, 2011; Goodwin-Gill, 2011).

The International Covenant on Civil and Political Rights (ICCPR) Article 26 further guarantees the right to non-discrimination, emphasizing the importance of preventing discrimination to safeguard various rights such as family life, freedom of movement, religion, employment, and access to justice (Dowd, 2011).

The principle of non-penalization, enshrined in the 1951 Convention Article 31, protects asylum-seekers entering or residing in a country without authorization if they come directly from a territory where their life or freedom is at risk. This right is contingent upon asylum-seekers promptly presenting themselves to authorities and explaining their presence. Despite its intention to protect, controversy arises from the use of terms like "come directly" and "show good cause" (Goodwin-Gill, 2003). Issues such as false documents can lead to violations and penalties for asylum seekers (Patanè et al., 2020; Berry et al., 2015).

The 1951 Convention Article 33(1) guarantees the right of non-refoulement, prohibiting the return of asylum-seekers to territories where their life or freedom is threatened. This obligation is mandatory for states adopting such treaties and is considered a basic minimum standard for refugee treatment (Goodwin-Gill, 2011; Goodwin-Gill & McAdam, 2007). However, states are not obliged to grant entry to asylum seekers, and admissibility conditions determine the validity of claims. Article 33(2) allows refusal if there are "reasonable grounds" to consider the individual a security threat or if the refugee has a criminal conviction (Goodwin-Gill, 2011).

While the UNHCR bears the responsibility for ensuring compliance with these treaties when states grant asylum, criticism has been directed at certain EU countries, such as Italy, for violating these principles through bilateral agreements enabling forced returns to countries of embarkation, notably Libya (Barnes, 2004).

Critically, this chapter highlighted the fundamental tension between the rights guaranteed by the 1951 Refugee Convention and the discretion exercised by states in granting asylum. Instances of non-compliance, as observed in certain European countries, raise concerns about the effective enforcement of these principles.

The upcoming exploration of scholarly literature promises to shed light on the broader context of migration, border control, and the construction of the "deviant migrant" narrative, providing deeper insights into the challenges and dynamics surrounding asylum practices, as demonstrated next.

PART II

Globalization and Migration Dynamics: Navigating the European Refugee Challenge Within the Context of Democracy and Human Rights

After World War II, European states, devastated and in need of labor for reconstruction, cautiously selected individuals for their working class (Anderson, 2013). Despite the humanitarian context, Europe never embraced an "open arms" policy, with public opinions showing limited sympathy for reception policies even in involuntary displacement (Aas & Bosworth, 2013). Recent multinational detention operations and anti-terrorist activities prompted scrutiny of state obligations concerning the transfer of those arrested (Aas & Gundhus, 2015; Aas, 2011; 2013).

The refugee crisis in Europe since 2014 intensified debates on migration, highlighting the tensions between humanitarian concerns and the imperative to secure EU borders (Alston & Knuckey, 2016; Athanasopoulos, 2017). European states, including the USA, are increasingly blending criminal justice and immigration policies in response to labeled "dangerous" migration, reflecting the crimmigration law debate (Guia & Pedroso, 2015).

Crimmigration, originating in the USA in the 1980s and expanding to Europe, involves the progressive loss of migrants' rights and increased criminalization of their behavior (Guia, 2015). This practice, intensifying in the last decades, disproportionately affects individuals from the global south. Meanwhile, media perpetuates divisions between "us versus them", reinforcing collective identities of European citizens.

Amidst globalization and the creation of a "space of flows", where constant movement shortens distances, Europe's response seems contradictory to its history of immigration (Castells, 1996; 2020). Although globalization favors the flow of capital, goods, and people, it remains unequal. This social and cultural change weakened the nation-state and heightened processes of inclusion and exclusion (Castells, 2006). The resulting "bulimic society" creates two categories: tourists, who travel without restrictions, and vagabonds, facing mobility restrictions based on ethnicity, nationality, or race (Bauman, 1998).

Vagabonds, facing injustice, bring attention to Merton's concept of "relative deprivation", where dissatisfaction arises from welcoming certain groups while limiting their social mobility (Merton, 1949). This complex landscape has led criminology to delve into migration with a focused perspective, giving rise to the subfield of Border Criminologies[1] (Aliverti, 2020; Aas, 2019; Barker, 2018; Fassin, 2018; Bosworth, 2011).

Recent studies, such as those by Guia (2015), indicate an increase in border control practices, with the establishment of "superborders" and the classification of citizens based on border-crossing activities. Aas (2013; 2014) scrutinized changing territoriality within the "space of flows", revealing conflicting trends reinforcing symbolic border needs. Aas (2019) demonstrated the extension of state power beyond physical borders, emphasizing deportation mechanisms as an alternative to criminal proceedings.

The association between immigration and criminality intensified post-9/11, shaping contemporary societies' views on national security (Lyon, 2003). The "war on terror" justified increased bureaucracies for migration control (Vilmer et al., 2018). Technologies like biometric visas and profiling became widespread, contributing to a shift toward an autonomous system determining individual belonging (Curry, 2004).

Melossi (2003; 2015) linked the criminalization of migrants to globalization, deindustrialization, and identity crises, particularly in Europe. The identity crisis extended to citizens, leading to the task of constantly meeting standardization parameters. The perceived danger of the European Union coincided with rising xenophobia and racism (Berry, Garcia-Blanco & Moore, 2015).

Simmel's (1996) concept of "the stranger" aligns with the modern figure of the refugee, intensifying divisions between "us and them" in societies marked by globalization, terrorism, and civil wars (Aas, 2013; Melossi, 2003). The portrayal of the criminal immigrant is complex, especially concerning asylum seekers and refugees, despite legal distinctions (Melossi, 2003, pp.376).

Aas's (2019) concept of the "crimmigrant other" explores the malleable nature of this term, emphasizing border representatives' role in shaping judgments about "good" and "bad" migrants. The penal power wielded against "crimmigrant others" is depicted as a moral force, turning global privilege issues into matters of morality (Aas, 2019, pp.19). Initially coined by Stumpf (2006) in the United States, "crimmigration" has been expanded in European border criminology by Aas (2019), who focuses on "crimmigrants" to highlight the critical examination of "immigrant criminality".

Aas's (2019) creation of "bordered penalty" underscores a shift in penal power from panoptic to banoptic, where the "crimmigrant other" is both punishable and deportable, reinforcing social exclusion within an inclusive society (Aas, 2019, pp.70; 111). This concept has influenced EU member-states, leading to the establishment of the independent agency Frontex, dedicated to defending Europe's external borders

(Aas, 2019). Zedner (2020) notes that only a minority of non-citizens are labeled as crimmigrants, highlighting the malleability of this construct (Aas, 2019, pp.197).

Aas (2019) emphasizes that understanding "immigrant criminality" is crucial for evaluating governments' and populations' capacity to empathize with outsiders, challenging borders, and conducting a comprehensive analysis of crimmigration practices. Aas's work synthesizes her previous studies on 'crimmigrants' in Europe, bordered penalty in Norway, and normative tensions in Europe's externalized border zone (Aas, 2011; 2014; Aas & Gundhus, 2015), contributing to a groundbreaking exploration of social inequality and contested membership in contemporary societies (Aas, 2019).

Examining Garland's (2001) idea that the penalty has little to do with crime, this study delves into the historical roots of immigrant criminality. Since the early 1970s, structural changes in the capitalist order influenced popular views of lawbreaking, leading to tough-on-crime tactics (Melossi, 2015). Garland's theories of social control emerged in response, focusing on imposing control and viewing crime as a breakdown of order.

Understanding the evolution of crime and criminology is essential for comprehending "the crimmigrant other" and Europe's response to unwanted migrants, characterized by an unequal relationship between the Global North and South (Aas, 2019, pp. 198). Theories of social control shed light on the current trend of criminalizing migrants, categorizing asylum seekers and refugees as deviant, and excluding them from the "good" cluster of citizens. The use of penal power at the border reflects the contentious nature of Northern citizenship and residence rights in a deeply unequal global order (Aas, 2019, pp. 198).

The security treatment of migration is not exclusive to punitive measures but extends across various institutional devices, practices, and discourses. Migration is characterized by the classification of flows, acts, subjects, and docile bodies rather than solely repressive measures. The focus is on categorizing the escape itself, whether voluntary or not, making migration the target of securitization practices.

The precarious status of refugees, contingent on being perceived as innocent victims reliant on humanitarian aid, is further compounded by the risk of negative classification as unwanted immigrants, often facing stigmatization as liars or criminals and subject to stringent state and community controls. This examination of migration and criminality gains valuable insights from classical sociological and criminological perspectives, notably articulated by scholars such as Becker (1971; 1963), Cohen (1985; 1979; 1972), Foucault (1977), and Durkheim (2005; 1984; 1961), as elucidated below.

Categorization, Labeling, and Control in Contemporary Societal Frameworks

Insights from Becker (1971; 1963) and Cohen's theories (1985; 1979; 1972), help understand the labeling, segregation, and control of individuals, particularly refugees, within societal frameworks.

Becker's interactionist theory (1971; 1963) shifts criminology from a focus on "crime" to "deviation" as a social relation. Deviance is not inherent but a result of labeling acts as deviant. Social groups construct deviance through rules, labeling individuals as outsiders. This labeling process influences self-perception and behavior. Recent studies apply Becker's labeling theory to asylum-seekers, revealing social isolation and marginalization based on imposed "outsider" status.

Cohen's "moral panic" theory (1985; 1979; 1972) involves labeling certain conditions or groups as threats, disproportionately amplifying perceived threats. "Folk devils" embody these threats, sustaining moral panics. Globalization expands local moral panics globally. The concept of the "crimmigrant other" reflects societal anxieties about immigrants and border security, leading to exclusionary asylum systems. Cohen's concerns about "community control" highlight the blurred lines between deviant and non-deviant, impacting asylum-seekers through detention and restrictive measures.

Foucault (1977, pp. 137) introduced "discipline" as a method enabling meticulous control over the body, ensuring its constant subjection and a docility-utility relationship. Discipline operates in two ways: shaping "docile bodies" that can be subjected, used, transformed, and improved, and providing resources for "good training", contributing to the formation of a factory of broken subjectivities (Foucault, 1977, pp. 136). Discipline, as per Foucault (1977), doesn't reduce forces but selects and dissociates power from the body, turning it into an 'aptitude' to be increased and a strict subjection relationship (pp. 138). Power, according to Foucault (1977), produces more than it suppresses, forming, training, exercising, and leading. However, his theorization may seem outdated in the face of contemporary border policies, reflecting a shift from disciplining bodies to preventing the mobility of asylum-seekers and expelling them (Aas, 2019; Kastoryano, 2018; Aarstad, 2015; Aas, 2014; Aas & Bosworth, 2013; Aas, 2013; 2011).

Foucault's (1997) panopticon concept, where constant visibility leads to individualization, is applied to asylum-seekers. The escape itself becomes the object of control devices, with security measures aiming to deactivate subversive potential within migration, intertwining with norms, knowledge, and powers governing security devices, territories, and populations.

Foucault (1978) linked scientific knowledge and technological development to the prison, defining a micro-physics of power that is strategic and tactical.

Immigration detention, relevant to criminology, mirrors and expands penal power's influence on race, gender, and postcolonial relations globally (Bosworth & Guild, 2008). Crimmigration, encompassing judicial processes, detention, imprisonment, conviction, and expulsion, epitomizes brutal control over the undesired 'other' (Guia, 2015).

Durkheim's (2005; 1984; 1961) structural functionalism views society as a living organism, emphasizing necessary functions fulfilled by inherent structures. Immigration, as seen through Durkheim's lens, is vital for social cohesion, contributing to the fusion of social segments (Durkheim, 1984). Applying this to asylum-seekers, despite potential benefits to European societies, there is a tendency to view them as a problem rather than a solution, marked as 'external' rather than 'structural' (Matlin et al., 2018).

Durkheim (2005; 1961) defines "social regulation" as limiting individual wishes and ambitions, preventing anomie. However, asylum-seekers face integration challenges, contradicting the idea of an impartial social order. Merton's (1994) concept of anomie, where people lack resources to achieve defined objectives, applies to asylum-seekers and refugees denied means available to nationals (Gagliardi et al., 2021; Giacco et al., 2018).

The concept of "social integration" (Durkheim, 2005; 1961) is crucial, fostering attachment to shared values and beliefs. European states, often adopting an 'us' versus 'them' stance, contribute to the segregation of asylum-seekers and refugees, hindering social integration and leaving them to rely solely on themselves for survival.

Durkheim (2005) emphasizes socialization and common values as vital for societal ties. Historically, migrants in the United States, socializing with similar ethnic backgrounds, experienced group solidarity, reducing anomie and contributing positively to social capital (Durkheim, 2005). However, the contemporary influx of asylum-seekers raises concerns about their integration and societal cohesion, contradicting historical evidence of positive impacts (Durkheim, 2005) and prompting discussions on the installation of social control in societies.

Contemporary society continues to exhibit social selection, integrating desired elements and expelling perceived threats. The expansion of control extends across various frontiers, encompassing social, individual, geographical, and virtual realms. States are redefining borders, projecting influence beyond their territories to monitor and manage the movement of people in advance (Bosworth, 2008).

Despite the potential utility of asylum seekers and refugees, there is a growing global trend, observed in both European and non-European countries, toward exclusion, stigmatization, and heightened border and social controls (Aas, 2019). While both men and women seek asylum for diverse reasons, women face distinct obstacles and dangers, exacerbated by gender inequalities intensified through globalization (Aas, 2013).

The United Nations Division for the Advancement of Women (2003) highlights the particular vulnerability of migrant women to deprivation, suffering, discrimination, and abuse. The concept of intersectionality emphasizes the dual vulnerability of asylum-seeking women to violence, considering both their legal status and gender (Carastathis, 2014).

This chapter stressed the multifaceted nature of the European response to the refugee challenge, incorporating historical, legal, sociological, and criminological perspectives. The intersection of globalization, identity crises, crimmigration, and security treatment of migration underscores the complexity of navigating democracy and human rights in the context of migration dynamics.

In the upcoming section, this research will delve into the challenges faced by asylum-seekers in host countries, with a specific focus on gender-related issues.

PART III

Gendering the Challenges and Struggles of Asylum-Seekers in Host Countries

The scientific literature, as highlighted earlier, illuminates the often-restrictive stance of resettlement states towards unwanted migrant clusters, including asylum seekers and refugees (Griswold et al., 2021). Emphasizing fundamental values such as democracy and respect for fundamental rights, the European Union underscores the importance of these principles in the reception and integration of asylum-seekers and refugees, aiming for simultaneous protection and inclusion in the local societies of host countries.

Crucial practical measures during the initial reception, including pre-departure orientation, documentation, initial housing, and healthcare, play a vital role (Griswold et al., 2021). Similarly, bureaucratic measures, such as legislation and policy instruments, along with stakeholder collaboration, are essential for securing legal status, rights allocation, and access to naturalization (UNESCO, 2016).

Stakeholder consultation, involving various levels of government and civil society, ensures that asylum-seekers and refugees can access both basic and specialized services in their new communities (Yıldız, & Sert, 2019). Integration, being a dynamic two-way process, demands mutual adaptation – asylum-seekers adjusting to the host society's lifestyle while the host society embraces and responds to asylum-seekers' needs (Huschke & Pottie, 2020).

Creating a welcoming environment necessitates host states and civil society support to help asylum-seekers achieve long-term economic stability, nurture a sense of belonging, and inspire involvement in new communities (UNESCO, 2016).

Integration programs, focusing on seven levels, are vital for asylum-seekers and refugees to enjoy equality in their host countries (Griswold et al., 2021; Yıldız, & Sert, 2019). Effective integration policies require long-term investment in fair measures, demanding political, social, and financial commitment to benefit all communities (European Parliament, 2016).

Despite historical and ongoing global efforts, challenges persist in assisting asylum-seeking individuals. They often face intimidation and violent attacks due to misconceptions among national citizens, who may perceive them as dangerous or different, leading to tensions (Borges & Faria, 2022; Aliverti, 2020; Barnes, 2004). This hostile environment not only adds to their difficulties but contributes to their heightened vulnerability, particularly evident in the gendered experiences of asylum-seeking and refugee women exposed to various forms of gender-based violence (GBV).

Internationally recognized institutions like the United Nations (UN), the World Health Organization (WHO), and the United Nations International Children's Emergency Fund (UNICEF) actively address GBV against women. The UN (2006) emphasizes that violence against women is deeply rooted in structural relationships of inequality, recognizing GBV as an urgent public health priority. UNICEF (2018) reports that globally, one in three girls/women will experience physical and/or sexual violence in their lifetime, with conflicts and disasters exacerbating these violations in emergency situations.

Women, compared to asylum-seeking and refugee men, have less access to resources and social support, increasing their risks of GBV, including psychological, physical, and sexual violence. The perpetrators include military forces, men (intimate partners or strangers), security forces, government officials, aid agency officials, and residents of the host community, all of whom abuse power towards vulnerable asylum-seeking and refugee women (Freedman, 2016a; 2016b). GBV often leads to unwanted pregnancies, abandonment, health issues, HIV/AIDS, social ostracism, and death (Cochrane, 2018; Sapia, 2018; Baczynska & Ledwith, 2016; 2015; Hathaway & Foster, 2014).

In the host country, GBV against asylum-seeking and refugee women is often exacerbated by outdated and inadequate reception and accommodation conditions. Some countries may respond to asylum-seekers with hostility, neglecting those seeking permission to enter and settle (Baczynska & Ledwith, 2016). Border control systems contribute to gendered harm, as outlined in Canning's study (2017) on the British asylum system, emphasizing the brutality of the system, its policies, and the actors involved.

Surveys conducted in resettlement, residence, or transit countries, primarily based on clinical settings and refugee camps, delve into the trauma experienced by asylum-seeking and refugee women. The aftermath of trauma commonly manifests as psychosocial problems, depression, anxiety disorders, and post-traumatic stress disorder (PTSD) (Davaki, 2021; Dionis, Timar & Domscheit-Berg, 2016; Laban et al., 2005).

Physical and mental health care deficiencies, along with unsafe and unsanitary conditions within reception and detention centers, have been extensively documented (Sapia, 2018; Freedman et al., 2020; Triggs, 2015). Davaki (2021) emphasizes the need for public health nurses to assist asylum-seeking women in coping with trauma, particularly older women with significant family responsibilities.

Increased vulnerability of asylum-seeking refugee women and the harsh conditions they endure can be attributed to government fatigue, insufficient funding, administrative challenges, and social unrest marked by citizen intolerance (Freedman et al., 2020). Sapia's study (2018) highlights a lack of understanding among politicians and professionals about refugees' sociocultural backgrounds and the need for preventive strategies involving victims, families, communities, and society.

From inadequate facilities to violence fears due to overcrowded spaces, asylum-seekers, especially women, face numerous challenges. Freedman's study (2016a) reveals women's concerns about sharing space with unknown men, leading to specific fears. Gender-based violence consistently occurs in official asylum-seeking accommodations, turning supposed safe havens into sites of attacks on asylum-seeking women (Borges & Faria, 2022).

These conditions result in gender-specific outcomes, including sexual assault episodes, long queues for hygienic items, and prolonged stays in facilities meant to be temporary (Triggs, 2015).

Recognizing the diversity of experiences among asylum-seeking and refugee women is paramount, as each individual's journey is shaped by a unique intersection of factors such as cultural background, age, education, and personal history. While not all women within these communities face violence in the same way, the urgency lies in comprehending the intricacies of their conditions to tailor effective and targeted interventions.

To address the multifaceted challenges encountered by these women, strategies must be developed within the asylum-seeking and refugee community. A comprehensive approach involves collaborative efforts between various stakeholders, including governmental bodies, non-governmental organizations (NGOs), international agencies, and local communities.

CONCLUSION

In conclusion, the 1951 Refugee Convention, a foundational pillar of international instruments (Goodwin-Gill & McAdam, 2007), stands as a significant commitment to safeguarding the rights and well-being of asylum-seekers and refugees globally. However, the practical application of the Convention brings to light discernible gaps between its ambitious ideals and the intricate realities of defining refugee status, particularly amid contemporary challenges like climate-induced displacement (Fawzy et al., 2020; Scott, 2020).

Essential safeguards enshrined within international human rights, refugee, and customary law, including non-discrimination, non-penalization, and non-refoulement, play a crucial role in ensuring parity and averting forced returns to perilous territories (Dowd, 2011; Goodwin-Gill, 2011). Despite their paramount significance, controversies surrounding the interpretation and implementation of these principles pose challenges, potentially leading to violations and penalties for asylum-seekers (Patanè et al., 2020; Berry et al., 2015).

The complex dynamics influencing Europe's response to the refugee challenge, shaped by globalization, migration, democracy, and human rights, underscore the ongoing impact of historical contexts, including post-World War II labor needs and constrained sympathy for reception policies, on contemporary migration debates.

The emergence of the term "crimmigration" signals a convergence of criminal justice and immigration policies, forcing Europe to grapple with the tension between humanitarian concerns and border security imperatives (Aas, 2019). Exploring the concept of a "space of flows" reveals the constant movement in a globalized world, triggering social and cultural changes that challenge the traditional nation-state framework and result in the categorization of unrestricted travelers and those facing mobility restrictions (Aas, 2013; 2014).

The criminalization of migrants in Europe, rooted in globalization, deindustrialization, and identity crises, amplifies xenophobia and racism. Aas's (2019) concept of the "crimmigrant other" and the notion of a "bordered penalty" highlight the flexible nature of these terms and the pivotal role of border representatives in shaping judgments about migrants.

An examination of the historical roots of immigrant criminality, influenced by changes in the capitalist order since the early 1970s, provides insight into popular perceptions of lawbreaking. Insights from classical sociological and criminological perspectives, including Becker (1971; 1963), Cohen (1985; 1979; 1972), Foucault (1977), and Durkheim (2005; 1984; 1961), contribute to comprehending the intricate interplay between migration and criminality.

The scientific literature underscores the often-restrictive stance of resettlement states toward unwanted migrant clusters, including asylum-seekers and refugees. Practical measures during the initial reception, encompassing bureaucratic processes, legislation, and stakeholder collaboration, are pivotal for securing legal status, rights, and access to naturalization (Hathaway, 2005).

Integration, viewed as a dynamic two-way process, necessitates mutual adaptation, with asylum-seekers adjusting to the host society's lifestyle and the host society embracing and responding to asylum-seekers' needs (Cochrane, 2018; Canning, 2017). However, persistent challenges, such as intimidation and violent attacks, heighten vulnerability, especially among asylum-seeking and refugee women exposed to various forms of gender-based violence (GBV) (Sapia, 2018; Baczynska & Ledwith, 2016; Freedman, 2019; 2016a; 2016b; Hathaway & Foster, 2014).

Internationally recognized institutions actively addressing GBV against women, recognizing it as a public health priority, emphasize the increased risks faced by asylum-seeking and refugee women due to limited access to resources and social support, leading to various physical and mental health issues (Hathaway, 2005; Atlani & Rousseau, 2000). Deficiencies in physical and mental health care, coupled with unsafe conditions within reception and detention centers, accentuate the vulnerability of asylum-seeking refugee women.

From inadequate facilities to fears of violence due to overcrowded spaces, tailored interventions involving collaborative efforts between stakeholders emerge as crucial for addressing the unique challenges faced by asylum-seeking and refugee women on their journey. The establishment of comprehensive and culturally sensitive support programs, encompassing mental health services, educational initiatives, and legal assistance, is essential.

By fostering partnerships between governments, non-governmental organizations (NGOs), international agencies, and local communities, we can create an environment that not only protects the basic rights of asylum-seeking and refugee women but also empowers them to rebuild their lives with dignity and resilience.

This collaborative approach, rooted in empathy and understanding, will contribute to the development of inclusive and sustainable solutions that go beyond mere reception and aim for the genuine integration and well-being of these vulnerable individuals in their host societies.

REFERENCES

Aas, K. (2011). 'Crimmigrant' bodies and the bona fide traveler: Surveillance, citizenship and global governance. *Theoretical Criminology*, *15*(3), 331–346. doi:10.1177/1362480610396643

Aas, K. F. (2013). *Globalization & crime: Key approaches to criminology*. Sage Publications.

Aas, K. F. (2019). *The crimmigrant other: Migration and Penal Power*. Routledge.

Aas, K. F., & Bosworth, M. (2013). *The borders of punishment: Migration, Citizenship, and Social Exclusion*. Oxford University Press. doi:10.1093/acprof:oso/9780199669394.001.0001

Aas, K. F., & Gundhus, H. O. I. (2015). Policing humanitarian borderlands: Frontex, human rights and the precariousness of life. *British Journal of Criminology*, *55*(1), 1–18. doi:10.1093/bjc/azu086

Aliverti, A. (2020). Benevolent policing? Vulnerability and the moral pains of border controls. *British Journal of Criminology*, *60*(5), 1117–1135. doi:10.1093/bjc/azaa026

Alston, P. P., & Knuckey, S. (Eds.). (2016). *The transformation of human rights fact-finding*. Oxford University Press. doi:10.1093/acprof:oso/9780190239480.001.0001

Anderson, B. (2013). *Us and them: The dangerous politics of immigration control*. Oxford University Press. doi:10.1093/acprof:oso/9780199691593.001.0001

Athanasopoulos, A. (2017). Fortress Europe?: The Aegean Sea Frontier and the Strengthening of EU's External Borders. In G. Wahlers (Ed.), *Borders* (pp. 14–25). Konrad Adenauer Stiftung.

Atlani, L., & Rousseau, C. (2000). The politics of culture in humanitarian aid to women refugees who have experienced sexual violence. *Transcultural Psychiatry*, *37*(3), 435–449. doi:10.1177/136346150003700309

Baczynska, G., & Ledwith, S. (2016). How Europe built fences to keep people out. *Reuters*. Retrieved from: https://www.reuters.com/article/us-europe-migrants-fences-insight-idUSKCN0X10U7

Barker, V. (2018). *Nordic nationalism and penal order walling the welfare state*. Routledge. doi:10.1093/iclq/53.1.47

Barnes, R. (2004). Refugee Law at Sea. *The International and Comparative Law Quarterly*, *53*(1), 47–77. doi:10.1093/iclq/53.1.47

Bauman, Z. (1998). *Globalization: The human consequences*. Columbia University Press.

Bauman, Z. (2016). *Strangers at our door*. Cambridge Polity Press.

Becker, H. S. (1963). *Outsiders: Studies in the sociology of deviance*. Free Press Glencoe.

Berry, M., Garcia-Blanco, I., & Moore, K. (2015). *Press coverage of the refugee and migrant crisis in the EU: A content analysis of five european countries. report prepared for the United Nations High Commission for Refugees*. Cardiff School of Journalism, Media and Cultural Studies Press.

Borges, G. M., & Faria, R. (2022). Breathing Under Water: Gendering the Violence Against Refugee Women. In *Research Anthology on Child and Domestic Abuse and Its Prevention* (pp. 19–37). IGI Global. doi:10.4018/978-1-6684-5598-2.ch002

Bosworth, M. (2008). Border control and the limits of the sovereign state. *Social & Legal Studies, 17*(2), 199–215. doi:10.1177/0964663908089611

Bosworth, M. (2011). Human rights and immigration detention. In Are Human Rights for Migrants? Critical Reflections on the Status of Irregular Migrants in Europe and the United States (pp. 165-183). Routledge.

Bosworth, M., & Guild, M. (2008). Governing through migration control: Security and citizenship in Britain. *British Journal of Criminology, 48*(6), 703–719. doi:10.1093/bjc/azn059

Canning, V. (2017). *Gendered harm and structural violence in the British asylum system*. Taylor & Francis eBooks.

Canning, V. (2020). Corrosive Control: State-Corporate and Gendered Harm in Bordered Britain. *Critical Criminology, 28*(2), 259–275. doi:10.1007/s10612-020-09509-1

Carastathis, A. (2014). The concept of intersectionality in feminist theory. *Philosophy Compass, 9*(5), 304–314. doi:10.1111/phc3.12129

Castells, M. (1996). *The Rise of the Network Society, The Information Age: Economy, Society and Culture*. Blackwell.

Castells, M. (2020). Space of Flows, Space of Places: Materials for a Theory of Urbanism in the Information Age. In T. Richard & F. S. LeGates (Eds.), *The city reader* (pp. 14–25). Routledge. doi:10.4324/9780429261732-30

Cochrane, B. (2018). Harms at the crossroads of carework and irregular migration. *Journal of Refugee Studies, 33*(3), 500–520. doi:10.1093/jrs/fey056

Cohen, S. (2011). *Folk Devils and Moral Panics: The Creation of the Mods and Rockers*. Routledge. doi:10.4324/9780203828250

Davaki, K. (2021). *The traumas endured by refugee women and their consequences for integration and participation in the EU host country.* Policy Department for Citizens' Rights and Constitutional Affairs Directorate-General for Internal Policies.

Dionis, M. S., Timar, M., & Domscheit-Berg, A. (2016). *Protecting refugee Women and girls from violence: A collection of good practices.* World Future Council.

Dowd, R. (2011). Dissecting discrimination in refugee law: An analysis of its meaning and its cumulative effect. *International Journal of Refugee Law, 23*(1), 28–53. doi:10.1093/ijrl/eeq043

Edwards, A. (2005). Human rights, refugees and the right "to enjoy" asylum. *International Journal of Refugee Law, 17*(2), 293–330. doi:10.1093/ijrl/eei011

Fassin, D. (2018). *The will to punish.* Oxford University Press. doi:10.1093/oso/9780190888589.001.0001

Freedman, J. (2015). *Gendering the international asylum and refugee debate.* Palgrave Macmillan. doi:10.1057/9781137456236

Freedman, J. (2016a). Sexual and gender-based violence against refugee women: A hidden aspect of the refugee "crisis". *Reproductive Health Matters, 4*(47), 18–26. doi:10.1016/j.rhm.2016.05.003 PMID:27578335

Freedman, J. (2016b). Engendering security at the borders of Europe: Women migrants and the Mediterranean crisis. *Journal of Refugee Studies, 29*(4), 568–582. doi:10.1093/jrs/few019

Freedman, J. (2019). Grand challenges: Refugees and conflict. *Frontiers in Human Dynamics, 3,* 1–3. doi:10.3389/fhumd.2019.00001

Freedman, J., Crankshaw, T. L., & Mutambara, V. M. (2020). Sexual and reproductive health of asylum seeking and refugee women in South Africa: Understanding the determinants of vulnerability. *Sexual and Reproductive Health Matters, 28*(1), 323–334. doi:10.1080/26410397.2020.1758440 PMID:32425112

Goodwin-Gill, G. S. (2003). *Refugees and Responsibility in the Twenty-First Century: More Lessons Learned from the South Pacific.* Available at: https://digitalcommons.law.uw.edu/wilj/vol12/iss1/5

Goodwin-Gill, G. S. (2009). *Introduction to the 1951 Convention/1967 Protocol relating to the Status of Refugees.* UN Audio-Visual Library of International Law.

Goodwin-Gill, G. S. (2011). The right to seek asylum: Interception at sea and the principle of *non-refoulement. International Journal of Refugee Law*, *23*(3), 443–457. doi:10.1093/ijrl/eer018

Goodwin-Gill, G. S., & McAdam, J. (2007). *The refugee in international law* (3rd ed.). Oxford University Press.

Griswold, K. S., Vest, B. M., Lynch-Jiles, A., Sawch, D., Kolesnikova, K., Byimana, L., & Kefi, P. (2021). "I just need to be with my family": Resettlement experiences of asylum seeker and refugee survivors of torture. *Globalization and Health*, *17*(27), 1–7. doi:10.1186/s12992-021-00681-9 PMID:33750402

Guia, M. J. (2015). *Imigração, 'Crimigração' e Crime Violento: Os Reclusos Condenados e as Representações sobre Imigração e Crime.* Tese de Doutoramento em Direito, Justiça e Cidadania no Séc. XXI, apresentada à Faculdade de Economia da Universidade de Coimbra.

Guia, M. J., & Pedroso, J. (2015). A insustentável resposta da "crimigração" Face à irregularidadedos migrantes: Uma perspetiva da União Europeia. *REMHU –. Revista Interdisciplinar da Mobilidade Humana*, *45*(45), 129–144. doi:10.1590/1980-8585250319880004507

Hathaway, J. C. (2005). *The rights of refugees under international law*. Cambridge University Press. doi:10.1017/CBO9780511614859

Hathaway, J. C., & Fosterm, M. (2014). *The law of refugee status* (2nd ed.). Cambridge University Press. doi:10.1017/CBO9780511998300

Melossi, D. (2003). 'In a Peaceful Life': Migration and the crime of modernity in Europe/Italy. *Punishment & Society*, *5*(4), 371–397. doi:10.1177/14624745030054001

Melossi, D. (2015). *Crime, punishment and migration*. Sage Publications. doi:10.4135/9781473920965

Meltzer, H., Doos, L., Vostanis, P. P., Ford, T., & Goodman, R. (2009). The mental health of children who witness domestic violence. *Child & Family Social Work*, *14*(4), 491–501. doi:10.1111/j.1365-2206.2009.00633.x

Patanè, F., Bolhuis, M. P. P., van Wijk, J., & Kreiensiek, H. (2020). Asylum-seekers prosecuted for human smuggling: A case study of *Sacristy* in Italy. *Refugee Survey Quarterly*, *39*(2), 123–152. doi:10.1093/rsq/hdaa008

Sapia, M. R. (2018). Refugee women, victims of GBV - which issues for the health care system? A qualitative study. *European Journal of Public Health*, *27*(3), 411–419. doi:10.1093/eurpub/cky048.184

Stumpf, J. (2006). The crimmigration crisis: Immigrants, crime, and sovereign power. *The American University Law Review*, *56*(2), 367–419.

The European Parliament. (2016). *Action Plan on the integration of third country nationals*. Communication from the commission to the European Parliament, the Council, the European Economic and Social Committee and the Committee of the Regions.

Triggs, G. (2015). *The forgotten children: National inquiry into children in immigration detention 2014*. Australian Human Rights Commission Sydney.

UNESCO. (2016). *Cities welcoming refugees and migrants*. The United Nations Educational, Scientific and Cultural Organization.

UNICEF. (2018). *Child protection from violence, exploitation and abuse*. UNICEF.

United Nations Division for the Advancement of Women. (2003). *Sexual Violence and Armed Conflict: United Nations Response. Women 2000 and Beyond and UNDAW*. Author.

United Nations (UN). (2006). *Ending violence against women: from words to action Study of the Secretary-General*. Author.

Yıldız, U., & Sert, D. (2019). Dynamics of mobility-stasis in refugee journeys: Case of resettlement from Turkey to Canada. *Migration Studies*, 1–20. doi:10.1093/migration/mnz005

Zedner, L. (2020). *Reading the crimmigrant other*. Border Criminologies.

ENDNOTE

[1]   Established in 2013 and based at the Centre for Criminology at the University of Oxford, "Border Criminologies" is not only s field of study, as well as an international network of researchers, practitioners, and those who have experienced border control.

Chapter 4
Breathing the Asylum System:
Gendering Portugal's Reception Conditions and Integration Practices

Gabriela Mesquita Borges
University of Lusíada, Portugal

ABSTRACT

Establishing a life in an asylum country presents an exceptionally daunting challenge, particularly for women. In asylum countries, women encounter numerous hurdles like healthcare, language barriers, economic empowerment, childcare, education, cultural adjustment, legal issues, and more. This chapter comprehensively analyzes reception conditions and integration practices in the Portuguese asylum system from a gender perspective, covering seven critical areas: housing, financial support, healthcare, psychological assistance, education, labor market integration, and legal aid. Through 49 interviews (with asylum-seeking women and with professionals working in the Portuguese asylum system), this research unveils deficiencies in support, mainly due to the absence of gender-specific approaches. The chapter aims to promote gender-sensitive policies and practices to aid asylum-seeking women.

INTRODUCTION

In recent years, a significant increase in asylum seekers' arrivals at various international borders has drawn scholarly and practitioner attention (Borges, 2023; Aliverti, 2020; Aas, 2019; Barker, 2018; Fassin, 2018; Bosworth, 2011). This surge has led to stricter border control measures and biased portrayals of migrants (Aas, 2019; 2011), reinforcing stereotypes of "violent asylum seekers, smuggling, trafficking

DOI: 10.4018/979-8-3693-5436-0.ch004

networks, Muslim terrorists, Nigerian and East European prostitutes, and ethnic youth gangs" (Aas, 2013, pp.79). States may use the rhetoric of "there is no alternative" to stifle substantial discussions on how to mitigate systemic harms (Aas, & Bosworth, 2013; Bosworth, & Kaufman, 2011). Consequently, governments frequently resort to repressive and exclusionary tactics within their asylum procedures, with official support services often falling short in mitigating the adverse consequences of these actions (Bosworth, 2008; Bosworth, & Guild, 2008).

Asylum-seeking women face heightened vulnerability to gender-based violence, including physical and psychological harm (Cochrane, 2018; Freedman, 2016b; 2015). Sexual violence is also a prevalent concern, occurring in various contexts (Freedman, Crankshaw & Mutambara, 2020; Sapia, 2018). The vulnerability of asylum-seeking women is further heightened by systemic issues such as inadequate support services, language barriers, and fear of reporting violence due to potential repercussions, perpetuating their vulnerability (Dionis et al. 2016; Sansonetti, 2016). These forms of violence are often interconnected, with one type of violence intensifying the impact of another (Canning, 2020; Kelly, 1998; 2008).

While asylum narratives have often centered on men, failing to encompass the unique and often marginalized experiences of individuals who do not conform to the heteronormative, male-centric refugee stereotype (Kanal & Rottmann, 2021), there is a growing recognition of the need to collect and analyze women's narratives (Borges & Faria, 2022; Borges, 2023). To enhance the well-being of asylum-seeking women in host countries, a comprehensive approach is essential. This chapter offers insights from 49 interviews with 24 asylum-seeking women residing in Portugal, and with 25 professionals actively involved in the Portuguese asylum system.

This chapter presents valuable insights for the academic community, policymakers, and government authorities, with the aim of improving the well-being and preserving the dignity of asylum-seeking women, both within Portugal and on a global scale. as elucidated in the forthcoming sections.

BACKGROUND

Law no. 27/2008, as amended by Law no. 26/2014 (also known as "The Asylum Act"), defines 'applicants in need of special procedural guarantees'. While the Act does not provide an exhaustive list of criteria for such individuals, it references factors like age, gender, gender identity, sexual orientation, disability, serious illness, mental disorders, torture, rape, or other severe forms of psychological, physical, or sexual violence as potential determinants of special procedural guarantees (Oliveira, 2020). The Asylum Act emphasizes safeguarding individuals targeted for persecution due to gender-based reasons, as specified in subparagraph f of article

5, addressing acts of persecution. Notably, it's important to highlight the scarcity of publicly available statistics specifically related to cases of gender-based violence among asylum-seeking women.

In fact, 2019 is the only year for which information regarding gender-based violence as a reason for asylum requests by women was accessible. In 2019, 24 international protection requests were submitted by women (21) and underage daughters (3) facing gender-based discrimination or persecution, accounting for 4.8% of the total 496 requests made by women that year, a substantial increase from 2018 (SEF, 2020). These 24 cases included 9 instances of female genital mutilation, 6 cases of forced marriage, 6 cases of women vulnerable due to widowhood, and 3 cases of discrimination based on sexual orientation (EUROSTAT, 2014-2019).

In the host country, gender-based violence against asylum-seeking women is often worsened by outdated and inadequate reception and accommodation conditions (Borges & Faria, 2022; Cochrane, 2018; Baczynska & Ledwith, 2016; Freedman, 2016b; Hathaway & Foster, 2014). Some countries may respond to asylum seekers with hostility and reluctance to grant permission to enter and settle (Baczynska & Ledwith, 2016). Freedman (2016a) conducted qualitative research in Greece, Serbia, and France, interviewing 40 female and 20 male refugees, as well as key informants. Hersh and Obser (2016) carried out a similar investigation in Berlin, Cologne, and Stockholm. Dionis et al. (2016) concentrated on proposing measures to safeguard refugee women, while Sansonetti (2016) presented an overview of the challenges encountered by asylum-seeking women in Europe.

All of these studies documented cases where institutions fell short in addressing the unique needs of asylum-seeking and refugee women, leaving them vulnerable to gender-specific forms of violence.

Canning's (2017) research in the British asylum system also reveals the systemic gender-specific harm inflicted on asylum seekers, especially women. This study highlights how policies and practices intensify gender-based harm and dehumanization. Inspired by Canning's insights, this article aims to infuse a gender perspective into the analysis of the asylum-seeking process in Portugal. It will explore asylum procedures, practical challenges, and limited access to support systems, as this chapter unfolds.

METHODOLOGY

Sampling

In the study, a multi-informant approach was adopted (Archibald et al., 2019; Alvesson & Skoldberg, 2009), selecting two distinct groups of informants: asylum-seeking women in Portugal and professionals in the Portuguese asylum system. However, it's essential to emphasize that the central focus of the study remains on the narratives of asylum-seeking women.

For asylum-seeking women, selection criteria included: i) women aged 18 years or older; ii) official recognition by the Portuguese asylum system; iii) arrival in Portugal during the recent European refugee crises (2014 to present); and iv) proficiency in Portuguese or English or willingness to have a translator present. The study included 24 women from various countries, aged 21 to 48, with different marital and educational backgrounds, asylum seeker statuses, and lengths of stay in Portugal.

In the case of professionals, criteria included: i) gathering information about Portuguese reception and integration institutions online, identifying professionals connected to the asylum system; and ii) selecting professionals from diverse roles and institutions.

Data Collection

At the beginning of each interview, participants were reminded of the research objectives, assured of data confidentiality, and provided informed consent. Interviews with asylum-seeking women totaled twenty-four, with thirteen involving translators (French and Arabic). The initial five interviews were face-to-face in January and February 2020, but COVID-19 disrupted the schedule. Post-lockdown, the remaining nineteen interviews were conducted online via Zoom.

Professional interviews occurred from November 2020 to March 2021 and were conducted online due to pandemic measures. The initial aim was to recruit fifteen participants from various institutions in the Portuguese asylum system. Still, the sample expanded to twenty-eight due to referrals and a snowball sampling technique. However, it's essential to note that although twenty-eight professionals were included in the study, only twenty-five semi-structured interviews took place. In one instance, four professionals participated in a collective interview unexpectedly. Five interviews were conducted but not included in the final sample as they primarily worked with migrant women in general, lacking the expertise required for the interview questions.

Data Analysis

All interviews in this study were transcribed verbatim. Field notes capturing non-verbal signs and environmental information were added to the transcripts. The study used a constructivist grounded theory approach, emphasizing participants' construction of meaning (Charmaz & Thornberg, 2021; Charmaz et al., 2017), supplemented by the abduction approach for discovering novel concepts (Kennedy

& Thornberg, 2018). Initial coding identified significant themes, followed by focused coding for more conceptual meaning units (Charmaz et al., 2021). Data categorization and cataloging classified fundamental words and word groups. Concurrent data generation and analysis took place within the purposive sample. Researcher memos were used to record thoughts during data collection. Theoretical sampling guided constant comparative analysis. Intermediary coding facilitated analysis from incidents to categories and beyond. Categories were fully developed through sub-category correction and exploration of their dimensions. Finally, these categories were interconnected. Qualitative data analysis software, QDA Miner, was employed for handling large amounts of data.

Reflexivity

This chapter's study was approved by the Research Ethics Committee at the University of Porto (Portugal), emphasizing the importance of ethical research beyond approval. The researcher employed reflexivity (Cowburn et al., 2017) to consider fundamental research integrity principles (Berger, 2016) and ethical reflection, addressing topics such as translator use, emotional impact, researcher-participant dynamics, data collection during a global pandemic (Borges & Faria, 2023), and gatekeeper influence (Borges, Guerreiro & Conde, 2022).

Participants were informed and provided consent, with audio-recorded interviews, often conducted via Zoom. Pre-interview sessions ensured technical considerations and participant comfort. Data were securely protected and deleted after transcription. Participants had the right to withdraw, and their images and audio recordings could be promptly deleted upon request.

Regarding asylum-seeking women, their preferences guided the decision to be alone during interviews, avoiding coercion. Safety measures included a 'safe word' for potential threats, with real-time video for comfort, though no incidents occurred.

Professional participation varied in relation to knowledge and time constraints. Some referred others or cooperated, providing valuable data. However, some lacked involvement, affecting data quality, while non-responses were sometimes unclear, possibly due to a lack of knowledge or external instructions. Some professionals assigned by gatekeepers were uncooperative. Smaller institutions offered more knowledgeable and involved participants.

RESULTS

Before delving into the results, let's provide context on the Portuguese asylum system. As mentioned earlier, Law no. 27/2008, amended by Law no. 26/2014, defines conditions and procedures for granting asylum or subsidiary protection, as well as the legal status of asylum seekers, refugees, and those under subsidiary protection. Upon arrival in Portugal, asylum seekers must submit a request to the Portuguese Immigration and Borders Service (*Serviço de Estrangeiros e Fronteiras*, SEF). Law no. 27/2008, Article 11, allows applicants to stay in Portugal until their application's admissibility decision. A positive outcome results in a residence permit.

Portugal adheres to EU standards through directives like Directive 2008/115/EC, which establishes unified EU norms for forced return and voluntary departure; Directive 2011/95/EU, which specifies the criteria for third-country nationals or stateless individuals to qualify for international protection, delineating a standardized status for refugees and subsidiary protection beneficiaries, and outlining the scope of the protection provided; and Directive 2013/33/EU, which sets forth rules governing the reception of international protection applicants.

Reception and integration for spontaneous asylum seekers involve multiple ministries and institutions. The Portuguese Council for Refugees (*Conselho Português para os Refugiados*, CPR) provides initial support and services, including legal counsel, housing, and a monthly living allowance. Additionally, it offers early integration services such as Portuguese language training, job market preparation workshops, as well as cultural and art activities. Asylum seekers under EU relocation and resettlement programs are referred to hosting entities responsible for their reception and integration. These entities, often municipalities, parishes, foundations, and NGOs, offer housing, utilities, and financial support. Integration services are available to all migrants through the High Commission for Migration *(Alto-Comissário para as Migrações* – ACM) through its Support Unit for the Integration of Refugees (*Gabinete de apoio à integração de pessoas refugiadas* - NAIR) (Oliveira, 2020).

The study data reveals that both spontaneous asylum seekers and those under the European relocation and resettlement programs face similar challenges in asylum procedures, practical difficulties, and the consequences of restricted access to support systems. These shared challenges persist despite differing management by various ministries and institutions. Therefore, the subsequent sections will present findings in seven key areas - housing, financial assistance, healthcare, psychological support, education, labor market integration, and legal aid, all drawn from interviews with women (without distinguishing between the two groups), as well as from the professionals interviewed.

For anonymity, pseudonyms for interviewees were used, both women and professionals. "Portugal" next to a name indicates a professional, while other countries next to names represent the asylum-seeking women's countries of origin.

Housing

Housing is not only a basic necessity but also a pivotal dimension of refugee integration and a prerequisite for the enjoyment of other essential rights, as stated in Directive 2013/33/EU. The location, conditions, and size of housing, along with frequent relocations, significantly impact refugees' access to language courses, education, employment, and social welfare support (Mangrio, Zdravkovic & Carlson, 2019; Demarchi & Lenehan, 2019; Fotaki, 2019).

The findings of this study highlight the disparities in housing allocation for asylum seekers in Portugal. The majority of the women interviewed were placed in private or shared apartments upon their arrival, and some women reported being initially accommodated in reception centers. These discrepancies in housing allocation result in a diverse starting point for individuals within the same legal cluster. Within the same category of accommodation, notable discrepancies emerged, concerning health, hygiene, privacy, and comfort.

While some professionals held the view that the apartments allocated to asylum seekers adhered to basic standards and "were equipped with everything needed to foster a sense of comfort and normalcy in domestic life." (Ema, Portugal) this sentiment did not universally align with the experiences reported by the women interviewed. Shamsa (Syria) vividly described her allocated apartment as having "terrible conditions", leading her and her family to vehemently reject the accommodation, even for a single night, as it was considered "an unsuitable and unhealthy environment for their children." On the other hand, some women found the apartments to be comparatively satisfactory, as articulated by Rana (Syria), who deemed them "good" when contrasted with accommodations provided to other asylum seekers.

In shared accommodations, differences in the conditions adversely affect the integration process, impacting health, hygiene, privacy, and comfort (Boccagni, 2017). The women residing in shared apartments voiced vehement criticisms regarding the accommodation facilities. Issues such as overcrowding, and a pronounced absence of privacy were particularly notable. Fatima (Iraq) offered a poignant perspective, lamenting, "The situation in the apartment is dire: there are six families coexisting within this confined space. Additionally, two men share our living quarters. This situation creates profound challenges, not only in terms of privacy but also due to conflicts with our deeply ingrained cultural traditions. My feelings of anger and desperation are palpable". Likewise, in Freedman's study (2016a), women expressed concerns about sharing space with unfamiliar men, especially single men, seen as a specific threat.

The unanimous testimony of women placed in reception centers highlighted the distressing reality of an environment marked by unhygienic and unsanitary conditions, exacerbated by pronounced issues concerning cleanliness and the shared use of space. The presence of unsafe and unsanitary conditions within reception centres has been also documented by Davaki (2021). This includes a lack of running water, electricity, insufficient numbers of toilets, beds, and blankets, and a much lower support capacity than needed. For the majority of the women, the experience of staying in reception centers was far from favorable, characterized by disarray and a conspicuous lack of hygiene, as noted by Shamshi (Somalia), who stated: "Everything was a mess! It was very dirty. People were not hygienic."

Promesse (Congo) vividly described the disorganized and unclean state of the reception center, stressing that "it was overcrowded with numerous occupants, and the kitchen area was in a state of disarray." Similarly, Alice (Angola) recounted an alarming situation with multiple people sharing sleeping quarters. She vividly remembered the persistent presence of "biting insects" and the notable absence of "basic bedding", which forced her to resort to draping her own clothing over the bare mattresses in order "to find some semblance of comfort and rest."

In response to the overwhelming number of applicants, host institutions often resorted to renting hostels as an alternative form of accommodation, as explained by Margarida (Portugal). However, the conditions in these hostels were described as equally dire as those in the reception center, with the additional drawback of lacking institutional support. This predicament left some, like Glória (Congo), feeling abandoned and disheartened, as she recounted: "The hostels' conditions were just as terrible as at the reception center, if not worse, because there was no one from the institution present to assist us. It felt like I had been left there to fend for myself."

Moreover, for all the women interviewed who shared living spaces with other asylum seekers, whether in reception centers, hostels, or shared apartments, the coexistence of diverse individuals inevitably gave rise to conflicts. As Madalena (Angola) recounted: "Verbal abuse and fights were constant. I was living among people with different traditions and ways of life, so it's almost expected that such clashes would occur." This challenge was also acknowledged by professionals, including Diana (Portugal), who recognized that "living in such close quarters often led to cultural clashes and disputes."

These findings align with prior studies (Horn et al., 2021; Hermans, Kooistra & Cannegieter, 2017; Demarchi & Lenehan, 2019; Fotaki, 2019; Freedman, 2015; Ticktin, 2016; Pichou, 2016; Bacon et al., 2013) that have consistently reported inadequacies in asylum accommodations, encompassing issues such as overcrowding, lack of privacy, risks of sexual and gender-based violence, insufficient attention to vulnerabilities, subpar hygiene conditions, and social isolation.

Similarly, a significant portion of the women interviewed went through the process of being relocated to different cities. However, during this process, they were not adequately informed about the reasons for relocation or given the opportunity to express their opinions or preferences regarding this significant change in their living arrangements. This lack of communication and consultation left them "feeling uncertain" Maara (Syria) and possibly disadvantaged in making informed decisions about their own lives and well-being. Moreover, this had profound adverse consequences, including family separation, job loss, and disruption of their social networks.

This internal relocation, which took place frequently, has been shown in other studies (Merikoski, 2021; Bendixsen & Wyller, 2019; Kreichauf, 2018; Boccagni, 2017; Bulley, 2017) to generate significant challenges. The absence of transparent information concerning these transfers can be interpreted as a form of mistreatment. Also, the frequent dismissal of these women's opinions and objections regarding these transfers suggests a demeaning and paternalistic attitude on the part of the professionals overseeing their asylum proceedings.

Financial Assistance

The monthly allowances provided to the women interviewed came under heavy scrutiny and were unanimously criticized as insufficient to cover their basic living expenses. This financial shortfall persisted even when these women were accommodated in institutional facilities. However, this issue was particularly pronounced for women with children, as illustrated by Shaimma (Iraq), who, as a mother of four, emphasized the significant "financial demands of providing essentials like clothing, food, and school supplies for my children". The situation was undoubtedly exacerbated by the monthly allowance's inadequacy.

In response to this financial struggle, some of the women found themselves in the position of seeking assistance from non-governmental organizations, with Institute of the Santa Casa da Misericórdia (*Institute of the Santa Casa da Misericórdia*, ISCM) emerging as a crucial lifeline. Adilah (Morocco) shared that she and her husband and three children had to rely on ISCM "for food. They gave us free meals", as they were grappling with the insufficiency of their monthly allowances.

In addition to offering food assistance, the professionals highlighted another vital role played by ISCM: ensuring access to necessary healthcare services. As stated by Pedro (Portugal) "although the law provides for access to health care, without a national health system (SNS) number, doctors are unable to prescribe medicines to asylum seekers."

Access to healthcare for asylum seekers can be a complex issue, as it often hinges on the possession of a national health system (SNS) number. Without this identification, doctors might be unable to prescribe essential medicines, despite the asylum seekers being legally entitled to healthcare services. In such scenarios, ISCM steps in to bridge the gap by providing these much-needed medicines, serving as a crucial intermediary between the asylum seekers and their right to adequate healthcare.

As Article 18(9) of Directive 2013/33/EU states, asylum applicants have the right to their fundamental needs met under material reception conditions. Moreover, Article 29 of Directive 2011/95/EU explicitly outlines the right to receive social assistance benefits through public funds, aligning with Article 23 of the 1951 Refugee Convention. The role of ISCM in addressing financial and healthcare needs reveals systemic issues in the asylum support framework, indicating a gap in the state's ability to fulfill its obligations to those in need.

Sadly, the non-compliance with the mentioned directives can be seen as a form of violence by the Portuguese state. This violence is a result of systemic failures in supporting asylum seekers. The financial resources provided to the women and their families were insufficient for their basic needs, raising concerns about the state's obligations to ensure their well-being and dignity. Inadequate financial support not only hampers integration but also exacerbates their existing challenges and vulnerabilities.

This emphasizes the need to address these systemic issues and reevaluate the mechanisms for fulfilling humanitarian responsibilities related to offering asylum.

Like Mariam (Syria), women found themselves "subjected to unwelcome pressure from institutional professionals." Mariam (Syria) candidly shared her frustration, stating, "I grew weary of the professionals' constant insistence that we should save money. The reality, however, is that the funds provided to us fall far short of covering our monthly expenses, let alone allowing us to set aside savings." Mariam's sentiments are echoed by many others who shared her discomfort and anger over the imposed financial expectations.

The professionals interviewed acknowledged that this practice was indeed quite common among their ranks. They articulated their intent, emphasizing that "it was aimed at encouraging asylum seekers to cultivate financial responsibility." (Clara, Portugal). The rationale was "to equip these individuals with the skills to manage their finances effectively, particularly with an eye toward self-sufficiency, should the day come when the Portuguese state ceases to provide financial support." (Filipa, Portugal). In the absence of stable employment, they believed that having some financial cushion would empower asylum seekers to navigate life more independently, reducing their reliance on state subsidies.

While the intention behind this practice may be rooted in a desire to promote financial literacy and autonomy, it is crucial to consider the broader context. The limitations of the monthly allowances provided to asylum seekers must be recognized, as this financial pressure on already vulnerable individuals can yield unintended consequences. The line between encouraging financial responsibility and creating added distress should be carefully examined, and it becomes apparent that any such practice should ideally align with the realities of the financial support available to asylum seekers.

According to Merton's anomie theory (1967), a disconnection emerges between culturally assigned objectives, typically rooted in economic success, and the accessibility of lawful means to realize these objectives. This disparity places significant stress on the cultural norms that dictate the acceptable methods for achieving these prescribed objectives. Merton (1967) termed this erosion of cultural norms "anomie", a concept originating from Durkheim's (1897) observations of the diminishing influence of the normative order within society. Essentially, it reflects how established social norms can lose their efficacy in governing individual behavior.

Drawing inspiration from both Merton's (1967) and Durkheim's (1897) theories, this thesis introduces the concept of "institutionalized regulatory practices". This concept characterizes how professionals endeavor to oversee the conduct of asylum seekers while exerting pressure on them to attain specific objectives. This pressure often transpires without offering them legitimate avenues to achieve these objectives, setting up a paradox where they are expected to achieve goals without being provided with the necessary means to do so. Rather than fostering positive self-management and autonomy, this pressure inflicted harm and caused psychological instability among the women interviewed.

It seems that the normative system that compels these women to achieve specific outcomes, such as saving money, is the very system that restricts their capacity to act independently. This dual burden is aptly illustrated in Alexandra's (Portugal) remarks: "I don't acquiesce to every request. I encourage these individuals to reflect and cultivate greater self-reliance. They must grasp that they cannot depend on us for every little need."

Healthcare

According to Article 13 of the Directive 2013/33/EU, all states must ensure the effective exercise of refugees' right to social and medical assistance. Furthermore, it guarantees that every refugee must receive adequate assistance and medical treatment if they become ill. Nevertheless, a comprehensive analysis of the findings reveals that the provision of medical assistance to the sample of refugee women upon their arrival in Portugal differs significantly according to the institution responsible for their care.

In a small minority of the women interviewed, medical examinations were administered promptly upon their arrival. Amal (Iraq) described her experience, stating: "A group of doctors at the reception center examined us, and it was an excellent experience". In contrast, for the majority of women, several months elapsed before they had the opportunity to see a physician: "It took six months before they [referring to the professionals from the host institution] arranged for us to visit a doctor." (Eisaa, Syria). As a consequence, for the women who fell ill, their ordeal stretched over several months. This was exemplified in the case of Alice (Angola), who "endured months of discomfort" due to her back pain while waiting for a doctor's appointment, ultimately exacerbating her Crohn's disease.

In sharp contrast, the professionals underscored the priority placed on medical examinations. Alexandra (Portugal) affirmed, "A dedicated team of doctors meticulously assesses individuals in more delicate health conditions and administers vaccinations where necessary." Moreover, they reiterated that their responsibility includes ensuring that medical examinations are carried out and streamlining the registration process for asylum seekers and refugees at local hospitals, with Sofia (Portugal) stating that: "This streamlined approach is essential to expedite access to healthcare."

However, the women did not report receiving this kind of assistance from the professionals overseeing their cases. They even asserted that they had to navigate the intricacies of hospital registration independently, as highlighted by Maara (Syria), who explained: "I had to take charge of my hospital registration because the institution's staff were unresponsive in this regard." Rana (Syria) shared a similar sentiment, stating that she was puzzled when she and her children had to venture to the hospital unaccompanied and manage their registration on their own.

Furthermore, the women who undertook their medical registration at local hospitals faced various challenges, especially stemming from cultural biases and language barriers. As Pedro, one of the professionals interviewed noted, "Refugees often report that when they have to register at the hospital or make a regular appointment on their own, they wait a long time to be seen, and other Portuguese patients who arrived later are prioritized. This bias appears to be due to prejudices and communication difficulties".

Likewise, some refugee women encountered refusals when they requested a doctor's consultation, as observed in Fatima's (Iraq) case: "We all had the flu, so we asked to see a doctor, but they only provided us with medications." Others confronted insufficient treatment for chronic illnesses, like Ama (Togo), who disclosed that the institution responsible for her case did not support ophthalmological expenses. Consequently, she had no choice but to utilize her monthly allowance to purchase necessary medication, mirroring the experiences of several others, including Amélia (Angola): "I fell ill and had to dip into the money I receive each month to cover the cost of my medication."

In contrast, interviewed professionals lacked awareness of such situations, with Ema (Portugal) emphasizing the institution's responsibility to cover medication expenses. This lack of awareness highlights a communication gap within the system, underscoring the need for improved information sharing and coordination to ensure equitable access to healthcare services without personal expenses or treatment denials (Sapia et al., 2020). Such discrepancies emphasize the importance of streamlining processes for consistent access to medical care for all asylum seekers and refugees (Winters, 2018; Reilly, Sahraoui, & McGarry, 2021).

Professionals within the system acknowledge that the intricate bureaucracy of the Portuguese National Health Service poses significant challenges to their work. Maria (Portugal) stressed this point, saying, "In theory, these individuals are entitled to medical care, but in practice, they require a national health number, which is contingent upon having a social security number. As newcomers in Portugal awaiting refugee status, they face significant barriers in obtaining this documentation".

This complex bureaucratic system obstructs asylum seekers' healthcare access in Portugal, contrary to Article 13 of Directive 2013/33/EU, worsening their vulnerabilities. This aligns with prior research (Lebano, Hamed & Bradby 2020; Chiarenza, Dauvrin & Chiesa, 2019; Reilly, Sahraoui, & McGarry, 2021) highlighting healthcare disparities due to legislative, financial, and administrative barriers. These issues are compounded by interpretation and cultural mediation shortcomings, a lack of awareness about services, and insufficient organization among healthcare providers. Reports also point to unmet healthcare needs, especially in mental health treatments, language barriers, and discrimination within healthcare services (Sapia et al., 2020; Matlin et al., 2018; Bradby et al., 2015).

On a more positive note, pregnant women and those who had babies in Portugal received swift, sustained, and specialized healthcare support, exemplified by Mariam (Syria), who reported that: "Upon revealing my pregnancy, the hosting institution promptly arranged for my medical care and scheduled regular appointments with an obstetrician."

Psychological Support

Refugee populations commonly suffer from mental health issues like anxiety, post-traumatic stress, and depression (Davaki, 2021; Sepia, 2017; Canning, 2017; Dionis, Timar & Domscheit-Berg, 2016). These problems result from pre-displacement, displacement, and post-displacement experiences (Rohlof, Knipscheer & Kleber, 2014; Jensen et al., 2013), including exploitation, discrimination, family separation, and health threats during their journeys (Hynie, 2018; Gartley & Due, 2017; Mangrio & Forss, 2017). Upon reaching resettlement countries, their mental well-being may be further affected by legal uncertainty, poor reception conditions, detention, asylum claim rejections, deportation fears, family separation, isolation, and integration challenges, potentially re-traumatizing those with pre-existing mental health issues (Slewa-Younan et al., 2017; Valibhoy, Kaplan & Szwarc, 2017; Robertshaw, Dhesi & Jones, 2017; Wright et al., 2016).

The majority of the women interviewed expressed a need for psychological support due to the trauma they had experienced and the anxiety and stress they faced during their integration in Portugal. This aligns with findings in other studies (Due, Green & Ziersch, 2020; Valibhoy, Kaplan & Szwarc, 2017; Robertshaw, Dhesi & Jones, 2017) that indicate asylum seekers and refugees are more likely to develop mental illnesses compared to the general population. However, most of the women we interviewed reported that psychological support was never offered to them or their families upon arrival in Portugal or during the integration process.

Maara (Syria) questioned why "despite everything we had already been through, even in Portugal, in the detention center, nobody offered us psychological support." Concerns about their children's mental well-being were also expressed by mothers, such as Fatima (Iraq), who was especially worried because "my son developed very serious psychological problems when we were living in Turkey" and Mariam (Syria), who "pleaded with the school to provide psychological support for my daughter because she was having a hard time adapting to our new reality."

According to the professionals, psychological support is "the area facing the most serious implementation problems." (Rita, Portugal). However, this issue reflects the broader situation of psychological support in Portugal, affecting both citizens and refugees, as Camila (Portugal) explained: "Psychological support is failing in Portugal for all Portuguese people, not just refugees, because it continues to be under-prioritized. The Order of Psychologists has been critical of this over the years".

Studies (Due, Green & Ziersch, 2020; Hynie, 2018; Gartley & Due, 2017; Rohlof, Knipscheer & Kleber, 2014; Jensen et al., 2013) link the host country's healthcare system to mental health care for asylum seekers and refugees. The issue isn't the specific mental care given to asylum seekers but the overall provision of mental health support by the state. This structural problem affects those unable to afford private healthcare, including asylum seekers and refugees (Due, Green & Ziersch, 2020). Additionally, even when psychological therapies are available, a shortage of trauma specialists limits support services in practice (Hynie, 2018; Slewa-Younan et al., 2017; Valibhoy, Kaplan & Szwarc, 2017; Robertshaw, Dhesi & Jones, 2017).

Another aspect that can render sessions with psychologists ineffective is the absence of interpreters (Freedman, 2019; Gartley & Due, 2017). As reported by the few women who received psychological support, the lack of an interpreter made the therapy sessions unproductive. Hanan (Syria) found it "very frustrating" as she couldn't communicate with the psychologist effectively due to language barriers. Jassim (Syria) also faced similar issues: "I asked for psychological help multiple times, and finally, they got me a psychologist. But the psychologist couldn't ask me questions because she didn't speak English or Arabic. I was very upset and sad and never returned".

Sapia's study (2018) revealed a knowledge gap among politicians and professionals about refugee backgrounds, symptoms, and coping strategies, emphasizing the need for intercultural interpreters to bridge language barriers. Professionals often use free tools "like Google Translate or ACM's translator line" (João, Portugal), considering them sufficient. However, refugee women criticized the lack of translators, affecting their communication with professionals and during psychological appointments. Inadequate mental health support for trauma-experienced applicants hinders successful integration (Robertshaw, Dhesi & Jones, 2017; Jensen et al., 2013).

Interpreters and translators, as evidenced by studies (Boylen et al., 2020; Berbel, 2020; MacFarlane, Huschke & Pottie, 2020; Ivars & Pinilla, 2018; Kindermann & Derreza-Greeven, 2017), play a crucial role in shaping the integration of asylum seekers and refugees in their new country. They do more than translating; they build cultural bridges, considering context, emotions, and expressions. Their role extends beyond word-for-word translation, adapting cultural terms, expressions, and idioms to provide comprehensive content meaning. This underscores their indispensable contribution to the integration process.

Education

Timely access to inclusive and formal education and training is a potent tool for fostering integration. Proficiency in the language of the host country is pivotal to successful social inclusion, the exercise of rights, and the addressing of specific needs (Borges & Faria, 2022; Horn et al., 2021). The Directive 2013/33/EU, though lacking specific provisions for language courses, generally sees most EU member states offering such courses to asylum seekers and refugees. These classes are often organized informally in reception or accommodation centers, with support from civil society, volunteers, or directly provided by institutional professionals (Lochmann, Rapoport & Speciale, 2019; Åslund, & Engdahl, 2018).

In Portugal, the national asylum system recognizes the importance of language acquisition for successful integration and mandates access to Portuguese classes upon arrival. Initially, asylum seekers are provided instruction, either by volunteers at reception centers or through the "Portuguese for All" program offered by the Institute of Employment and Training A notable example is the "Portuguese for all" program (*Português para Todos* - PPT), a Portuguese language initiative offered in collaboration with the Portuguese Institute for Employment and Professional Training (*Instituto do Emprego e Formação Profissional* - IEFP). However, a notable challenge arises from the fact that the "Portuguese for All" program requires a minimum of twenty participants because, due to the decentralized approach adopted within the Portuguese asylum system, only a limited number of asylum seekers find themselves accommodated within the same city.

Consequently, the stipulation of requiring twenty students per class implies that the majority of asylum seekers may not be able to avail themselves of this program, mirroring the experience of the vast majority of women interviewed. According to the professionals perspective, "while this program seems flawless in theory, the practical challenges are formidable, particularly outside major urban areas, where it's rare to find a concentration of twenty individuals residing in the same locality" (Carolina, Portugal). In fact, none of the women interviewed had the opportunity to participate in such classes.

The majority of the women interviewed received only brief, rudimentary courses in Portuguese that did not afford them a comprehensive grasp of the language. Amal (Iraq) explained: "The course we had in the reception center only covered the basics of the Portuguese language, and I ceased to receive any form of classes after leaving the reception center." Some women were fortunate enough to have volunteer teachers who visited their homes to provide instruction. As Eisaa (Syria) shared: "A teacher came to our home to teach us. She was a volunteer, and she visited us twice a week."

The professionals also reported have resorted to volunteer-led classes, a practice that has become somewhat customary in Portugal. However, this approach has its inherent limitations, primarily because it often offers only rudimentary instruction and struggles to accommodate individuals with varying language proficiency levels within group settings. This was succinctly encapsulated by Alda (Portugal), who stated that volunteer-led classes "often provide only basic instruction and face difficulties in catering to individuals with diverse language skills."

The heavy reliance on civil society's goodwill to fulfill the integration requirements laid out in the Directive 2013/33/EU has been deemed an unsustainable solution. This is further underscored by the experiences of the majority of the women interviewed, who expressed their dissatisfaction with the quality of Portuguese courses they received. They felt "ill-prepared in terms of language skills required for effective integration", as Alia (Sudan) noted. In contrast, a substantial number of women were denied the chance to enroll in Portuguese language classes, much like Yaya (Gambia), who lamented, "My family and I were never provided with the opportunity to access Portuguese language courses."

When it comes to professional training, the available opportunities in Portugal are quite restricted, with a focus on asylum seekers who have experienced prolonged periods in the country and encountered significant challenges in finding employment. A striking example of this can be found in the experience of Madalena (Angola), who shared her story: "I've been in this country for nearly two years, and right from the moment I arrived, I've consistently requested the opportunity to enroll in a hairdressing course. It was only after a substantial two-year period of unsuccessful job searches that they eventually agreed to provide me with the training I'd been seeking".

Access to professional development is closely tied to the length of one's stay and employment difficulties, potentially delaying skill acquisition and integration. More flexible and accessible training opportunities are needed for newcomers to ensure effective integration. Women with higher education face challenges in having their qualifications recognized, which directly affects their access to the labor market, causing delays and frustration in their integration process.

The Lisbon Recognition Convention (LRC) of 1997 promotes recognizing qualifications held by refugees, displaced persons, and those in refugee-like situations with flexibility. In 2017, the LRC Committee recommended ratifying states to adopt these measures. This flexible approach prioritizes practical skills and competencies over formal qualifications, improving the integration prospects for well-educated refugees by expediting recognition processes.

It's important to note, however, that despite Portugal being a signatory to the Lisbon Recognition Convention (LRC), the country has yet to fully incorporate these progressive practices within its recognition system. This discrepancy between the international commitment and its practical implementation highlights an area where improvements are needed to facilitate the seamless integration of refugees with higher education backgrounds into the Portuguese workforce and society at large.

Labor Market Integration

Studies on the labor market integration of asylum seekers and refugees are limited (Hillmann & Koca, 2021; Kofman, 2020; Pallmann, Ziegler & Pfeffer-Hoffmann, 2019; Hainmueller, Hangartner, Lawrence, 2016). Brell, Dustmann, and Preston (2020) offered an extensive overview of labor market integration in various high-income countries. They found that, except for the United Kingdom, the United States, and Canada, employment rates for asylum seekers and refugees are usually below 20% in the first two years after their arrival. Although there is some improvement in the short term, asylum seekers and refugees still lag behind native and other immigrant populations in employment rates over a decade. This indicates that refugees face a more prolonged and challenging integration compared to other immigrant groups, with women earning less than their counterparts.

Undoubtedly, the majority of women had faced significant challenges in securing employment in Portugal at the time of the interviews. As expressed by Promesse (Congo): "I've been sending out CVs ever since I received the temporary resident permit, but finding a job remains an elusive goal. It's a major concern because without employment, my future is uncertain. I honestly don't know what lies ahead."

Among the limited group of women who had managed to find work, most had resorted to working in unregistered, informal positions. Amélia (Angola) mentioned,

"I took on caregiving duties for an elderly woman who paid me, but I didn't have a formal employment contract".

An even smaller subset of women had received assistance from institutional professionals in their journey toward labor market integration. Shamshi (Somalia) shared her experience: "Initially, I worked for the institution that provided me shelter, primarily handling translations. Subsequently, they arranged a paid internship for me, and I'm now employed as a seamstress".

Health issues, such as back problems or mental health concerns, have also acted as barriers to employment, as supported by other studies (Hynie, 2018; Chen, Hall & Renzaho, 2017; Shishehgar et al., 2017; Hainmueller, Hangartner & Lawrence, 2016; Schick et al., 2016). Khadija (Syria) expressed, "I would genuinely like to work, but I'm confronted with a back problem that prevents me from taking on any job, especially those that require significant strain on my spine".

The challenges in labor market integration for asylum seekers and refugees are often linked to two key theories: human capital theory, focusing on skill deficiencies, and social capital theory, highlighting the importance of valuable social connections (Campion, 2018). However, many women in this study lacked substantial relationships with Portuguese citizens or fully integrated refugees, limiting their social capital. Recent research emphasizes the role of native friends or well-integrated family members in improving employment prospects (Eggenhofer-Rehart et al., 2018), which was not the case for the women in this study.

In terms of human capital, women often grappled with challenges arising from disparities in the educational systems of their home countries compared to Portugal. They also faced limited work experience, insufficient professional training, and language barriers. Ammar (Syria) aptly highlighted these hurdles: "I aspire to work here in Portugal, perhaps as a seamstress or a hairdresser, but my predicament lies in having no prior experience in these fields, coupled with my lack of proficiency in the Portuguese language".

Furthermore, many of them had not engaged in employment outside their homes. Consequently, this dearth of labor market exposure can be viewed as a facet of human capital that adversely affects the economic integration of women.

The collected data on the labor market integration also unveiled another dimension of human capital that detrimentally impacted their employment prospects: their proficiency (or lack thereof) in the language of the host country. Given that the Portuguese language is not commonly spoken in the countries of origin of most women interviewed, they arrived in Portugal without any prior knowledge of Portuguese. Jassim (Syria) articulated the challenge succinctly, stating, "I genuinely want to find a job, but the language barriers make it very difficult".

Language skills play a pivotal role in the labor market performance of immigrants since most professions in the host country require reasonable proficiency in the local language (Dustmann et al., 2017). Amal (Iraq) reiterated this point, noting, "The issue with finding work is that all employers expect me to speak Portuguese, and I still haven't acquired that skill". Lang (2021) underlines the positive impact of enhanced language skills on the economic success of refugees, expanding the range of jobs they are qualified for in the labor market.

Moreover, the majority of women expressed dissatisfaction with the lack of institutional support for their labor market integration. In contrast, none of the professionals admitted to neglecting their duty of assisting women in finding employment; in fact, they acknowledged it as one of their primary responsibilities. However, the professionals also contended that other tasks took precedence over job placement, with Rita (Portugal) stating: "We must empower them to seek employment on their own. If we secure a job for someone, and they later wish to change jobs or face termination, they won't have the skills to seek new opportunities independently."

The professionals further argued that it was comparatively easier to integrate refugee men into the Portuguese labor market due to their physical capabilities and prior work experience. The professionals' discourse also reflects certain prejudices about the cultural and traditional norms of asylum seekers and refugee women. They suggested that "many men did not approve of their wives working outside the home" (António, Portugal), citing cultural norms as a contributing factor.

Contrary to these biases, the women interviewed who were married expressed that their husbands were supportive of their employment aspirations. These contrasting perspectives underscore the need to dispel cultural biases.

Legal Aid

Legal aid plays a crucial role in asylum proceedings, where both excessively fast and lengthy procedures can jeopardize fundamental rights (Buxton, 2020; Hvidtfeldt, Petersen & Norredam, 2020; Demarchi & Lenehan, 2019; Brekke, 2010). Hastily made decisions leave insufficient time for preparation and legal assistance, infringing on the right to access asylum, as defined in Articles 18 and 19 of The Charter of Fundamental Rights of the European Union (CFR, 2000). In appeal proceedings, this affects the right to an effective remedy, as enshrined in Article 47. Conversely, protracted proceedings leave asylum seekers in a state of uncertainty, compromising their right to good administration, a fundamental EU law principle (Hainmueller, Hangartner & Lawrence, 2016).

The impact of time on asylum seekers' rights and well-being is evident through their experiences. Many women expressed frustration with the delays in international protection application processing. For example, Promesse (Congo) mentioned, "it took more than four months since I arrived in Portugal for [name of the institution] to start processing my case." Delays in decision-making, requiring repeated renewals of temporary residence permits, were also a significant concern. Darya (Syria) highlighted her uncertainty: "It is the third time that I renew my temporary residence permit, and I still don't know how much longer it will take for the Portuguese state to decide if they accept us or not."

Asylum seekers in Portugal typically receive a temporary residence permit known as "ARP" ("*Autorização de Residência Provisória*"), which is valid for six months while their international protection requests are being processed. These permits are usually issued by the SEF and must be renewed if the final decision on the asylum application is not reached within the permit's validity period. This prolonged waiting negatively affects asylum seekers' rights to access essential services, hindering their integration (Buxton, 2020; Hvidtfeldt, Petersen & Norredam, 2020).

Moreover, the women interviewed also highlighted bureaucratic challenges when renewing temporary residence permit documents. As expressed by Glória (Congo): "The process can be quite arduous – we find ourselves navigating a labyrinth of bureaucracy, starting with the need to secure an appointment with the SEF. Regrettably, it often becomes a waiting game, with considerable delays before they can accommodate us."

Professionals echoed this concern, with Susana (Portugal) stating that "the SEF does not consider the expiration dates of the temporary residence permits", resulting in asylum seekers often being caught in legal limbo while waiting for renewal. This situation is highly problematic since an expired temporary residence permit "means they are no longer entitled to essential services like healthcare, employment, and subsistence support" (Maria, Portugal).

Time plays a crucial role in the integration of asylum seekers and refugees, impacting their access to employment, social welfare, healthcare, and services (Shishehgar et al., 2017). Delays in Portugal's international protection process are in line with Buxton's (2020) critique of temporary refugee protection, leading to precarious asylum status, affecting rights and mental health. Buxton (2020) argues that the only solution to this injustice is to grant asylum seekers permanent refugee status.

Some of the women interviewed faced the rejection of their international protection requests and found themselves in a state of "awaiting the outcome of my appeal" (Madalena, Angola). In Portugal, asylum seekers who receive negative decisions on their international protection requests have the option to file appeals without a set limit. If individuals choose not to appeal or depart voluntarily, the compulsion to leave Portugal only arises when they come to the attention of law enforcement through involvement in criminal activities.

The legal aspect of refusal aligns with Directive 2008/115/EC and Portuguese Law No. 26/2014, which emphasizes respecting fundamental rights, including the principle of 'non-refoulement,' prohibiting the expulsion of asylum seekers to life-threatening situations. Resolution of the Council of Ministers of Portugal, No. 103/2020, requires state support for individuals appealing inadmissibility decisions. However, rejected asylum seekers lack state support and must rely on non-profit organizations. Indefinite appeals subject asylum seekers to precarious legal status and its harmful consequences.

The Resolution of the Council of Ministers of Portugal, No. 103/2020, introduced a unified system for the reception and integration of individuals applying for and benefiting from international protection. This was followed by the enactment of Decree-law 26/2021, which established the National Urgent and Temporary Housing Scholarship program. The National Housing Plan encompasses a wide range of risk situations and social emergencies, including but not limited to unscheduled migratory flows, individuals who have fallen victim to human trafficking, and those under international protection.

Additionally, Ordinance No. 120/2021 delineates the operational and management framework of the National Urgent and Temporary Housing Exchange, which was established pursuant to Decree-Law No. 26/2021. Furthermore, Order No. 47/2022 delegates specific authorities to the Secretary of State for Internal Administration, specifically in relation to administrative procedures within the framework of the legal provisions governing international protection.

The women interviewed often expressed concerns about the persistent delays in family reunification processes. These delays can result in numerous challenges, such as limited access to services, mental health issues, and susceptibility to illegal employment and criminal activities (Kraus, Sauer & Wenzel, 2019). As per the insights shared by professionals, these challenges are not unique to Portugal. They noted that asylum seekers are "required to furnish documentation validating their family connections and, in addition, bear the expenses associated with the travel of their family members" (Diana, Portugal).

Simplifying the family reunification process is vital for refugee integration and offers significant long-term benefits for the host country. Since 2015, family reunification has become more difficult due to various legal and practical obstacles, such as complex procedures, limited access to diplomatic missions outside the EU, and financial burdens for obtaining necessary documents (Löbel & Jacobsen, 2021). Requiring asylum seekers and refugees to prove family ties and cover their families' travel expenses worsens these challenges. This approach also overlooks the positive impact of family reunification on integration and its role in reducing human smuggling and secondary movements.

DISCUSSION: ADVANCING GENDER EQUALITY IN THE PORTUGUESE ASYLUM SYSTEM

This chapter underscores the need for an urgent reevaluation of Portugal's asylum support framework, especially regarding gender issues. While Resolution No. 103/2020 aimed to unify the protection framework, there are concerns about consistency and adherence to international standards (Directive 2008/115/EC, 2011/95/EU, and Directive 2013/33/EU).

As illustrated in this chapter, the support system for asylum seekers in Portugal remains fragmented, leading to notable disparities in the quality and accessibility of the assistance offered to asylum-seeking women. Portugal lacks specific mechanisms, standard procedures, or dedicated units for systematically identifying asylum seekers requiring special procedural guarantees.

The screening of vulnerability relies on a questionnaire used by SEF, but its effectiveness is questionable. Asylum seekers claiming to be victims of torture are assessed on a case-by-case basis, and victims of human trafficking need better training and support. In 2020, the UN Human Rights Committee expressed concern over this absence and recommended establishing an effective mechanism for identifying vulnerable applicants (Oliveira, 2020).

To address the complexities faced by asylum-seeking women, specific needs should be identified during the asylum application process, preventing challenges that hinder their access to fundamental human rights. These challenges include insufficient assessment, limited access to welfare resources, and reduced support for survivors of violence.

Within the context of violence experienced by asylum-seeking women, Canning (2017) introduces the concept of "intersectional continuums of violence", a term that encapsulates violence persisting across a spectrum of social actors, including government forces, militia, smugglers, traffickers, allies, friends, partners, and husbands. This conceptual framework seeks to broaden our understanding by recognizing the diversity of experiences among these women, thus moving beyond the confines of categorizing them as a homogeneous group.

This approach underscores the urgent necessity of acknowledging the various forms that violence can assume in the lives of asylum-seeking women and the distinctions within their experiences of violence.

Drawing upon the invaluable insights provided by Canning's thoughtful theorization (2017) and the findings presented here, this chapter acknowledges that, while variations may exist in the experiences of violence among asylum-seeking women, it is highly probable that each will, in some form, confront the chilling grasp of institutional violence within the host country. It is essential to recognize that these incidents are not isolated but rather emblematic of a systemic pattern.

The term "institutional violence" typically refers to a spectrum of harm inflicted upon individuals or groups as a result of policies, practices, or actions within institutions or organizations (Galtung, 1969; Farmer, 2005). This harm can manifest in various forms, including physical, psychological, structural, or systemic, often perpetuated by the very systems designed to provide support, security, or services (Butler, 2016).

This chapter's revelations expose a persistent gap between policy objectives and their practical implementation in Portugal, a discrepancy that often results in the perpetuation of institutional forms of violence against asylum-seeking women. Furthermore, Portugal's asylum system lacks gender-specific practices, with consequences for asylum-seeking women. Gender-focused initiatives for asylum seekers and refugee women are limited, emphasizing the need for comprehensive gender-sensitive practices and specialized assistance to address their unique challenges.

In 2022, a sub-group focusing on vulnerabilities within the asylum system was created, composed of several relevant authorities (CPR, 2022). This sub-group was expected to identify services and mechanisms to address specific vulnerabilities during the first semester of 2023. However, as of the writing of this article in December 2023, no report from this group has been made publicly available for consultation.

The attainment of gender equality and safety for asylum-seeking women in Portugal hinges on comprehensive gender-specific data collection and gender-sensitive integration practices, as emphasized in the AIDA report of 2018.

The Istanbul Convention of 2014, along with other human rights treaties, operates on the principles of "Prevention, Protection, and Prosecution" as a response to gender-based violence. Effective action in prevention, protection, and prosecution demands comprehensive measures to address gender-based violence against asylum seekers and refugee women (Peroni, 2016).

Having shed light on the deficiencies in gender-related policies and practices in Portugal through our data analysis, next this chapter provides best practice recommendations to improve gender-sensitive integration practices within the Portuguese asylum system, focusing on addressing the challenges faced by asylum-seeking women.

Advancing Best Practices

The compilation of nineteen recommendations in this section functions as a strategic framework for nurturing an environment that is both more equitable and secure for asylum-seeking women. At its core, the pivotal action entails the implementation of asylum system policies that intricately consider the historical experiences of discrimination and violence endured by these women.

1. **Clear asylum procedure guidance:** Offer clear and comprehensive information and guidance on the asylum procedure to help asylum seekers understand and navigate the process.
2. **Separate reception centers:** Create dedicated reception centers for all asylum-seekers, featuring separate facilities for women and families to ensure safety and privacy.
3. **Specialized financial support:** Provide financial support to asylum seekers while considering the specific needs of women, children and the elderly.
4. **Health assessment on arrival:** Conduct comprehensive physical and mental health assessments for asylum seekers upon their arrival.
5. **Gender-specific health programs:** Offer tailored health programs that include reproductive rights information and address the unique health needs of women.
6. **Tailored language courses:** Provide Portuguese language courses with a gender perspective, considering the specific linguistic needs and challenges faced by women.
7. **Gender-focused employment support:** Offer employment support services with a particular emphasis on the needs and challenges of women in the labor market.
8. **Recognition of qualifications:** Effectively implementing the Lisbon Recognition Convention is a practical step toward expediting the process of recognizing qualifications acquired in one's home country. This, in turn, facilitates the smoother integration of asylum-seeking women into the workforce.
9. **Mentoring programs:** Establish mentoring programs designed to support women in the labor market and help them navigate career pathways.
10. **Psychological support:** Provide psychological support that is sensitive to gender-related trauma and experiences, particularly for survivors of violence.
11. **Victim support office:** Set up a dedicated office to support asylum-seeking and refugee women who have been victims of violence and abuse.
12. **Balancing language learning and childcare:** Develop programs that assist mothers in balancing language learning with childcare responsibilities.
13. **Legal representation and counselling:** Ensure access to legal representation and counselling for all asylum seekers to navigate the asylum procedure.
14. **Prioritizing family reunification:** Emphasize the importance of reuniting families separated during the asylum-seeking process by fostering collaboration with the relevant authorities in the home countries of asylum-seekers.
15. **Gender education for men:** Implement educational programs for asylum-seeking men to promote gender awareness and equality.
16. **Culturally competent mediators**: Employ intercultural mediators who are culturally and linguistically competent to facilitate communication and understanding between asylum seekers and host communities.

17. **Social support to combat isolation:** Provide support to address social isolation and help asylum-seeking women build personal networks within their host community.

18. **Promoting agency through creative expression:** Encourage asylum-seeking and refugee women to express themselves creatively and engage in workshops that empower them to reclaim their agency and identity.

Adhering to these recommendations aligns with recent advice from the Working Group on the Universal Periodic Review, a body of the Human Rights Council, which encourages the development of comprehensive strategies to eliminate gender-based discrimination and overcome stereotypes regarding gender roles. While the recommendations provided by this chapter are tailored for Portugal, their broader objective is to address gender-related issues among asylum seekers, aiming to prevent re-victimization, secondary victimization, insecurity, and increased vulnerability on a global scale.

CONCLUSION

Based on the findings in this chapter, Portugal urgently needs a comprehensive reevaluation of its asylum support framework to rectify mistreatment and inadequacies. Reforms in the seven key intervention areas are necessary to uphold the dignity and fundamental rights of asylum seekers. Portugal and other nations must prioritize humane treatment and meet the needs of asylum seekers as they start new lives in their host countries. Comprehensive policy changes are crucial to facilitate their integration, fully implementing international commitments like the Lisbon Recognition Convention, and improving coordination and consistent support among stakeholders.

This chapter also highlights a significant gender gap in the Portuguese asylum system, despite international legal instruments promoting gender equality. Efforts to address gender-based violence and discrimination have limitations and challenges. The absence of gender-specific provisions within the asylum system hinders effective support for asylum-seeking women. Tailored support services, specialized assistance, psychological support, initiatives targeting gender equality among asylum-seeking men, gender-sensitive data collection, and national integration policies challenging traditional gender roles and stereotypes are needed.

While this research contributes to criminology, gender, and migration studies, it has limitations due to its qualitative methodologies. Subjectivity raises concerns about validity, reliability, and objectivity, emphasizing the importance of reflexivity to address biases and ethical considerations. The in-depth nature may limit generalizability to broader populations, which could be improved with a larger and more diverse sample.

Deeper exploration of asylum-seeking women's experiences and the causes behind the gender approach insufficiency, along with documentary analysis of asylum applications, research on the emotional impact on professionals, and public perceptions and knowledge about asylum seekers and refugees, is necessary for effective strategies and a supportive community.

For survivors of gender-based violence, Portugal should enact integration measures championing gender equality and prioritizing the well-being of asylum seekers, fostering inclusivity, and celebrating their contributions while upholding fundamental rights.

REFERENCES

Aas, K. (2011). 'Crimmigrant' bodies and the bona fide traveler: Surveillance, citizenship and global governance. *Theoretical Criminology*, *15*(3), 331–346. doi:10.1177/1362480610396643

Aas, K. F. (2019). *The crimmigrant other: Migration and Penal Power*. Routledge.

Aas, K. F., & Bosworth, M. (2013). *The borders of punishment: Migration, Citizenship, and Social Exclusion*. Oxford University Press. doi:10.1093/acprof:oso/9780199669394.001.0001

Åslund, O., & Engdahl, M. (2018). The value of earning for learning: Performance bonuses in immigrant language training. *Economics of Education Review*, *62*, 192–204. doi:10.1016/j.econedurev.2017.11.010

Baczynska, G., & Ledwith, S. (2016). How Europe built fences to keep people out. *Reuters*. Retrieved from: https://www.reuters.com/article/us-europe-migrants-fences-insight-idUSKCN0X10U7

Barker, V. (2018). *Nordic nationalism and penal order walling the welfare state*. Routledge.

Berger, R. (2016). Now I see it, now I don't: Researcher's position and reflexivity in qualitative research. *Qualitative Research*, *15*(2), 1–16. doi:10.1177/1468794112468475

Borges, G., & Faria, R. (2023). Language, emotions, and access to refugee women: Ingredients for reflexivity. In A. M. Díaz Fernández, C. Del-Real, & L. Molnar (Eds.), *Fieldwork Experiences in Criminology and Security Studies: Methods, Ethics, and Emotions.* Springer Nature. doi:10.1007/978-3-031-41574-6_17

Borges, G. M. (2023). *Journey of Violence: Refugee Women's Experiences Across Three Stages and Places.* Int. Migration & Integration. doi:10.1007/s12134-023-01102-z

Borges, G. M., & Faria, R. (2022). Breathing Under Water: Gendering the Violence Against Refugee Women. In *Research Anthology on Child and Domestic Abuse and Its Prevention* (pp. 19–37). IGI Global. doi:10.4018/978-1-6684-5598-2.ch002

Borges, G. M., Guerreiro, A., Conde, L. (2022). Stroking reflexivity into practice: The pros and cons of resorting to gatekeepers to conduct qualitative criminological research. *Journal of Qualitative Criminal Justice & Criminology.* doi:10.21428/88de04a1.31b36875

Bosworth, M. (2008). Border control and the limits of the sovereign state. *Social & Legal Studies, 17*(2), 199–215. doi:10.1177/0964663908089611

Bosworth, M. (2011). Human rights and immigration detention. In Are Human Rights for Migrants? Critical Reflections on the Status of Irregular Migrants in Europe and the United States (pp. 165-183). Routledge.

Bosworth, M., & Guild, M. (2008). Governing through migration control: Security and citizenship in Britain. *British Journal of Criminology, 48*(6), 703–719. doi:10.1093/bjc/azn059

Brell, C., Dustmann, C., & Preston, I. (2020). The labor market integration of refugee migrants in high-income countries. *The Journal of Economic Perspectives, 34*(1), 94–121. doi:10.1257/jep.34.1.94

Butler, J. (2016). *Frames of war: When is life grievable?* Verso Books.

Buxton, R. (2023). Justice in waiting: The harms and wrongs of temporary refugee protection. *European Journal of Political Theory, 22*(1), 51–72. doi:10.1177/1474885120973578

Campion, E. D. (2018). The career adaptive refugee: Exploring the structural and personal barriers to refugee resettlement. *Journal of Vocational Behavior, 105*(2), 6–16. doi:10.1016/j.jvb.2017.10.008

Canning, V. (2017). *Gendered harm and structural violence in the British asylum system*. Taylor & Francis eBooks.

Canning, V. (2020). Corrosive Control: State-Corporate and Gendered Harm in Bordered Britain. *Critical Criminology*, *28*(2), 259–275. doi:10.1007/s10612-020-09509-1

Charmaz, K., & Thornberg, R. (2021). The pursuit of quality in grounded theory. *Qualitative Research in Psychology*, *18*(3), 305–327. doi:10.1080/14780887.2020.1780357

Charmaz, K., Thornberg, R., & Keane, E. (2017). Evolving grounded theory and social justice inquiry. In N. K. Denzin & Y. S. Lincoln (Eds.), *The SAGE handbook of qualitative research* (pp. 411–443). Sage Publications.

Chen, W., Hall, B. J., & Renzaho, A. M. N. (2017). Pre-migration and post-migration factors associated with mental health in humanitarian migrants in Australia and the moderation effect of post-migration stressors: Findings from the first wave data of the BNLA cohort study. *The Lancet. Psychiatry*, *4*(3), 219–229. doi:10.1016/S2215-0366(17)30032-9 PMID:28161455

Chiarenza, A., Dauvrin, M., Chiesa, V., Baatout, S., & Verrept, H. (2019). Supporting access to healthcare for refugees and migrants in European countries under particular migratory pressure. *BMC Health Services Research*, *19*(1), 513. doi:10.1186/s12913-019-4353-1 PMID:31337406

Cochrane, B. (2018). Harms at the crossroads of carework and irregular migration. *Journal of Refugee Studies*, *33*(3), 500–520. doi:10.1093/jrs/fey056

CPR. (2022). Aida: Asylum Information Database. Country Report: Portugal.

Davaki, K. (2021). *The traumas endured by refugee women and their consequences for integration and participation in the EU host country*. Policy Department for Citizens' Rights and Constitutional Affairs Directorate-General for Internal Policies.

Demarchi, G., & Lenehan, S. (2019). *Gender in waiting: Men and women asylum seekers in European reception facilities*. The World Bank. doi:10.1596/31209

Dionis, M. S., Timar, M., & Domscheit-Berg, A. (2016). *Protecting refugee Women and girls from violence: A collection of good practices*. World Future Council.

Due, C., Green, E., & Ziersch, A. (2020). Psychological trauma and access to primary healthcare for people from refugee and asylum-seeker backgrounds: A mixed methods systematic review. *International Journal of Mental Health Systems*, *14*(71), 1–18. doi:10.1186/s13033-020-00404-4 PMID:32944067

Dustmann, C., Fasani, F., Frattini, T., Minale, L., & Schönberg, U. (2017). On the economics and politics of refugee migration. *Economic Policy*, *32*(91), 497–550. doi:10.1093/epolic/eix008

Eggenhofer-Rehart, P. P. M., Latzke, M., Pernkopf, K., Zellhofer, D., Mayhofer, W., & Stevre, J. (2018). Refugees' career capital welcome? Afghan and Syrian eefugee job seekers in Austria. *Journal of Vocational Behavior*, *105*, 31–45. doi:10.1016/j.jvb.2018.01.004

EUROSTAT. (2014-2019). *Asylum and managed migration*. European Commission.

Farmer, P. (2005). *Pathologies of power: Health, human rights, and the new war on the poor*. University of California Press.

Fassin, D. (2018). *The will to punish*. Oxford University Press. doi:10.1093/oso/9780190888589.001.0001

Fotaki, M. (2019). A crisis of humanitarianism: Refugees at the gates of Europe. *International Journal of Health Policy and Management, 8*(6), 321–324. doi:10.15171/ijhpm.2019.22 PMID:31256563

Freedman, J. (2015). *Gendering the international asylum and refugee debate*. Palgrave Macmillan. doi:10.1057/9781137456236

Freedman, J. (2016a). Sexual and gender-based violence against refugee women: A hidden aspect of the refugee "crisis". *Reproductive Health Matters*, *4*(47), 18–26. doi:10.1016/j.rhm.2016.05.003 PMID:27578335

Freedman, J. (2016b). Engendering security at the borders of Europe: Women migrants and the Mediterranean crisis. *Journal of Refugee Studies*, *29*(4), 568–582. doi:10.1093/jrs/few019

Freedman, J. (2019). Grand challenges: Refugees and conflict. *Frontiers in Human Dynamics*, *3*, 1–3. doi:10.3389/fhumd.2019.00001

Freedman, J., Crankshaw, T. L., & Mutambara, V. M. (2020). Sexual and reproductive health of asylum seeking and refugee women in South Africa: Understanding the determinants of vulnerability. *Sexual and Reproductive Health Matters*, *28*(1), 323–334. doi:10.1080/26410397.2020.1758440 PMID:32425112

Galtung, J. (1969). Violence, peace, and peace research. *Journal of Peace Research*, *6*(3), 167–191. doi:10.1177/002234336900600301

Gartley, T., & Due, C. (2017). The interpreter is not an invisible being: A thematic analysis of the impact of interpreters in mental health service provision with refugee clients. *Australian Psychologist*, *52*(1), 31–40. doi:10.1111/ap.12181

Hainmueller, J., Hangartner, D., & Lawrence, D. (2016). When lives are put on hold: Lengthy asylum processes decrease employment among refugees. *Science Advances*, *2*(8), 1–7. doi:10.1126/sciadv.1600432 PMID:27493995

Hathaway, J. C., & Fosterm, M. (2014). *The law of refugee status* (2nd ed.). Cambridge University Press. doi:10.1017/CBO9780511998300

Hermans, M. P. P. J., Kooistra, J., Cannegieter, S. C., Rosendaal, F. R., Mook-Kanamori, D. O., & Nemeth, B. (2017). Healthcare and disease burden among refugees in long-stay refugee camps at Lesbos, Greece. *European Journal of Epidemiology*, *32*(9), 851–854. doi:10.1007/s10654-017-0269-4 PMID:28597126

Hersh, M., & Obser, K. (2016). *Falling through the cracks: Refugee women and girls in Germany and Sweden*. Women's Refugee Commission.

Hillmann, F., & Koca, B. T. (2021). By women, for women, and with women": On the integration of highly qualified female refugees into the labour Markets of Berlin and Brandenburg. *Comparative Migration Studies*, *9*(3), 1–12. doi:10.1186/s40878-020-00211-3

Horn, R., Wachter, K., Friis-Healy, E. A., Ngugi, S. W., Creighton, J., & Puffer, E. S. (2021). Mapping complex systems: Responses to intimate partner violence against women in three refugee camps. *Frontiers in Human Dynamics*, *3*, 1–15. doi:10.3389/fhumd.2021.613792

Hvidtfeldt, C., Petersen, J. H., & Norredam, M. (2020). Prolonged periods of waiting for an asylum decision and the risk of psychiatric diagnoses: A 22-year longitudinal cohort study from Denmark. *International Journal of Epidemiology*, *49*(2), 400–409. doi:10.1093/ije/dyz091 PMID:31106354

Hynie, M. (2018). The social determinants of refugee mental health in the post-migration context: A critical review. *Canadian Journal of Psychiatry*, *63*(5), 297–303. doi:10.1177/0706743717746666 PMID:29202665

Jensen, N. K., Norredam, M., Priebe, S., & Krasnik, A. (2013). How do general practitioners experience provide care to refugees with mental health problems? A qualitative study from Denmark. *BMC Family Practice*, *14*(17), 1–9. doi:10.1186/1471-2296-14-17 PMID:23356401

Kanal, M., & Rottmann, S. (2021). Everyday agency: Rethinking refugee women's agency in specific cultural contexts. *Frontiers in Psychology*, *12*, 1–14. doi:10.3389/fpsyg.2021.726729 PMID:34867608

Kelly, L. (1988). *Surviving sexual violence*. Polity Press.

Kelly, L. (2005). Inside outsiders: Mainstreaming violence against women in human rights discourse and practice. *International Feminist Journal of Politics*, *7*(4), 471–495. doi:10.1080/14616740500284391

Kennedy, B. L., & Thornberg, R. (2018). Deduction, induction, and abduction. In U. Flick (Ed.), *The sage handbook of qualitative data collection* (pp. 49–64). Sage Publications. doi:10.4135/9781526416070.n4

Kofman, E. (2020). Gender and the feminization of migration. In C. Inglis, W. Li, & B. Khadria (Eds.), The sage handbook of international migration (pp. 2016–2231). Sage Publications.

Kraus, E., Sauer, K. L., & Wenzel, L. (2019). Together or apart? Spousal migration and reunification practices of recent refugees to Germany. *ZtF. Zeitschrift für Familienforschung*, *31*(3), 303–332. doi:10.3224/zff.v31i3.04

Lebano, A., Hamed, S., Bradby, H., Gil-Salmerón, A., Durá-Ferrandis, E., Garcés-Ferrer, J., Azzedine, F., Riza, E., Karnaki, P., Zota, D., & Linos, A. (2020). Migrants' and refugees' health status and healthcare in Europe: A scoping literature review. *BMC Public Health*, *20*(1039), 1–16. doi:10.1186/s12889-020-08749-8 PMID:32605605

Löbel, L. M., & Jacobsen, J. (2021). Waiting for kin: A longitudinal study of family reunification and refugee mental health in Germany. *Journal of Ethnic and Migration Studies*, *47*(13), 2916–2937. doi:10.1080/1369183X.2021.1884538

Lochmann, A., Rapoport, H., & Speciale, B. (2019). The effect of language training on immigrants' economic integration: Empirical evidence from France. *European Economic Review*, *113*, 265–296. doi:10.1016/j.euroecorev.2019.01.008

Mangrio, E., & Forss, K. S. (2017). Refugees' experiences of healthcare in the host country: A scoping review. *BMC Health Services Research*, *17*(814), 1–18. doi:10.1186/s12913-017-2731-0 PMID:29216876

Mangrio, E., Zdravkovic, S., & Carlson, E. (2019). Refugee women's experience of the resettlement process: A qualitative study. *BMC Women's Health*, *19*(1), 147. doi:10.1186/s12905-019-0843-x PMID:31775733

Oliveira, C. (2020). *Entry, reception and integration of applicants and beneficiaries of international protection in Portugal - 2020 asylum statistical report*. Academic Press.

Pallmann, I., Ziegler, J., & Pfeffer-Hoffmann, C. (2019). *Refugee women as a target group of labour market policies*. Mensch & Buch.

Reilly, N., Sahraoui, N., & McGarry, O. (2021). Exclusion, minimization, inaction: A critical review of Ireland's policy response to gender-based violence as it affects migrant women. *Frontiers in Human Dynamics*, *3*, 1–17. doi:10.3389/fhumd.2021.642445

Robertshaw, L., Dhesi, S., & Jones, L. L. (2017). Challenges and facilitators for health professionals providing primary healthcare for refugees and asylum seekers in high-income countries: A systematic review and thematic synthesis of qualitative research. *BMJ Open*, *7*(8), 1–18. doi:10.1136/bmjopen-2017-015981 PMID:28780549

Rodella Sapia, M. D., Wangmo, T., Dagron, S., & Elger, B. S. (2020). Understanding access to professional healthcare among asylum seekers facing gender-based violence: A qualitative study from a stakeholder perspective. *BMC International Health and Human Rights*, *20*(1), 25. doi:10.1186/s12914-020-00244-w PMID:32957996

Rohlof, H. G., Knipscheer, J. W., & Kleber, R. J. (2014). Somatization in refugees: A review. *Social Psychiatry and Psychiatric Epidemiology*, *49*(11), 1793–1804. doi:10.1007/s00127-014-0877-1 PMID:24816685

Sansonetti, S. (2016). *Female refugees and asylum seekers: the issue of integration*. Women's Rights & Gender Equality.

Sapia, M. R. (2018). Refugee women, victims of GBV - which issues for the health care system? A qualitative study. *European Journal of Public Health*, *27*(3), 411–419. doi:10.1093/eurpub/cky048.184

Shishehgar, S., Gholizadeh, L., DiGiacomo, M., Green, A., & Davidson, P. M. (2017). Health and socio-cultural experiences of refugee women: An integrative review. *Journal of Immigrant and Minority Health*, *19*(4), 959–973. doi:10.1007/s10903-016-0379-1 PMID:26976004

Surmiak, A. (2018). Confidentiality in qualitative research involving vulnerable participants: Researchers' perspectives. *FQS*, *19*(3), 1–26.

Valibhoy, M. C., Kaplan, I., & Szwarc, J. (2017). It comes down to just how human someone can be: A qualitative study with young people from refugee backgrounds about their experiences of Australian mental health services. *Transcultural Psychiatry*, *54*(1), 23–45. doi:10.1177/1363461516662810 PMID:27550374

Winters, M., Rechel, B., de Jong, L., & Pavlova, M. (2018). A systematic review on the use of healthcare services by undocumented migrants in Europe. *BMC Health Services Research*, *18*(1), 1–30. doi:10.1186/s12913-018-2838-y PMID:29347933

Chapter 5

"Because I Was the One to Blame, Right?":
Secondary Victimisation of Migrant Women

Nathália Castro da Silva
University of Porto, Portugal

Rita Faria
ⓘ https://orcid.org/0000-0003-0093-0550
School of Criminology, University of Porto, Portugal

ABSTRACT

Gender and migration status add to the risk of certain people being victims and have been considered, from an intersectionality perspective, added vulnerabilities to some social groups. Likewise, it can negatively affect the experience that victims have with the police when reporting a crime suffered to the authorities, which can generate secondary victimisation and impact people's lives. This chapter presents the results of empirical research about the experiences of victimised migrant women with the criminal police in Portugal, analysed from a narrative victimology approach under the intersectional lens. Data was collected using semi-structured interviews, and by conducting a narrative analysis, it was found that most migrants suffered secondary victimisation, this situation also being influenced by gender and migrant status. Critical methodological issues will also be dealt with, including the recruitment of participants and the reflexivity of the first author, a migrant herself, researching migrant women.

DOI: 10.4018/979-8-3693-5436-0.ch005

INTRODUCTION

Understood as a cultural construction of the appropriate roles for men and women in society (Scott, 1995), gender is a central and organising category of migration and adaptation processes in the host country. Women and men can experience the migratory journey differently due to gender, with women being significantly impacted by violence and discrimination in this process, which does not end with the immediate arrival in a new country (Boyd & Grieco, 2003; Jerónimo, 2019).

According to the literature, various factors or conditions of people may make them more at risk of becoming victims of certain types of crime. Gender and migration status are often included in the list of acknowledged vulnerabilities, as well as economic status, race and nationality. Any analysis of vulnerabilities must consist of an observation of the broader social conditions that affect potentially vulnerable individuals or social groups (Green, 2012). In this sense, analysing from a single angle can hide other spaces of vulnerability, which is why an intersectional analysis is vital to challenge single understandings that homogenise discourses, as well as to make visible phenomenological experiences where various social structures intersect, without fragmenting such events (Dhamoon, 2011; Carastathis, 2014).

It is also well known that people who were victimised continue to feel the impact of the victimisation event (s) for relatively long periods. This process of persistent suffering can stem from the trauma of the crime, as well as from the fact that society overall and social institutions, in particular, fail to recognise and concede the status of victims to specific individuals or social groups (Condry, 2010). One possible institutional reaction that has been well developed in scientific literature is secondary victimisation, which, according to Manzanares (2014), highlights the process of interaction between victims and the formal systems of state control, particularly the damage and inconvenience it causes and that may increase suffering resulting from primary victimisation or the experience of the criminal event in the first place.

Based on empirical studies and theories explaining the phenomenon, such as *"Belief of a Just World"* (Lerner, 1980) and *"The Ideal Victim"* (Christie, 2018), this chapter is structured as follows: first, a brief literature review on secondary victimisation is presented; next the empirical study conducted about the experiences of migrant women with the police in Portugal will be presented, namely some details about the qualitative methodology adopted; notably the Narrative Analysis carried under the framework of Narrative Victimology (Pemberton & Aarten, 2018), as well as challenges regarding recruitment of participants and positionality of the first author. Participants of the study are Brazilian women who had been victims of crimes in Portugal (primarily gender-based violence) and who reported the crime to Portuguese police authorities.

The third part of the paper will present the results of this analysis and provide claims, from an intersectional perspective, about the extent to which the migrant status, intersecting with gender, race and nationality, are elements enhancing the occurrence of secondary victimisation and the impacts it has on identity, emotions and culture. Lastly, proposals will made to improve the practices of professionals in the criminal justice system and for future studies that push forward Narrative Victimology by stressing the centrality of people and the events they experience as the investigative essence (Sandelowski, 1995), thus placing migrant women at the centre of victimological studies, allowing them to feel empowered to provide new meanings to their experiences of victimisation.

1. SECONDARY VICTIMISATION OF MIGRANT WOMEN

Victimology first enunciated the notion of secondary victimisation in 1980, when Martin Symonds (*cit. in* Wemmers, 2013) called it "a second injury", occurring after individuals experience crime and feel rejected and unsupported by the community, agencies, institutions, family members and society in general. The pioneering analysis of the term developed for victims of violent crime (Symonds, 2010) and, following an article by Joyce Williams in 1984 (cit. in Pemberton & Mulder, 2023), secondary victimisation was consolidated as a concept addressing the consequences of the interaction between victims of any crime and social institutions. At the time, Williams defined it as an aggravated result persisting over time and stemming from negative attitudes and behaviours directed at the victim, translating into a lack of support and, sometimes, reprimands against or social alienation of the victim.

Secondary victimisation may be generated from a variety of behaviours by criminal justice professionals and social institutions, namely: attempting to blame the victim; not providing the victim with relevant information about criminal and judicial procedures; depersonalisation of care; lack of reparation for the harms suffered; and finally, the inability to resolve the victim's claim. Such situations can lead to the persistence of the victimisation experienced in the first place (Peixoto, 2012).

However, Pemberton and Mulder (2023) have recently offered a critical analysis of the concept and studies about secondary victimisation. The authors claim that existing literature considers the negative emotional consequences rather than other outcomes resulting from secondary victimisation. Furthermore, studies have focused predominantly on active attitudes towards the victims, failing to highlight the harms resulting from inertia and mere lack of institutional support. Pemberton and Mulder (2023) thus suggest using Fricker's notion of epistemic injustice to broaden the understanding of secondary victimisation.

Fricker (2017) considers epistemic injustice to be a form of discrimination that can manifest itself in testimonial or hermeneutic injustice. Testimonial injustice happens when, for instance, the listener discredits the speaker (witness or the victim) based on prejudices. This causes the words/statements of individuals from specific social groups to be considered less relevant due to the place of belonging from which they speak. In hermeneutic injustice, on the other hand, the listener fails to perceive the speaker (that is, the witness or the victim) as an epistemic subject due to the lack of understanding of basic information about the social reality in which they are inserted, which can be result an unequal opportunities for specific subjects or social groups.

In view of this, Pemberton and Mulder (2023) explain that secondary victimisation must encompass certain actions and behaviours that place victims in situations of injustice and manage to re-victimize them. Such actions and behaviours may include the person being wronged in the credibility of their word, or the exclusion of the victim on knowing relevant information about the process they are experiencing, and even the lack to opening a criminal inquiry due to ignorance of professionals regarding the difficulties that victims face in their social environment when was suffering a crime. An example of this is a migrant women who suffers some kind of domestic violence, tries to report it to the police and the agencies do not register it as crime because they descredibilise such actions, justifying are natural and pertinent to the victim cultural context, misleading the victim into believing that they have not suffered an offence under the law.

In another reflection on the subject, mainly derived from research with victims of gender-based violence contacting the justice system, Bodelón (2014) states that secondary victimisation is also a form of institutional violence insofar as the lack of adequate professional training, gender sensitisation and attention to victims' demands are reflected in the victim-institution interaction. This is due to the lack of coordination that prevents social institutions from including legal changes for gender protection and are thus kept androcentric and impose new ways of violence against women who have been victimised.

From this perspective, in a study about police conduct in a Portuguese police district, Coelho (2010) found a correlation between high levels of erroneous beliefs about violence against women among professionals and their perception that domestic violence events are less severe than other crimes. Moreover, police officers felt less pressured to intervene in domestic violence events despite existing laws for the protection of gender-based violence victims.

The studies clearly show that social stereotypes about victims may be reflected in the work of justice system professionals, leading them to consider that some women suffering from domestic violence do not correspond to the model of a battered woman (Bodelón, 2014), especially those that resist assigned gender roles and the corresponding socially constructed features of victim identity.

The supposed victim identity has been the subject of victimological discussion for some time. Nils Christie formulated one of the most relevant theories, known as "The Ideal Victim", in 1986. Christie listed a series of attributes that would promptly lead a person suffering a crime to be given victim status by society. In these terms, to be considered an ideal victim, the person would have to: be seen as fragile; be carrying out a relevant project at the time of the victimisation; not be in a suspicious, blame-worthy, place; be physically assaulted by someone unknown to them, bigger and stronger than them. In addition, and paradoxically, the victim ought to be weak while strong and powerful enough only to be listened to.

Continuing on Christie's work, authors have stressed that these idealised images of the victim do not necessarily correspond to their respective concrete realities (Green, 2012). When a person is victimised and does not possess similar elements of innocence and passivity, society may not provide them with social recognition and victim status, instead leading others to question and disqualify them as victims. Strobl (2010) states that this is particularly prevalent with victims from groups socially marginalised groups despite them having the objective/legal requirement to receive the status of victim, that is, having suffered a crime. In sum, they are more at risk of not having the socially constructed image corresponding to the ideal victim deserving protection and justice.

According to Lerner's theory, "Belief of a Just World", this attitude towards the victim stems from the fact that specific individuals need to reorganise their world to remain stable, reliable, safe and free from injustices. According to the author, a just world is an essential belief that allows individuals to live stable and confident lives. This means that people must believe in a reality where people "get what they deserve" according to their actions and behaviours. When something risks this belief, it disrupts the sense of reliability that people have in the world as they know it, triggering adjustment reactions to reduce the anguish felt about their expectations of respect and security (Lerner, 1980). When it is impossible to eliminate the injustice, individuals try reorganising the event so that the situation seems fair cognitively. To do so, they may resort to devaluing the victim and denying their suffering (Correia & Vala, 2003).

To best understand secondary victimisation, it is also necessary to state the obvious: that women who are victims of crime are not a homogenous group. They have particularities and axes of identity that intersect, such as race, gender, nationality, and age. The notion of intersectionality formulated by Crenshaw has made it possible to see how different categories operate in concrete situations of oppression and how these interact to produce something different from any single discriminatory situation (Dhamoon, 2011). This is what Crenshaw distinguishes as structural intersectionality, which corresponds to a thorough analysis of how the positionality of black women, intersected by gender and race, leads to actual experiences of violence that are different from those felt by white women. These concrete experiences also demonstrate that essentialising distinct categories can reproduce hegemonic identity views that hide marginalised histories of members of a specific social category (Yuval-Davis, 2006). In this scenario, and according to the literature, the position of migrant women who are victims presents peculiarities. For Duarte and Oliveira (2012), migrant women are at higher risk of being targeted for social stereotypes which have repercussions in their daily lives, but that may also be reproduced in relevant contexts, such as in care services and contact with the criminal justice system. In addition, migrants face many challenges in the hosting country, some of which may impact their chance of suffering from violence, including lack of knowledge about their rights, language differences imposing strains in communication, economic difficulties that prevent them from hiring legal counselling, as well as potential social isolation from the migrant community in which they live (Steibelt, 2009).

In international studies carried out on migrant women, victimisation and police, the following results were relevant: police officers believe that recent migrant women in the host country report crimes suffered less frequently compared to other victims (David & Erez, 1998), and a study with migrant women victimised by intimate partners in the United States found that, in order to add greater cultural competence and sensitivity to police officers, it is important to verify whether the violence suffered by the victim is a crime in their country of origin and socially accepted as commonplace in their community, as well as it is necessary to overcome linguistic and cultural barriers in the police service. (Erez et al., 2003)

In sum, a series of vulnerabilities inhabit migrant women, making them more at risk of becoming victims of a "secondary injury" when contacting the criminal justice system in their host countries, particularly when reporting the crime to the police. The way the police deal with such victims is critical because, often, it is the first institution the victims turn to right after the crime has taken place. The experience with the police may have severe impacts on how the victims develop (or do not) trust towards the criminal justice institutions, as well as on their expectations of justice and, in broader terms, in their efforts of integration into the host country.

2. THE NARRATIVE TURN IN VICTIMOLOGY

Narrative Victimology is a methodological approach and analytical tool that Pemberton, Aarten and Mulder have recently developed. The narrative turn in social sciences has paved the way for narratives to be recognised as legitimate and relevant in qualitative research. After studies on life stories with the Chicago School (Goodson & Gill, 2011), narratives regained strength in various scientific fields from the 1970s onwards, opposing positivist structures that favoured statistical data that was more distanced from the objects of study. This movement was based on more humanising qualitative approaches and on highlighting the voices of new actors and social groups, as well as their subjective experiences, which had previously been sidelined by conventional analyses (Sarah, 2013). The narrative turn, therefore, flourishes with the need to investigate social dynamics through a reflexive and critical lens (Goodson & Gill, 2011).

Despite these strengthening of narrative in the social sciences, it was only in 2009 with Louis Presser that the Narrative Criminology was born, seeking yo understand the power of life stories in the construction of crime (Presser & Sandberg, 2019). In 2019, narrative analysis has also beginning to develop strongly in the field of Victimology, especially from the article of Pemberton, Aarten and Mulder (2019a) namely *"Stories of Injustice: Towards a Narrative Victimology"*, which the authors developed the aspects that compose this new methodology approach. In the similar direction, the studies of Walklate and colleagues (2019; Cook & Walklate, 2019) also sought a change in the perception of victimisation stories. The studies arising from this approach have moved beyond the mere debate about typologies of victims or how they might influence suffering and instead have begun to focus on narratives of victimisation formulated by the victims themselves, exploring the meaning they give to the suffering they have experienced and understanding why some narratives gain prominence over others (Cook & Walklate, 2019). Narrative Victimology, thus, considers that the victims' narratives may provide elements that highlight the motivations behind the actions suffered and contribute to re-signifying the impacts of victimisation for those who have experienced it (Hourigan, 2019).

Narrative Victimology shares some aspects with Narrative Criminology, such as the role of narratives in shaping identities and that narrated experiences don't need to correspond to an objective truth of events: attention should be given to the processes of meaning-making from those who experience them. Particularly, Narrative Victimology is concerned with understanding how victimising processes affect the sense of control over our own life story and the possibility of perspectives about the future of someone who has been victimised (Janoff-Bulman, 1992, cit. in Pemberton et al., 2019a).

While analysis of narratives in Victimology seems to be something recent, Bakan (1966) had already stated that victimisation processes could damage the "Big Two" dimensions of human behaviour: agency and communion. Agency refers to the individuals' sense of competence, power and achievement, and communion consists of peoples' longing to relate to each other in the community (cit. in Pemberton et al., 2017). Thus, when someone goes through a process of victimisation, it is expected that, at some point, they will redirect their efforts towards reconstructing this narrative identity, namely in these two dimensions.

As well as enabling a process of identity reconstruction through the recovery of agency and communion, narratives allow victims' experiences to be heard on their terms. This demonstrates the relevance of narrative for strengthening victimology since harmful events analysed exclusively from victimisation surveys can now be examined by looking into the subjectivities contained in victimisation narratives (Cook & Walklate, 2019).

However, attempts by the victim to rebuild their identity may suffer social interference, which can act as a pressure mechanism. According to Pemberton et al. (2019b), examples of such pressure include the differences between the story told by the victim and by the perpetrator and this being used against victims, especially since accounts of victimisation carry strong emotions and sometimes temporal disconnects with them. Moreover, instances of victim blaming originating on the "Belief of a Just World" can cause secondary victimisation and impact meaning-making about the criminal event experienced, as well as about the victim's identity, agency and communion, which may be particularly relevant in the case of migrant women who are dealing with processes of integration and re-identification in the hosting country.

In view of this, in this study, the intersectional approach will provide an understanding of victimisation processes as part of the coexistence of axes of power that run through the lives of victims and can affect their experiences in different ways, such as gender, race, migrant status and nationality. As Crenshaw (cit. in Dhamoon, 2011) points out, analysing from a single structural perspective ends up hiding other spaces of vulnerability. Essentially, narratives are intersectional stories, a significant part of how we make sense of the events that happen to us (Fathi, 2017).

3. METHODOLOGICAL FRAMEWORK AND RESEARCH DESIGN

This section will present the methodological structure and research design formulated for understand the victimisation experiences of migrant women and eventual secondary victimisation when reporting the crime to the police. The goal was to collect the victims' narratives and access the meaning attributed to experiences with the police, especially inquiring about if and how their migrant and gender status, together with other intersected dimensions, influenced experiences and narratives of secondary victimisation.

A qualitative approach was used (Strauss & Corbin, 1998; Minayo & Sanchez, 1993) by considering that specific social experiences can be better understood when researchers access the participants' emotions, subjectivities and narratives, allowing them to use their voices and perspectives to (as much as possible) to convey their experiences, sense of identity, agency and communion. For that, how explained in before section, the Narrative Victimology was adopted as a methodological approach in this study. At this point, it will thoroughly explain the methodological procedures applied in the research.

3.1 Sampling, Procedures, and Instrument

A non-probabilistic sample was used, and recruitment was done with women who were migrants in Portugal, had suffered a crime in the host country and, consequently, had sought police support. Both Purposeful and Snowball samplings were used, with the aim of selecting participants who had information and experiences relevant to the research object. In the case of the Snowball Sampling, this technique was important to facilitate the access to a hard-to-reach population, as occurred in this study.

The final sample included nine women who had migrated from Brazil to Portugal in the last ten years. There was no restriction on the nationality of the migrants taking part in the study, but only Brazilian migrant women spontaneously joined. It is possible that the fact they shared a cultural identity with the migrant researcher led to feelings of trust or curiosity enhancing to their participation. Furthermore, according to the 2022 Report produced by the former Foreigners and Borders Service of Portugal (2023), Brazilian women currently make up the most significant number of migrant women in Portugal, with 128,998 residing in the country, a factor that may have contributed to the greater adherence of migrants to research. So, the sample composed exclusively of Brazilian women also indicates the importance/relevance of this nationality in the current Portuguese migrant trends.

Recruitment was challenging, and a series of strategies had to be used. Initially, these included formal and informal contacts with non-governmental institutions supporting migrants and victims of crime in the hopes they would forward researchers to potential participants. However, there were difficulties in getting consistent replies and support from institutions, leading the researchers to use alternative ways to access the sample. The research was then publicised on social media via an Instagram page created specifically for this purpose (instagram.com/nathalia_vozmigrante). The virtual medium was the most effective in accessing migrant women, as it overcame geographical barriers, was easy to understand and access, allowed prospective participants to make their own mind independently of gatekeepers. Also allowed the researcher to exert better control over the process. Even so, recruitment took some time, with numerous calls for participation. In addition, the study was also publicised and recruitment attempted with the delivery of leaflets to people near strategic locations such as migrant support centres, religious groups and events (e.g. an Intercultural Exhibition by a municipality) where a significant presence of migrants was likely. It can be hypothesized that further support from non-governmental institutions would facilitate the recruitment of participants.

Online semi-structured interviews were happened to instrumentalise the qualitative research, allowing victimisation and experiences with the police to be presented and made meaningful from the participants' perspective (Noaks & Wincup, 2004). The interview guide consisted of four dimensions: I) introductions and initial questions; II) characterisation of the victimisation suffered and the assistance received by the police; III) verification of the occurrence of secondary victimisation of migrant women; IV) final questions. This script contained questions about the original victimisation suffered and experiences with the police when reporting the crime, which made it possible to: verify the level of satisfaction of migrant women with the assistance received, capture narratives of secondary victimisation and how they perceived migrant status, gender, the type of crime suffered and nationality as elements capable of influencing possible secondary victimisation experienced.

Collecting data with and for victims requires great care to avoid any potential psychological and emotional harm to participants, especially considering the vulnerabilities of the sample group chosen for the study – migrant women. This scenario required the fulfilment of basic ethical requirements and an integral, flexible ethical stance to be taken by researchers in concrete situations presented throughout the research process (Faria, 2022). For example, when the interviews were carried out, the possibility of withdrawing from participation throughout the process was ensured if the interviewee no longer felt comfortable sharing her experiences. Care was also taken in designing questions that were attentive both to the object of study and to not creating situations of re-victimisation. As a way of managing participants' emotions, pauses were created at times when migrant women felt moved by the recollection of their experiences, and the possibility of terminating the interview was ensured in the event of discomfort. Moreover, especially as the researcher collecting the data familiarized herself more with the process, information about psychological and emotional support was also shared. In this sense, all ethical dimensions were ensured throughout the study, namely by asking participants for their informed consent, guaranteeing anonymity and data confidentiality, as well as by establishing a respectful and warm rapport with each participant during the interview and validating their experiences and feelings (Noaks & Wincup, 2004).

Reflexivity from the researcher was also used as a tool to understand better and make sense of the data, helping to critically reflect on issues of positionality as the researcher – and first author of this paper – is a migrant woman as much as the participants. It is believed that this facilitated the creation of a good rapport with interviewees and allowed candid replies about intense experiences. It also allowed a better understanding of the narrative and a more in-depth data analysis. Considering their status, she was able to understand, with a certain familiarity due to shared cultural identity, the first impressions gathered from the participants regarding the feeling of becoming a migrant, difficulties and acceptance in a country different from their own. This understanding was clear to the interviewees and was an element that made them feel comfortable sharing painful experiences of victimization. Thus, by using reflexivity and critical stance towards the researcher's positionality, it is possible to conclude that a total distance between researcher and researched is not necessary or even realistic and advisable for guaranteeing quality in investigation (Palaganas et al., 2017).

3.2 Qualitative Data Analysis

Data were analysed using narrative analysis under the specific framework of Narrative Victimology with an intersectional approach. The aim was to understand how the interviewees gave new meaning to the significant events they experienced and how they were represented in their narratives (Riessman, 2000).

This process began concretely with the first interview, as the dynamics developed in this dialogue led to refining the questions and the way the were asked for the next interviews (Butina, 2015). By listening to the participants' experiences, it was reflected on the emotions felt by the victims. Another important step was transcription of data that allowed a closer contact with the participants' feelings, representing both a form of data interpretation and an analytical technique (Riessman, 1993). The third step was the interpretation of narratives considered from a time-frame perspective in the sense that participants were asked about the time before, during and after reaching out to the police. Which means that the interaction with the police served as the time reference for the analysis.

The following step was integrating the broader narrative analysis process with the Narrative Victimology framework, by developing a deep examination of excerpts about victimization using the three axes of analysis identified by Pemberton and Aarten (2018) - Identity, Emotions and Culture. The first dimension allowed understanding the impact of victimisation on the victims' sense of identity and the role of narrative in identity reconstruction. In the field of emotions, critical events were perceived as turning points in the victim's life journey, why and that is the reason why emotions were a central dimension of analysis and made up the core of a narrative (Aarten et al., 2018). The dimension of culture, in turn, proved to be relevant for understanding the narratives as a space of connection between individual experiences of victimisation and the broader collective and cultural context.

This analysis in a narrative structure, connected to the concepts and theories central to the study, made it possible to understand the experiences of migrant women from the different aspects that can be impacted by victimisation. Furthermore, as a way of bringing the analysis closer to the real experiences of the victims and also in order to complete all the investigation's objectives, an intersectional perspective was used, which allowed to observe how gender, migrant status and nationality can interact and enhance the occurrence of secondary victimisation for migrant women.

RESULTS

Narratives of Victimised Migrant Women

Considering the methods, procedures and methodological approach adopted, part of the narratives of the nine migrants will be analysed here. It was observed that many critical moments for the victims occurred during police assistance, which generated secondary victimisation processes. One of the elements that stands out in these experiences is the professionals' contestation of the victim's identity. Despite having suffered a crime, migrant Firmina realised that the police did not see her as a victim, contesting her identity in this position. She expressed that *"(…) It seems that I was the perpetrator of the crime (…) so I went there to tell the police officer my statement...' oh, but yes, you could have defended yourself'."*

To be seen by society as a victim, it is not enough to have suffered a crime; it is also necessary to be inserted in a place where the victimised person obtains a specific identity as a victim (Herrera Moreno, 2014). This place is the result of an internal process of the person who suffered harm when recognising themselves as a victim and an external process of society understanding that that individual can be identified as a victim. In the situation experienced by Firmina, the victim's identity was challenged by the police officer, who sought to hold her responsible for having suffered the harmful event. The fact that Firmina does not have similarity with the ideal of a passive and innocent victim, as presented by Christie, impacted her police treatment, as well as affecting her identity: she expressed that her experiences of primary and secondary victimisation were traumatic, which led to a psychosomatic pain that he called the *"pain of Portugal"*. Furthermore, the victimisation she suffered changed her life trajectory, as she feels restricted in her freedom of movement in the city and anxiously awaits the trial of the case.

In another scenario, migrant Rosa also experienced her identity as a victim being challenged by police officers. She stated that *"(…) they implied that I was trying to seduce him and then I didn't want to, or I was in fact having a relationship with him and then I wanted to break up and I was making up stories, like blaming him without, 'poor guy didn't do anything'."* We observe the reproduction of a hypersexualising gender stereotype about Rosa, a woman and migrant who, in the professionals' view, could not have been the victim of a threat by a Portuguese man, but rather, by being a woman, she must have "seduced" the one who was accused of being the perpetrator of the crime. According to the expansion of the Ideal Victim theory by Bosma et al. (2018) using the Stereotype Content Model (SCM), Rosa would not have been seen as a victim by society and the police since he defended himself from the crime suffered when seeking police assistance, he was competent and not very cordial. Possibly, these factors led to the devaluation and deterioration of his image as a victim (Correia & Vala, 2003). Thus, the police reformulated Rosa as someone who received what she deserved (Pemberton, 2019a), accordingly reorganising the professionals' belief in a just world (Lerner, 1980).

This process of secondary victimisation suffered by Rosa, which included blaming the victim and constant questioning of the facts by the police, impacted the migrant's identity. At that point, she expressed that *"it was a traumatising situation in some way, so there is also always this issue of erasing a bit of what happened."* According to Brison (2002, cit. in, Pemberton et al., 2019a), when a trauma resulting from victimisation occurs, identity can be fractured, and this process also involves a rupture in the memory of the events, such as what happened to the migrant Rosa.

Among the treatment received by the victims, it was found that the presence of numerous unfair, discouraging and inattentive behaviours committed by police officers led to experiences of secondary victimisation suffered by migrant women. For Simone, the formalisation of a criminal case was only possible due to her insistence with the police officer that the crime be investigated. She explained that he, the police officer, put *"a thousand difficulties for me. He made it clear that, yes, it would be very difficult for me to win, that I had no way of proving it, that lawyers were expensive (...). He dissuaded me in every way he could. And then I said 'you can open it, you can open it'. So he opened the process."* In sum, the police officer tried to convince Simone to open a case when she legitimately had the right to know and participate in it. Pemberton and Mulder (2023) describe this as epistemic injustice in secondary victimisations.

The development of this event generated negative emotions in Simone due to the time-consuming procedures, lack of adequate guidance, financial limitations in hiring a lawyer and lack of free legal assistance in the short term. She decided to withdraw, and the case was filed. She explained: *"since I received this letter, I decided to give up this process and I feel terrible because, yes, I am a romantic person, I believe in justice."* It can be seen here that both primary and secondary victimisations have the potential to trigger strong emotions in those who experience the event (Pemberton et al., 2018). On the other hand, the act of telling her story and narrating her emotions by interacting with the justice system professionals could have been a way of rebuilding communion for Simone. Given this impossibility, this event may have reinforced the primary victimisation she had already suffered (Erez, 2004, cit. in Pemberton et al., 2019a).

In a similar experience, migrant Patrícia stated that she found a police environment full of difficulties and professional neglect. Patrícia explained that *"I started to complain about the noise, I started to complain that it wasn't conducive, that he wasn't listening to me properly, there was information that I gave him about who he is, I asked again (...) And then when I imposed myself, I mean, you, you are a victim, you are there violated and you are still there (...) It's very cluelessness, right?"*

In her narrative, the migrant expressed indignation both with the direct actions of the police officer and due to his inertia in assisting, especially because the agency where she sought the service was supposedly specialised in domestic violence. She stated that she did not have any female police officer to assist her and that she gave her statement in an inappropriate environment, where other police officers were laughing and talking loudly, without any empathy when dealing with sensitive gender issues. Due to this treatment received, and because she felt disregarded as a victim because she was a woman, it appears that Patrícia experienced secondary victimisation in the form of testimonial injustice, with police officers not trusting her word due to her gender and the type of crime suffered, with suffocation of their testimony and reduction of their experience to a yes or no communication with professionals in the justice system (Herman, 2003, cit. in Pemberton & Mulder, 2023).

The secondary victimisations contained in the narratives demonstrate that numerous critical moments for the migrants resulted from the connection of individual experiences to broader cultural and collective contexts. Brazilian nationality was an element that emerged in inappropriate speeches and behaviours in police encounters as an attribute that negatively influenced the occurrence of secondary victimisation. In Nísia's speech, she expresses how she was treated by the police when reporting the crime: *"I said it was public defamation and was against the newspaper (...) there were two or three photos of us, and big ones, like, our face, our profile was well profiled in the newspaper, which was also embarrassing. And he said there was nothing wrong with that. And my husband is like "no, he's saying she's hot". And he even asked me "yeah, isn't she Brazilian?"*

Scientific literature has been paying attention to this phenomenon of hypersexualisation of Brazilian women that occurs especially within Portuguese society. According to Malheiros (2007), Brazilian women are victims of the reproduction of stereotypes in Portugal, which places them in a position of "easy" women, where the distance between being considered "warm and exuberant" and being considered "prostitutes" is small, being This stigma is also reinforced by the media, as was the case experienced by Nísia.

In the case of this migrant, other factors came together to increase the occurrence of secondary victimisation: in addition to gender and nationality, the colour of her skin was felt to be an element that contributed to her having suffered victimisation. She expressed that she was the only black woman among the couples who participated in the newspaper report and that there were only detailed comments about her body. For Nísia, *"(...) I think that the black body is very associated with sexuality (...) it was not what I am, but my body, and the message that my body transmits and the permissions that people think that has."*

The intersectionality present here demonstrates that the police and the defamation suffered questioned crime experienced by the migrant, which was naturalised as if it were something acceptable, expected and unworthy of being considered a crime. It is as if the fact that Nísia is a woman, Brazilian, and black were attributes that allowed society to violate and victimise her. Furthermore, the intersectional lens allowed us to uncover how specific socially marginal categories can contain internal positions of privilege, such as that of migrant women. In this context, different elements can interact within this category. They can place a migrant in a place of greater vulnerability to suffer victimisation and more painful experiences, as happened with Nísia, where all the elements already mentioned put her in a place of more significant lack of protection (Fathi, 2017).

In turn, the migrant status was perceived for Maria as a factor that allowed the police officer to establish an unprofessional and intimate relationship with you as a victim. The migrant expressed that *"(…) the way the officer in particular, is, gave himself the freedom to create a bond with me I think so. There, I think, if it had been a Portuguese woman, he wouldn't have done it that way. He wouldn't have given himself the freedom to text or call, you know?"* In this experience, a fundamental element for fair police treatment of victims was not verified, as found in the study developed by Elliot et al. (2014): post-service empowerment. Maria did not feel strengthened and safe after the police contact, as the professional behaved in an invasive way in the victim's private life, making her feel coerced. In the migrant's view, the fact that she was not a Portuguese woman influenced the behaviour adopted by the police officer, which demonstrates that her status as a migrant was not disconnected from the broader cultural and social context of challenges that are faced, especially by migrant women in the host country, especially marked and affected by gender-based violence (Jerónimo, 2019).

It was also possible to notice in the migrant narratives that the essential dimensions of human personality conceptualised by Bakan – agency and communion, are affected in the process of criminal victimisation (1966, cit. in Pemberton et al., 2017). The victims' search for assistance and reparation in the criminal justice system can be understood as a way of repairing the fracture caused in these two dimensions due to the crime suffered (Pemberton et al., 2017), both in terms of acting and asserting themselves as competent individual in the world through agency, as in the scope of the capabilities to establish social connections and relationships through communion (Leonard, 1997).

At times, it was observed in the migrants' speeches that they sought to rescue these dimensions affected by victimisation. After having suffered a crime, Sílvia sought police assistance to report what had happened, and she felt the need to share the event she suffered with her son and people in her social circle: *"(...) I arrived home very ill. Only in the afternoon, only at home, with my son. (...) I felt terrible, I revealed. I started writing about that incident because...I was horrified, I wrote to people at Organization Y (...) I joined forces. I joined all possible forces to try to locate the attacker."*

The experience of narrating the victimisation suffered can be an opportunity for the victim to reconstruct their affected identity, as happened with Sílvia, who, through communicating the event to her son and other people in her social environment, presented a resilient, strong version and competent of herself, even after victimisation. In addition to this recovery of her agency, the fact that she shared the event with people who had work and community relationships can be understood as an attempt to maintain communion.

In Nísia's experience, the victimisation profoundly affected her dimension of communion, which materialised in fractures of family social relationships, as she explained in her speech: *"(...) soon I will have to sit in front of the judge, prove what the psychological damage was, you know? (...) how do you prove psychological damage? I have to show how many medications I take...is it a social life that I don't have?"* Given what she experienced, she saw the search for the justice system as an opportunity to repair what had happened, saying: *"(...) it's not a cool experience, but that's it, like, I just think we have rather than using the issue of legal access as our ally and unfortunately being in these places too, you know?"* Regarding the decision to narrate her experiences of victimisation, she stated that *"(...) one of the reasons I decided to do it, to contribute to your research (...) because I think it is important (...) and also an issue to tell women too that, migrant women, that we have to go after (...)"*.

It is clear from the migrant's words that both the search for police assistance and the sharing of her experiences in the research were reflections of rescuing her agency and communion. The victim's voice is thus shown to be a way of reaffirming her position, occupying a space in the justice system, and receiving recognition and respect for this, that is, to rescue your agency. Sharing experiences with other migrants who may have gone through similar experiences was expressed as a means of establishing connections in the social environment in which they are inserted, connecting an individual experience to broader narratives and, this way, conducting the reconstruction of communion (Pemberton et al., 2017; McAdams, 2013).

In experiences like those reported by the migrants in the study, the central need to express their emotions and be heard and welcomed by institutions is observed. Thus, accessing the justice system can indicate more than a desire for reparation but also a way of connecting and being heard on one's terms by the social actors present there, thus contributing to the reconstruction of agency and communion (Pemberton, 2016; Pemberton et al, 2017).

DISCUSSION

When analysing the experiences of victimisation and police contact narrated by the nine Brazilian migrants, it was observed that most of them felt dissatisfied with the treatment they received. This dissatisfaction was due to a series of inappropriate conduct and behaviours practised by police officers when assisting victims. In summary, the following problems were found to occur: continuous questioning about the facts presented by the migrants; lack of a suitable environment with reserve, empathy and tranquillity to give a police statement; lack of female police officers to respond to crimes involving gender-based violence; victim blaming; reproduction of gender stereotypes and those related to the intersection of gender and Brazilian nationality; ironic behaviour in the face of victims' testimonies; lack of procedural guidance and information about the investigation or process.

These inappropriate behaviours generated emotional, psychological, social and even physical impacts for most victims. Many migrants expressed that police assistance caused emotional shock, frustration, a feeling of disrespect and of being attacked again, of helplessness and trauma. When connecting these impacts with the dimensions analyzed in narrative structure (identity, emotions and culture), it appears that the dimension of emotions was the one that presented the most negative manifestations resulting from the contact of victims with the police, confirming what Aarten et al. (2018) points out about the power of victimizations to cause strong emotions, which is why they can occupy central spaces in a narrative.

Considering the conduct of the police officers, in addition to the impacts and experiences by the victims, it appears that most migrants were not perceived by agents as suitable ideal victims. This relates to the notion of "victimity" which, according to Herrera Moreno (2014), consists of political and sociocultural attributes the victim is expected to possess to be recognised in society. This means that it is not always enough that the victim has suffered harm; it is also necessary that she is perceived as capable of acquiring victim's status. Despite their vulnerability, they were not passive and reacted to the victimisation suffered, being incompatible with the ideal victim model elaborated by Christie (2018). Based on the Stereotype Content Model (SCM) Theory, the migrants showed themselves with high cordiality and competence, making it more difficult for them to be perceived as victim deserving support (Bosma et al., 2018). Using derogatory actions of blaming, many police officers sought to invalidate the facts reported by the migrants, reformulating the image of victims as people who deserved what they got. This allows police officers a cognitive reorganisation of their idealised understanding of the fair world (Correia & Vala, 2003).

In the case of migrant victims of crime, Strobl (2010) is right: they may not always be perceived as worthy of the victim status, as they do not fit into the idealised image of the victim. Victims' opportunities to be seen with sympathy and empathy are reduced when desires and expectations projected onto them by society are not met (Miers, cit. in Green, 2012).

Consequently, and considering the results of this research, migrant women suffered secondary victimisation caused by the police. This resulted from an institutional reaction to the first victimisation suffered (having been a victim of crime) and which caused substantive emotional, social and physical impacts and persistent suffering after the victimisation experience (Manzanares, 2014). Furthermore, the possibility of expanding the concept of secondary victimisation proposed by Pemberton and Mulder (2023) is significant for this analysis, understanding it as acts of epistemic injustice towards the victim. In the narratives of the participants, several actions by the police fitted into forms of testimonial injustice: discrediting the victim's testimony because it came from a specific place of speech in which she found herself inserted due to her gender, nationality and migrant status.

CONCLUSION

Through the analysis developed from an intersectional perspective, it was possible to conclude that some participants had more painful experiences of victimisation due to different dimensions that structurally intersected when they looked for police support, especially gender, migrant status and nationality (Brazilian in this case). Also through these perspective, it can be stated that the fact that participants all shared the same social group should not lead to the automatic conclusion that they will have the same experiences of victimisation. Instead, results allow us to argue that migrant victims do not share a single identity and narrative but rather showcase distinct specificities, which leads them to experience victimisation in different ways and to be impacted differently as well (Dhamoon, 2011).

By accessing victims' narratives, it is possible to contact the phenomenon of secondary victimisation of migrant women in their particularities. More than just the reproduction of events experienced by migrants, personal narratives are, essentially, units of discourse that enable the meaning and resignification of past events (Riessman, 2000). Considering the positionality and subjectivity arising from the narrative, Victimology appropriated this tool to understand the meaning that victims give to the suffering experienced (Cook & Walklate, 2009); how they experience harmful events; and how these processes of victimisation affect essential aspects of the individual themselves and in connection with society, including their sense of identity, agency, their emotions, communion, and established cultural connections.

It is known that this approach, as a qualitative methodology, does not seek to generalize data and does not want an objective truth about the facts narrated by the participants. Moreover, empirical investigations from the perspective of Narrative Victimology may be damaged when the information brought by the participants does not provide sufficient information to access the subjectivities pertinent to the victimization experiences.

Despite this, when researching experiences of victimisation and placing victims' voices at the centre of the analysis (Cook & Walklate, 2009), it is clear that Narrative Victimology becomes a fundamental methodological and analytical approach to access and understanding the subjective dimensions of victims in greater details, when the data was well collected and reaching empirical saturation. This study shows that, with an intersectional lens, events become visible in their differences, particularly those that result from the intersect of gender, race, nationality and migrant status in the real life experiences of these women.

In this dialogical process, researchers also become part of the narrative process, as they collaborate with participants to construct meaning of the established communication (Connelly & Clandinin, 1990). That is why it is vital to highlight reflexivity as an essential element in conducting this research, especially for the first author, a migrant woman carrying out research on migrant women, and thus, with an insider status. More than ethical considerations about the well-being of participants (present in any investigation with victims, this research needed consideration about emotional risks for researchers studying phenomena experienced by members of the social group of which they are part (Faria, 2022), as was the case for the first author of this paper. The modulation of an empathetic attitude with the necessary judgement-free stance was a challenging balance but much needed in order to access detailed and nuances accounts, followed by original and thought-provoking analysis. It is important to clarify that, despite the first author's positionality and some shared perspectives with participants about feelings and experiences of being a migrant, the researcher felt she avoided bias in interpreting results, thus respecting the participants' account in the analysis. As an example, it was observed that participants did not to define clearly the influence of their status on the occurrence of secondary victimisation, a fact that was objectively dealt with during the interview and in the data analysis. What was only demarcated was that, in the researchers' perception, the intersections of gender, migrant status and nationality especially made the experiences of secondary victimisation more painful for some of them. This analysis, in particular, demonstrates how reflexivity made it possible to combine critical awareness of the insider researcher position with her contribution to the construction of meanings of the experiences narrated in the study (Palaganas et al., 2017). Also, there was a challenge for the first author to manage feelings of anguish and concern while listening to participants' narratives, but the sense of scientific responsibility in achieving an authentic dialog with the victims was the guiding element in the reflective process.

Authentic dialog presupposes a solidary and pedagogical encounter in the terms of Freire (2009), with the establishment of a horizontal relationship between the parties and a humble, open and trusting position in the knowledge produced with those in dialogue. In addition, a clear interview script allowed the researcher to focus on the participants' experiences. It is important to mention that in this process of communicative interaction called data collection, the participants stated the positive impacts of the research, namely attributed to the fact that they felt they were given a chance to collaborate on a relevant social problem that could affect many other migrant women. In sum, interviews allowed them to share their experience in the hopes that results from the research would help other people in similar situations.

For all the above, the importance of this investigation for the scientific community is evident. Firstly, it contributes to the development of Narrative Victimology as a methodology capable of accessing subjective dimensions of victimisation previously unreached by the victimological field. Secondly, it depicts the experiences of victimisation from especially vulnerable groups: migrant women suffering crimes in the host country and as well as analysing how gender, migrant status and nationality can interact to generate different and more painful victimisation processes for these women. Thirdly, results clarify the importance of police officers in preventing or, on the contrary, generating secondary victimisation with its harmful effects on victims and, consequently, on their sense of justice and fairness or even, eventually, on their sense of integration into a new community. Lastly, the research allowed us to better understand, through narrative analysis from an intersectional perspective, processes of identity reconstruction, recomposition of emotions and resignification of victimisation experiences, illustrating narrative as a significant venue for empowerment and better support for victims of crime.

REFERENCES

Aarten, P. G., Mulder, E., & Pemberton, A. (2018). The Narrative of Victimization and deradicalization: An expert view. *Studies in Conflict and Terrorism, 41*(7), 577–572. doi:10.1080/1057610X.2017.1311111

Bodelón, E. G. (2014). Institutional violence and gender violence. *Anales de La Cátedra Francisco Suárez, 48*, 131–155. doi:10.30827/acfs.v48i0.2783

Bosma, A., Mulder, E., & Pemberton, A. (2018). The Ideal Victim through other (s') eyes. In M. Duggan, M. (Ed.), Revisiting the "Ideal Victim": Developments in Critical Victimology (pp. 27-42). Bristol University Press.

Boyd, M., & Grieco, E. (2003). Women and migration: Incorporating gender into international migration theory. *Migration Information Source*, 1-7. www. migrationinformation.org/feature/print.cfm?ID=106

Butina, M. (2015). A narrative approach to qualitative inquiry. *Clinical Laboratory Science*, *18*(3), 190–196. doi:10.29074/ascls.28.3.190

Carastathis, A. (2014). The concept of intersecctionality in feminist theory. *Philosophy Compass*, *9*(5), 304–314. doi:10.1111/phc3.12129

Christie, N. (2018). The Ideal Victim. In M. Duggan (Ed.), Revisiting the "Ideal Victim": Developments in Critical Victimology (pp. 11-24). Bristol University Press.

Coelho, A. (2010). *Beliefs and attitudes of police officers towards violence against women* [Master's thesis, University of Porto]. University of Porto Institutional Repository. https://repositorio-aberto.up.pt/bitstream/10216/55356/2/Dis sertaoCincias%20Forenses.pdf

Condry, R. (2010). Secondary Victims and Secondary Victimization. International Handbook of Victimology, 219-249. doi:10.1201/EBK1420085471-c8

Connelly, F. M., & Clandinin, D. J. (1990). Stories of experience and Narrative inquiry. *Educational Researcher*, *19*(5), 2–14. doi:10.2307/1176100

Cook, E., & Walklate, S. (2019). Excavating Victim Stories: making sense of agency, suffering and redemption. In E. Cook, S. Walklate, J. Fleetwood, L. Presser, S. Sandberg, & T. Ugelvik (Eds.), *The Emerald Handbook of Narrative Criminology* (pp. 239–257). Emerald Publishing Limited. doi:10.1108/978-1-78769-005-920191023

Correia, I., & Vala, J. (2003). When Will a Victim Be Secondarily Victimized? The Effect of Observer's Belief in a Just World, Victim's Innocence and Persistence of Suffering. *Social Justice Research*, *16*(4), 379–400. doi:10.1023/A:1026313716185

Davis, R. C., & Erez, E. (1998). *Immigrant Population as Victims: Toward a Multicultural Criminal Justice System*. https://www.ojp.gov/pdffiles/167571.pdf

Dhamoon, R. K. (2011). Considerations on Mainstreaming Intersectionality. *Political Research Quarterly*, *64*(1), 230–243. doi:10.1177/1065912910379227

Duarte, M., & Oliveira, A. (2012). Women on the margins: domestic violence and immigrant women. *Sociology: Journal of the Faculty of Letters of the University of Porto, 23*, 223-237. https://ojs.letras.up.pt/index.php/Sociologia/article/view/1428

Erez, E., Ammar, N., & Orloff, L. E. (2003). *Violence against Immigrant Women and Systemic Responses: An exploratory study*. Report submitted to National Institute of Justice in fulfillment of requirements for Grant. https://www.ojp.gov/pdffiles1/nij/grants/202561.pdf

Faria, R. (2022). "Being" Ethical in Research. In R. Faria & M. Dodge (Eds.), *Qualitative Research in Criminology: Cutting-Edge Methods* (pp. 229–240). Springer International Publishing. doi:10.1007/978-3-031-18401-7_14

Fathi, M. (2017). *Intersectionality, Class and Migration – narratives of iranian women migrants in the U.K.* Springer. doi:10.1057/978-1-137-52530-7

Foreigners and Borders Service. (2023). *Immigration, Borders and Asylum Report 2022*. https://www.sef.pt/pt/Documents/RIFA2022%20vF2a.pdf

Freire, P. (2009). *Pedagogy of the oppressed* (48th ed.). Paz e Terra.

Fricker, M. (2017). Evolving concepts of epistemic injustice. In Routledge Handbook of Epistemic Injustice. Routledge. doi:10.4324/9781315212043-5

Gonçalves, M., & Matos, M. (2020). Victimized immigrant women in Portugal: Factors associated with formal and informal help-seeking. *Revista de Psicología Social, 35*(2), 370–412. doi:10.1080/02134748.2020.1725360

Goodson, I. F., & Gill, S. R. (2011). The narrative turn in social research. *Counterpoints, 386*, 17-33. https://www.jstor.org/stable/42981362

Green, S. (2012). Crime, victimisation and vulnerability. In S. Walklate (Ed.), *Handbook Of Victims and Victimology* (pp. 91–117). Willan.

Herrera Moreno, M. (2014). ¿Quién Teme A La Victimidad? El Debate Identitario En Victimología. *Revista De Derecho Penal y Criminología*, (12), 343-404. https://revistas.uned.es/index.php/RDPC/article/view/24528

Jerónimo, P. (2019). *Gender Equality: Old and New Challenges*. University of Minho Law School. https://repositorium.sdum.uminho.pt/handle/1822/79497

Leonard, R. (1997). Theorizing the relationship between agency and communion. *Theory & Psychology, 7*(6), 823–835. doi:10.1177/0959354397076005

Lerner, M. J. (1980). The Belief in a Just World. In *The Belief in a Just World. Perspectives in Social Psychology*. Springer. doi:10.1007/978-1-4899-0448-5_2

Malheiros, J. M. (Org.). (2007). *Imigração brasileira em Portugal. Alto Comissariado para a Imigração e Diálogo Intercultural (ACIDI, I. P.).* https://www.om.acm.gov.pt/documents/58428/179693/1_ImigrBras ileira.pdf/7d926056-f322-427a-8393-73fb1848da37

Manzanares, R.C. (Dir.); Mayo, M. J. S., & Tarrío, C. T. (Coord.). (2014). *Justicia Restaurativa y violência de género: más allá de la Ley Orgánica 1/2004.* Universidade de Santiago de Compostela, Servizo de Publicacións e Intercambio Científico.

McAdams, D. P. (2013). The psychological self as actor, agent, and author. *Perspectives on Psychological Science*, *8*(3), 272–295. doi:10.1177/1745691612464657 PMID:26172971

Minayo, M. C. S., & Sanches, O. (1993). Quantitative and Qualitative Methods: Opposition or Complementarity? *Cad. Saúde Pub., Rio de Janeiro*, *9*(3), 239-262. https://www.scielo.br/j/csp/a/Bgpmz7T7cNv8K9Hg4J9fJDb/?forma t=pdf&lang=pt

Narrative Victimology: Speaker, audience, timing. (2019). In Hourigan, K. L. (Ed.), *The Emerald Handbook of Narrative Criminology* (pp. 259–277). Emerald Publishing Limited. doi:10.1108/978-1-78769-005-920191024

Noaks, L., & Wincup, E. (2004). *Criminological research.* SAGE Publications Ltd., doi:10.4135/9781849208789

Palaganas, E., Sanchez, M. C., Molintas, M. V. P., & Caricativo, R. D. (2017). Reflexivity in Qualitative Research: A Journey of Learning. *The Qualitative Report*, *22*(2), 426–438. doi:10.46743/2160-3715/2017.2552

Peixoto, A. (2012). *Propensity, experiences and consequences of Victimization: social representations* [Doctoral dissertation, New University of Lisbon]. New University of Lisbon Institutional Repository. http://hdl.handle.net/10362/7880

Pemberton, A. (2016). Empathy for victims in criminal justice: Revisiting Susan Bandes in Victimology. In H. Conway & J. Stannard (Eds.), *Emotional Dynamics of Law and Legal Discourse.* Hart Publishing.

Pemberton, A., Aarten, P. G., & Mulder, E. (2017). Beyond retribution, restoration and procedural justice: The Big Two of communion and agency in victims' perspectives on justice. *Psychology, Crime & Law*, *23*(7), 682–698. doi:10.1080/1 068316X.2017.1298760

Pemberton, A., & Aarten, P. P. G. M. (2018). Narrative in the study of victimological processes in terrorism and political violence: An initial exploration. *Studies in Conflict and Terrorism*, *41*(7), 541–556. doi:10.1080/1057610X.2017.1311110

Pemberton, A., & Mulder, E. (2023). Bringing injustice back in: Secondary Victimization as epistemic injustice. *Criminology & Criminal Justice*. Advance online publication. doi:10.1177/17488958231181345

Pemberton, A., Mulder, E., & Aarten, P. G. (2019a). Stories of injustice: Towards a narrative victimology. *European Journal of Criminology*, *16*(4), 391–412. doi:10.1177/1477370818770843

Pemberton, A., Mulder, E., & Aarten, P. G. (2019b). Stories as property: Narrative ownership as a key concept in victims' experiences with criminal justice. *Criminology & Criminal Justice*, *19*(4), 404–420. doi:10.1177/1748895818778320

Presser, L., & Sandberg, S. (2019). Narrative Criminology as Critical Criminology. *Critical Criminology*, *27*(1), 131–143. doi:10.1007/s10612-019-09437-9

Riessman, C. K. (1993). *Narrative analysis*. SAGE Publishings.

Riessman, C. K. (2000). Analysis of personal narratives. *Inside interviewing: New lenses, new concerns*, 331-346. https://uel.ac.uk/sites/default/files/analysis-of-personal-narratives.pdf

Sandelowski, M. (1995). Sample size in qualitative research. *Research in Nursing & Health*, *18*(2), 179–183. doi:10.1002/nur.4770180211 PMID:7899572

Sarah, R. (2013). The narrative turn: interdisciplinary methods and perspectives. *Student Anthropologist, 3*(3), 64-80). DOI: doi:10.1002/j.sda2.20130303.0005

Scott, J. W. (1995). Gender: A useful category for historical analysis. *Educação e Realidade*, *20*(2), 71–99. https://seer.ufrgs.br/index.php/educacaoerealidade/article/download/71721/40667/297572

Steibelt, E. (2009). The context of gender-based violence for Vietnamese women migrant factory workers in Southern Vietnam. *Gender Asia in*, 217-61. https://publications.iom.int/es/system/files/pdf/gender_and_labour_migration_asia.pdf#page=217

Strauss, A., & Corbin, J. (1998). *Basics of Qualitative Research: Techniques and Procedures for Developing Grounded Theory*. Sage Publications.

Strobl, R. (2010). Becoming a Victim. In G. S. Shlomo, P. Knepper, & M. Kett (Eds.), *Internation Handbook Of Victimology* (pp. 3–23). CRC Press Taylor & Francis Group. doi:10.1201/EBK1420085471-c1

Symonds, M. (2010). The "Second Injury" to Victims of Violent Acts. *American Journal of Psychoanalysis*, *70*(1), 34–41. doi:10.1057/ajp.2009.38 PMID:20212437

Tewksbury, R. (2011). Qualitative Methodology. In C. D. Bryant (Ed.), *The Routledge Handbook of Deviant Behavior*. Routledge Handbooks Online. doi:10.4324/9780203880548.ch9

Walklate, S., Maher, J., McCulloch, J., Fitz-Gibbon, K., & Beavis, K. (2019). Victim stories and victim policy: Is there a case for a narrative Victimology? *Crime, Media, Culture*, *15*(2), 199–215. doi:10.1177/1741659018760105

Wemmers, J.-A. (2013). Victims' experiences in the criminal justice system and their recovery from crime. *International Review of Victimology*, *19*(3), 221–233. doi:10.1177/0269758013492755

Yuval-Davis, N. (2006). Intersectionality and Feminist Politics. *European Journal of Women's Studies*, *13*(3), 193–209. doi:10.1177/1350506806065752

Chapter 6
Shadows of Silence:
Investigating Police Responses to Intimate and Gender–Based Violence

Joana Torres
University of Maia, Portugal

Jorge Gracia Ibáñez
Universidad San Jorge, Spain

Sónia Maria Martins Caridade
🆔 https://orcid.org/0000-0003-0387-7900
Psychology Research Center, School of Psychology, University of Minho, Braga, Portugal

ABSTRACT

The Istanbul Convention stands out as a crucial and pioneering tool in addressing gender-based violence (GBV) and violence against women (VAW) within the European context. Recognizing the significance of police responses to such violence, this qualitative study aims to analyze and comprehend the implementation of police officers' responses to intimate partner violence in Portugal, while considering the principles outlined in the Istanbul Convention. Thirteen interviews (M = 46; S.D. = 13.3) were conducted with professionals involved in police response, evenly distributed across Portugal. The objective was to explore their experiences in providing responses to intimate and GBV, which were then scrutinized against the recommendations outlined in the Group of Experts' Report to Combat Violence Against Women and Domestic Violence. The findings revealed a significant gap in knowledge among first-line response personnel regarding the phenomenon. While the establishment of specialized groups within the police force, such as the Investigation and Support Centers for Specific Victims (NIAVE), was viewed as an important and positive resource, it was deemed insufficient due to heavy workloads, resulting in the prioritization of higher-risk cases. Despite the implementation of a risk assessment instrument, there was a notable lack of understanding among professionals regarding its application. The investigation yielded several recommendations for enhancing these responses, including a substantial investment in training for police responses to GBV and bolstering the capacity of NIAVE to ensure effective management of all domestic violence (DV) cases.

DOI: 10.4018/979-8-3693-5436-0.ch006

INTRODUCTION

From the 1970s onwards, feminist and battered women's movements began petitioning and lobbying legislators to criminalize domestic violence (DV), which until then had been considered a private matter, outside the scope of state intervention (Labriola et al., 2009). In the subsequent decades, social justice movements confronted states with their responsibility to guarantee proactive political responses to combat DV (Busch & Valentine, 2000).

The progressive social visibility of the phenomenon, along with the growing number of cases being publicized, compelled states to implement systems, procedures, and policies to respond to the phenomenon (Pinchevsky, 2017). However, while on the one hand, there was a pressing need to respond to these cases, on the other hand, the whole scenario of their emergence seems to have facilitated a lack of planning, contributing to a fragmented system that raises questions about the effectiveness of the support provided to victims (Johnson & Stylianou, 2022). In an attempt to make responses to gender based-violence (GBV) more effective, there has been an investment in adopting more specialized responses, through measures such as the creation of specialized units or the selection of specific approaches (Quintas & Sousa, 2017), or the development of coordinated community response systems capable of extending the reach of interventions (Post et al., 2010) and maximizing the effectiveness and efficiency of responses (Klevens et al., 2008).

In addition to the challenges listed, relating to the structures and articulation of responses, there are also challenges relating to the type of approaches used in responses, which often reflect deep-rooted patriarchal beliefs and values that are reflected in institutional policies and professional practice (Montesanti & Thurston, 2015; Rodríguez-Blanes et al., 2017).

Parallel to the institutional responses made available to tackle GBV, women's human rights instruments were created and adopted (e.g., Declaration on the Elimination of Discrimination Against Women, 1967; Convention on the Elimination of All Forms of Discrimination Against Women, 1979), which outline both women's rights and the duties of states to guarantee them.

In the European context, the Istanbul Convention stands as the first regional human rights instrument solely dedicated to promoting a Europe free of violence against women (VAW) and domestic violence (DV). This instrument unequivocally declares in its preamble that such violence constitutes a violation of human rights, stemming from structural gender asymmetry. Article 5 of the Istanbul Convention explicitly mandates that States Parties refrain from committing any acts of VAW and ensure the same behavior throughout their entire systems or entities acting on their behalf (Article 5, nr. 1). Additionally, Member States bear the responsibility of adopting legislative or other necessary measures to ensure the prevention, investigation, punishment, and redress of cases of violence under the Convention perpetrated by non-state actors (Article 5, para. 2). To monitor and control progress and effective compliance with the commitments of the States Parties, the Istanbul Convention includes the creation of the Group of Experts on Action Against Women and Domestic Violence (GREVIO) (Article 66 of the Istanbul Convention), an independent specialized body that has been in operation since September 2015 (Council of Europe, 2020). The functions of GREVIO include: i) the adoption/implementation of policies; data collection; adoption of preventive measures/programs; ii) adoption of protection and support measures; iii) provision of general and specialized support; iv) legal framework; v) civil restoration of victims; vi) investigation, accusation, procedural law, and protection measures (Council of Europe, 2020).

In turn, the Member States are also subject to submitting informative periodic reports on the implementation of the provisions of the Istanbul Convention to the Council of Europe. The content of this report submitted by the States is guided by the "Questionnaire on Legislative Measures and Other Measures Implementing the Provisions of the Council of Europe Convention on Preventing and Combating Violence Against Women and Domestic Violence (Istanbul Convention)", developed by GREVIO (Group of Experts on Action Against Women and Domestic Violence [GREVIO], 2016). It covers, following the order of provisions of the Convention itself, aspects to consider verifying if these are effectively being implemented (Council of Europe, 2020). In addition to the questionnaire, a moment is established for dialogues with the authorities of the States under assessment; and finally, observations/visits to the States are carried out (Council of Europe, 2020).

In the specific case of Portugal, the first (baseline) assessment conducted by GREVIO (2019) resulted from an evaluation based on: the assessment of implementation measures taken by Portuguese authorities; additional information presented by a coalition of NGOs (the shadow report of NGOs) and the results of this group's dialogue with State representatives from Portugal in 2018 in Strasbourg; and finally, data collected during a 5-day assessment visit to Portugal (March 2018) with a group of delegates appointed for this purpose. This visit served the purpose of deepening knowledge through meetings with governmental and non-governmental representatives working in the field of preventing and combating VAW (e.g., justice professionals, medical professionals, social workers, representatives of the media) (GREVIO, 2019).

This chapter aims to analyze the police responses to GBV in intimate relationships. We begin by conducting a theoretical review of the background regarding police responses to GBV in intimate relationships. Next, we present the design of the empirical study and its results. In the discussion and conclusion, we seek to reflect on the practical implications of the results in combating violence against women (VAW) and GBV.

BACKGROUND

Police Responses to Gender-Based Violence in Intimate Relationships

The 1980s marked a turning point in police responses to GBV (Buzawa & Buzawa 2003). The traditional perception of GBV as a private and family issue, widespread within police responses and manifested in the omission of actions by these professionals, has been evolving. This change is notably due to the pressure exerted by feminist movements for violence against women to be effectively treated as a crime (Stalans & Lurigio, 1995). Presently, the seriousness of this criminal phenomenon is widely acknowledged by police forces (DeJong et al., 2008; Gover et al., 2011). However, it is also recognized that, in terms of police responses, there is still progressed to be made, particularly in ensuring adequate protection for victims. This deficiency is often motivated by a devaluation of the violence suffered (Jordan, 2004; Poiares, 2016). Police structures harbor prejudices towards "domestic crime" anchored in issues of masculine policing ethos (Douglas, 2008; Lewis 2004) and its association with "soft" policing (Douglas, 2012; Loftus, 2009).

In Portugal, the National Republican Guard (NRG) and the Public Security Police (PSP) are the criminal police organizations (CPO) with the most contact with DV incidents, representing 99.96% of DV reports registered by the OPC in 2021. Additionally, within these mentioned CPOs, offices were established with professionals specialized in DV to offer support, information, and referrals to victims: the Proximity and Victim Support Teams (PVST) in the case of the PSP, and the Investigation and Support Centres for Specific Victims (SCSV) in the NRG.

According to the Annual Domestic Violence Monitoring Report - ADVMR (Internal Security System [ISS], 2022), by the end of 2021, the security forces had 1,325 permanent DV support staff (799 in the NRG and 526 in the PSP). In the NRG, there were 122 military personnel assigned to the SCSV, and 677 military personnel assigned to the Investigation and Inquiry Teams (ISS, 2022). The key aspects of intervention by these security forces in DV include: i) considering DV as a serious crime impacting individuals and society, requiring an effective and efficient response from the judicial system; ii) cooperating with other organizations involved in the process to reduce and prevent the violence and, when requested, exercising the criminal measures imposed by the current criminal justice system on the aggressor; iii) adapting responses to the specificities of the victims (e.g., safeguarding ethnic, cultural, and age aspects); iv) coordinating with communities and actively participating in preventing the phenomenon; v) protecting children and young people directly or indirectly involved; vi) and ensuring impartial intervention, conducted constructively and free of value judgments (ISS, 2014). In the DV process, it is up to the police to collect and gather all evidence of the crime and send it to the Public Prosecutor's Office as soon as possible (Art. 243, Decree-Law 78/87 of 17 February).

According to ADVMR-2021 (ISS, 2022), 26,517 DV reports were registered by the security forces (12,754 by the NRG and 13,763 by the PSP) - an average of 2,210 reports per month, 73 per day, and 3 per hour. Approximately 80% of DV incidents were reported to the security forces on the same day or the following day: 47.4% of cases were reported in person; 25.0% were reported by telephone; and 20.1% were reported as part of a neighborhood policing intervention. Police intervention was generally motivated by a request from the victim (75.0%) and in 11.8% of cases by family members/neighbors or an anonymous complaint (3.1%). In 19.3% of the recorded cases, there had been previous occurrence(s) formalized through another report(s). Psychological violence was present in 81.5% of situations, physical violence in 65.2%, social violence in 15.6%, economic violence in 7.1%, and sexual violence in 2.6% of cases.

It is the responsibility of the police forces, when acting on the front line, to take the first measures to protect the victim. These measures include, when there is direct contact with the aggressor, immediately stopping the aggression or, if the service is carried out in the police structure, referring the victim to the victim support office to carry out the necessary steps, safeguarding their safety and that of others involved (e.g., children) (ISS, 2014).

Over the last decade, the Ministry of Internal Administration has made means and resources available to respond to the phenomenon of DV, creating a set of instruments aimed at improving the responses of the security forces, namely the violence risk assessment form (RVD) implemented in 2014 (ISS, 2014). The ADVMR - 2021 (ISS, 2022) indicates that 71% of NRG and PSP posts and police stations had specific victim service rooms, and together, both police forces carried out 26,997 risk assessments (20.3% of cases assessed as "high" risk) (ISS, 2022). Poiares (2016) (n=70), in his study on the responses of DV systems in Portugal, identified a sense of persuasion reported by victims, particularly from first-line intervention professionals (referred to as "patrol officers"), to convince them to drop their complaints. This issue was not prevalent among second-line police officers who had specialized training in DV (Poiares, 2016). The study also highlighted a significant challenge faced by police officers in providing victims with a genuine sense of security during initial contact. This difficulty was attributed to value judgments, lack of patience, re-victimization, inadequate information provision, and superficial handling of the situation (Poiares, 2016). The described data is particularly relevant when considering that first-line police officers may be the initial point of contact for victims disclosing violence or seeking help, and the response provided at that moment is crucial throughout the process (Barnett et al., 2010). In some instances, police practices can be harmful to victims and insensitive to gender issues, emphasizing victim blaming and contributing to underreporting (Felson et al., 2002). Generally, even when perpetrators acknowledge the importance of their actions and meet victims' expectations, they may fail to offer adequate protection, underestimate the violence, and neglect certain requests for help due to not considering them serious or a priority (Barnett et al., 2010). Victims often contact the police with the expectation of interrupting the cycle of violence, and some hope that police intervention will encourage the aggressor to cease abusive behavior or send a disapproving message about their actions (Leisenring, 2012). As a result, it's not surprising that the literature indicates high rates of victims giving up, not cooperating, or not pursuing complaints in these cases, contributing to police officers perceiving this type of case as a waste of time (Davis & Smith, 1995). The disengagement and/or inadequacy of the approach among police officers are also linked to their beliefs about victims, influencing their actions regarding filing complaints, cooperation, or dropping charges (Gauthier, 2010).

Despite the existence of legal guidelines guiding these professionals' interventions, personal factors coexist and can influence various police responses, such as the belief that GBV is a private family matter, individual perceptions of the severity of situations, and externalization of guilt by attributing causes like unemployment, alcohol and drug use, or economic difficulties (Coelho, 2010; Robinson & Chandek, 2000). The racial background of the perpetrator and the victim can also condition police officers' responses if they hold deep-rooted prejudices (Coelho, 2010; Robinson & Chandek, 2000). Coelho (2019) in a quantitative study carried out in Portugal (n=1,871) with the aim of identifying the beliefs, attitudes, and values of NRG military personnel in relation to GBV and understanding how these interpretations affect their performance, found that, in general, there is greater awareness and less tolerance of the phenomenon. However, it also found that beliefs persist among these professionals related to the externalisation of guilt on the part of aggressors: stereotyped and simplistic views of the phenomenon; beliefs that this violence is due to alcohol consumption, drugs, lack of money, unemployment, or extramarital relationships (Coelho, 2019). Differences in understanding and action were identified between female and male NRG soldiers in terms of DV, namely: the degree of legitimisation and trivialisation of GBV is lower among women; in terms of intervention, it is female soldiers who attribute the highest severity value to occurrences, intervening more actively in these cases, while male soldiers are less involved (Coelho, 2019). Finally, the study shows that it is military personnel with specific training in DV who have the lowest percentage of beliefs legitimising this violence, which demonstrates the importance of public policies continuing to invest in training (Coelho, 2019). In fact, in Portugal, the professionals themselves admit that the training they receive is not sufficient to meet the professional demands that arise in cases of DV, contributing to them limiting themselves to complying with the steps indicated by the Public Prosecutor's Office as part of the investigation (Poiares, 2016). In terms of training, the ADVMR - 2021 (ISS, 2022) indicates that within the scope of the annual joint training plan, the main purpose of which is to promote training in matters of Violence against Women and Domestic Violence, 11 courses were held, corresponding to 80 training sessions in which 769 trainees took part, 294 from the NRG and 475 from the PSP (ISS, 2022).

The scientific evidence within this topic also points to a lack of consensus regarding victims' perceptions of the responses they receive from police services (e.g., Apsler et al., 2003; Fleury-Steiner et al., 2006, p. 335). Among the situations in which victims tend to report unsatisfactory service are minimising their suffering; police officers not believing in what they are sharing (Stephens & Sinden, 2000); blaming them for the violence; reprimanding them for previous cases that they did not pursue; and advising them to try to resolve the issue with the aggressor (Fleury-Steiner et al., 2006, p. 335). However, it has also been found that satisfaction with the service is influenced by the degree of agreement between the police officers' behaviour and the victims' expectations (Apsler et al., 2003; Buzawa & Austin, 1993; Rajah et al., 2006).

With regard to changes to improve the intervention of the police forces with GBV victims, the study by Poiares (2016) points out the following areas for investment: the quality of care, especially in the first line of intervention; strengthening the security of police forces in procedures; not attending victims at the counter; ensuring greater privacy; treating victims with an interest in their story; not making value judgements; not re-victimizing the victim; increasing the number of professionals with specialized training, particularly on the front line; reinforcing continuous training and following a standardized training plan; including more women in the response to this form of violence; and avoiding a possible proximity between the biased stance of these agents and the stance of the aggressor (Poiares, 2016). Optimizing this response to GBV cases is an important contribution to empowering victims, to their satisfaction and feeling of support from the support provided and to ensuring their safety (Sani & Morais, 2015). Positive police responses encourage victims to seek legal remedies, as well as their willingness to resort to this response in the future (Apsler et al., 2003; Fleury-Steiner et al., 2006; Harne & Radford, 2008). For this to be promoted, the work to be carried out involves ensuring that information, counselling and support are made available, as well as appropriate referral and promoting the victims' ability to deal with the situations that led to the complaint themselves (Sani & Morais, 2015). The response should therefore counteract negative police attitudes which, in turn, contribute to victims not reporting the violence they have suffered (Erez & Belknap, 1998; Felson et al., 2002), since it is known that failure to report tends to be related to an increase in re-victimisation rates, with reporting acting as a deterrent to this violence (Felson et al., 2005). Sani et al. (2018), in an exploratory study, found that police intervention tends to be based on the law, which understands the phenomenon in a criminal context, with the need for immediate action to protect the victim, with DV being understood as a priority issue for these responses. In Portugal, the "One Step Further" programme, which has been running in the city of Porto since 2013, is an experiment in the specialisation of justice and police services in the response to crimes of DV and ill-treatment, whose evaluation, carried out by the School of Criminology at the University of Porto, found that the professionals in the specialised police structure (in this case, the PSP Victim Assistance and Information Office in Porto) consider: their own useful work; the proximal action with the entire institutional network involved as enhancing the bureaucratisation of work and promoting greater monitoring and support for victims in their decisions (Quintas & Sousa, 2017, p. 9). Victims covered by the programme also indicate greater satisfaction and an increased feeling of insecurity when compared to victims who are in the normal response system (Quintas & Sousa, 2017), which corroborates the idea that adopting an integrated team perspective is a source of empowerment and satisfaction for victims and these professionals (Russell & Light, 2006). The close monitoring of victims by the police and justice system agencies contributes to delaying the commission of repeated offences against the same victims, and this is only possible with a reorganisation of the structures involved, coordination of services and greater specialisation and dedication on the part of professionals, although the report also warns that sustained changes over time should involve investment in maintaining the victim support structure, as well as reducing the rate of recidivism (Quintas & Sousa, 2017).

METHODOLOGY

Study Design

The present study aims to analyze police officers' experiences in terms of responses GBV, which are subsequently examined based on the recommendations outlined in the Group of Experts' report to Combat Violence against Women and Domestic Violence (2019). The goal is to deepen understanding and propose more robust interventions in the field of GBV. For this purpose, a phenomenological qualitative investigation was conducted, focusing precisely on the lived experience regarding institutional responses to GBV (Creswell, 2007). In line with this, the study emphasizes experience, particularly in the intersection between certain objective conditions and their lived experiences by expert witnesses. Consequently, this qualitative approach did not adhere to positivist concerns of subject-object separation, nor did it rely on the construction of universal laws or follow a hypothetico-deductive model that perceives reality as external to the research process (Bakker, 2019).

As ontological and epistemic starting assumptions, it is advocated that knowledge production is contextualized and emergent. When seeking to understand social relations based on lived experience, we are already immersed in that social reality, and it cannot be external to the researcher and the research (Mason, 2002). Research is an active moment in knowledge production, and its practical agenda is primarily transformative (Creswell, 2007, 2014), aiming at informed practical reforms in the field of GBV whenever deemed necessary.

Sampling

The study used a purposive sampling process, specifically, participants were recruited according to specific characteristics - a sampling process based on criteria and stratified by professional groups (e.g., Morgan, 2008; Ritchie, Lewis et al., 2003). The inclusion criterion was working or having worked in institutions that provide support to victims of GBV. Thirteen interviews were conducted (M=46; S.D. = 13.3), with 11 men and 2 women, professionals from the police force, evenly distributed across the entire territory of mainland Portugal. On average, they had been working for 14 years (M=14.2; S.D.= 7.54).

Data Collection

The study with these professionals was based on a semi-structured interview script developed for the purpose, based on the work of GREVIO and the literature on the subject. The script was later revised and tested by experts. The dimensions contained in the script were: sociodemographic data; degree of awareness of professionals and their role in the phenomenon; difficulties faced by the professional class in responding to GBV; available means of responding to GBV and their effectiveness; feeling of support from the system in place; degree of training and preparation for action; feeling about the support received for their action.

For the conduction of the interviews, initial contacts were made via email with the General Secretariat of the Ministry of Internal Administration, presenting the project through a description of the research and a formal request for collaboration. After institutional and individual authorization, individual contacts were made to schedule the interviews. Regarding data collection, individual semi-structured qualitative interviews were conducted (Fontana & Frey, 2005). Prior to the interviews, participants completed and signed informed consents, which included an overview of the project, its objectives, the research team, data collection procedures, as well as the principles of voluntary participation and the ability to terminate the interview at any time without justification. The interviews took place on the day and time most convenient for all participants involved, in an environment as soundproof, private, and comfortable as possible, typically in participants' workplace institutions (e.g., offices, meeting rooms). Due to the pandemic situation, some interviews were conducted through digital platforms. The interviews had an average duration of 1 hour, were recorded in audio, and transcribed in full. Fictitious names were used to safeguard the identity of the participants. This process took place between March 2021 and April 2022.

Data Analysis

Data analysis followed a semi-inductive approach to content analysis with an affinity to some of the principles, techniques and strategies associated with grounded theory (Bakker, 2019; Charmaz, 2005). It began with a floating reading (e.g., pre-coding) of the data from the interviews (Creswell, 2014) and continued with a coding and categorisation model, as proposed by Saldaña (2011) - there was a progressive shift from more descriptive coding processes (vivo strategy) to conceptual coding processes (focused, axial and theoretical). The codes were assigned to a unit of analysis or record - a standard cut-out of the data (Berg, 2001). The unit of analysis was defined as the idea (a particular articulated content that reflects a concept or formulation).

The context unit was defined as a paragraph and serves the purpose of contextualizing the meaning of the unit of analysis (Bardin, 1977). It is through coding, in this circular and travelling process of the data, that we began to detect patterns which, in turn, led us to an interpretation that took the form of categories (Saldaña, 2009). Both were interpretative and circular processes in which the theory favored by the researcher, the objectives of the research process and the emerging data merged.

Theoretical saturation was reached when the data from the interviews began to become redundant, without generating the need to compose new categories or motivating the reformulation of existing ones (Strauss & Corbin, 1990). The final skeleton of categories is shown in Table 1, later explained in text.

Results

Data analysis translates into a category system, organized into three generations (cf. Table 1). The first generation, "Perceptions of professional practice", pertains to the overarching topic of analyzing interview results. From this initial major category, five second-generation categories and seven third-generation categories emerged (cf. Table 1), reflecting the refinement process in the analysis of interview results.

Table 1. Category system framework after data analysis by three generations

First generation categories	Second generation categories	Third generation categories
Perceptions of professional practice	Level of awareness of professionals	Knowledge of professionals about GBV
	Difficulties in dealing with the issue	Preparation to respond to the phenomenon
	Resources available	Political, legislative and institutional
	Efficiency	Works
		Does not work/needs improvement
	Training	Initial preparation
		Continuous training

So, starting with the second-generation category "degree of awareness among professionals", the participants report a evolution in the level of awareness among the professionals who make up the NRG (*"And the security forces have kept up with this and have tried to provide themselves with the means to accompany people more and more".* – P1), identifying that this is related to the generational change of the professionals (*"I can see that the staff, in my opinion, who are younger, are already more sensitized. The older staff, as it wasn't a topic that was probably touched on during the course, it seems that on a professional level they are not so..."* – P2). They recognize that the institution itself has a certain culture of conservatism (*"I feel that we as the security forces have a subculture with individuals who are not very 'given' to these developments."* – P3).

Some of the participants identify the very entrenchment of the patriarchal system among their peers as a difficulty in dealing with the phenomenon (*"kay, okay...', or 'It's all DV, this is their way of specializing in the divorce process, because they want freedom.".* – P3).

Regarding the instruments available to respond to this crime in their professional practice, the police officers interviewed indicate that there are means of response, although they present them as insufficient given the volume and complexity of the cases (*"We have few resources for the level of occurrences that exist and sometimes due to the evolution of the occurrence, in which it often starts in a normal way and, from one moment to the next, evolves, we have to ask for reinforcements and they take a long time to arrive".* – P4). They refer positively to the work carried out by the SCSV teams, highlighting the importance of this specialized group in supporting the professional practice of other police officers who don't have a specialization (*"So far, the times I have had to call SCSV, they are come, or they have told me how to proceed."* – P5).

However, there are also perceptions that the SCSV need greater investment, in order to allow for greater response capacity and a specialised response to all cases, without differentiating by risk level (*"We need to invest more in material goods, human goods and, in this case, we need to increase the centres because, I think, the* SCSV *should deal with all DV cases, they shouldn't be police stations (...) and they shouldn't only deal with those cases that are considered more serious and complex."* - P6).

In terms of the service provided at police stations, some of them have rooms to receive victims and professionals responsible for handling DV enquiries (*"At the moment there's a victim support room, from 9am to 5pm there's always a comrade who also does the enquiries for people with DV"*. - P5), but the fragility of this solution is also exposed, as it limits the service dedicated to assisting victims to one working shift (*"We need to understand that there is DV from 9am to 5pm. In fact, most cases happen outside these hours, because that's when people are at home."* - P7).

Most of the participants emphasize the importance of the "Safety Plan", which they draw up together with the victim, and the risk assessment tool they have ("W*e give the Safety Plan, depending on the risk the victim is at, and we make the RVD form, which is very important in the investigation phase, so that they can then assess or reassess the case (...)"*. - P8).

Specifically, about the effectiveness of the means and their intervention, the participants consider safety plans to be a good form of guidance for victims (*"Safety plans are essential for victims to know what they are going to do if the other person reacts in a certain way, (...)"*). - P9); that teleassistance is a tool that increases victim protection (*"This is confidential, we can't give much information about teleassistance, but it's an asset for the victim"*. - P9); they emphasise the importance of the work of the bodies that provide support to victims (*"There are various bodies dedicated to minimising and supporting victims, and I think they have done an important job."* - P1), although they also point out that the coordination between organizations responding to DV doesn't always work in the same way and with the same effectiveness ("For example, in this municipality this network works very well, but in others the network doesn't work well, or not at all." - P4); and, they report that the justice system is more sensitised and the responses in their field are progressively quicker and more sensitive to the specifics of the crime in question (*"I think the courts are more attentive, more capable, when I started with DV (...) it was almost impossible for there to be a measure of coercion."* - P4).

In the interviews, all the social representations anchored to the police and the police station are also presented as possible obstacles to effective intervention (*"If she was immediately referred to a place where she felt protected, supported... It's not that she won't be protected here, but it's different. It's the uniform, it's the police..."*. - P1), and the arbitrary nature of the care given to the victim (*"Sometimes people can get a sensitive guard, and others may not be so lucky, and situations that could be resolved straight away aren't."* P1). In addition, the interviews also show a lack of understanding in the speeches of some of the professionals interviewed about the dynamics of the phenomenon (*"Sometimes it seems like they make fun of our work and I'm not even talking about the uniform."* - P10).

They often point to the need to improve their working conditions so that their work can be carried out with greater quality (*"We are the first line, or the first person there to help, and if we are overloaded and overworked, we are not going to be much help."*- P10). They say that the information they receive on the subject, through manuals sent to emails and which they recognise as important, is not appropriate for the professionals (*"I believe that all the new procedures that have emerged are disseminated, now the question is the form of dissemination, which should be more face-to-face and periodic training."*- P9).

Lastly, regarding training, participants often said they had no training in the area in question ("Training is scarce in this aspect of DV, but we try to do our best on the street, even without specific training."- *P5*). Among the topics where they pointed out that it would be pertinent to invest in training, they mentioned how to approach victims (*"We don't have any training to talk to victims, and it would make perfect sense."* - *P8*), and some of the participants highlighted their concern about the lack of preparation to approach children in these scenarios (*"A more pedagogical way of talking to people who have been victims of a crime, including children."* - *P11*); liaison between organizations that respond to DV (*"In terms of liaising with structures."* - *P10*); and the construction of the report (*"(...) sometimes reports come in that don't contain the information that is pertinent to starting the investigation."* - *P9*).

DISCUSSION

The main aim of this study was to analyse and better understand how these GBV responses and services are being made available among security force professionals, in order to deepen understanding and propose more robust GBV interventions. By adopting a qualitative perspective, this study sought to build an in-depth view of the subjective experiences and perceptions of police officers, and more specifically, frontline police officers (patrol officers), who do not have specialised training in the subject under study.

The participants in the study reported that, in general, there has been an evolution in terms of professionals' awareness of the phenomenon and they associate this with the generational change among professionals. However, they mention the existence of an institutional culture that tends towards conservatism, and some of the participants also identified the entrenchment of the patriarchal system among their peers as one of the difficulties these professionals have in dealing with the phenomenon. Sani et al. (2018) in their research with NRG professionals found that, in general, these professionals do not legitimise some of the ideas that mystify GBV, but they also identified the persistence of socially valid gender beliefs among these police officers, resulting from the very patriarchal social context in which they operate.

In this sense, institutional and professional contexts that act in the context of responses to GBV and have beliefs that legitimise this violence tend to justify and naturalise violent practices, which sustain systems of power that make victims invisible and have a negative impact on the responses provided (Cabral & Javier Rodríguez-Díaz, 2017). Knowing the structure and culture of the police is particularly important when assessing the attitudes and experiences of these professionals in relation to GBV, as it influences their practices (Grant & Rowe, 2011).

Therefore, this type of study is significant, as it not only brings to discussion the type of responses that professionals provide, but also calls for a deeper reflection on how institutional culture and professional beliefs and practices intersect in a patriarchal system. The GREVIO (2019), in its assessment of Portugal, points out that the country should ensure that the handling of cases of VAW by law enforcement and judicial services is firmly anchored in an understanding of the gender-based nature of VAW and is centered on the safety and human rights of women and their children.

In general, the participants in the study believe that there are resources available to deal with GBV in their professional practice, but they describe them as insufficient, given the volume and complexity of the cases. This is particularly emphasised when they talk about the work carried out by the SCSV, which they consider to be extremely important, particularly in the support they provide to first-line police officers, but which they believe needs to be invested in and expanded.

The literature describes the positive contributions of specialised GBV response units in relieving case congestion, resulting in a more targeted, informed and well-managed police response (Segrave et al., 2018). Foster (2003) points to the need to ensure the promotion and recognition of the work of these units within the police force as a whole, avoiding marginalisation based on the vision of "soft policing", which tends to be devalued. As presented in the ADVMR - 2021 (ISS, 2022) data, they mention, in a positive way, the existence of rooms to receive victims and the fact that there are professionals responsible for investigating these crimes, but they emphasise that the response from these professionals is limited to the day shift and does not guarantee this response throughout the day. They also refer to the "Safety Plan" and the risk assessment tool as important working tools for carrying out their work.

In terms of the effectiveness of the means and their intervention, they consider that the safety plans are good guidelines for victims; that teleassistance increases victim protection; that the organisations that provide support to victims do a good job, although the coordination between organisations is not always effective; and they indicate that the justice system is more sensitised, and its responses are progressively faster and more sensitive to the specificities of the crime in question.

Regarding the coordination of responses, GREVIO (2019) states in its report that the ADVMR - 2021 (ISS, 2022) has not yet fulfilled its mission of enabling truly effective cooperation between all the relevant players, although it also recognises that there are good examples where partial coordination is practised. However, he also adds that the success of coordination is essentially down to the individual initiative of the organisations concerned (GREVIO, 2019). About teleassistance, a measure that requires victims to have a device to call for help when they feel at risk, the GREVIO (2019) report considers that, with this measure, the state favours making victims responsible for their own safety over measures against the aggressor (GREVIO, 2019).

In the interviews, all the social representations anchored to the police and the police station and the randomness of the type of care provided to the victim emerged as possible obstacles to effective intervention. Russell and Light (2006) mention this randomness in terms of the quality of care a victim receives when they turn to the police, which is mediated by the assessment these professionals make of whether they deserve attention; the authors state that this randomness can be counteracted, particularly through training.

Sensitive responses are likely to give victims a sense of legitimacy in their complaint and provide a relevant guide for accessing specialised victim support services; inadequate responses can dissuade victims from seeking help in the future, unprotecting them and exposing them to a greater risk of violence, and sending a message to the aggressor that their behaviour is acceptable (Harne & Radford, 2008).

The interviews also show a lack of understanding of the dynamics of the phenomenon in the speeches of some of the professionals interviewed, which may be at the root of the feeling of frustration they share with regard to the behaviour of the victims. The tendency for these professionals to become frustrated with the victims' behaviour has been documented (e.g., Leisenring, 2012), and is often associated with repeated requests for support for the same case of violence, demonstrating an inability/unawareness to understand the violent dynamics involved (Gover et al., 2011; Horwitz et al., 2011), and the perception that the victims are often uncooperative (DeJong et al., 2008; Gover et al., 2011).

About victim co-operation, it is worth emphasising the importance of considering the individual context of each victim, as this co-operation can be influenced, for example, by dependence on the aggressor, economic and/or housing issues (for themselves and their children) (Bohmer et al., 2002; Leisenring, 2012). They often point to the need to improve their working conditions so that their work can be carried out to a higher standard. And they say that the information they receive on the subject, through manuals sent to emails and which they recognise as important, is not used by professionals. We are thus led to the subject of training, and it is assumed in the speeches that this is a gap, as it only covers a small fringe of frontline professionals.

These perceptions are in line with the results of the study carried out by Poiares (2016), which already pointed out the need to strengthen initial training and lifelong learning, particularly with regard to approaching and referring victims, as well as the legal aspects relating to this crime, which was highlighted as a need for police officers. In fact, among the topics indicated by the participants as pertinent for training plans were how to approach the victim and children in these scenarios; liaison between organisations that respond to domestic violence; and the construction of the police report. This professional's concern seems legitimate if we consider that, according to ADVMR – 2021 (ISS, 2022), in 31.1% of cases the occurrences were witnessed by minors.

Despite the significant contributions made by this study to improving GBV responses, it is crucial to recognise certain limitations. Data collection took place at a time of pandemic, characterised by various contact limitations and atypical workflows. Another limitation stems from the characteristics of the sample, since the study exclusively involved the NRG security force, which was the organisation that agreed to collaborate with the research. However, for a better understanding of the system, it would be important to extend the study to PSP professionals and then, in future research, to study the specific responses to DV within each of these security forces.

CONCLUSION

This research, which focuses on the institutional responses of police officers to GBV in Portugal, points to an evolution in terms of recognising the quality of the responses provided to this violence. However, there are still many challenges to achieving the desired level of quality in dealing with GBV cases.

Firstly, the professionals themselves still need to invest in deconstructing the gender beliefs that legitimise GBV. Despite the country's efforts after ratifying the Istanbul Convention to align legislation and build public policies in line with the Convention's presuppositions, its application is always dependent on professionals and, more specifically, on the level of knowledge, awareness and deconstruction that professionals have of their patriarchal references. It is therefore important that police responses benefit from greater investment in training (especially for first responders), which focuses on the conceptualisation and dynamics of the phenomenon, as well as understanding the points on which risk assessment is based and how to apply it effectively.

In turn, having identified the importance of SCSV work, it is also understood that its response capacity should be expanded to allow all DV offences to pass through its services. Currently, due to the scarcity of resources, these specialised professionals focus on the most serious cases, according to the risk assessment. This practice, considering the weaknesses in risk assessment assumed by a significant proportion of the first-line professionals who took part in the study, could leave out serious cases if the assessments fail. Furthermore, it would be important to guarantee the same standards of care for all victims. In this sense, the study also highlights the relevance of training all police response professionals in applying this instrument and translating the concerns expressed in the interviews, in victim care competences.

In addition to the results obtained from the research, it is relevant to highlight that it presented some limitations. Firstly, given that DV is essentially addressed by two security forces in Portugal (NRG and PSP), it would be important to obtain the perspective of both. However, as no response was received from the PSP regarding the request for collaboration in the research, the research team was compelled to proceed as presented. Secondly, the sample included a significant difference between the number of "patrolling" police officers (11 personnel) and police officers belonging to specialized DV response services (2 personnel). Therefore, considering the mentioned limitations and the research findings, it would be important for future investigations to focus on the procedures of the two security forces that respond most to DV in Portugal (NRG and PSP), in order to study and, from there, identify weaknesses and best practices in responses, contributing to a potential improvement and harmonization of procedures. It would also be relevant for future studies to examine in more detail the responses of specialized teams in Gender-Based Violence (GBV) within both mentioned security forces.

Finally, it is important to acknowledge that conducting scientific investigations involving the relevant public presents certain ethical challenges. This reflects the necessity to strike a balance between the study's objectives and the rights and well-being of participants. Alongside obtaining informed consent and ensuring confidentiality, anonymity, and responsible disclosure, it is crucial to address concerns such as the potential impact on participants' professional careers or personal lives, ensure representativeness to prevent bias, and establish ethical, collaborative, and trustworthy relationships with police enforcement institutions.

Qualitatively investigating institutional responses to intimate gender-based violence is crucial for a better understanding of the dynamics and processes underlying the responses that professionals provide to the phenomenon. This allows for improvements in the development of institutional policies and public policies.

REFERENCES

Apsler, R., Cummins, M. R., & Carl, C. (2003). Perceptions of the police by female victims of domestic partner violence. *Violence Against Women*, *9*(11), 1318–1335. Advance online publication. doi:10.1177/1077801203255554

Bakker, J. I. (2019). Grounded theory methodology and grounded theory method: introduction to the special issue. *Sociological Focus, 52*(2), 91-106. doi:10.1080/00380237.2019.1550592

Barnett, O. W., Miller-Perrin, C. L., & Perrin, R. D. (2010). *Family violence across the lifespan: an introduction*. SAGE Publications.

Berg, B. L. (2001). *Qualitative research methods for the social sciences*. Allyn and Bacon.

Busch, N. B., & Valentine, D. (2000). Empowerment practice: A focus on battered women. *Affilia*, *15*(1), 82–95. doi:10.1177/08861090022093840

Buzawa, E. S., & Austin, T. (1993). Determining police response to domestic violence victims: The role of victim preference. *The American Behavioral Scientist*, *36*(5), 610–623. doi:10.1177/0002764293036005006

Buzawa, E. S., & Buzawa, C. G. (1996). *Domestic violence: the criminal justice response*. SAGE Publications.

Cabral, P., & Rodríguez-Díaz, F. (2017). Violência conjugal: Crenças de atuais e futuros profissionais, implicados na sua reposta e prevenção - direito, saúde e educação [Marital violence: beliefs of current and future professionals, involved in its response and prevention - law, health and education]. *Saber & Educar*, *23*(23), 152–167. doi:10.17346/se.vol23.275

Charmaz, K. (2005). Grounded theory in the 21st century: applications for advancing social justice studies. In N. Denzin, & Y. Lincoln (Eds.), The sage handbook of qualitative research (pp. 507-535). SAGE Publications.

Coelho, A. M. (2010). *Crenças e atitudes dos agentes policiais face à violência contra a mulher* [Beliefs and attitudes of police officers towards violence against women] [Dissertação de mestrado não publicada]. Universidade do Porto.

Coelho, R. P. P. S. (2019). *Violência doméstica e de género: crenças, atitudes e valores dos militares da GNR* [Domestic and gender-based violence: beliefs, attitudes and values of GNR soldiers] [Dissertação de mestrado não publicado]. Universidade Aberta.

Correia, A. L., & Sani, A. I. (2015). As casas de abrigo em Portugal: Caraterização estrutural e funcional destas respostas sociais [Shelters in Portugal: structural and functional characterization of these social responses]. *Análise Psicológica*, *33*(1), 89–96. doi:10.14417/ap.918

Creswell, J. W. (2007). *Qualitative inquiry and research design: choosing among five approaches*. SAGE Publications.

Creswell, J. W. (2014). *Research design: qualitative, quantitative, and mixed methods approaches*. SAGE Publications.

Davis, R. C., & Smith, B. (1995). Domestic violence reforms: Empty promises or fulfilled expectations? *Crime and Delinquency*, *41*(4), 541–552. doi:10.1177/0011128795041004010

DeJong, C., Burgess-Proctor, A., & Elis, L. (2008). Police officer perceptions of intimate partner violence: An analysis of observational data. *Violence and Victims*, *23*(6), 683–696. doi:10.1891/0886-6708.23.6.683 PMID:19069561

Douglas, H. (2008). The criminal law's response to domestic violence: What's going on? *The Sydney Law Review*, *30*(3), 439–469.

Erez, E., & Belknap, J. (1998). In their own words: Battered women's assessment of the criminal processing system's responses. *Violence and Victims*, *13*(3), 251–268. doi:10.1891/0886-6708.13.3.251 PMID:9836413

Felson, R. B., Ackerman, J. M., & Gallagher, C. A. (2005). Police intervention and the repeat of domestic assault. *Criminology*, *43*(3), 563–588. doi:10.1111/j.0011-1348.2005.00017.x

Felson, R. B., Messner, S. F., Hoskin, A. W., & Deane, G. (2002). Reasons for reporting and not reporting domestic violence to the police. *Criminology*, *40*(3), 617–648. doi:10.1111/j.1745-9125.2002.tb00968.x

Fleury-Steiner, R. E., Bybee, D., Sullivan, C. M., Belknap, J., & Melton, H. C. (2006). Contextual factors impacting battered women's intentions to reuse the criminal legal system. *Journal of Community Psychology*, *34*(3), 327–342. doi:10.1002/jcop.20102

Flick, U. (2018). Triangulation. In N. Denzin, & Y. Lincoln (Eds.), The Sage handbook of qualitative research. SAGE Publications.

Fontana, A., & Frey, J. H. (2005). The interview: from neutral stance to political involvement. In N. K. Denzin & Y. S. Lincoln (Eds.), *The Sage handbook of qualitative research* (pp. 695–727). SAGE Publications.

Foster, J. (2003). Police cultures. In T. Newburn (Ed.), *Handbook of policing* (pp. 196–227). Willan Publishing.

Gauthier, S. (2010). The perceptions of judicial and psychosocial interveners of the consequences of dropped charges in domestic violence cases. *Violence Against Women, 16*(12), 1375–1395. doi:10.1177/1077801210389163 PMID:21164215

Gover, A. R., Paul, D. P., & Dodge, M. (2011). Law enforcement officers' attitudes about domestic violence. *Violence Against Women, 17*(5), 619–636. doi:10.1177/1077801211407477 PMID:21551213

Grant, S., & Rowe, M. (2011). Running the risk: Police officer discretion and family violence in New Zealand. *Policing and Society, 21*(1), 49–66. Advance online publication. doi:10.1080/10439463.2010.540662

Group of Experts on Action against Violence against Women and Domestic Violence. (2019). *Baseline evaluation report: Portugal.* Council of Europe. https://www.cig. gov.pt/wp- content/uploads/2019/01/Relat%C3%B3rio-GREVIO.pdf

Harne, L., & Radford, J. (2008). *Tackling domestic violence: theories, policies and practice.* Open University Press.

Horwitz, S. H., Mitchell, D., LaRussa-Trott, M., Santiago, L., Pearson, J., Skiff, D. M., & Cerulli, C. (2011). An inside view of police officers' experience with domestic violence. *Journal of Family Violence, 26*(8), 617–625. doi:10.1007/s10896-011-9396-y

Internal Security System - ISS. (2014). *Violência doméstica: relatório anual de monitorização. Ministério da Administração Interna* [Domestic violence: annual monitoring report. Ministry of Internal Affairs]. https://www.cig.gov.pt/siic/2014/12/violencia-domestica-2013-relatorio-anual-de- monitorizacao-mai-agosto-de-2014/

Internal Security System - ISS. (2022). *Violência Doméstica - 2021. Relatório anual de monitorização. Ministério da Administração Interna* [Domestic Violence - 2021. Annual monitoring report. Ministry of Internal Affairs]. https://www.sg.mai.gov. pt/Documents/Relat%C3%B3rio%20de%20Monitoriza%C3%A7%C3%A3o%20 de%202021.pdf

Johnson, L., & Stylianou, A. M. (2022). Coordinated community responses to domestic violence: A systematic review of the literature. *Trauma, Violence & Abuse, 23*(2), 506–522. doi:10.1177/1524838020957984 PMID:32954993

Jordan, J. (2004). *The word of a woman?: police, rape and belief.* Palgrave MacMillan. doi:10.1057/9780230511057

Kallivayalil, D. (2004). Gender and cultural socialization in Indian immigrant families in the United States. *Feminism & Psychology*, *14*(4), 535–559. doi:10.1177/0959353504046871

Klevens, J., Baker, C. K., Shelley, G. A., & Ingram, E. M. (2008). Exploring the links between components of coordinated community responses and their impact on contact with intimate partner violence services. *Violence Against Women*, *14*(3), 346–358. Advance online publication. doi:10.1177/1077801207313968 PMID:18292374

Labriola, M., Bradley, S., O'Sullivan, C. S., Rempel, M., & Moore, S. (2009). *A national portrait of domestic violence courts*. Center for Court Innovation. https://www.ncjrs.gov/pdffiles1/nij/grants/229659.pdf

Leisenring, A. (2012). Victims' perceptions of police response to intimate partner violence. *Journal of Police Crisis Negotiations*, *12*(2), 146–164. doi:10.1080/15332586.2012.728926

Lewis, R. (2004). Making justice work: Effective legal interventions for domestic violence. *British Journal of Criminology*, *44*(2), 204–224. doi:10.1093/bjc/44.2.204

Mason, J. (2002). *Qualitative researching*. SAGE Publications.

Montesanti, S. R., & Thurston, W. E. (2015). Mapping the role of structural and interpersonal violence in the lives of women: Implications for public health interventions and policy. *BMC Women's Health*, *15*(1), 100. doi:10.1186/s12905-015-0256-4 PMID:26554358

Morgan, D. (2008). Sampling. In L. Given (Ed.), *The sage encyclopedia of qualitative research method* (pp. 799–800). SAGE Publications.

Pinchevsky, G. M. (2017). Understanding decision-making in specialized domestic violence courts: Can contemporary theoretical frameworks help guide these decisions? *Violence Against Women*, *23*(6), 749–771. doi:10.1177/1077801216648792 PMID:27216474

Poiares, N. (2016). *A letra e os espíritos da lei: a violência doméstica em Portugal* [The letter and spirit of the law: domestic violence in Portugal]. Chiado.

Post, L. A., Klevens, J., Maxwell, C. D., Shelley, G. A., & Ingram, E. (2010). An examination of whether coordinated community responses affect intimate partner violence. *Journal of Interpersonal Violence*, *25*(1), 75–93. doi:10.1177/0886260508329125 PMID:19196879

Quintas, J., & Sousa, P. (2017). *Avaliação científica do programa 'UM PASSO MAIS': relatório*. Universidade do Porto.

Rajah, V., Frye, V., & Haviland, M. (2006). "Aren't I a victim?": Notes on identity challenges relating to police action in a mandatory arrest jurisdiction. *Violence Against Women, 12*(10), 897–916. doi:10.1177/1077801206292872 PMID:16957172

Ritchie, J., Lewis, J., & Elam, G. (2003). Designing and Selecting Samples: Qualitative research in practice. In J. Ritchie, & J. Lewis (Eds.), Qualitative research practice: a guide for social science students and researchers (pp. 77-104). SAGE Publications.

Robinson, A. L., & Stroshine Chandek, M. (2000). Philosophy into practice? Community policing units and domestic violence victim participation. *Policing, 23*(3), 280–302. doi:10.1108/13639510010342985

Rodríguez-Blanes, G. M., Vives-Cases, C., Miralles-Bueno, J. J., San Sebastián, M., & Goicolea, I. (2017). Detección de violencia del compañero íntimo en atención primaria de salud y sus factores asociados. *Gaceta Sanitaria, 31*(5), 410–415. doi:10.1016/j.gaceta.2016.11.008 PMID:28188013

Russell, M., & Light, L. (2006). Police and victim perspectives on empowerment of domestic violence victims. *Police Quarterly, 9*(4), 375–396. Advance online publication. doi:10.1177/1098611104264495

Saldaña, J. (2011). *Fundamentals of qualitative research*. Oxford university press.

Saldaña, J. (2012). *The coding manual for qualitative researchers*. SAGE Publications.

Sani, A., & Morais, C. (2015). A polícia no apoio às vítimas de violência doméstica: Estudo exploratório com polícias e vítimas [The police in supporting victims of domestic violence: exploratory study with police and victims]. *Direito e Democracia, 16*(1), 5–18.

Sani, A. I., Coelho, A., & Manita, C. (2018). Intervention in domestic violence situations: Police attitudes and beliefs. *Psychology, Community & Health, 7*(1), 72–86. doi:10.5964/pch.v7i1.247

Stalans, L. J., & Lurigio, A. J. (1995). Responding to domestic violence against women. *Crime and Delinquency, 41*(4), 387–398. doi:10.1177/0011128795041004001

Stephens, B. J., & Sinden, P. G. (2000). Victims' voices: Domestic assault victims' perceptions of police demeanor. *Journal of Interpersonal Violence, 15*(5), 534–547. doi:10.1177/088626000015005006

Chapter 7

Understanding Women's Fear of Crime:
The Role of Intimate Partner Violence

Camila Iglesias
Faculty of Law, University of Porto, Portugal

ABSTRACT

In recent decades, research on the fear of crime has significantly expanded within the fields of criminology and victimology. Similarly, studies on gender-based violence have also increased, particularly concerning domestic violence and intimate partner violence (IPV) perpetrated against women. Criminological evidence has consistently shown that women report high levels of fear of crime, despite having a lower risk of becoming victims of common (or street) crimes. The disparity between women's fear and risk has given rise to what is known as the "fear-victimization paradox," and several theories have been proposed over time to explain this paradox. However, an apparent dichotomy between public and private spaces still influences empirical evidence, and researchers have often overlooked the effects of domestic violence and IPV on women's fear of crime. This theoretical chapter aims to shed light on a better understanding of this fear-victimization paradox. It seeks to provide an integrated approach to the concepts of women's fear of crime and IPV. Moreover, it will delve into the potential repercussions of this type of victimization and fear on women's quality of life and daily routines, thereby illuminating promising avenues for future research in this crucial area.

INTRODUCTION

Recent data highlights a troubling truth: women experiencing intimate partner violence often have nowhere safe to turn (UNFPA, 2023). Their closest relationship,

DOI: 10.4018/979-8-3693-5436-0.ch007

meant to be a haven of safety and comfort, can instead become a frightening and threatening place. For these women, home, which should offer protection and care, becomes a dangerous space where their safety and well-being are at risk.

When the conventional notion of safety is inverted in the lived experiences of women victimized by their intimate partners, spaces intended for safety become arenas for violence. This violence extends beyond sporadic encounters in public domains; instead, it infiltrates intimate relationships and personal spaces, intensifying the feelings of threat and fear experienced by these women. (Stanko, 1995).

Taking this into consideration, when addressing women's fear, it's imperative to acknowledge the actual scale of victimization they face within and beyond their household boundaries. This nuanced understanding is vital to avoid dismissing women's fears as unfounded or exaggerated. Instead, it underscores the persistent feeling of insecurity arising from vulnerability to gender-based violence encountered in both private and public spheres, with a specific focus on cases of domestic and intimate partner violence.

Despite this reality, research in the field of fear of crime and its correlates has consistently overlooked the impact of these forms of violence on women's fear of crime. Consequently, studies linking these two subjects are scarce. This can be attributed in part to the continued conceptualization and examination of the fear of crime exclusively as a response or reaction to the public environment (street crime). Furthermore, enduring misconceptions surrounding the privacy of violence occurring behind closed doors further contribute to this research gap.

Therefore, in this chapter, we aim to provide a deeper understanding regarding the scale and repercussions of the violence to which women are exposed, specifically domestic violence and intimate partner violence, intending to explore their impact on the fear of crime experienced and reported by these women.

1.   Gender-based violence against women: The reality behind closed doors

(...) the phrase "behind closed doors" is intended to capture that kind of criminal behaviour that is likely to be recognized as such, by the victim in particular, and as a consequence less likely to come to the attention of the criminal justice system (Walklate, 2006, pp. 65)

Gender-based violence stands as one of the prevailing forms of violence globally (Morrison & Orlando, 2004), disproportionately impacting women and girls within societies. These types of violence fundamentally violate the human rights of women and girls, presenting themselves in diverse manifestations. Among the most prevalent are domestic violence, namely intimate partner violence (IPV) in its various forms – e.g., sexual, psychological, and physical violence. For the purpose of this chapter, IPV will be defined as *"(all) abusive behavior by a person within an intimate relationship including current or past marriages, domestic partnerships, or de facto relationships"* (Fitz-Gibbon, Walklate, McCulloch, & Maher, 2018, pp. 01). Throughout history, women and girls have been subjected to various forms of violence due to the inherently patriarchal and misogynistic structure upon which societies were built (Fox, 2002). This structure has proven to be particularly oppressive within domestic, familial, and intimate relational settings. Within these spheres, women often assumed subservient roles relative to men, enduring profound control over their bodies. Presently, this social structure exerts its power by subjecting thousands of women and girls to diverse forms of violence, with gender inequality serving as a foundational element perpetuating these incidents (Ackerson & Subramanian, 2016; Rahman, Nakamura, Seino, & Kizuki, 2013; Willie & Kershaw, 2019). Importantly, these acts of violence span societal strata and are not confined to specific subsets of women[1]. According to estimates by the World Health Organization (WHO), nearly one-third (27%) of women aged 15-49 who have been in a relationship report facing some form of physical and/or sexual violence from their intimate partner (WHO, 2021). Experiencing these forms of violence has adverse effects on the physical and mental health of its victims (Bacchus, Ranganathan, Watts, & Devries, 2018; Campbell, 2002; Campbell et al., 2002). A recent meta-analysis examining the global prevalence and mental health repercussions of IPV among women reveals that nearly 4 in 10 (37.3%) women aged 16 and above have encountered some form of IPV in their lifetime. Moreover, 1 in 4 women (24%) reported experiencing it within the past year (White et al., 2024). The same study also demonstrated compelling evidence indicating that exposure to IPV significantly affects women's mental health, elevating the risk of adverse outcomes. These include depression, suicidal thoughts and attempts, anxiety, post-traumatic stress disorder (PTSD), and psychological distress. Over an extended period, occurrences of such violence and their consequences for victims were relegated to the realm of privacy, devoid of societal censure and state oversight (Walklate, 2006). This approach, to a considerable degree, obscured these violent acts and perpetuated a culture of impunity, resulting in the marginalization and silencing of victims and their narratives while also masking the effects of these forms of violence on victims and their costs for society.

2.   Understanding fear of crime

The experience of fear is a common aspect of human existence, characterized by a profound emotional response upon perceiving or anticipating a threat or danger directed toward oneself. This experience is universally encountered to some extent, across diverse contexts and circumstances. From a psychological standpoint, fear can either be functional or dysfunctional; it can act as a useful defense mechanism against identified risks or become a trap that diminishes an individual's quality of life (Gray, Jackson, & Farrall, 2011; Lupton & Tulloch, 2003). Fear can be triggered by various stimuli. In the case of fear of crime, the stimulus object is the crime itself or symbols that people associate to crime (K. Ferraro, 1995). However, it is important to consider that fear of crime is not necessarily a response directly proportional to the recorded crime rates in a specific time and place (Rader, 2017). Instead, it reflects individual perceptions of this criminal activity. In the realm of crime discourse, particularly concerning fear of crime, it's essential to recognize its complexity and the absence of a universally accepted definition. The conceptualization of this term, as well as its methodological approach to measuring fear, varies significantly depending on the theoretical frameworks embraced by different scholarly authors (Ditton & Farrall, 2016). Fear of crime is a complex and dynamic concept that is influenced by spatial, temporal, and social contexts (Koskela & Pain, 2000b). While lacking a singular definition, scholars commonly view fear of crime as a tripartite concept. It comprises an emotional aspect (the fear itself), a cognitive dimension (involving risk perception), and a behavioral element encompassing precautionary measures individuals adopt to safeguard themselves against crime and potential threats (Guedes, 2012; Rader, 2017). Also, as summarized by Hale (1996), among the most prevalent theoretical and methodological approaches to understand fear of crime are: i) the vulnerability thesis (see Killias, 1990 and Killias & Clerici, 2000), which suggests that individuals who perceive themselves as incapable of effectively protecting themselves against (the threat of) crime due to certain limitations report higher levels of fear. In this context, due to their increased susceptibility, women, the elderly, and individuals living in poverty are regarded as vulnerable groups; ii) the victimization thesis, proposing that fear of crime arises from the level of criminal activity or exposure to information about such activity within the community. At an individual level, evidence regarding the relationship between fear and victimization is mixed - there is supporting evidence for a positive association between victimization and fear, alongside scientific evidence suggesting the contrary; iii) the environmental aspects thesis, which contends that the social and physical environment in which individuals reside influences reported fear of crime; and finally, iv) the psychological factors thesis, suggesting that for certain individuals, fear of crime is not solely an emotional response to perceived danger but rather a reflection of a generalized unease about the world, stemming from individual personality traits. These approaches have been tested over time and collectively overlook the impact of violence experienced within the private sphere in explaining and understanding female fear. This aspect will be expounded upon in the subsequent section.

3.   The 'paradoxical' nature of women's fear: What is the IPV role?

Despite the crime statistics which suggest women are more at risk at home and from men they know, women are still encouraged to perceive the home (private sphere) as a haven of safety and refuge and to associate the public world where the behaviour of strangers is unpredictable with male violence. Similarly, the social construction of masculinity has on the one hand defined the male stranger as potentially aggressive and powerful, and on the other hand defined the male partner as not only the family provider but also as its protector with conjugal rights. (Valentine, 1992, pp. 23-24)

Research on this topic have been demonstrate that while men have a higher probability of being victims of so-called 'street crimes,' it is women who consistently report higher levels of fear (Chataway & Hart, 2018; Fox, Nobles, & Piquero, 2009; Hale, 1996; May, Rader, & Goodrum, 2010a; Reid & Konrad, 2004; Smith & Torstensson, 1997; Smith, Torstensson, & Johansson, 2001). The disparity between the actual levels of victimization experienced by women and their reported fear of crime is referred to as the fear-victimization paradox.

In response to this paradox, there were simplistic and stereotypical suggestions within 'malestream scholarship'[2] that women's fear is irrational and exaggerated. Nevertheless, this perspective has been progressively discarded in light of compelling scientific evidence to the contrary (Koskela & Pain, 2000a; Logan & Walker, 2021; May, Rader, & Goodrum, 2010b; Rachel Pain, 2001, 2014; Stanko, 1995; Yodanis et al., 2004).

According to Smith and Torstensson, (1997) there are four possible explanations for this paradox, first, the apparent lower victimization rates of women can be misleading, so they are not 'irrationally' fearful of crime; instead, their fear may be attributed to the under-reporting of victimization, which remains 'hidden'; despite the little empirical support, a second explanation given by the authors would be that due cognitive process, women tend to 'generalize' across situations more than men, encompassing temporal, geographic, and types of victimization experiences. This implies that, particularly for women, victimization yields its effects irrespective of its type, the time it occurred, or the place where the victimization took place—whether in private or public spaces. A third possible explanation would be that women tend to generalize across various types of victimization experiences, meaning that *"if a woman experiences burglary in her home, she will be more fearful of assault in her home"* (Smith & Torstensson, 1997, pp. 610).

Agreeing to this approach, the heightened vulnerability of women to various forms of violence not only serves as a warning signal about their own condition but also contributes to a more pronounced perception of risk compared to men. In this context, the authors identified a phenomenon they termed the "double interaction effect" wherein gender and the environment interact to intensify women's perception of risk. This heightened risk, when combined with gender, further exacerbates their fear of crime. Finally, a fourth perspective presented by the authors concerns the male role in understanding female fear. This is because male socialization often instructs boys and young men to neutralize their fears, either by being unable to recognize or admit to this sentiment, which would render them immune or invulnerable, or by overemphasizing their physical abilities to combat threats and maintain their protective role over women. This, in turn, hinders them from acknowledging or revealing their true level of fear.

Also, some evidence suggests an interaction effect between gender, not only in terms of fear but also in relation to risk perception. As women tend to be more sensitive to perceived risk than men, they report higher levels of fear (Warr, 1984). Another important explanation for this gender-fear gap can be found by considering the 'shadow of sexual assault' theory (Ferraro, 1995; Ferraro, 1996). Corresponding to this formulation, women's fear of crime is, in fact, the fear that all offenses can escalate to sexual violence or rape. This theory has been tested, and the findings support the argument (Fisher & Sloan, 2003; Hirtenlehner, Farrall, & Groß, 2023; May, 2001; Mellgren & Ivert, 2019; Özascilar, 2013). Not only in the specific case of sexual violence but also in the context of interpersonal violence, it is known that a woman is more likely to experience these forms of violence at the hands of a man she knows than from a stranger (Koskela & Pain, 2000a; Pain, 1997).

As highlighted by Logan and Walker it poses challenges to omit specific references to such forms of violence in studies that investigate women's fear and safety responses (2021), namely due to the fact that *"fear is one of the primary mechanisms through which abusive partners seek to control their partner—fear of actual or threatened injury, death or other consequences—to the women and her children"* (Signorelli et al., 2022, pp. 2537).

However, a dichotomy persists in studies on the fear of crime, as the concept is predominantly examined and explored as a reaction to public crime, neglecting some specific forms of interpersonal victimization, particularly that which occurs among intimate partners (Broll, 2014; Iglesias, Cardoso, & Sousa, 2020). Nevertheless, there is scientific evidence supporting the positive association between intimate partner victimization and women's insecurity – fear of crime, also impacting their everyday-life routine and quality of life (see Broll, 2014; Madriz, 1997; Stanko, 1993).

CONCLUSION

This chapter endeavored to forge a concise theoretical link between the constructs of fear of crime and intimate partner violence (IPV). It encourages contemplation on the recognition that women's fear of crime necessitates an examination of the extensive spectrum of victimizations to which they are consistently exposed. This exposure is not confined solely to public spaces but is predominantly entrenched within private settings (Hale, 1996).

The analysis of women's fear of crime cannot be detached from the reality of the scale of violence against women. As Lupton and Tulloch (2003, pp. 509), points out, *"Women's fears should not, therefore, be discounted as 'irrational' but rather be viewed as rational responses to lived situations they find frightening"*. In this context, it becomes imperative to transcend the dichotomy that separates public and private spaces.

For women victimized within the realm of intimate relationships, the conventional notion of security undergoes a profound deconstruction, casting its reverberations onto their daily routines, influencing interactions within both public and private spheres, and leaving an indelible mark on their social engagements.

This intricate interplay between personal experiences and spatial dynamics underscores the multifaceted nature of security concerns for women, challenging traditional conceptualizations and necessitating a nuanced understanding that extends beyond conventional boundaries.

REFERENCES

Ackerson, L. K., & Subramanian, S. V. (2016). State Gender Inequality, Socioeconomic Status and Intimate Partner Violence (IPV) in India : A Multilevel Analysis. *The Australian Journal of Social Issues*, 81–103.

Bacchus, L. J., Ranganathan, M., Watts, C., & Devries, K. (2018). Recent intimate partner violence against women and health: A systematic review and meta-analysis of cohort studies. *BMJ Open*, *8*(7), e019995. Advance online publication. doi:10.1136/bmjopen-2017-019995 PMID:30056376

Broll, R. (2014). "Criminals Are Inside of Our Homes": Intimate Partner Violence and Fear of Crime. *Canadian Journal of Criminology and Criminal Justice/La Revue Canadienne de Criminologie et de Justice Pénale, 56*, 1–22. doi:10.3138/cjccj.2011.E24

Campbell, J. C. (2002). Health consequences of intimate partner violence. *Lancet, 359*(9314), 1331–1336. doi:10.1016/S0140-6736(02)08336-8 PMID:11965295

Campbell, J. C., Jones, A. S., Dienemann, J., Kub, J., Schollenberger, J., O'Campo, P. J., Gielen, A. C., & Wynne, C. (2002). Intimate partner violence and physical health consequences. *Archives of Internal Medicine, 162*(10), 1157–1163. doi:10.1001/archinte.162.10.1157 PMID:12020187

Chataway, M. L., & Hart, T. C. (2018). *A Social-Psychological Process of "Fear of Crime" for Men and Women: Revisiting Gender Differences from a New Perspective.* doi:10.1080/15564886.2018.1552221

Crenshaw, K. (1991). Mapping the Margins: Intersectionality, Identity Politics, and Violence against Women of Color. *Stanford Law Review, 43*(6), 1241–1299. doi:10.2307/1229039

Ditton, J., & Farrall, S. (2016). *The fear of crime*. Routledge.

Ferraro, K. (1995). Fear of crime: Interpreting victimization risk. State University of New York Press.

Ferraro, K. (1996). Women's Fear of Victimization: Shadow of Sexual Assault?*. *Social Forces, 75*(2), 667–690. doi:10.2307/2580418

Fisher, B. S., & Sloan, J. J. (2003). Unraveling the fear of victimization among college women: Is the "shadow of sexual assault hypothesis" supported?. *Justice Quarterly, 20*(3), 633–659. https://doi.org/https://doi.org/10.1080/07418820300095641

Fitz-Gibbon, K., Walklate, S., McCulloch, J., & Maher, J. (2018). *Intimate Partner Violence, Risk and Security: Securing Women's Lives in a Global World* (1st ed.). Routledge. doi:10.4324/9781315204765

Fox, K. A., Nobles, M. R., & Piquero, A. R. (2009). Gender, crime victimization and fear of crime. *Security Journal, 22*(1), 24–39. doi:10.1057/sj.2008.13

Fox, V. (2002). Historical Perspectives on Violence Against Women. *Journal of International Women's Studies, 4*(November), 15–34. https://vc.bridgew.edu/jiws/vol4/iss1/2

Gray, E., Jackson, J., & Farrall, S. (2011). Feelings and Functions in the Fear of Crime: Applying a New Approach to Victimisation Insecurity. *British Journal of Criminology, 51*(1), 75–94. doi:10.1093/bjc/azq066

Guedes, I. M. E. de S. (2012). *Sentimento de Insegurança, Personalidade e Emoções Disposicionais: que relações?* Universidade do Porto.

Hale, C. (1996). Fear of Crime: A Review of the Literature. *International Review of Victimology, 4*(2), 79–150. doi:10.1177/026975809600400201

Hirtenlehner, H., Farrall, S., & Groß, E. (2023). Are women of all age groups equally affected by the shadow of sexual assault? *European Journal of Criminology, 20*(3), 834–855. doi:10.1177/14773708231156330

Iglesias, C., Cardoso, C., & Sousa, P. (2020). *Macrosystem and Women's Fear of Crime in Intimate Relations: An Integrated Model.* doi:10.1017/cri.2020.10

Killias, M. (1990). Vulnerability: Towards a better understanding of a key variable in the genesis of fear of crime. *Violence and Victims, 5*(2), 97–108. doi:10.1891/0886-6708.5.2.97 PMID:2278956

Killias, M., & Clerici, C. (2000). Different Measures of Vulnerability in their Relation to Different Dimensions of Fear of Crime. *British Journal of Criminology, 40*(3), 437–450. doi:10.1093/bjc/40.3.437

Koskela, H., & Pain, R. (2000a). *Revisiting fear and place : women's fear of attack and the built environment.* Academic Press.

Koskela, H., & Pain, R. (2000b). Revisiting fear and place: Women's fear of attack and the built environment. *Geoforum, 31*(2), 269–280. doi:10.1016/S0016-7185(99)00033-0

Logan, T. K., & Walker, R. (2021). The Gender Safety Gap: Examining the Impact of Victimization History, Perceived Risk, and Personal Control. *Journal of Interpersonal Violence, 36*(1–2), 603–631. doi:10.1177/0886260517729405 PMID:29294904

Lupton, D., & Tulloch, J. (2003). Theorizing fear of crime: Beyond the rational/irrational opposition. *The British Journal of Sociology, 50*(3), 507–523. doi:10.1111/j.1468-4446.1999.00507.x PMID:15259198

Madriz, E. (1997). Images of Criminals and Victims: a Study on Women's Fear and Social Control. *Sage Publications, 11*(3), 342–356.

May, D. C. (2001). The effect of fear of sexual victimization on adolescent fear of crime. *Sociological Spectrum, 21*(2), 141–174. doi:10.1080/02732170119080

May, D. C., Rader, N. E., & Goodrum, S. (2010). A gendered assessment of the "'threat of victimization'": Examining gender differences in fear of crime, perceived risk, avoidance, and defensive behaviors. *Criminal Justice Review, 35*(2), 159–182. doi:10.1177/0734016809349166

Mellgren, C., & Ivert, A. K. (2019). Is Women's Fear of Crime Fear of Sexual Assault? A Test of the Shadow of Sexual Assault Hypothesis in a Sample of Swedish University Students. *Violence Against Women, 25*(5), 511–527. doi:10.1177/1077801218793226 PMID:30156127

Morrison, A., & Orlando, M. B. (2004). *The costs and impacts of gender-based violence in developing countries*. Academic Press.

Özascilar, M. (2013). Predicting fear of crime: A test of the shadow of sexual assault hypothesis. *International Review of Victimology, 19*(3), 269–284. doi:10.1177/0269758013492754

Pain, R. (1997). Whither women's fear? perceptions of sexual violence in public and private space. *International Review of Victimology, 4*(4), 297–312. doi:10.1177/026975809700400404

Pain, R. (2001). Gender, Race, Age and Fear in the City. *Urban Studies (Edinburgh, Scotland), 38*(5–6), 899–913. doi:10.1080/00420980120046590

Pain, R. (2014). Everyday terrorism Connecting domestic violence and global terrorism. *Progress in Human Geography, 38*(4), 531–550. doi:10.1177/0309132513512231

Rader, N. (2017). *Fear of Crime*. Oxford University Press. doi:10.1093/acrefore/9780190264079.013.10

Rahman, M., Nakamura, K., Seino, K., & Kizuki, M. (2013). Does Gender Inequity Increase the Risk of Intimate Partner Violence among Women? Evidence from a National Bangladeshi Sample. *PLoS One, 8*(12), e82423. doi:10.1371/journal.pone.0082423 PMID:24376536

Reid, L. W., & Konrad, M. (2004). The gender gap in fear: Assessing the interactive effects of gender and perceived risk on fear of crime. *Sociological Spectrum, 24*(4), 399–425. doi:10.1080/02732170490431331

Signorelli, M., Taft, A., Gartland, D., Hooker, L., McKee, C., MacMillan, H., Brown, S., & Hegarty, K. (2022). How Valid is the Question of Fear of a Partner in Identifying Intimate Partner Abuse? A Cross-Sectional Analysis of Four Studies. *Journal of Interpersonal Violence, 37*(5–6), 2535–2556. doi:10.1177/0886260520934439 PMID:32646314

Smith, W. R., & Torstensson, M. (1997). Gender differences in risk perception and neutralizing fear of crime: Toward resolving the paradoxes. *British Journal of Criminology, 37*(4), 608–634. doi:10.1093/oxfordjournals.bjc.a014201

Smith, W. R., Torstensson, M., & Johansson, K. (2001). Perceived Risk and Fear of Crime: Gender Differences in Contextual Sensitivity. *International Review of Victimology, 8*(2), 159–181. doi:10.1177/026975800100800204

Stanko, E. A. (1993). The case of fearful women: Gender, personal safety and fear of crime. *Women & Criminal Justice, 4*(1), 117–135. doi:10.1300/J012v04n01_06

Stanko, E. A. (1995). Women, Crime, and Fear. *The Annals of the American Academy of Political and Social Science, 539*(1), 46–58. doi:10.1177/0002716295539001004

UNFPA. (2023). *Violence against women and girls has invaded all spaces, including virtual ones, and this must end.* Retrieved from https://www.unfpa.org/press/ violence-against-women-and-girls-has-invaded-all-spaces-including-virtual-ones-and-must-end

Walklate, S. (2006). *Criminology: the basics.* Routledge. doi:10.4324/9780203448212

Warr, M. (1984). Fear of Victimization: Why are Women and the Elderly More Affraid? *Social Science Quarterly,* 681–702.

White, S. J., Sin, J., Sweeney, A., Salisbury, T., Wahlich, C., Margarita, C., ... Mantovani, N. (2024). Global Prevalence and Mental Health Outcomes of Intimate Partner Violence Among Women : A Systematic Review and Meta-Analysis. *Trauma, Violence & Abuse, 25*(1), 494–511. doi:10.1177/15248380231155529 PMID:36825800

WHO. (2021). *Violence against women Prevalence Estimates, 2018. Global, regional and national prevalence estimates for intimate partner violence against women and global and regional prevalence estimates for non-partner sexual violence against women.* WHO.

Willie, T. C., & Kershaw, T. S. (2019). An ecological analysis of gender inequality and intimate partner violence in the United States. *Preventive Medicine, 118,* 257–263. doi:10.1016/j.ypmed.2018.10.019 PMID:30393017

Yodanis, C. L., Woodhouse, B. B., Warr, M., Smith, W. R., Torstensson, M., Johansson, K., ... Britton, D. M. (2004). Dangerous Places and the Unpredictable Stranger: Constructions of Fear of Crime. *Social Science Quarterly, 33*(2), 209–226.

ENDNOTES

[1] These forms of violence have a broad impact on women from diverse backgrounds, emphasizing the pivotal role of intersectionality in understanding gender-based

violence (Crenshaw, 1991). Intersectionality acknowledges the multi-layered vulnerabilities and invisibilities experienced by women, stemming not only from their gender but also from intersecting factors that intensify the violent repercussions within patriarchal societies. Factors such as skin color, ethnic origin, and sexual orientation magnify these impacts, illustrating the intricate interplay of various identity markers in shaping experiences of violence.

[2] The expression was original used by Smith et al., 2001:159).

Chapter 8
Intimate Partner Violence in Portugal:
Reflections on the Last Three Decades

Ariana Correia
ⓘD https://orcid.org/0000-0002-8432-6790
University of Maia, Portugal & CIEG (ISCSP-ULisbon), Portugal

Mafalda Ferreira
ⓘD https://orcid.org/0000-0002-9240-0348
CIEG (ISCSP-ULisbon), Portugal

Joana Topa
ⓘD https://orcid.org/0000-0003-0663-973X
University of Maia, Portugal & CIEG (ISCSP-ULisbon), Portugal

Estefânia Gonçalves Silva
University of Maia, Portugal & CIEG (ISCSP-ULisbon), Portugal

Sofia Neves
ⓘD https://orcid.org/0000-0001-6180-4932
University of Maia, Portugal & CIEG (ISCSP-ULisbon), Portugal

ABSTRACT

This chapter presents the main characteristics of intimate partner violence perpetrated in Portugal, discussing policy, legal, and academic advances in the last three decades. Although relevant steps have been taken concerning victims' rights, with children and women benefiting from policies, legislation, mechanisms, and resources, domestic violence and partner homicide rates are still high, suggesting that measures and strategies to prevent and combat this have not been effective. Future directions are discussed regarding cultural, social, and scientific issues.

DOI: 10.4018/979-8-3693-5436-0.ch008

INTRODUCTION

In the last five decades, Portugal has been facing profound social and political transformations (Azambuja et al., 2013; Marques, 2021). The fascist dictatorship led by António de Oliveira Salazar for almost 50 years was particularly harmful to vulnerable social groups, such as women, who were not considered full citizens until 1974, when democracy was instituted. Based on the principle of family preservation, the New State deprived women of certain rights concerning their public life, consigning them to the domestic context, where they should meet their duties, mainly as mothers and wives. Having supported the notion of *female nature* (Chokova, 2013), Salazar's regime emphasized the ideal of women's subordination, which contributed to the legitimation of gender-based discrimination and violence that persists.

Despite the 1976 Constitution recognizing women's liberties and guarantees, and even though Portugal ratified the Convention on the Elimination of All Forms of Discrimination Against Women (United Nations, 1979) in 1980, only in the 1990s did legal and political measures gain prominence in the field of preventing and combating violence against women (Lisboa et al., 2020; Neves & Brasil, 2018). Even though Article 153 of the 1982 Penal Code had already contemplated the maltreatment of partners as a crime in the Portuguese legal system ("Abuse or overload of minors and subordinates or between spouses"), only in 1991 (Law no. 61/91, 13 August) did legislation strengthen the mechanisms for legally protecting women victims of domestic violence. In 2000, the crime became public (Law no. 7/2000, 27 May), which means investigation and prosecution do not depend on the victims' complaints, and in 2007, domestic violence was considered autonomous under Article 152 of the Portuguese Penal Code (Law no. 59/2007) (Duarte, 2012). Following the Law, manifestations of physical, psychological, and sexual violence, including rape, are criminalized, and penalties for domestic violence aggressors range from one to five years of imprisonment. Protective measures for victims are mostly taken in the framework of criminal proceedings.

In 2013, Portugal became the first member state of the Council of Europe to ratify the Council of Europe Convention on Preventing and Combating Violence against Women and Domestic Violence (Istanbul Convention) (Council of Europe, 2011), affirming the commitment taken since the creation of the First National Plan against Domestic Violence (1999–2002)[1]. In 2018, a new governmental approach towards gender equality was taken with the National Strategy for Equality and Non-Discrimination 2018–2030[2], encompassing three action plans that echo the commitments taken in the Istanbul Convention and the Sustainable Development Goals developed by the United Nations in 2015.

In this paper, the Portuguese legal, social, cultural, and historical path against intimate partner violence is analyzed, highlighting its strengths and fragilities, with a focus on the last three decades.

1. PORTUGUESE GOVERNMENT AND LEGAL FOOTPRINT AGAINST DOMESTIC VIOLENCE

Intimate partner violence is a structural phenomenon; it is historically constructed and embedded in conservative and patriarchal cultural values about family and intimacy and constitutes a significant social problem in Portugal. Nevertheless, it's a faltering journey, from an invisible and non-criminal time up to a time of government intersectional coordination.

Still, official data regarding domestic violence, i.e., formal complaints through national authorities, reveals that despite governmental efforts in recent decades, the number of domestic violence complaints, more than 80% due to intimate partner violence, has not decreased in the last 15 years or even increased in some years (e.g., 2022). More than 500 women have died because of intimate partner violence in the past 20 years, and another 500 have managed to survive attempts at femicide (Neves, 2008; Neves & Nogueira, 2010; SSI, 2023); this is a trend that is also evident in other forms of violence against women.

Next, a chronological frame of a historical and legal overview of domestic violence in Portugal is presented, going back to 1974, in a post-revolution country that was shredded by a fascist, conservative, and misogynist dictatorship indoctrinating its beliefs for almost half a century.

1.1. From Invisibility to Public Matter: Slow but Steady Steps

The Carnation Revolution (1974), through which democracy was regained after decades of obscurantism during which women's rights in Portugal stagnated", boosted the start of a course towards gender equality, starting with the approval of the new Constitution in 1976 that recognized women as full citizens. In the following year, the Feminine Condition Commission (Comissão da Condição Feminina – CCF), created before the revolution, was legally recognized, allowing data to be collected from Portuguese women in all dimensions – family, educational, professional, and health - and therefore focusing on and fulfilling their needs (Costa, 2018).

In 1982, domestic violence was criminalized for the first time, addressed in Article 153 of the Penal Code as *Abuse or overload of minors and subordinates or between spouses*, implying a sentence of up to three years' imprisonment. However, for the crime to be acknowledged, and by this, it meant physical and repeated violence, it would have to fulfill the criteria, which means it had to be proven that it was committed due to *selfishness* or *wickedness*. The subjective character of the criteria constrained the effectiveness of the law, leaving it to a conservative legal power that was shy to intervene in domains that were still believed to be mostly private (Neves & Brasil, 2018). Portugal's accession to the European Economic Community in 1986 is considered a significant milestone for affirming and recognizing domestic violence as a social problem (Costa, 2018).

The early nineties, with the approval of Law no. 61/91, marked the beginning of the regulation towards the protection of victims of violence and laid the foundations for combating violence against women. This included a specialized hotline for domestic violence victims, specialized police departments, and specific protection measures for victims, like restraining orders. However, most of these proceedings only came into effect in 1999, a symptom of the gap between what is conceived and what is operationalized. In the same year, the CCF became the Commission for Equality and Women's Rights (Comissão para a Igualdade para os Direitos das Mulheres – CIDM), maintaining its original focus. Also, in Article 152, *selfishness* or *wickedness* were finally removed as criteria for maltreatment, and psychological violence was legally considered, as well as violence perpetrated within non-legal unions, bringing to light a plentiful number of situations. The penal frame went up to five years of imprisonment. It was also in the 1990s that specific social responses appeared, aiming to combat the problem of violence and protect victims through the strength and initiative of women's rights organizations (Tavares, 2011).

In 1997, two years after the Beijing Declaration and Platform for Action highlighted violence against women as an obstacle to the achievement of the objectives of equality, the first national study on violence against women was published, allowing a nationwide vision regarding its extent, and leveraging social concern about the phenomenon. Using data analyses from 1000 inquiries with a heterogeneous profile regarding socioeconomics, age, and area of residence, the report drew attention to the fact that 52.2% of the women surveyed had been victimized at least once, mostly in private contexts (43%) with mainly psychological violence (76.4%), but also physical violence (10.6%) and sexual violence (10.6%). The respondents also reported violence that occurred in public contexts (34%), highlighting sexual violence (50.9%), mostly situations of sexual harassment. This study put the current or previous partner at the center of violence against women, evidencing private contexts as the most harmful and bringing visibility to their structural character and the urgency to broaden political and legal policies (Lourenço et al., 1997).

In 1998 (Law no. 65/98), the transition to a semi-public crime was made, where the Public Prosecution Service gained the possibility to initiate the diligence and procedures when the victim's interests required it, ensuring previously that there was no opposition from the victim (Marques, 2021).

The year 1999 stands as a remarkable year in addressing domestic violence since Decree-Law no. 107/99 created a public network of support houses for victims of violence against women. Also, under the 50th celebration of the Universal Declaration of Human Rights (WHO, 1948), the first National Plan Against Domestic Violence was launched, acting between 1999 and 2002 and aligned with the most recent international guidelines at that time, crossing the millennium and focusing on prevention, intervention, and expanding knowledge about domestic violence. It was followed by four more national plans that established penal, legal, educational, and social measures and respective indicators against domestic violence (1999–2017) (Lisboa et al., 2020).

Simultaneously, in the late 1990s, intervention programs with the perpetrators of domestic violence emerged at the Universities of Porto and Minho as a complement to victim support, aiming at their protection and reducing the incidence and high rates of recidivism of the crime of domestic violence (Manita, 2008). Also created were the Programme for Domestic Violence Offenders (PAVD) and CONTIGO Programme promoted by the DGRSP, addressed to defendants or convicted offenders of domestic violence committed against spouse, companion, or girlfriend that have as their main objectives: the acquisition of skills and the change of attitudes; the awareness and assumption of responsibility for the violent behavior; and the use of alternative strategies, promoting the reduction of recidivism (DGRSP, 2022).

1.2. The 2000s: The Road to Istanbul

Although it has been 18 years since domestic violence was criminalized (1982) – under the designation of *abuse or overload of minors and subordinates or between spouses* – only in the year 2000 (Law no. 7/2000) did the crime assume a public nature, still in effect to this day. This milestone embodies a major shift, underscoring this crime as a social and political matter, defying the private domain the crime was consigned to, and relieving the pressure from the victim, with whom until that moment the responsibility lay to initiate the legal process or not, apart from some exceptions (Marques, 2021).

Another major change took place seven years later, in 2007, when Law no. 59/2007 singled out domestic violence as a specific type of crime. It no longer required a continuous character to be considered domestic violence, nor did the cohabitation between the parties, whether in an actual or previous intimate relationship, broaden the scope of the legal intervention (Costa, 2018).

In an extension of the first National Survey on Violence against Women (Lourenço et al., 1997), another study was carried out in 2009, reporting that 38% of women aged 18 or older, in an intimate relationship, had been subject to acts of physical, psychological, and/or sexual violence. Also, about one in three women, aged 18 or over, reported being a victim, either in the same or in the previous year, of at least one episode of violence. Social discrimination (52.9%), physical violence (22.6%), and sexual violence (19.1%) are the most prevalent forms of violence against women, with psychological violence (53.9%) coming in second. The aggressor's feelings of possession, jealousy, and male cultural values concerning gender inequality were the most frequent reasons pointed out by victims to explain intimate partner violence. This study underpins the home as the most dangerous place for women (Lisboa et al., 2009).

Law no. 112/2009 from September 16, the so-called Law of Domestic Violence, updated in 2020, established the applicable legal regime towards the prevention of domestic violence and the protection and assistance of its victims, configuring a broader and holistic legal framework in support and protection of domestic violence victims. This law brought the *Status of Victim*, given by the judicial authorities or the competent authorities, when the crime of domestic violence is reported and provided the technical means to improve the safety of victims; it included teleassistance services; it provided protection and coercion measures within 72 hours after the formal report; it created urgent measures to be applied within 48 hours after the indictment of the perpetrator; it recognized the urgent nature of the domestic violence process, with detention for perpetrators caught in flagrante delicto, risk assessment and safety plans; it reinforced the necessity for more attending rooms; and it required the mandatory communication of data (victim status and final decisions in criminal cases), integrating knowledge and intervention on the phenomenon (Machado et al., 2021).

Law no. 26/2010 changed the scope of the crime of domestic violence, assuming its classification within violent criminality. The public prosecutor is now obliged to inform the victims about compensation, immediate financial support, and the network of support to which victims of the crime can apply for assistance.

In 2013, Portugal became the first European Union country to ratify the Council of Europe Convention on Preventing and Combating Violence against Women and Domestic Violence, commonly referred to as the Istanbul Convention (Council of Europe, 2011). It was described as a new landmark treaty for the Council of Europe and confers minimum standards in the operationalization of responses by each of the member states to preventing and eradicating gender-based violence in all its forms, recognizing that (Article 3):

"(a) violence against women is understood as a violation of human rights and a form of discrimination against women and shall mean all acts of gender-based violence that result in, or are likely to result in, physical, sexual, psychological, or economic harm or suffering to women, including threats of such acts, coercion, or arbitrary deprivation of liberty, whether occurring in public or private life".

"(b) domestic violence' shall mean all acts of physical, sexual, psychological, or economic violence that occur within the family or domestic unit or between former or current spouses or partners, whether the perpetrator shares or has shared the same residence with the victim".

The Fifth National Plan, in effect between 2014 and 2017[3], considered the guidelines from the Istanbul Convention for the National Plan for Domestic and Gender Violence, broadening the scope of action with goals regarding female genital mutilation or sexual harassment and pointing out the urgency of collecting and sharing standardized data to reveal the extent of the phenomenon.

Following previous commitments, in 2018 a new approach was initiated in public policies for equality and non-discrimination between men and women, with approval of the National Strategy for Equality and Non-Discrimination 2018–2030 – "Portugal + Equal"[4]. This is a structure of three action plans that define axes and strategic objectives until 2030: the Action Plan for Equality between Women and Men (PAIMH); the Action Plan to Combat Discrimination Based on Sexual Orientation, Gender Identity and Expression, and Sexual Characteristics (PAOIEC) and the Action Plan to Prevent and Combat Violence against Women and Domestic Violence (PAVMVD).

At this time, all the member states ratifying the Istanbul Convention would have to undertake legal, political, and social changes on a national level. To be in keeping with the principles of the Convention, this implementation is periodically evaluated through a monitoring mechanism – the Group of Independent Experts on Action against Violence against Women and Domestic Violence (GREVIO), composed of 10 independent, impartial experts appointed due to their recognized expertise in the fields of human rights, gender equality, violence against women, and/or assistance to and protection of victims. The GREVIO report on the Portuguese implementation of the Istanbul Convention (Council of Europe, 2019) highlights the commitment by national authorities over the years to tackling violence against women and, simultaneously, the effort to promote gender equality. It points out the fact that the scope of public policies was widened beyond domestic violence, criminalizing other forms of violence against women with a clear gendered connotation, such as stalking, female genital mutilation, and forced marriage. However, it stressed the low levels of reporting to authorities, which means the official data is just a portion of the extent of domestic violence. At the operational level, the report underlines the impact of Law no. 112/2009 on domestic violence, which codifies the duty of cooperation and communication between social services, child protection services, law enforcement agencies, and health officials, and points out the need to improve this cooperation and communication, especially with local authorities. It also highlights the need to improve inter-ministerial coordination and interagency cooperation to ensure equal access to support and protect all victims. It further underlines the need for Portugal to continue to approach all forms of violence holistically, concerning all forms of gender-based violence, gender equality, and LGBTIQ+ rights (Council of Europe, 2019).

There are three different levels of responders to domestic violence who may be asked for help and advice in specific circumstances by the victims. The first-level responders are responsible for the direct and immediate response to occurrences of domestic violence, namely the Portuguese National Guard (GNR), a group that specializes in human resources for prevention, investigation, and monitoring of situations of violence against women, children, and other specific groups of victims (IAVE Project). In Portugal, there are 24 IAVEs and 350 teams operating in a logic of proximity policing; the Portuguese Public Security Police (PSP) are the traditional service at the police station and are part of the Model of Proximity Policing: the Victim Information and Assistance Office (GAIV), which allows more direct liaison between the police and the victim; the Judiciary Police (PJ; only in cases of homicide); and the Public Prosecution Service (PPS). In this service, under the protocol between the Ministry of Justice (MJ) and the Attorney General's Office (PGR), the Victims of Gender Violence Assistance Offices (GAV) were created, including victim support technicians from NGOs. Currently, there are six GAVs. Despite not having an intervention and not being mobilized in domestic violence situations, the second level is services to which the victims appeal for help or assistance, namely: local police service desks in central hospitals; hospitals; health centers; the National Network of Support to Victims of Domestic Violence (RNAVVD); the CPCJ local bureaus (state local Commissions for the Protection of Children and Young Persons); and the Directorate-General of Reintegration and Prison Services. Finally, the third-level responders provide specialized responses to help domestic violence victims with specific needs, for example, social security, employment agencies, and/or education (Machado et al., 2021).

In March 2019, the Portuguese government created the Multidisciplinary Technical Commission for the Improvement of the Prevention and Combat of Domestic Violence (CTM). This commission, according to Council of Ministers Resolution no. 139/2019[5], produced a report with several recommendations on data and statistical indicators. Following this report, a governmental order was approved, defining the priority actions to be carried out as well as other measures to be taken in areas such as health, education, and social security. Among the measures determined, the following should be underlined: a) the implementation of a database on violence against women and domestic violence; b) the creation of a joint training plan for professionals regarding violence against women and domestic violence; and c) a guide of functional procedures to be followed within 72 hours after the report to Law Enforcement Authorities.

In 2021, the amendments to the Penal Code and the Domestic Violence Act (Law no. 57/2021) introduced economic/patrimonial violence in the legal definitions of domestic violence and considered that children who are dependent on the perpetrator or another victim of domestic violence are also considered victims of domestic violence, even if they do not cohabitate with the perpetrator (Machado et al., 2021).

With its current national strategy, Portugal goes far beyond legislative instruments, extending the intervention to multiple dimensions. The country has 39 shelters, with 661 places for women and six for men, and 26 emergency shelters, which have 176 places for women and four for men. There are 133 structures registered in the national network of support for victims of domestic violence (Comissão para a Cidadania e Igualdade de Género, n.d.).

The political and legal changes from recent decades have been leveraged by academic research, whose data consistently present domestic and gender-based violence as a public health matter proportionate to an epidemic (United Nations Women, 2021).

1.3. Domestic Violence Through an Academic Lens

Violence against women gained greater awareness through the feminist movements of the 1960s, being defined as any act of violence, including threats, coercion, or other arbitrary deprivation of liberty that is based on gender, that results in or may result in harm or suffering of a physical, sexual, or psychological nature, and that occurs in public or private life (Neves & Nogueira, 2005).

Psychological violence is intended to damage the victim's identity and self-esteem using humiliation, insults, shouting, threats, contempt, or coercion (Day et al., 2003) and is frequently the most harmful typology of violence (Dias, 2005). Physical violence occurs through any act or intention that aims to cause physical injury to the victim and can be perpetrated through physical force or other instruments or weapons (Day et al., 2003).

Sexual violence occurs when any behavior of a sexual nature is forced on the victim against their will, from psychological threats to the use of physical force, weapons, or drugs, exposure to pornographic content, or prostitution (Day et al., 2003; Manita, 2007). Social violence emerges as a strategy of the aggressor to remove the victim from their social support network, placing them in places of great vulnerability, and, finally, economic violence results from the victim's restricted access to primary goods or money, controlling their expenses or even the possibility of employment (Koss, 1990). These typologies, which frequently co-occur, are present in a cyclical pattern and tend to escalate potentially into femicide, recognized as the most extreme form of gender-based violence (Russell, 1976).

As stated in an EU-wide survey (FRA, 2014), in Portugal, 19% of women have been victims of domestic violence, and 93% of every Portuguese woman surveyed considered that violence against women is either very common or common in the country.

According to a study by the European Institute for Gender Equality (2022), gender-based violence costs the EU EUR 366 billion annually, demonstrating that women from all EU member states continue to experience discrimination, sexual abuse, harassment, poor working conditions, rape, and, in some extreme cases, death. In 2020, 775 women died because of homicide by a family member or intimate partner in the 17 EU member states, which means that on average, more than two women died every day in those member states at the hands of a family member or intimate partner. Across the EU, almost half of women (44%) have suffered psychological violence from a partner in their lifetime (EIGE, 2022).

Recent Portuguese scientific literature has focused on many topics about this scourge. A study carried out by Carmona-Torres et al. in 2017 found that abuse against vulnerable adults within the family and community environment in the Azores islands was identified in 24.5% of the participants, and psychological abuse was the most common, being mostly perpetrated by their children. Some risk factors for the occurrence of domestic violence were identified, such as being a woman and belonging to a dysfunctional family, although the high level of domestic violence against the elderly in the Azores islands is like in continental Portugal. On the other hand, Tomás et al. (2018) showed that although domestic violence has become a more noticeable phenomenon in the academic and social world, children have so far been considered peripheral victims of domestic violence compared to adults, especially women. Thus, to guarantee justice for children, their specific needs must be considered and differentiated from those of adult victims, combating domestic violence from an inclusive perspective.

Regarding the authorities, in 2018, Sani and Carvalho developed a mixed exploratory study based on the analysis of reports received by the Public Security Police (PSP) for domestic violence and news reports during the year 2010 in Portugal. To determine whether children were directly or indirectly involved in these situations, the researchers found that 45% of the 167 analyzed reports indicated that there were children in these families and that in 29% of the situations, these children witnessed violence. Most reports (141) also revealed that these children suffered direct physical and psychological violence (e.g., manipulation). These data evidence the need for police officers to reinforce their training on children at risk. Also in 2018, Sani et al. studied the beliefs of Portuguese police officers regarding domestic violence against women to understand how their beliefs influenced their actions. The sample consisted of 453 police officers from the Public Security Police of Porto, Portugal. Two instruments were administered (Marital Violence Beliefs Scale and Intervention Scale), and the results show disagreement regarding legitimizing myths related to intimate partner violence; most participants show that they tend to perform all necessary procedures unconditionally, especially when faced with physical violence situations. There is, in fact, a correlation between higher levels of legitimizing beliefs towards marital violence and a more affected police action, which means that there is an association between both dimensions.

In the same year, Morais-Gonçalves et al. (2018) administered the Risk Monitoring Grid in Cases of Recidivism of Victims of Domestic Violence to analyze the presence of risk factors that increase recurrence and prevent victims from ending the cycle of violence. According to the analysis of data from the Portuguese National Institute of Forensic Medicine and Sciences (INMLCF), between 2012 and 2017, 88.4% of female victims returned to their abusers. Results evidence the need for continuous and dynamic monitoring and risk assessment to prevent violence.

Considering protective measures for victims, a study by Rola and Oliveira (2019) focused on the necessary changes to Law no. 130/2015 that attribute a special statute to all victims of domestic violence, especially children living in a household context where violence is taking place; this is not only a legal requirement but also a social and ethical imperative. This is because, according to the Istanbul Convention, which states that it is necessary to recognize that children are victims of domestic violence, particularly as witnesses of violence in the family, the protection of criminal proceedings and all victims is decisive. This study contributes to altering the law about children when they live in these contexts or witness them, something that will allow an understanding not only of the aggressions that children experience but also all the violence that comes with experience in this context. This is an opportunity to promote a holistic approach to the protection of children, even though it does not always occur, as shown by a qualitative study (Sani & Correia, 2019) focused on the perspectives and interventions of 11 technicians from nine different domestic violence shelters in Portugal regarding children that were temporarily in domestic violence shelters. Data collection from the intentional sample consisted of a structured interview, and the results showed that the priorities of their interventions are mainly related to the mothers of these children, namely by training their educational practices, parental skills, rules, routines, and attachment towards their children.

Considering the current importance of media and social networks, a study developed by Nogueira et al. (2020) showed that publicity is one of the most controversial means of social communication of the century. The government, security forces, or NGOs that assist these victims are primarily responsible for carrying out these campaigns, according to this group of researchers who focused on the discourse analysis of publicity campaigns intended to combat domestic violence in Portugal. However, other private companies (e.g., fashion, communication, entertainment, TV) have started to focus on this topic since feminist movements are increasingly visible in the media. In research aiming to characterize intimate partner femicide in Portugal, starting from media narrative analysis published in the national newspaper between the years 2000 and 2017, it was highlighted that the national top-selling newspaper tends to narrate the crimes as passionate and unpredictable ones, associated with jealousy and the non-acceptance of the couple's separation, appealing to parallel narratives that exonerate these crimes. These sensationalist narratives, which frame gender-based crimes within individual and/or interpersonal attributions, promote a skewed social construction of intimate partner femicide, with effects not only on public opinion but on the victims of intimate partner violence and offenders (Correia & Neves, 2021). Also, while trying to understand the dialectic between domestic violence and social networks, Poiares (2020) focused on the possibility of the crime of domestic violence being related to other types of crime such as the wanton destruction of private life (Article 192 of the Portuguese Penal Code) or illegal photographs and recordings (Article 199). In these scenarios, the agent must be punished for the most serious crime committed since there is a subsidiary relationship between these legal types.

Ferreira (2020) looked at the results of a national policy that aimed to stop intimate partner violence, provide special protection, and offer support to victims. They discovered that there was an increase in the prosecution and punishment of offenders, but failures were found when looking at the policy's ability to reduce the prevalence of this social scourge.

Between April and October 2020, Gama et al. (2021) conducted an online survey in Portugal aiming to collect data about the experience of domestic violence and help-seeking during the pandemic. A total of 1062 respondents answered this survey, and 13.7% reported having suffered domestic violence during the pandemic, including psychological (13%), sexual (1%), and physical violence (0.9%).

In 2021, Martins et al. discussed the importance of using electronic surveillance in Portugal as a strategic element for criminal policy and a reaction to provide alternative tools of social control that not only support the development of cyber-justice but also respond to a need when faced with overcrowded prisons. However, the use of this type of technology may raise some ethical implications since it is crucial to ensure that it does not violate the principle of human dignity or cause any damage to the individual.

In the same year, judicial decisions from the Courts of Appeal of Lisbon and Porto about the crime of rape perpetrated against female victims were analyzed to ascertain whether the actions of Portuguese jurisprudence maintain or construct gender hierarchies. No reproduction or creation of stereotypes was perceived in the cases studied (Sousa et al., 2021).

To collect the beliefs and practices of first-line professionals that intervene in domestic violence situations, 25 Portuguese professionals were interviewed (e.g., authorities, criminal investigators, domestic violence intervention specialists, legal medical practitioners), concretely 11 females and 14 males, with an average age of 42 years (SD = 7.05). A thematic discourse analysis was carried out, through which the inefficiency of the system emerged. Here, the lack of specialized training in domestic violence, especially in conducting and scoring risk assessment scales and their consequent management, was pointed out as a serious constraint with obvious impacts. Also, domestic violence specialists in the intervention are alert to the fact that risk assessment is a dynamic process and, therefore, artificial, and flexible and that it is urgent not to depend only on this information but to have cooperation and communication between all institutions that intervene in domestic violence, whether with victims and/or perpetrators. This intervention requires robust involvement and coordination by all actors.

Therefore, GREVIO (2019) emphasizes the importance of a detached intervention with no effective results, which means there is a higher risk of revictimization. As major constraints in domestic violence intervention, the study specifically points out poor risk monitoring, victim-blaming beliefs by professionals, subjective proceedings, and a focus on crime evidence. Also, the gap between the written law and its appliance and the *ad eternum* legal and justice proceedings is frequently non-compatible with the victim's protection or safety (Correia, 2021).

1.4. Statistical Evidence

According to the 2022 Annual Statistics Report of the Portuguese Association for Victim Support (APAV), the crime of domestic violence constituted 77.4% of the crimes reported to this institution. 77.7% of victims who contacted them were Portuguese females with an average age of 40, 7.3% of whom had attended higher education. The relationship of the victims with the perpetrators of the crime is intimate (e.g., spouse or ex-spouse, boyfriend/girlfriend, or ex-boyfriend/girlfriend) in 1% of the situations. Victimization was reiterated in 49.1% of cases, lasting approximately between two and three years, and occurred in 54.1% of situations in the common residence of the aggressor and the victim. Of all the situations reported to the Portuguese Association for Victim Support, 49.2% resulted in a formal complaint to the competent authorities, an increase in percentage compared to the previous year (APAV, 2023).

In the 2022 Annual Internal Security Report, the crime of domestic violence in the context of intimacy continues to be the most reported type of crime in Portugal, with an increase of 15% compared to the previous year and 86% of the reports due to intimate partner violence, with 72.4% of the victims being female, and 80.2% of the perpetrator's male (SSI, 2023). However, within its 30 488 reports, in 63.7% (22711) charges were archived and, following only 14% (5028) of the reports, charges were deduced. In 5.9% (5774) of the situations, charges were provisionally suspended, a pre-sentence deal that prevents criminal proceedings to lead to court and, frequently leads to the process archive. Now, it becomes very clear that, even though the portuguese legal system had been trying to embrace international guidelines regarding gender-based violence (e.g., CEDAW, Istanbul Convention, United Nations 2030 Agenda), the outcome does not fulfill the main goal, being decreasing gender-based violence numbers, including intimate gender-based violence.

Dating violence, frequently related to teens but also young adults (e.g., college students), presents as a risk factor for intimate violence in adulthood, with substantial, long-term consequences, including low academic achievement, depression, suicidal ideation, substance use disorders, and violence among intimate partners in adulthood (Vives-Cases et al., 2021). The likelihood of dating violence seems higher in youngsters who are migrants or who have foreign parents and/or those who have prior experiences of violence in childhood and who have been victims of bullying and cyberbullying, showing the urgency of an intersectional lens in dealing with this phenomenon (Vives-Cases, 2021).

Focusing on dating violence among college students, one earlier study found that approximately 21% of all college students had experienced violence in their intimate relationships, and 61% reported that they knew someone who had been personally affected by dating violence (Makepeace, 1981). Later studies consistently showed college students as being vulnerable to dating violence due to the social environment in which they live and interact with other students (Smith et al., 2017). The Portuguese National Study on Dating Violence Amongst College Students, with a sample of 4696 students, 81.9% girls, 17.8% boys, and 0.3% non-binary participants, mainly heterosexual (86.5%), reported that half of the participants (53.7) had experienced at least one form of dating violence, and 34% admitted to having been abusive within an actual or past dating relationship, with psychological victimization standing out (51.2%), but also sexual victimization, with 14.8% of the girls having experienced non-consensual sexual behavior (Neves et al., 2023). One of the main findings of this study was a statistical association between victimization and perpetration and conservative gender beliefs and, consequently, the legitimization and normalization of these practices (Neves et al., 2023).

Because it is widely recognized that domestic violence victims are more vulnerable to femicide, it is imperative to raise the visibility of this crime. So, according to the Global Study on Homicide, homicides perpetrated by partners or family members are increasing, representing 57% of female homicide victims in 2017, which is why the house is still the most lethal place for women because of inequalities and the perpetuation of gender stereotypes (UNODC, 2019).

According to (non-official) data from 2004–2018, collected by the Portuguese Observatory of Murdered Women, an initiative led by the non-governmental organization UMAR, more than 500 women were killed by their partners or ex-partners, and more than 400 suffered a femicide attempt with 500 associated victims, namely their children. Also, 419 children were orphaned due to the femicide and suicide of the perpetrator or imprisonment (OMA, 2004–2019). Since 2019, according to indications from GREVIO and CTM, reports of domestic violence and intimate partner homicides (including femicides) are formally available online in a governmental database, although little information is available except the gender of the victims and perpetrators. According to these data, the number of femicides dropped during the pandemic context but quickly increased by 1/3 in 2022. The consistently high rate of femicide, that pervades the past decades of legal adjustments, may be related to an obvious unconformity between the victim's needs, i.e., protection and justice, and what the legal system provides, i.e., ¾ of the domestic violence reports to authorities that leads to nowhere, even amplifying the victims' vulnerabilities and disbelief in the legal system.

Adding to the constrains on (tertiary) intervention with this phenomenon, it should be highlighted the inefficiency of primary intervention, whereas gender equality, citizenship and human rights are taught in a detached, unarticulated and intermittently way, consequently being unproductive to youngsters (Neves et al., 2023).

These data show the urgency of preventing and combating domestic violence, namely through early education for gender equality and through the implementation of adequate support for all victims and punishment for offenders.

CONCLUSION

In the last century, Portugal was locked in a fascist dictatorship (the New State) for almost 50 years, ruled on the principle of family preservation. Using this norm, the New State disenfranchised women from certain rights concerning their public life, allowing them to exist only in the domestic context. Having supported the notion of female nature (Chokova, 2013), the regime emphasized the ideal of women's subordination, which contributed to the legitimation of gender-based discrimination and, consequently, the naturalization of violence against women and other vulnerable social groups (e.g., LGBT) that were impeded from living according to their true selves, being forced either to escape or to perform a cis and heteronormative life.

After the 1974 revolution, women's rights started to settle progressively and made clear advances throughout the 1980s, with two milestones: the Portuguese ratification of the Convention on the Elimination of All Forms of Discrimination Against Women (United Nations, 1979) in 1980 and the criminalization of domestic violence in 1982, back then legally recognized as *Abuse or overload of minors and subordinates or between spouses* (Article no. 153 of the Portuguese Penal Code).

Also, the approval of a new constitution passed in 1986 and the revision of the Penal Code made a major impact on all citizens, promoting their rights and guarantees, but especially women.

As a new democracy, Portugal had been adjusting to the new times, focusing on social, political, and legal development, with women's rights matters taking off in the nineties, especially concerning domestic violence. In 1991 (Law no. 112/2009), *selfishness* or *wickedness* was finally removed as criteria for maltreatment, and psychological violence is legally considered, as well as violence perpetrated within non-legal unions, bringing many situations to light. Despite several proceedings only coming into effect in 1999, with a gap between theory and practice present to this day, the nineties unveiled a social problem by making scientific data available with the first national study on violence against women. This was essential in addressing the phenomenon, adding to the recent Beijing Declaration and Platform for Action, adopted by 189 member states, including Portugal, in 1995.

After 18 years of criminalization of domestic violence, the crime assumed a public nature and was autonomized in 2007; it remains so to this day. Law no. 112/2009, the so-called Law of Domestic Violence, brought remarkable changes regarding the protection of and assistance for victims, and the ratification of the Istanbul Convention symbolized a new era in addressing violence against women, now formally and undoubtedly conceptualized as gender-based violence, underpinning an intersectional matrix to public policies regarding this matter.

However, after three decades of democracy, it is crucial to make a critical reflection on this journey and its ups and downs and address its effectiveness. The number of official reports on domestic violence would be expected to have dropped significantly, yet in fact, in 2022 there was an increase, reaching 30,000 annual reports after three years of decrease, most probably related to lockdowns in 2020 and 2021 (Berniell & Facchini, 2021). Nevertheless, between 2009 and 2018, the number of reports remained consistently above 30,000 annually, and before, there was a massive gap, with the annual reports being as low as 6,958 in the year 2000 and, until 2006, never above 11,000 official reports. Although this remarkable rise from 2009 until 2018 can plausibly be related to Law no. 61/91, which brought unreported situations to light, the femicide rate remains disturbingly high, with more than 500 women killed by their partners or ex-partners and more than 400 suffering a femicide attempt. Data (non-official) is only available from 2004 (from the Women Killed Observatory managed by the NGO UMAR) to 2018, and since 2019, domestic violence reports and intimate partner homicides (including femicides) are formally available according to indications from GREVIO (SSI, 1999–2023; OMA, 2004–2019) On the other hand, domestic violence remains an underreported crime rooted in fear of retaliation and social judgment. Awareness-raising efforts are essential to tackle the widespread problem of underreporting.

The reasons that underlie these constraints were partly pointed out by GREVIO (Council of Europe, 2019), specifically conservative social beliefs held by professionals that intervene with victims, which address individual or interpersonal causes of violence: these feed a victim-blaming approach that distorts the system and brings it into disbelief, adding vulnerabilities to these victims. Professional training on domestic violence, which could be a way to deconstruct these myths, is lacking, contributing to this circle of revictimization and inoperative practices. Furthermore, comprehensive training of law enforcement authorities is essential to ensure the effectiveness of legal action. Also, the lack of coordination, liaison, and communication between justice, health, and social security should be pointed out; this adds to a system of justice that is evidence-based and amplifies the probability of non-collaboration from the victim. Also, the combination of the lack of accountability in this regard, which means the different sectors frequently pass responsibilities onto the others, as well as the legal and justice proceedings being highly bureaucratic, leads to the maintenance of a high number of reports (excluding the ones that remain uncounted) and the lack of protection of these victims, which facilitates femicide (Council of Europe, 2019; Gama et al., 2021; Neves & Correia, 2022; Martins et al., 2021). In fact, knowing the number of reports that remain is insufficient to understand and monitor the evolution of the phenomenon, because do these reports already represent most cases? To know this dimension of the phenomenon and understanding if there are variations in the characteristics of the acts perpetrated is essential if effective measures are to be taken to combat this scourge. In this sense, it is also important to know the characteristics of the perpetrators of violence and in what contexts these acts occur, as well as to know the risk that victims run and the type of behavior they adopt.

The measures adopted in the National Plans, although subject to evaluation, still need to be analyzed in terms of their effects and effectiveness, particularly with regard to the actions of the justice system and other structures for combating, protecting and preventing. At this level, the knowledge about the effectiveness of the action and coordination of the various state bodies and other countries is still scarce.

It is also crucial to address the primary prevention of gender equality and citizenship in a cross-curricular way, promoting a bystander approach that brings awareness to the importance of the report, which is also pointed out as a shortcoming in implementation (Council of Europe, 2019). The existing prevention and intervention programmes, while important, are still weak, mainly because they are not regulated and properly coordinated, and are insufficient to have an impact on reducing indicators of victimization and perpetration. Treatment programmes available for perpetrators of violence are still scarce in the country and should promote a culture of accountability that preserves the deterrent function of sentences. Prevention should focus on eradicating social tolerance to the various manifestations of violence, raise awareness of its impacts and promote a culture of non-violence, human rights, equality, and non-discrimination.

Decentralize support services for victims of domestic violence. Currently concentrated in major cities and district capitals, these services need to be extended to rural areas where a significant proportion of vulnerable women, especially the elderly, remain unprotected.

While GREVIO' acknowledge the merits of Portugal's main legislation on domestic violence, namely Law No. 112/2009, which makes domestic violence a public crime, GREVIO's report highlights some shortcomings in the implementation of this law. One of these is the subsidiary nature of domestic violence compared to more serious crimes: when a more serious crime, i.e., rape, is committed in the context of an intimate relationship, legal action is usually taken for the more serious crime, a practice that camouflages the gender dimension of domestic violence. However, despite the importance of decentralization, authorities and support services for these victims must coordinate with each other, speeding up processes and avoiding secondary victimization.

Finally, the results of public policies will only be lasting and impactful if we know the perception and experience of victims, men and women, in relation to security and the measures made available. These policies must approach all forms of violence comprehensively, in terms of prevention, protection and legal action, thus contributing to increasing complaint rates among authorities.

Overall, the importance that various social actors (academics, NGOs, and activists) assume for gender equality and tackling and preventing domestic and gender-based violence cannot be overlooked. However, it is paramount to guarantee that the practice is consistent with the theory in a society that has been under a strictly patriarchal dictatorship. There continue to be glimpses of this in everyday life, from conservative beliefs to victim-blaming approaches to individual or interpersonal attributions to gender-based crimes such as honor or jealousy, skewing all the efforts made in the last three decades (Correia & Neves, 2021; Neves, 2016).

REFERENCES

APAV (2023). *Estatísticas APAV - Relatório Anual 2022*. Associação Portuguesa de Apoio à Vítima.

Azambuja, M., Nogueira, C., Neves, S., & Oliveira, J. (2013). Gender Violence in Portugal: Discourses, Knowledge, and Practices. *Indian Journal of Gender Studies*, *20*(1), 31–50. doi:10.1177/0971521512465935

Berniell, I., & Facchini, G. (2021). COVID-19 lockdown and domestic violence: Evidence from internet-search behavior in 11 countries. *European Economic Review, 136*, 103775. doi:10.1016/j.euroecorev.2021.103775 PMID:35721306

Carmona-TorresJ.Carvalhal-SilvaR. M.Viera-MendesM. H.Recio-AndradeB. GoergenT.Rodríguez-BorregoM. A. (2017). Elder abuse within the family environment in the Azores Islands. *Revista Latino-Americana de Enfermagem, 25*. https://doi.org/ doi:10.1590/1518-8345.1871.2932

Chokova, M., Ward, D., & Teixeira, A. C. (2013). *The Female Condition During Mussolini's and Salazar's Regimes.* https://repository.wellesley.edu/object/ir409

Correia, A., & Neves, S. (2021). Narrativas mediáticas sobre o femicídio na intimidade em Portugal - Implicações e desafios. *Media & Jornalismo, 21*(39), 229–245. doi:10.14195/2183-5462_39_12

Costa, D. (2018). A evolução de políticas públicas em Portugal na área da Violência Doméstica. In I. Dias (Ed.), *Violência Doméstica e de Género: uma abordagem multidisciplinar* (pp. 123–156). Pactor.

Council of Europe. (2011). *Council of Europe Convention on preventing and combating violence against women and domestic violence.* https://rm.coe.int/168008482e

Council of Europe. (2019). GREVIO baseline evaluation report: Portugal. Strasbourg: Secretariat of the monitoring mechanism of the Council of Europe Convention on Preventing and Combating Violence against Women and Domestic Violence, Council of Europe.

DayV.TellesL.ZorattoP.AzambujaM.MachadoD.SilveiraM.DebiaggiM.ReisM. CardosoR.BlankP. (2003). Violência doméstica e suas diferentes manifestações. *Revista de Psiquiatria do Rio Grande do Sul, 25*(1). https://doi.org/ doi:10.1590/ S0101-81082003000400003

Dias, I. (2005). *Violência na Família: Uma abordagem sociológica.* Edições Afrontamento.

Direção Geral de Reinserção e Serviços Prisionais (DGRSP). (2022). *Programas específicos de reabilitação.* https://dgrsp.justica.gov.pt/Justi%C3%A7a-de-adultos/ Penas-e-medidas-privativas-de-liberdade/Programas-e-projetos/Programas-espec%C3%ADficos-de-reabilita%C3%A7%C3%A3o#MedidasAlternativasPriso

European Institute for Gender Equality. (2022). *Pandemic and Care.* European Institute for Gender Equality.

European Union Agency for Fundamental Rights (FRA) (2014). *Violence against women: an EU-wide survey*. Luxemburg: Publication Office of the European Union.

Ferreira, E. (2020). Intimate Partner Violence - findings and lessons from a national deterrence policy. *European Law Enforcement Research Bulletin, 20.*

Gama, A., Pedro, A. R., Carvalho, M. J., Guerreiro, A., Duarte, V., Quintas, J., Matias, A., Keygnaertg, I., & Dias, S. (2021). Domestic Violence during the COVID-19 Pandemic in Portugal. *Portuguese Journal of Public Health*, *38*(1, Suppl. 1), 32–40. doi:10.1159/000514341

Lisboa, M., Barroso, Z., Patrício, J., & Leandro, A. (2009a). *Violência e género – Inquérito nacional sobre a violência exercida contra mulheres e homens*. Comissão para a Cidadania e Igualdade de Género.

Lisboa, M., Barroso, Z., Patrício, J., Leandro, A. (2009b). *Inquérito Nacional sobre a Violência Exercida contra Mulheres e Homens*. Comissão para a Cidadania e Igualdade de Género.

Lisboa, M., Cerejo, D., & Brasil, E. (2020). De onde vimos e para onde vamos? Conhecimento e políticas públicas em Portugal sobre a violência doméstica, nas últimas três décadas. In S. Neves (Coord.), Violências de Género na Intimidade (pp. 13–39). Edições ISMAI.

Lourenço, N., Gama Lisboa, M., & Pais, E. (1997). *Violência contra as mulheres*. Comissão para a Igualdade e para os Direitos das Mulheres.

Machado, P., Pais, L. G., Felgueiras, S., & Quaresma, C. (2021). Frontline Response to High Impact Domestic Violence in Portugal. In B. Lobnikar, C. Vogt, & J. Kersten (Eds.), *Improving Frontline Responses to Domestic Violence in Europe* (pp. 215–238). University of Maribor. doi:10.18690/978-961-286-543-6.13

Machado, P., Pais, L. G., Morgado, S., & Felgueiras, S. (2021). An inter-organisational response to domestic violence: The pivotal role of police in Porto, Portugal. *European Law Enforcement Research Bulletin, 21.*

Manita, C. (2007). *Dinâmicas e consequências da violência doméstica: o(s) valor(es) da liberdade e da vida*. Conferência Regional Parlamentos Unidos contra a Violência Doméstica contra as Mulheres.

Manita, C. (2008). Programas de intervenção em agressores de violência conjugal: Intervenção psicológica e prevenção da violência doméstica. *Ousar Integrar: Revista de Reinserção Social e Prova, 1,* 21–32.

Marques, J. (2021). A look at Domestic and Gender-based Violence in Portugal: from law to discourses. In NORDSCI (Orgs), *Conference Proceedings-International Conference on Social Sciences* (pp. 245–253). Bulgaria: SAIMA Consult. 10.32008/NORDSCI2021/B2/V4/21

Martins, N., Correia, P., & Pereira, S. (2021). Ciberjustiça em Portugal: A Vigilância Eletrónica como Estratégia da Política Criminal. *Lex Humana*, *13*, 177–189.

Morais-Gonçalves, D., Lopes-Borges, S., & Gaspar, H. (2018). Reincidência, Fatores de Risco e Avaliação de Risco em Vítimas de Violência Doméstica. *Trabajo Social Global –. Global Social Work*, *8*(15), 78–113. doi:10.30827/tsg-gsw.v8i15.7424

Neves, J. (2008). Violência doméstica – bem jurídico e boas práticas. *Revista do Centro de Estudos Judiciários*, *8*, 43–63.

Neves, S. (2016). Femicídio: O fim da linha da violência de género. *Ex Aequo (Oeiras)*, *34*(34). Advance online publication. doi:10.22355/exaequo.2016.34.01

Neves, S., & Brasil, E. (2018). A intervenção junto de mulheres vítimas de violência doméstica em Portugal: percursos, paradigmas, práticas e desafios. In I. Dias (Ed.), *Violência Doméstica e de Género: uma abordagem multidisciplinar* (pp. 175–188). Pactor.

Neves, S., & Correia, A. (2022). Intimate Partner Femicide in Portugal. The perception of intervention professionals with intimate partner violence. *Observatorio (OBS*)*, *16*(2), 117–137. doi:10.15847/obsOBS16220221916

Neves, S., & Nogueira, C. (2005). Metodologias Feministas: A reflexividade ao serviço da Investigação nas Ciências Sociais. *Psicologia: Reflexão e Crítica*, *18*(3), 408–412. doi:10.1590/S0102-79722005000300015

Neves, S., & Nogueira, C. (2010). Deconstructing gendered discourses of love, power and violence in intimate relationships. In D. Jack & A. Ali (Eds.), *Silencing the Self Across Cultures Depression and Gender in the Social World* (pp. 241–261). Oxford University Press. doi:10.1093/acprof:oso/9780195398090.003.0012

Neves, S., Santos, I., & Topa, J. (2023). The Implementation of Dating Violence Prevention Programmes in Portugal and Their Effectiveness: Perspectives of Professionals. *Social Sciences (Basel, Switzerland)*, *12*(9), 9. Advance online publication. doi:10.3390/socsci12010009

Nogueira, E., Simões, E., & Sani, A. (2020). A publicidade institucional e a sua repercussão mediática: uma análise de campanhas publicitárias no combate à violência doméstica. In M. Batista & A. Almeida (Eds). Performatividades de género na democracia ameaçada (pp.147–155). Grácio Editor.

Poiares, N. (2020). Violência doméstica e redes sociais: a proteção jurídico-penal da vida privada na internet. In T. Castro (Ed.), Revista Científica Sobre Cyberlaw do Centro de Investigação Jurídica do Ciberespaço. Faculdade de Direito da Universidade de Lisboa.

Rola, R., & Oliveira, M. (2019). *O estatuto de vítima na violência doméstica. A atribuição do estatuto de vítima às crianças que vivem o crime*. Revista Electrónica de Estudios Penales y de la Seguridad.

Russell, D. (1976). *Crimes against women: international tribunal proceedings*. Les-Femmes Publishing.

Sani, A., & Carvalho, C. (2018). Violência Doméstica e Crianças em Risco: Estudo Empírico com Autos da Polícia Portuguesa. *Psicologia: Teoria e Pesquisa (Brasília)*, *34*(34). Advance online publication. doi:10.1590/0102.3772e34417

Sani, A., Coelho, A., & Manita, C. (2018). Intervenção em Situações de Violência Doméstica: Atitudes e Crenças de Polícias. *Psychology, Community & Health*, *7*(1), 72–86. doi:10.5964/pch.v7i1.247

Sani, A., & Correia, A. (2019). A intervenção técnica junto de crianças em acolhimento residencial em casa de abrigo para vítimas de violência doméstica. *Revista de Ciências Sociais Configurações*, *23*(23), 138–158. doi:10.4000/configuracoes.7214

Sistema de Segurança Interna (SSI). (2023). *Relatório Anual de Segurança Interna 2022 – RASI*. Sistema de Segurança Interna.

Sousa, J. (2021). (In)Existência de Estereótipos de Gênero na Jurisprudência Portuguesa. *Revista de Gênero. Sexualidade e Direito*, *7*(1), 130–150. doi:10.26668/2525-9849/Index_Law_Journals/2021.v7i1.7716

Tavares, M. (2011). *Feminismos - Percursos e Desafios (1947-2007)*. Texto Editores.

Tomás, C. A., Fernandes, N., Sani, A. I., & Martins, P. C. (2018). A (in)visibilidade das crianças na violência doméstica em Portugal. *SER Social*, *20*(43), 387–410. doi:10.26512/ser_social.v20i43.18867

UMAR. (2019). *Observatório das Mulheres Assassinadas*. UMAR.

UMAR. (2021). *Relatório Anual 2020 (1 de janeiro de 2020 a 31 de dezembro de 2020)*. Observatório de Mulheres Assassinadas. UMAR.

United Nations. (1979). *Convenção sobre a Eliminação de todas as Formas de Discriminação Contra as Mulheres.* https://gddc.ministeriopublico.pt/sites/default/files/documentos/instrumentos/convencao_eliminacao_todas_formas_discriminacao_contra_mulheres.pdf

United Nations Office on Drugs and Crime (UNODC). (2019). *Global study on homicide: Gender-related killing of women and girls.* Division for Policy Analysis and Public Affairs.

United Nations Women. (2021). *Measuring the Shadow Pandemic: Violence Against Women During Covid-19.* United Nations Women.

ENDNOTES

[1] https://dre.pt/dre/detalhe/resolucao-conselho-ministros/55-1999-308998

[2] https://www.portugal.gov.pt/pt/gc21/consulta-publica?i=231

[3] https://dre.pt/dre/detalhe/resolucao-conselho-ministros/102-2013-483890

[4] https://www.portugal.gov.pt/pt/gc21/consulta-publica?i=231

[5] https://dre.pt/dre/detalhe/resolucao-conselho-ministros/139-2019-124044596

Chapter 9

From Forms of Violence to the Specificities of the Impact on LGBTI+ Victims

Cynthia Leite da Silva
ⓘ https://orcid.org/0000-0001-8871-6000
University of Porto, Portugal

ABSTRACT

LGBTI+ people are victims of different forms of violence all over the world, from situations of hate, discrimination, LGBTI+ phobic bullying, domestic violence, and even violence within intimate relationships. A large part of this violence sends a message to the community: a message of intolerance and non-acceptance. These are acts that undermine the dignity and identity of the victims. This chapter therefore aims to specify these forms of violence, outlining and understanding the differential impact that violence has on LGBTI+ victims. At the same time, it seeks to list some measures that can contribute to combating or reducing the occurrence of this violence.

INTRODUCTION

Despite all progress in increasing recognition and fulfilment of the rights of LGBTI+ people, this community remains at high risk of becoming victim of violence due to sexual orientation, gender identity and/or gender expression. The LGBTI+ population is especially vulnerable to different forms of violence, from acts of discrimination, to hate speech, to bullying and cyberbullying. Even within their dating relationships, abusive dynamics can take on particularly difficult contours, with truly harmful consequences for the victims.

DOI: 10.4018/979-8-3693-5436-0.ch009

In the public and private spheres, at social, family, work, educational and legal levels, among others, asymmetries persist, which serves to reinforce that the formal and legal rights already achieved do not mean, nor guarantee, in themselves, its effective execution (Sousa et al., 2023).

This chapter aims to address the specificities of violence directed at LGBTI+ people and how the impact of victimization can be particularly devastating for victims. On the other hand, it is also intended to highlight how important raising awareness on this topic can be, especially to promote the demystification of stereotypes, beliefs and social and cultural values that promote and legitimize precisely some acts of violence. Information, knowledge and even in a more structured way, prevention, can be key tools for reducing these acts. The family and the educational community are essential figures, especially for children and young people, but the whole of society must assume a central role in combating this violence. Regardless of whether we know or are close to LGBTI+ people, it is everyone's duty to contribute to ensuring that their rights are shared by all. It is everyone's duty to foster a more balanced and egalitarian society, which is respectful and welcoming of difference as natural and positive.

1. SPECIFICITIES OF THE LGBTI+ COMMUNITY

Gender norms are socially constructed, learned, and transmitted, varying culturally and historically. These norms are unwritten rules about acceptable and ideal forms of conduct and behaviour and will influence the attitudes of individuals in their family and intimate relationships (Carman et al., 2021). Furthermore, these norms influence the way society sees and acts towards the LGBTI+ community, feeling legitimized to exclude and marginalize anyone who is part of this population.

Gender and gender inequality are constructed based on the assumption that "real" men and women are necessarily heterosexual. Thus, LGB, trans and gender diverse people challenge the assumptions that support a binary and heterogeneous system of the model of the relationship between sex, gender, and sexuality. At the same time, they can threaten to expose patriarchy and the heterosexist foundations that sustain situations of violence. Also, gender norms are reinforced by the idea that the only "normal" and "natural" bodies/sexes and gender identities are "male" and "female". Binary gender norms are, therefore, associated with the cisnormativity that drives violence against trans and gender diverse people, and in some cases, motivates medical interventions aimed at "normalizing" intersex bodies (Carman et al., 2021).

Due to the existence of a highly heterosexist and cisnormative society, a large proportion of LGBTI+ people live within a triad of invisibility, isolation and social insult, with each vertex feeding the other. The social insult emerges within a heterosexist and heteronormative society that excludes and discriminates against all people who do not fit into this social standard. By way of example, it includes *"any individual perceived not to conform to prevailing norms about gender (such as physical appearance, choice of clothing, mannerisms) or sexuality (emotional and physical attraction to others) or sex characteristics"* (Magić & Selun, 2018, pp.17). This insult is culturally internalized and transmitted generationally. It is based on stereotypes and preconceived ideas that legitimize the perpetuation of these discriminatory behaviours and attitudes. Growing up in a society where social insults are legitimized, coming out and asserting one's identity can be difficult steps, contributing to people remaining invisible. This invisibility, in turn, increases the isolation of these people, especially if there is no strong and cohesive informal support network to serve as a back-up.

These social insults can fit into microaggressions, which are subtle or indirect behaviors that are derogatory and/or hostile towards those who are the target of them. Examples such as addressing the person as a gender that is not theirs or asking what their genitalia are, making the person uncomfortable and/or anxious. In many cases, microaggressions go unnoticed and are not considered violent (Sándor, 2021).

This triad therefore contributes to the fact that many situations of violence are not known. On the one hand, sexual orientation and gender identity can be weapons used by abusive partners to keep victims trapped in the relationship. The threat of disclosure, known as outing, is one of the strategies used to avoid ending a relationship, even when it is an abusive relationship. On the other hand, requests for help and complaints may be non-existent or rare for reasons of guilt, shame, fear of reprisals and fear of discredit felt by the victims and precisely because they live in invisibility.

A large number of people who do not fit into heteronormativity, namely gays, lesbians, and bisexuals, feel the need to hide their sexual orientation to avoid experiencing discrimination in different social contexts. In Dueñas and collaborators study (2021), in the sample of students who reported being aware of an act of violence directed at LGBTI+ people, 45% also reported being aware of at least one case in which an LGBTI+ person hid their sexual orientation or gender identity. This resistance to coming out may be associated with fear of stigma, prejudice, LGBTI+phobia and violence. Obviously, this invisibility can, in turn, imply mental health problems, such as depression and stress (Pachankis et al., 2020 *cit in* Dueñas et al., 2021).

Each victimization experience is unique, which means the impact will always be subjective. However, there are aspects that may be common in the life trajectories of LGBTI+ people. One of these transversal aspects is internalized LGBTI+phobia. This phenomenon is present when, during their growth, some people were exposed to various stereotypes and prejudices from society - often manifested in social insults - for being LGBTI+ people, leading people themselves to internalize these prejudices and create some repudiation or rejection regarding their own identity and/or sexual orientation (Sousa et al., 2023).

The presence of insult, isolation and invisibility contribute to the perpetuation of situations of discrimination, stigmatization, and violence against LGBTI+ people. Not only for the incidence of these acts, but also for their silencing, legitimization, fear of victims and their marginalization. Everything seems to work like a vicious cycle. Thus, the lack of freedom to express identity can be extremely overwhelming for people, so these aspects and other subtle forms of violence should not be normalized.

Another relevant aspect is that within the LGBTI+ community there is a general distrust in health professionals and services, for example. Many LGBTI+ people believe that service providers will be uninformed about their specific needs or may disregard them if they reveal their sexual orientation or gender identity (Rees et al., 2017). On the other hand, the results indicated that there are differences between the intentions of LGBTI+ and heterosexual participants to report crimes, with LGBTI+ people being less willing to report crimes than heterosexual people. Belief in police homophobia strongly influences LGBTI+ people's intention to underreport crimes to the police (Miles-Johnson, 2013).

In Dueñas and collaborators study (2021), there was a high percentage of violence not reported to the university or the police. This result is worrying because people who attack can be left with a feeling of impunity, generating frustration and helplessness in victims and potential victims. Furthermore, this low record of occurrences contributes to the phenomenon of underreporting of situations of violence against LGBTI+ people.

This resistance to ask for help and reporting violence may arise from prejudices and discrimination that lead to cases of secondary victimization, in which service providers, such as the police and health professionals, may trivialize the abuse because it was perpetrated by someone from the same sex, not providing appropriate and sensitive services or making homophobic comments. These overlapping factors can contribute to silencing lived experiences of violence (Lynch & Sanger, 2016).

On the other hand, when the relationship is known and sexual orientation is revealed, there may be other obstacles to reporting and/or requesting support in cases of abusive intimate relationships. Myths regarding same-sex relationships, namely the idea that there is equality in these relationships, contribute to people not asking for support or reporting them. Furthermore, there is the belief that violence does not occur in lesbian relationships or that, when it does occur, it is "mutual violence", and that violence between gay men should be tolerated and excused due to the perception that physical violence forces and power are equal (Carman et al., 2021).

2. THE CONTOURS OF VIOLENCE DIRECTED AT THE LGBTI+ COMMUNITY

Violence against LGBTI+ people can occur in the intra-family and extra-family context. The family, one of the basic pillars of support and acceptance, can often be an environment in which a person experiences pain, suffering and rejection. To avoid suffering, people may hide their gender identity, sexual orientation and/or sexual characteristics. Situations of domestic violence against descendants, due to gender identity and/or sexual orientation, are unfortunately very common and are not always reported. LGBTI+ young people experience the same stress and anxiety as all other young people growing up. Adolescence is a particularly difficult time for everyone. But an important difference is that LGBTI+ people must at the same time accept and deal with an identity or orientation for which they will be stigmatized, and they generally do so without having the support of their family who often become "enemies". At a time when everyone needs more support, this population faces additional labelling and discrimination (Bašić & Dizdar, 2018).

When coming out within families, LGBTI+ people can be subject to rejection, abuse, and violence. Experiences of rejection are linked to verbal and physical abuse and family attempts to "normalize" their gender and sexual orientation. These acts may occur particularly when the asserted gender identity differs from the sex assigned at birth (Carman et al., 2021). Other forms of rejection may include expulsion from home, isolation from peers, punishments and even conversion practices (Sousa et al., 2023).

In addition to rejection from the family, rejection from peers and society can also occur, leading to them becoming more isolated (due to the lack of an informal support network). This rejection often happens because they consider that same-gender attraction or bisexuality, for example, is a temporary situation, a problem that can be solved using psychological support or that it is simply a less valid sexual orientation (Sousa et al., 2023). LGBTI+ people can also suffer from prejudice and discrimination from professionals when requesting support. This double victimization can be highly deterrent for the victim, for example, from filing a complaint regarding the violence experienced or seeking new support in future situations.

Homophobic and transphobic violence, which can be found for example in LGBTI+phobic bullying, punishes "gender deviance": such violence imposes "ordered" gender categories and the consequent social expectations for each category. Heterosexuality is seen as the standard, natural and ethical sexual orientation and that being gay is being deviant, pathological, and depraved. In fact, in many countries, homosexuality is still illegal. Even in countries with legal protections, social violence and discrimination often remain widespread (Loken & Hagen, 2022).

In the study by Mavhandu-Mudzusi (2017), participants mentioned that LGBTI+ students feel "forced" to engage in heterosexual relationships publicly, while in private they have a partner according to their sexual orientation. This happens to mask true sexual orientation in order to avoid stigma and discrimination. It is important to emphasize that the university, in this case, is a micro society that reflects the values and beliefs that exist in the macro society.

From another perspective, other forms of violence may arise with the increasing use of social networks in terms of content production, in many cases, to only consolidate the dominant rhetoric and ideology or social point of view taken in the offline context. The group, which is considered the majority, labels what it considers different as "other" and alienates it from society. Therefore, hate speech on social media and the effects of hate speech in real life must be taken seriously. The message shared on social media can promote a wrong perception in society. Furthermore, the individual or community labelled as "the other" in this message may be exposed to physical and psychological violence by the majority, leading to consequences that can hardly be compensated. Also, the sharing and dissemination of discourses that alter, discriminate, and alienate can cause not only personal victimization, but also social fragmentation in the community as a whole. The most destructive form of hate speech is that which seeks to justify the intention of excluding, discriminating, or murdering another group, portraying the "other" in the context of the messages as an enemy, inhumane, immoral or not worthy of existence. Hate speech and hate crimes are acts committed because of who the victims are or what they believe they are. Therefore, this phenomenon must be considered as a growing threat that undermines peace and tolerance between different groups in the community (Akmese & Deniz, 2017; Nyman & Provozin, 2019).

One of the points to explore through this chapter is how violence directed against LGBTI+ people distinguish itself from other acts of violence. The keyword will be intentionality. Each and every act of violence directed at this community is intentional, as there is a subliminal message that wants to be transmitted. Thinking about a situation of hate speech that is directed at a particular person. Sometimes, the hatred practiced does not happen for that specific person, but for belonging to a group that is neither desired nor socially accepted. Thus, the message behind that act is directed at the group to which the direct victim belongs. Furthermore, it is also important to highlight that these acts of violence are committed against what is most intimate to us, our identity, what defines us as human beings.

The disproportionate, lifelong exposure of the LGBTI+ population to physical and verbal violence, sexual violence and discrimination can contribute to the cumulative impact of violence on people's psychological and physical health and social isolation, the inability to recognize and let go abusive relationships (with partners or family) and distrust and disbelief in support from services, including health and community services, the police and the legal system (O'Halloran, 2015).

Finally, a last form of violence to address is the violence between intimate partners among LGBTI+ people that typically occurs in populations that already suffer high rates of violence and discrimination and lower levels of psychological and physical health than the general population, and where people have distrust in health services and other services. Intimate partner violence is associated with abuse of power, a factor that is universally found among perpetrators. However, there are specific factors that can be identified in intimate partner violence involving same-sex couples and in relationships involving transgender people. Examples of dynamics of violence between intimate partners specific to LGBTI+ are threats by the violent partner to "out" the victim (i.e., to reveal their sexual orientation or gender identity). The threat of "outing" can be used as a powerful form of control. Coerced sex through manipulation of the victim's emotional vulnerability related to shame or guilt over sexual orientation or gender identity. Failure to recognize the experience of abuse as violence between intimate partners, on the part of the victim or the perpetrator. Threats from the abuser that the police or judicial system are homophobic or transphobic and will not help them. The impact of these threats can also be reinforced by real experiences of discrimination in the past. Also, finally, transphobic abuse, in which a partner prevents the trans person from expressing their gender identity in preferred ways. It should be emphasized again that violence between intimate partners suffered by LGBTI+ people often occur in a broader scenario that includes other forms of abuse, including family violence, sexual violence and hate crimes. Violence between partners can undermine personal judgment and be unfairly experienced as normal or deserved. In this context, individuals may become increasingly isolated and less able to leave their perpetrators or seek help (Rees et al., 2017).

Although this is not the focus of this chapter, it is important to note that within the LGBTI+ community, there are groups that are more vulnerable than others to situations of violence and whose consequences can also be even more harmful. For example, trans people subjected to physical and sexual violence have been found to be more likely to attempt suicide and have greater suicidal ideation and a greater risk of substance abuse (Testa et al., 2012 *cit in* Dueñas et al., 2021).

In sum, experiences of family violence are often accompanied by experiences of abuse and violence in public spaces, educational environments, and workplaces, affecting LGBTI+ people in all areas and at all stages of their lives. Although violence is perpetrated against LGBTI+ people, it is important to highlight that violence is also perpetrated by and within LGBTI+ communities, and can often be motivated by homophobia, biphobia, transphobia and intersexphobia, as well as sexism and misogyny (Carman et al., 2021).

3. THE CONSEQUENCES OF VIOLENCE ON LGBTI+ VICTIMS

In this context, it is important to note first of all that "direct victim" will be the individual directly affected by a violent or discriminatory practice, and "indirect victim" refers to individuals who suffer consequences due to their inclusion in the targeted group. Direct victims' experiences may include physical harm, while both victims and indirect victims may face psychological effects such as feelings of insecurity, anxiety, isolation, fear, loneliness, and depression (Walters, 2014, 2019 *cit in* Domínguez Ruiz, 2022). There are those who also speak of "systemic trauma" as that which is historically suffered by a group, with particular consequences with regard to their feelings of security, belonging and dignity (Haines, 2019 *cit in idem*).

Some examples of physical reactions are dizziness, psychomotor disturbances, headaches, palpitations, high blood pressure, low blood sugar, digestive system problems, hyperexcitation, speech difficulties, difficulty breathing, shock. Cognitive reactions can include disorientation, confusion, concentration difficulties, expression difficulties, memory problems (Sándor, 2021).

It was found that experiences of family rejection have significant negative consequences on the mental health and well-being of LGBTI+ young people and, on the other hand, family acceptance has a positive impact and a protective effect against other forms of violence experienced by this population. Peer relationships and contact with LGBTI+ communities are important protective factors too in terms of health and well-being. Having other community, organizational, religious, cultural, and extended family connections can also be an important source of support for LGBTI+ people, not only in terms of prevention but also in situations where victimization has occurred, but it is important to act to minimize or eliminate the damage/impact (Carman et al., 2021).

One of the aspects that must be reinforced is that the way each victim deals with their experience of victimization is unique and subjective. There are common symptoms, but the impact can take on different shapes, which vary according to several factors, namely the type of criminal event, the characteristics of the victim and post-victimization experiences. However, considering that the victim's identity may be the main target of violence, one of the consequences that these victims may feel is the need to change or hide their own identity. If we talk about children and young victims, the impact that violence against their identity has can be truly devastating, especially because they are at a stage in life where they are discovering and developing that identity. Seeing this intimate and personal phase compromised in this way can be highly detrimental to their healthy development. In other words, *"not being able to express one's identity freely and comfortably may result in high levels of accumulated anxiety and may cause long-term negative consequences for*

LGBTI students at the very time they build their identity, self-esteem, and social skills" (Magić & Selun, 2018, pp.23).

The emotional and social consequences of being a victim of this type of violence can include emotional distress, humiliation, fear, and depression (Mallory et al. 2017; Davis et al. 2020 *cit in* Dueñas et al., 2021). Other significant harms can be the negative impact on self-esteem, silencing, restrictions on freedom of movement and expression and symptoms such as sleep deprivation, exhaustion, a feeling of fear when walking alone on the streets and strong feelings of discomfort (Nyman & Provozin, 2019). However, this impact is not only felt by direct victims. Other people, namely other LGBTI+ people, may feel the consequences of that act as being directed at them too.

Several studies indicate that the LGBTI+ community, compared to the heterosexual population, has lower levels of several mental health indicators, such as a greater need for and use of mental health services, higher levels of smoking, diagnoses of depression and anxiety widespread and substance use. Still regarding anxiety, it is suggested that chronic experiences of discrimination based on sexual orientation can negatively affect the ability to regulate emotional responses, which can lead to psychological disorders (Soriano-Moreno et al., 2022).

The inability to express one's identity freely and honestly and/or sexual orientation leads to numerous difficulties for the person within the family. It results not only in dysfunctional relationships and communication within the family, but also prevents the formation of solid relationships in all segments of life and is often followed by psycho-emotional anxiety (Bašić & Dizdar, 2018).

Other consequences felt, particularly by victims of hate, are symptoms of depression or withdrawal, anxiety, feelings of helplessness and a feeling of excessive isolation. The damage can be visible at the individual level, in the victim's group or community and in society in general, with increased insecurity felt and greater fragmentation (Akmese & Deniz, 2017).

The consequences can also be academic, namely lower academic performance, decreased interest in school activities, situations of school absenteeism and in some cases, early school leaving. The lack of support also has consequences for victims and makes it more difficult for them to become survivors and overcome the harmful effects suffered (Rios-Gonzalez et al., 2023; Sándor, 2021).

Highlighting the specific case of intersex people, in most European countries, intersex people are pathologized and their human rights are violated. Thus, whatever their age, intersex people can face stigma, structural and verbal discrimination, and harassment due to sexual characteristics, lack of adequate medical care, lack of access to necessary medication, lack of legal recognition and social invisibility of their bodies. If we consider this during childhood and youth, it is difficult to measure the severe impact this discrimination can have on the development of identity and expression (Sándor, 2021).

4. HOW TO COMBAT VIOLENCE DIRECTED AT THE LGBTI+ COMMUNITY

One of the main consequences of the dominant cis heteronormativity is the lack of knowledge among professionals in areas such as education and health that would enhance the provision of better support to LGBTI+ people, particularly children and young people (Santos, Esteves & Santos, 2020).

Formal and non-formal educational institutions can be hostile environments for many LGBTI+ young people who experience different forms of violence (Fundamental Rights Agency, 2020 *cit in* Rios-Gonzalez et al., 2023). One of the causes may be the lack of evidence of professional training for education professionals (Oliver, 2014; Yuste et al., 2014 *cit in* Rios-Gonzalez et al., 2023).

Children and young people need a team of professionals in an educational context who are properly trained in the area. Teachers have an important role in preventing any bullying situation – children need to have allies and see their teachers as references. It is also important to overcome isolation and invisibility, have more positive LGBTI+ role models and ensure the integration of gender diversity and sexual orientations into school curricula. This also includes the creation of documents and guides, the existence of appointments, psychological, legal, and psychosocial support. Efforts must also be made to adopt the social name of children and young people, even when there is no continuous procedure for changing their name (Santos, Esteves & Santos, 2020). Giving children and young people a voice is fundamental. Listening to their needs, concerns, fears and joys is allowing potential aggressors to put themselves in the victim's position.

Increasing knowledge, awareness, and training to work and/or intervene with LGBTI+ people is fundamental to providing more effective support. This knowledge must be transversal to education, health, justice professionals, among others. On the other hand, this training should be mandatory, given that these themes are still little explored by professionals. Some reasons for the lack of demand may be lack of interest in the area, lack of perceived relevance and shame. Addressing gender and LGBTI+ issues still seem like a taboo topic for many people.

The training will serve to promote the dissemination of inclusive practices that can be used daily to combat stereotypes and prejudices but will also provide professionals with useful tools to identify, intervene and prevent situations of violence perpetrated against LGBTI+ people (Sousa et al., 2023).

It is important, of course, to emphasize that training and information must not only be for educational institutions. It must also reach families, health services, the justice system, police agencies and the general population. Everyone can know someone who is part of the LGBTI+ community. Even if you do not, it is necessary to create conditions so that all people are treated fairly and equally, with respect and with freedom of expression of their identity and sexual orientation.

However, the inclusion of gender identity and sexual orientation in the family sphere is neither simple nor quick. Previous generations may present some resistance to knowledge and information. Therefore, receiving support and advice from specialized professionals can be an interesting solution.

Raising awareness aimed at informing others about the problems of online hate speech, for example, are also powerful expressions of solidarity with victims of hate speech (Keen & Georgescu, 2016). Furthermore, they can encourage victims themselves to report, as well as raise awareness of the importance of being a witness. Those who witness situations of violence and do not act condone and contribute to the perpetuation of these situations.

Violations of LGBTI+ human rights and the perpetuation of social insults are based on socially and culturally constructed and entrenched stereotypes and gender roles (Holtmaat & Post, 2018). Therefore, the role of awareness and prevention must involve deconstructing traditions, practices, and beliefs that in some way contribute to the maintenance of cisnormativity and heteronormativity.

There are protective factors that can and should be promoted. For example, a literature review by Espelage et al. (2019 *cit in* Rios-Gonzalez et al., 2023) showed that young people who suffer homophobic bullying, but have the support of family and friends, do not experience as many consequences. Furthermore, strong and positive school climates can prevent violence, as can the existence of trusted adults, involvement in prosocial activities, a cohesive informal support network, and access to formal support.

There is a need to develop several different types of information, education, and communication materials related to same-sex intimate partner violence. These materials need to focus on breaking the cycle of silence and shame associated with intimate partner violence, educating same-sex couples about their rights and how to identify warning signs, as well as providing information about counselling services and other resources available for them. For support services, it is necessary to provide entities with knowledge about the dynamics experienced in same-sex relationships, making the service provided more inclusive (Lynch & Sanger, 2016).

Furthermore, the integration of gender diversity and sexual orientation, the preparation of awareness campaigns and the broader involvement of social media and public spaces on the issue seem important steps that will work more effectively on the missing level – social change and cultural. For example, investing in greater representation of LGBTI+ people in the media can also lead to people from this community feeling freer and safer in their expression. This is the most macro level in the ecological model and the one that requires the most attention and time (Santos, Esteves & Santos, 2020).

Since violence is a complex and multidimensional phenomenon, the preventive approach should, whenever possible, take on an ecological character (Heise, 1998), address the different levels of human functioning, from the individual (where we work to reduce individual risk factors and promote protective factors), relationships (whether family, with peers, in the context of intimacy), the community (and the role of the support network) and society (from a perspective of changing beliefs, values and social and cultural norms that legitimize violence).

Other measures that contribute to the implementation of the rights of LGBTI+ people include compliance with existing legislation. As an example, Law No. 38/2018 of August 7, approves the Right to self-determination of gender identity and gender expression and the protection of each person's sexual characteristics. In this law, educational establishments must guarantee the necessary conditions so that children and young people feel respected in their gender identity and expression. Measures such as treating children and young people by their social names and creating neutral bathrooms are fundamental to this respect. Law No. 60/2009, of August 6, which establishes the regime for implementing sexual education in schools, also suggests respect for the differences between people and different sexual orientations. It also suggests the elimination of behaviours based on sexual discrimination or violence based on sex or sexual orientation.

Also, the use of gender-inclusive language, not looking for causes for gender orientation or identity, nor assuming them based on gender expressions, articulating with other entities and referring, whenever necessary situations of violence (considering that there may be a limitation of resources within the entity), promote respect for diversity, raise awareness of the recognition of insult as a form of discrimination and the impact on victims, promote school-family articulation, to alignment of forms of conduct is also very important, having knowledge and reflecting on the inner stereotypes that each person has should be highlighted. This deconstruction has to start with each person, internally.

Finally, it is suggested that many of the situations of violence that are directed at LGBTI+ people and that occur during adolescence and adulthood may begin during childhood, in subtler aspects, by dividing "masculine" and "feminine", the roles and characteristics that are attributed to the two categories. From colors, to clothes, to toys, activities and professions, the discourse perpetrated by the family, the school community, society and the media and the choices they make, when the child does not yet have decision-making power, can dictate the child's growth based on this gender binary. From here on, anyone who deviates from this pre-established norm may suffer harmful consequences. So, a seemingly obvious solution may be to allow children from an early age the freedom to explore all options, without judgment and rules. Here, especially the family and school must take a stance that promotes freedom and diversity and protects children and young people from disapproving looks and comments. Empathy and assertiveness are also skills that must be worked on early to enhance relationships based on respect, inclusion, and equality.

CONCLUSION

The experience of stigmatization and ostracism contributes to LGBTI+ people hiding their sexual orientation, which in turn makes them "invisible" to society. "Becoming invisible" may seem to LGBTI+ people to be a way of "surviving" acts of discrimination and violence, given the continuity of social stigmas and prejudices. However, a form of discrimination can also be the creation of an atmosphere of silence, where neglect or disrespect leads to the marginalization of LGBTI+ people (Špatenková & Olecká, 2020).

In addition to information and awareness-raising initiatives, specific training in this area aimed at professionals (e.g., education, health, justice) is also essential. As seen previously, the reporting of hateful situations, for example, may be scarce in relation to the number of existing cases. As seen in *National study on the needs of LGBTI people and discrimination based on sexual orientation, gender identity and expression and sexual characteristics* (2022), the low rate of reporting of hate crimes and incidents with homophobic and/or transphobic motivation is strongly associated with the lack of trust of victims and witnesses in public security forces, the fear of phobic reactions or blame for the incident suffered, negative experiences in previous contacts or the belief that nothing will be done. Therefore, in order to encourage LGBTI+ victims to report the hate crimes and incidents they suffer, barriers to reporting and recording hate crimes and incidents should be removed.

Generally speaking, some examples of preventive actions to be adopted are improving legislation, raising awareness through information campaigns, education on inclusion and opening up LGBTI+ people regarding their sexual orientation and gender identity (Nyman & Provozin, 2019).

Everyone, regardless of their sexual orientation and/or gender identity, must have the right to a home, family support, freedom of expression and movement. The impossibility or lack of protection for a child or young person exposed to violence due to their sexual orientation/gender identity/sexual characteristics is most likely the cruellest violation of their rights (Bašić & Dizdar, 2018).

These and other discussions and conclusions will, it is hoped, help to improve much-needed understanding and allow gaps to be explored, good practices shared and consensus-building around improving support and protection responses for LGBTI+ people. Among other things, it is also expected to contribute to a more inclusive society that respects diversity.

To complete, the school must be a free and safe place for all children and young people, so all professionals in the educational community must act as figures of reference and security. The family must also be a safe space for children and young people, where affection, respect and understanding are enhanced by dialogue and non-judgment. Obviously, the process of deconstructing myths and deep-rooted beliefs is neither simple nor quick. It is a long, complex path, but whose small steps are fundamental. Human rights, in theory, belong to all people. Access to these rights in practice as well, or should be.

REFERENCES

Akmeşe, Z., & Deniz, K. (2017). Hate Speech in social media: LGBTI persons. *15th International Symposium Communication in the Millennium.*

Carman, M., Fairchild, J., Parsons, M., Farrugia, C., Power, J., & Bourne, A. (2021). *Pride in prevention: A guide to primary prevention of family violence experienced by LGBTIQ communities.* Academic Press.

Domínguez Ruiz, I. E. (2022). Between the city and the country: Heterogeneous victimization experiences among LGBTI individuals. *Cogent Social Sciences*, *8*(1), 2107281. doi:10.1080/23311886.2022.2107281

Dueñas, J. M., Racionero-Plaza, S., Melgar, P., & Sanvicén-Torné, P. (2021). Identifying violence against the LGTBI+ community in Catalan universities. *Life Sciences, Society and Policy*, *17*(1), 1–10. doi:10.1186/s40504-021-00112-y PMID:33618762

Heise, L. L. (1998). Violence against women: An integrated, ecological framework. *Violence Against Women*, *4*(3), 262–290. doi:10.1177/1077801298004003002 PMID:12296014

Holtmaat, R., & Post, P. (2018). Enhancing LGBTI rights by changing the interpretation of the convention on the elimination of all forms of discrimination against women? In Human Rights, Sexual Orientation, and Gender Identity (pp. 53-70). Routledge.

Keen, E., & Georgescu, M. (2016). *Referências. Manual para o combate do discurso de ódio online através da educação para os direitos humanos*. Conselho da Europa: Fundação Calouste Gulbenkian.

Loken, M., & Hagen, J. J. (2022). Queering gender-based violence scholarship: An integrated research agenda. *International Studies Review*, *24*(4), viac050. doi:10.1093/isr/viac050

Lynch, I., & Sanger, N. (2016). *I'm your maker: power, heteronormativity and violence in women's same-sex relationships*. Academic Press.

Magić, B., & Selun, J. (2018). *Safe at school: Education sector responses to violence based on sexual orientation, gender identity/expression or sex characteristics in Europe*. Report Commissioned by the Council of Europe.

Mavhandu-Mudzusi, A. H. (2017). Impact of stigma and discrimination on sexual well- being of LGBTI students in a South African rural university. *South African Journal of Higher Education*, *31*(4), 208–218.

Miles-Johnson, T. (2013). LGBTI variations in crime reporting: How sexual identity influences decisions to call the cops. *SAGE Open*, *3*(2). doi:10.1177/2158244013490707

Nyman, H., & Provozin, A. (2019). *The harmful effects of online and offline anti LGBTI hate speech*. Academic Press.

O'Halloran, K. (2015). Family violence in an LGBTIQ context. *DVRCV Advocate*, (2), 10–13.

Rees, S., Horsley, P., Moussa, B., & Fisher, J. (2017). *Intimate partner violence and LGBTIQ people: Raising awareness in general practice*. Academic Press.

Rios-Gonzalez, O., Peña-Axt, J. C., Legorburo-Torres, G., Avgousti, A., & Sancho, L. N. (2023). Impact of an evidence-based training for educators on bystander intervention for the prevention of violence against LGBTI+ youth. *Humanities & Social Sciences Communications*, *10*(1), 1–13. doi:10.1057/s41599-023-02117-8

Saleiro, S., Ramalho, N., Menezes, M., & Gato, J. (2022). Estudo nacional sobre as necessidades das pessoas LGBTI e sobre a discriminação em razão da orientação sexual, identidade e expressão de género e características sexuais. Lisboa: Commission for Citizenship and Gender Equality.

Sándor, B. (2021). *Como Prevenir e Combater a Violência contra Crianças e Jovens LGBTI+ e de Género Diverso*. Academic Press.

Santos, A. C., Esteves, M., & Santos, A. (2020). National analysis on violence against LGBTI+ children: Portugal. Academic Press.

Soriano-Moreno, D. R., Saldaña-Cabanillas, D., Vasquez-Yeng, L., Valencia-Huamani, J. A., Alave-Rosas, J. L., & Soriano, A. N. (2022). Discrimination and mental health in the minority sexual population: Cross-sectional analysis of the first peruvian virtual survey. *PLoS One*, *17*(6), e0268755. doi:10.1371/journal.pone.0268755 PMID:35657953

Sousa, E., Neves, S., Ferreira, M., Topa, J., Vieira, C. P., Borges, J., Costa, R., & Lira, A. (2023). Domestic Violence against LGBTI People: Perspectives of Portuguese Education Professionals. *International Journal of Environmental Research and Public Health*, *20*(13), 6196. doi:10.3390/ijerph20136196 PMID:37444044

Špatenková, N., & Olecká, I. (2020). Invisible older people: LGBTI+. *Social Pathology & Prevention, 6*(2).

KEY TERMS AND DEFINITIONS

Biological Sex: Classification system based on an individual's genotypic or phenotypic characteristics. Individuals can generally be classified as male, female, or intersex.

Cisnormativity: When it is assumed that people should identify, in terms of gender, with the sex assigned to them at birth.

Coming Out: Is the process of understanding, accepting and revealing their gender identity and/or sexual orientation. Cis and heterosexual people do not have to go through this process, as the unspoken social norm is that all people are cis and heterosexual.

Discrimination: Unequal and unfair behaviour, attitudes and/or forms of treatment based, in this case, on sexual characteristics, sexual orientation and/or gender identity. In situations of discrimination, victims are deprived of their human rights.

Gender: Social construction resulting from the expectations that are created regarding what it means to be a "man" and to be a "woman". For each category, expectations are created regarding characteristics, roles and expressions. Although the concept of gender traditionally refers to gender roles within a binary system (male/female), the concept of gender also includes non-binary gender expressions/identities.

Gender Expression: Is the way a person expresses themselves publicly through clothing, hairstyle, body language, choice of name, preferred pronouns, among other things.

Gender Identity: It refers to personal self-recognition as a man or woman, as both, or as trans, regardless of the sex assigned at birth. It is even possible that there is no identification with any gender. Gender identity is something intimate that is only public knowledge if the person reveals it.

Gender Inequality: When men and women do not have access to the same opportunities, namely access to education, higher professional careers, health, among others.

Hate Crime: Criminal acts based on hatred, in this case, due to sexual characteristics, sexual orientation and/or gender identity. In Portugal, for a situation to be classified as a hate crime, that situation must be classified as a crime in Portuguese Penal Code and it must be proven that the crime was committed for reasons of hate.

Hate Speech: All forms of expression that incite, promote or justify hatred, in this case, based on sexual characteristics, sexual orientation and/or gender identity. These forms of expression that give rise to hatred are based on prejudices and stereotypes.

Heteronormativity: When it is assumed that the only sexual orientation is heterosexual, excluding and marginalizing any other sexual orientation.

Heterosexism: Ideological system that stigmatizes any non-heterosexual form of behaviour, identity, or relationship.

Internalized LGBTI+phobia: When the negative view of the LGBTI+ community is internalized and reproduced by people in the community themselves.

Intersex: Describes the multiplicity of bodies and sexual characteristics that do not fit the traditional definition of male or female sex, and this variety, which is perfectly natural, may or may not be visible.

LGBTI+: L (Lesbian); G (Gay); B (Bisexual); T (Trans); I (Intersex); + (To include all other gender identities and sexual orientations).

LGBTI+phobic Bullying: Repeated and intentional situations of violence directed at LGBTI+ people due to their (real or perceived) belonging to that group, motivated by prejudice towards that population.

Outing: The act or threat of publicly revealing that a person is LGBTI+ without that person's consent as a form of manipulation used by the aggressor towards the victim, often within abusive intimate relationships.

Secondary Victimization or Revictimization: Occurs when violence is reiterated and continued at the state level, institutions or through people who provide services. In these cases, the victim suffers violence continuously, not as a direct result of the act of violence suffered, but due to the way in which institutions and other people deal with the victim. Specifically, among LGBTI+ victims, it may include the use of inappropriate language, discrediting, LGBTI+phobic comments, discriminatory acts, among others.

Sexual Orientation: Linked to the affective part, refers to the person to whom we feel affectionately and/or sexually attracted. It includes sexual attraction, emotional involvement, sexual practices, and sexual identity.

Social Insult: These are insults transmitted, albeit unconsciously, about LGBTI+ people, based on stereotypes and prejudices based on heterosexist and heteronormative/cisnormative norms and values.

Chapter 10
Exploratory Research on Violence Against Transgender Prostitutes:
Limitations and Challenges in Participant Recruitment

Catarina Capucho Conde
Universidade Lusíada, Portugal

Fabiana Rodrigues Gonçalves
Universidade Lusíada, Portugal

Beatriz Filipa Andrade
Universidade Lusíada, Portugal

ABSTRACT

This chapter delves into the intricate intersectionality of transgender identity and involvement in prostitution, shedding light on the heightened vulnerability of transgender prostitutes to sexual and physical violence. The primary focus of this chapter is an exploration of the challenges encountered during a qualitative and criminological study aimed at collecting first-hand accounts through semi-structured interviews with transgender prostitutes. Despite the importance of this research, building a representative sample proved to be notably difficult, highlighting the complexity of engaging this marginalized population in research endeavors. By addressing these challenges, the chapter aims to contribute to the broader discourse on the victimological phenomenon affecting transgender prostitutes and emphasizes the critical importance of overcoming obstacles in conducting empirical research in this field. The ultimate goal is to facilitate future scientific inquiry by raising awareness about the intricacies of researching violence against transgender prostitutes.

DOI: 10.4018/979-8-3693-5436-0.ch010

INTRODUCTION

Throughout history, perceptions of prostitution have been intricately linked to the shift from matriarchal to patriarchal societies. In matriarchal eras, women were revered as life-givers and esteemed as "Goddesses" resulting in the emergence of prostitution without negative connotations; instead, it was viewed as a respected societal activity (Teodoro & Silva, 2015). Sacramento & Ribeiro (2014) emphasize that, in ancient times, there are multiple examples illustrating how prostitutes held a relevant social status, indicating that neither prostitution nor the women engaged in this practice were subject to stigmas or considered deviant.

However, the ascent of patriarchy led to the confinement of women to the private sphere and their subordination to men. Notably, women engaged in sex work retained a distinct status by receiving payment for their services (Costa, 2008). Despite this, evolving societal attitudes gradually turned negative, resulting in the criminalization of prostitution under the influence of patriarchal norms (Ceccarelli, 2008). This societal shift discredited the sanctity of women, creating a stark division between the *"woman of the street"* and the *"woman of the house"* (da Silva, 2011).

Traditionally, homosexuality was stigmatized as a "maleficent, marginal and capable of perverting the social order" (Borges, Perurena & Passamani, 2013). Consequently, research aimed at treatment and control paralleled the criminalization of homosexuality, especially in cases of same-sex interactions, as evidenced by studies by LeVay (1996), Rydstrom and Mustola (2007) and Nussbaum (2010).

The state, represented by the police as the primary law enforcement entity, played a pivotal role in administering and upholding legal structures related to homosexuality, leading to strained relations with the LGBTQIA+ community (Dwyer, Ball, & Crofts, 2016). This tension manifested in discrimination and occasional violence, as highlighted by Dwyer (2014). Furthermore, transgender individuals face pervasive challenges, including prejudice, denial of fundamental rights by various institutions, barriers to education and employment, and various forms of victimization collectively termed "transphobia" (Stenersen, Thomas & McKee, 2022). This underscores the systemic issues that contribute to the marginalization and vulnerability of transgender individuals within society (Jesus, 2013).

Discrimination within the context of transgender identity persists, but an intriguing reversal of societal attitudes is observed when comparing it with prostitution (Stotzer, 2009). Initially unburdened by negative connotations, prostitution has evolved to be perceived as "dirty work", while transgender identity has successfully shed its erroneous associations (Dwyer, Ball, & Crofts 2016). Transgender women working in the sex industry, particularly in prostitution, confront significantly elevated levels of sexual and physical violence compared to their cisgender counterparts (Cohan et al., 2006; Johnson, 2013; Nemoto,

Bodeker, & Iwamoto, 2011) This heightened risk is intricately tied to the concept of intersectionality, where the convergence of transgender identity and engagement in prostitution results in distinct forms of violence specifically targeting transgender prostitutes (Lombardi, Wilchins, Priessing & Malouf, 2001), particularly when operating on the streets (Lyons et al., 2017).

Despite the increasing interest in prostitution as a research topic within the LGBTQIA+ community (Stenersen, Thomas & McKee, 2022; Ribeiro, Neves Riani, & Antunes-Rocha, 2019; Laidlaw, 2018; Geist, 2017; Lyons et al., 2017; Moreira, Rolo, & Cardoso, 2016; Bucher, Manasse & Milton, 2015; Nadal, Davidoff, & Fujii-Doe, 2014; Jesus, 2013), there remain various aspects that are yet to be fully understood when delving into the intersection of prostitution and transgender identity. Within this context, a critical question arises: is the likelihood of victimization primarily influenced by entrenched biases existing independently in both situations; or does one factor significantly outweigh the other? This intersection prompts a nuanced exploration of the intricate dynamics at play, shedding light on the potential impact on the vulnerability of individuals involved.

In pursuit of a comprehensive examination of specific forms of violence against transgender prostitutes, an ambitious exploratory criminological and qualitative study was meticulously designed. The primary objective was to gather firsthand accounts through semi-structured interviews, aiming to unveil the nuanced experiences of this marginalized population in Portugal. Unfortunately, the endeavor encountered a substantial obstacle in the form of insufficient participation, rendering the execution of the study unfeasible.

This chapter serves as a critical exploration of the challenges confronted in the field during the recruitment process for the aforementioned study. A thorough analysis delineates the steps taken by researchers in their concerted efforts to engage participants, shedding light on the intricacies of this complex research landscape. The exploration delves into potential reasons underlying the hesitancy of the transgender sex worker population to actively participate in a study intended to deepen the understanding of the victimological phenomenon that profoundly affects them.

The overarching significance of this chapter lies in its contribution to the imperative task of expanding knowledge. By unraveling the challenges faced in fieldwork, this chapter offers invaluable insights for researchers, amplifying awareness about potential impediments and suggesting pragmatic strategies to overcome these barriers. In doing so, it advances the collective understanding of the complexities surrounding transgender prostitutes, fostering a more informed and compassionate approach to their experiences and struggles.

BACKGROUND

Prostitution can be broadly defined as the provision of sexual services involving a consistent exchange of economic remuneration or goods by women, men, transgender individuals, and youth (Monto, 2004; Note, 2009). Within the realm of prostitution, the engagement in sexual activities is often characterized by a lack of affection and emotionality among participants (Pasko, 2002).

The literature on prostitution has been substantially shaped by a feminist perspective (e.g. Freeman, 1996), especially within criminology. This influence has triggered a contentious debate within academia, with some viewing prostitution as a form of sexual victimization, while others advocate for its recognition as a regulated form of work (Moreira, Rolo, & Cardoso, 2016). Supporters of decriminalization and increased regulation consider it an individual's choice (Jordan, 2005), acknowledging potential downstream social inequalities and discrimination (Mossman, E., 2007). Conversely, anti-prostitution activists argue that the social context surrounding prostitution reduces all acts to non-consensual violence against women (Farley, 2004).

Regardless of one's perspective, violence is an undeniable facet of prostitution that varies with the context. Street prostitution often involves physical assaults, such as slapping, hair pulling, clothing damage, and threats with weapons (Bucher, Manasse & Milton, 2015). In contrast, indoor prostitution, despite a considerable number of reported sexual assaults, exhibits a higher prevalence of beatings (Raphael & Shapiro, 2004). The severity and sexual nature of violence tend to be more pronounced in private spaces compared to the more frequent and diverse violence in public settings (Farley et al., 1998; Katsulis et al., 2014; Raphael & Shapiro, 2004)

It is essential to note that violence against prostitutes must be considered within the context of societal marginalization and devaluation (Ribeiro, Neves Riani, & Antunes-Rocha, 2019; Moreira, Rolo, & Cardoso, 2016; Bucher, Manasse & Milton, 2015).

Traditionally, the normative idea that normality aligns with the congruence between biologically assigned sex and the gender with which individuals identify results in the marginalization, stigmatization, and persecution of the transgender population (Borrillo, 2010). Despite advancements in transgender rights, this population continues to face systemic, interpersonal, and institutional victimization due to persisting discrimination (Hill & Willoughby, 2005), contributing to vulnerabilities in their lives (Laidlaw, 2018; Nadal, Davidoff, & Fujii-Doe, 2014; Jesus, 2013).

According to Santos (2002), violence can be characterized as a power mechanism that manifests itself through various expressions, relying on the use of force and coercion, leading to social damage. Additionally, it operates in different spaces, taking on forms ranging from exclusion (effective or symbolic) to the imposition of stigmas (Hayeck, 2009). Thus, while violence is not exclusive to the transgender population, societal factors such as LGBTphobia, sexism, patriarchy, and cisheteronormativity contribute to the marginalization and vulnerability of transgender individuals, leading some to turn to prostitution as a means to cope with these challenges (Ribeiro, Neves Riani, & Antunes-Rocha, 2019).

Despite significant changes over time, the majority of research on prostitution continues to focus primarily on cisgender women, sidelining transgender and male prostitutes (Westbrook & Saperstein, 2015). This trend limits the literature and knowledge regarding the transgender population in this activity (Geist, 2017).

However, transgender prostitutes are frequently victims of physical and emotional violence, exposed to risky sexual practices, neglected by the criminal justice system (Santiago, Braz, & do Nascimento, 2021), and experience high rates of police-perpetrated violence, such as harassment (Fehrenbacheretal, 2020; Shermanetal, 2019). Additionally, they are more likely to suffer sexual violence from clients compared to cisgender prostitutes (Cohan et al., 2006; Johnson, 2013; Nemoto, Bodeker, & Iwamoto, 2011)

The intricate interplay of socio-structural factors accentuates the heightened vulnerability of transgender women in the sex industry (Lyons et al., 2017). This vulnerability is entwined with systemic issues, including discrimination, economic disparities, and societal prejudices (Laidlaw, 2018). To address these challenges, targeted interventions are essential, encompassing legal frameworks and initiatives promoting inclusivity, awareness, and community support. Enhancing awareness is pivotal for dismantling stereotypes and challenging stigmas that contribute to violence against transgender prostitutes (Nadal, Davidoff, & Fujii-Doe, 2014; Jesus, 2013).

Collaborative efforts involving community organizations, policymakers, healthcare providers, and advocacy groups can develop comprehensive strategies addressing root causes, empowering individuals, and creating safer environments (Ribeiro, Neves Riani, & Antunes-Rocha, 2019). Recognizing the convergence of socio-structural factors is a call to action, urging us to actively engage in initiatives for a more inclusive and equitable landscape for transgender women in the sex industry (Stenersen, Thomas & McKee, 2022).

METHODOLOGY

Study Design

The study sought to comprehensively explore the intersection of transgender identity and prostitution, particularly in relation to the dual exposure to physical and sexual violence, based on the premise that transgender women are inherently more susceptible to victimization, and engaging in prostitution further amplifies this risk

(Ribeiro, Neves Riani, & Antunes-Rocha, 2019; Laidlaw, 2018; Geist, 2017; Lyons et al., 2017; Moreira, Rolo, & Cardoso, 2016). To achieve this, we meticulously designed a qualitative study, utilizing semi-structured interviews as the preferred method for delving into the subjective aspects of human experience, encompassing beliefs, values, and perceptions acquired throughout development (Batista; Matos; Nascimento, 2017; Boni; Quaresma, 2005; Dejonckheere; Vaughn, 2019; Dicicco-Bloom; Crabtree, 2006; Marconi; Lakatos, 2003; McGrath; Palmgren; Liljedahl, 2019; Guazi, 2021).

During the conceptualization and execution of the aforementioned study, the authors of this chapter found themselves grappling with fundamental questions related to epistemology, specifically concerning the nature and attributes of scientific knowledge. These inquiries are inherent to researchers across disciplines, and they become particularly pronounced when employing data collection methods reliant on establishing a close rapport between the researcher and participants.

In the realm of positivist epistemology, which underpins much of quantitative empirical research, criteria such as validity, reliability, and objectivity are paramount. These benchmarks are typically achieved through the systematic elimination of subjective interpretations, ensuring the production of knowledge aligns with established standards (Imai, 2017). However, when conducting qualitative research within a constructivist framework, the adequacy of validity, reliability, and objectivity is often questioned, as they may not be sufficient for establishing trustworthiness (Chandra & Shag, 2017).

Taking an intermediary stance between positivism and constructivism, post-positivism contends that a researcher's ideas, perspectives, and even their identity can influence observations, thereby impacting research outcomes, conclusions, and insights (Panhwar, Ansari, & Shah, 2017). Post-positivists strive to enhance research trustworthiness by acknowledging and addressing personal biases. The crux of trustworthiness in qualitative research lies in ensuring credibility, transferability, dependability, and confirmability (Korstjens & Moser, 2018). Williams and Morrow (2009, p. 577) identify three main categories of trustworthiness that qualitative researchers should aim for: (1) integrity of data, (2) a delicate equilibrium between reflexivity and subjectivity, and (3) transparent communication of findings.

Regrettably, despite the theoretical and methodological considerations, the envisaged study faced insurmountable challenges in participant recruitment, particularly among transgender prostitutes. The complexities of establishing the necessary rapport and intimate relationships between researchers and participants in this context proved formidable, leading to the inability to collect meaningful data. As a result, despite the meticulous planning and adherence to rigorous methodological principles, the envisioned exploration of the intersection of transgender identity and prostitution, specifically in relation to the dual exposure to physical and sexual violence, could not be portrayed.

Henceforth, the forthcoming results section will not present data collected but will focus on elucidating the reasons behind this absence, elucidating the insurmountable barriers encountered during participant recruitment. It is crucial to emphasize, however, that the absence of results stemming from data collection does not diminish the importance of the research question or the commitment devoted to designing a comprehensive study. Instead, it underscores the formidable challenges inherent in the distinctive context of recruiting transgender prostitutes, shedding light on the profound implications these challenges bear on the capacity to glean insights into their lived experiences. Subsequent sections will delve into a reflective analysis of the encountered obstacles, emphasizing the necessity for ongoing discourse and innovative strategies to surmount these challenges and pave the way for future research endeavors in this critical area.

RESULTS

This section organized into several distinct sections, each addressing specific aspects that emerged during the course of our study, namely "Scarcity of scientific literature"; "Sampling strategies and challenges"; "Vulnerabilities and victimization"; "Voluntary participation and consent issues", "Fear of identification"; "Research participation expectations"; and "Participant compensation". Each of these sections aims to provide a comprehensive analysis of the ethical considerations and practical challenges encountered throughout the research process.

Scarcity of Scientific Literature

Our database search revealed a shortage of research on transgender prostitution, acknowledging the potential existence of inaccessible literature, especially in the Portuguese context. However, existing studies (Geist, 2017; Moreira, Rolo, & Cardoso, 2016; Bucher, Manasse & Milton, 2015; Nadal, Davidoff, & Fujii-Doe, 2014; Jesus, 2013) primarily focus on health issues, such as the transmission of sexual diseases (Herbst et al., 2008). While we acknowledge the importance of this research, it prompts us to question whether transgender prostitution should be primarily viewed as a public health concern. According to Stutterheim, van Dijk, Wang & Jonas (2021), the transgender population is disproportionately affected by these diseases rather than being solely a phenomenon increasing the likelihood of victimization through various forms of violence.

Furthermore, the scarcity of literature in this domain not only hampers our understanding and responsiveness to the needs of transgender individuals involved in prostitution but also leaves researchers ill-equipped to navigate the intricate challenges associated with participant recruitment and the execution of sensitive research. The absence of a robust knowledge base pertaining to the specificities of this population severely restricts researchers' ability to foresee and address potential pitfalls in recruiting participants and conducting research ethically.

The importance of understanding the nuanced experiences of transgender individuals engaged in prostitution extends beyond merely improving the overall quality of research; it is essential for ensuring that recruitment strategies and study protocols are intricately tailored to the unique characteristics of this population. Thus, advocating for heightened awareness among researchers about the pressing need for scientific studies on transgender prostitution becomes even more crucial. This serves as a foundational step toward building the knowledge base necessary for the development of successful and ethically sound research practices.

The lack of comprehensive literature not only impedes our grasp of the intricacies within this demographic but also exacerbates the challenges in designing and executing studies that are both impactful and ethical. By recognizing the imperative for research in this field, we lay the groundwork for future endeavors to not only contribute to academic scholarship but, more importantly, to directly inform interventions, policies, and support systems that can meaningfully address the needs of transgender individuals involved in prostitution. As we advocate for increased awareness, we pave the way for a more inclusive and informed research landscape, fostering a deeper understanding that transcends stereotypes and acknowledges the diverse and complex realities faced by this marginalized population.

Sampling Strategies and Challenges

As previously noted, in this study, we endeavored to recruit participants through three distinct strategies: i. engaging with institutions dedicated to transgender prostitutes (convenience sampling); ii. reaching out to individuals familiar to the researchers who have previous experience in the sex industry (purposive (or purposeful) sampling); and iii. actively seeking those with transgender peers (snowball sampling).

Engaging with institutions dedicated to transgender prostitutes aligns with convenience sampling, a practical method where participants are selected based on their accessibility through these specific organizations (Andrade 2021). While this approach was deemed suitable for our study, it comes with inherent constraints that warrant consideration. Initially, we established contact with an institution supporting transgender prostitutes to schedule a meeting and sought collaboration for sample constitution by presenting a detailed study design outlining the theme, objectives, and methodology. Any concerns from the institution were addressed to secure their agreement.

One significant limitation is the potential lack of representativeness, as participants are chosen for their convenience and accessibility through these institutions. This introduces a sampling bias, impacting the generalizability of the findings to the broader population of transgender prostitutes. Moreover, it's crucial to acknowledge that this process may introduce delays, contingent on the availability of both parties and the institution's acceptance. This temporal constraint is a common challenge associated with convenience sampling and may affect our study's adherence to deadlines, particularly in our case—a study involving interviews with transgender prostitutes conducted within a limited two-month timeframe.

Despite professionals' keen interest in gaining knowledge about the phenomenon they focus on; the issue of voluntariness becomes paramount. Individuals should not feel compelled to cooperate, underscoring the importance of their willingness to participate (Borges & Faria, 2023). Additionally, there's an inherent ambivalence between the desire to produce knowledge and the reluctance to potentially retraumatize those sharing abuse experiences, given the sensitivity of the topic. Institutions supporting these victims may express concerns that, instead of assisting, researchers are hindering professionals' efforts by asking victims to revisit traumatic situations, potentially prolonging their suffering (Pio & Singh, 2016).

In this study, despite the supportive role of the institution in providing contacts for transgender prostitutes and directing us to three relevant websites, namely "VipTransex", "ClassificadosX", and "OJE", a notable challenge surfaced. Despite our extensive outreach efforts, involving the contact of 52 individuals, the transgender community did not respond to the researchers' invitations to participate. This underscored a crucial limitation associated with relying solely on convenience sampling. Consequently, this circumstance emphasized the necessity to explore alternative sampling methods, leading us to adopt the purposive sampling technique.

Engaging with individuals familiar to the researchers who have prior experience in the sex industry, specifically transgender prostitutes, reflects purposive (or purposeful) sampling tailored to our study's objectives (Andrade, 2021). This approach, while valuable, introduces unique challenges, particularly when reaching out to known individuals within this specific context.

One significant challenge researchers may face is intricately tied to the study's theme. Delving into sensitive issues intentionally concealed by transgender individuals engaged in sex work becomes necessary, amplifying concerns about potential strain on the existing friendship. The investigator's evolving perception of the participant may inadvertently lead to unintended value judgments (Pio & Singh, 2016).

Moreover, there might be a perceived obligation for the individual, in this case, a person with prior sex work experience, to help the researchers to recruit a sample due to their friendship or acquaintance with the researcher, giving rise to concerns about potential coercion, even if unconscious (Borges, Guerreiro & Conde, 2022). It's crucial to recognize that the limitation may not solely rest in the study's adherence but could be attributed to the investigator.

This implies that, although there might be an initial interest in collaboration, individuals may choose to withdraw because of their reluctance to directly involve themselves in pointing others to the study or connecting the researchers with people they know. The sensitivity of the topic under research, especially related to transgender prostitution, may create discomfort, leading them to prefer not to be the intermediary for disclosing such sensitive information (Borges & Faria, 2023).

In our specific case, the acquaintance with firsthand experience in prostitution initially agreed to provide us with contacts of transgender prostitutes known during his time as a sex worker. However, he ultimately refrained, expressing, "I do not think it is fair of me to provide you with that kind of information without asking the transgender prostitutes first". Naturally, we respected this condition. Unfortunately, despite several messages seeking confirmation of these contacts, we did not receive any responses. This situation highlights the nuanced challenges in recruiting transgender prostitutes through purposive sampling, particularly when depending on known individuals within the community. As a result, we explored a third approach to participant recruitment: actively seeking transgender peers.

Actively seeking transgender peers as a means to identify known transgender prostitutes aligns with the principles of snowball sampling, a technique wherein existing participants or contacts aid in identifying and recruiting additional participants who meet the study criteria (Noy, 2008). The inclusion of peers in the research process is associated with certain advantages, such as reducing social desirability and enhancing the likelihood of obtaining truthful and authentic testimonies. These aspects contribute to a more nuanced understanding of the experiences being explored.

However, in the specific context of our study, this method encountered a notable challenge. The peers we approached, despite their willingness to assist, did not have direct connections with transgender individuals engaged in sex work. This unexpected limitation underscores the inherent unpredictability of snowball sampling, as its success is heavily contingent on the existing social networks of the initial participants (Noy, 2008). In our case, the absence of direct connections to the target population within the peers' networks resulted in the method being less effective than initially anticipated.

This experience highlights the need for researchers to acknowledge the inherent uncertainties associated with certain sampling methods and to adapt their approaches based on the specificities of the study population and context. Despite the challenges encountered, this iterative process of trial and adjustment is an integral aspect of refining research methodologies to ensure their relevance and effectiveness in addressing the research questions at hand.

Vulnerabilities and Victimization

There is a set of vulnerabilities that can increase the likelihood of victimization for these women, spanning various dimensions of their lives (Fernández-Rouco et al., 2017). When considering transgender identity and involvement in prostitution individually, we address topics that inherently deserve significant attention, as both present a myriad of risk factors identified for the victimization of these individuals.

One of the most prevalent forms of violence against transgender women, as documented by Duke & Davidson (2009), Grant et al. (2011), and Lombardi, Wilchins, Priesing, & Malouf (2001), is sexual violence. It is noteworthy that sexual violence is also identified as one of the crimes with higher rates of underreporting, attributable to various factors. Among these factors, hindering sample formation is the profound sense of humiliation, guilt, and shame associated with incidents of sexual violence. This not only contributes to the underreporting of such cases but also poses a significant obstacle to the active participation of transgender prostitutes who have experienced sexual abuse in research studies due to their reluctance to expose the situations of victimization they have endured.

Based on Campbell & Wasco (2005), there is extensive documentation indicating that sexual assault has significant negative effects not only on a physical but also psychological level. In addition to the impact of the act itself, the social reaction directed towards the victim when reporting the assault can contribute to emotional distress. The experience of being a victim of sexual abuse instills a pervasive sense of insecurity concerning safe spaces and raises doubts about the reliability of others (Maria, 2001). Consequently, a prevailing sense of distrust toward researchers and apprehensions about how they might be perceived become evident reasons for withdrawal and non-cooperation.

Coupled with this insecurity is the looming fear of potential reprisals, a natural reaction stemming from constant fear and terror, especially concerning the prospect of being subjected to abuse again by the same or another assailant (Fernández-Rouco et al., 2017). Moreover, within the broader context of violence, stereotypes often shape the perception of an ideal victim, conforming to established social and cultural standards. This standardized image of a victim can be a barrier for individuals whose experiences, like those of transgender prostitutes, do not align with societal norms (Pio & Singh, 2016).

Transgender identity and sex work, when considered individually, they do not conform to the normative standards of a society where transgender identity is stigmatized, and blame is often wrongly attributed to the victim for engaging in sex work. These biases, constituting a form of gender violence, compel victims to adopt self-protective measures to shield themselves from societal judgments and biases (Pio & Singh, 2016).

The notion of self-protection serves to prevent revictimization (Borges & Faria). Exploring instances of abuse, particularly through interviews, may trigger recollections of past traumas, making self-protection a paramount concern. This notion is further reinforced by the response obtained from a close contact who, when asked for assistance in reaching the intended sample and having the purpose of this research explained, stated that *"Regrettably, a significant number of trans women involved in sex work often endure a range of traumas and pressing survival challenges, which, unfortunately, hinders their ability to actively engage in this type of study"*.

Hence, by highlighting this limitation, the intention is to underscore the need for careful consideration in future research. It is essential to approach discussions involving victims with sensitivity, taking precautions to minimize the potential for contributing to the perpetuation of the suffering caused by the crimes they have experienced.

Voluntary Participation and Consent Issues

We underscore the paramount importance of conducting scientific studies founded on ethical and deontological principles, particularly given that criminology is an inherently social science entailing interactions with human subjects. Ethical considerations come to the forefront, especially during the data collection phase, particularly within the context of interviews where a relational dynamic between two individuals (interviewer and interviewee) is presumed (Borges & Faria, 2023; Borges, Guerreiro & Conde, 2022).

While criminology may lack specific regulations tailored to these issues, there exist universal principles that should guide all research endeavors. Aligned with the stipulations of the Deontological Code of the Portuguese Order of Psychologists (2021), three fundamental principles merit attention. Firstly, recognizing that it is the researcher who actively seeks and engages with participants, the crucial importance of respecting autonomy and self-determination is highlighted. Thus, even when there is a fervent desire to comprehend and disclose the studied phenomenon, potential conflicts with human and social values must be navigated. Secondly, the principle of beneficence and non-maleficence underscores the pivotal role of individuals, making the well-being of those involved the primary concern for the researcher. Lastly, the principle of social responsibility dictates that the development and dissemination of generated knowledge should be both valid and contribute significantly to the well-being of individuals (Deontological Code of the Portuguese Order of Psychologists, 2021).

According to this regulation, researchers must also adhere to the non-harm principle, ensuring that their practices avoid causing physical and/or psychological harm to participants. A significant concern arises in this context because obtaining information, not only about potential assaults but also regarding one's life history, prejudices, and stereotypes, could lead to a secondary victimization, thereby prolonging the suffering of those involved (Padilha, Ramos, Borenstein & Martins, 2005). Transgender prostitutes might be hesitant to participate in the research due to concerns that discussing their experiences, including potential violence, could be emotionally distressing and harmful. Additionally, the disclosure of sensitive information might contribute to prolonged suffering, especially if the research is perceived as invasive or judgmental.

Additionally, literature suggests that transgender women are more susceptible to developing clinical depression, and that exposure to physical and sexual violence, combined with a lack of social support, can negatively impact mental health (Nemoto, Bödeker & Iwamoto, 2011). Transgender women, as a group, may face higher susceptibility to clinical depression and exposure to violence (Dwyer, 2014). The researchers may encounter psychologically vulnerable individuals, and the participants may be concerned about the potential impact of the research on their mental health, particularly if it involves discussing traumatic experiences.

Addressing voluntary participation is equally important, with participants needing to be informed of their right to withdraw at any time. Despite potential frustration for researchers when facing a lack of participants, respecting each person's freely expressed will is paramount (Borges, Guerreiro & Conde, 2022). This acknowledgment should not be perceived as a constraint, given that the progress of research fundamentally hinges on voluntary participation.

Despite providing assurances regarding confidentiality and implementing the use of codenames, transgender prostitutes may harbor apprehensions about the potential for recognition and its potential consequences. The fear of being identified, even with the application of codes, may instigate hesitancy, as prospect participants may be anxious about the potential repercussions of their involvement becoming public knowledge and, consequently, may choose to refrain from participation.

Consent and the participant's capacity to provide it are imperatives in any research. When dealing with individuals facing vulnerabilities, as discussed by Padilha, Ramos, Borenstein and Martins (2005), questions arise about whether these vulnerabilities might constrain the free and conscious expression of will. Transgender prostitutes may be hesitant to participate if they feel that the research might compromise their autonomy or if they have doubts about the voluntary nature of their participation.

Thus, special care must be taken in cases where a participant's self-determination is reduced, as they may lack the expected capacity to provide entirely voluntary consent or comprehend the presented information.

Fear of Identification

An additional crucial aspect to examine is the substantial number of transgender prostitutes who are immigrants potentially residing unlawfully in Portugal. This circumstance contributes to a reluctance to engage in studies for a variety of reasons. Foremost among these is the fear of exposure, rooted in the persistent concern of being apprehended and reported to their country of origin. Consequently, these population adopt a defensive stance to safeguard their identity, striving to remain detached and inconspicuous (Laidlaw, 2018). Furthermore, they confront an array of challenges, encompassing limited access to essential services (such as health and education) and economic difficulties. These factors may drive them towards involvement in the sex industry, with all the associated consequences as previously outlined (Lyons et al., 2017).

Moreover, a dearth of community support and trust prevails, partly attributable to documented instances of power abuse by authorities presumed to be reliable, as suggested in the literature (Laidlaw, 2018). Instead of treating these individuals with the requisite respect for human dignity within a democratic state like Portugal, these authorities perpetuate discrimination, acting on preconceived notions and stigmas. This engenders fear of authority figures among these victims. The paradoxical situation where those in authority, entrusted with protection, become perpetrators of harm may lead this marginalized population to distance themselves and decline interaction or seeking support from other professionals (Pio & Singh, 2016) In essence, there's a risk of generalizing these negative experiences to interactions with other professionals, including within the domain of research.

Intrinsically, participants must be assured that no information jeopardizing their identity will be disclosed (Berger, 2016). Building trust is essential in any research involving sensitive topics (Borges & Faria, 2023). Transgender prostitutes may be hesitant if they do not trust the researchers or if they believe that the research might not be conducted without preconceived ideas and judgment. Despite diverse socializations contributing to specific beliefs, our work must be grounded in scientific knowledge, respect, and valuing human beings. Setting aside personal opinions and judgments is essential to prevent conveying a prejudiced and xenophobic attitude, which could further isolate individuals involved in the research (Pio & Singh, 2016). Transgender prostitutes may be concerned about researchers holding preconceived ideas, myths, or stereotypes about transgender individuals or prostitutes. Fear of being judged or stigmatized may contribute to their hesitancy to participate actively.

Research Participation Expectations

Furthermore, transgender prostitutes may question whether the research will genuinely contribute to their well-being and whether the knowledge generated will be used in a way that benefits them. This factor, although direct reports were not obtained, was conveyed to us by the contacted institution. It is the expectation of these individuals to witness a change in their living conditions. From this, we infer that there is a sense of hope, possibly previously invested, that by contributing to research, there will be reciprocity from the community, the state, and relevant services and institutions based on the knowledge acquired. In other words, by participating in studies aimed at exploring the phenomenon and providing their input to address various needs, what they anticipate is the realization of this change.

Like-wise, if they perceive the research as potentially harmful or irrelevant to their experiences, they may be less willing to participate actively. We can only speculate that transgender prostitutes expect that research translates into combating prejudice, ensuring equal rights, and supporting both formal and informal control systems. While this may be seen as a long-term goal, acknowledging that it develops gradually, we emphasize the importance that, in future studies, researchers accurately convey to participants that their contribution is indeed crucial for these issues. However, it is essential to do so without fostering unrealistic expectations that could lead to resistance in the active participation of this population due to the skepticism they may develop toward the research process (Borges & Faria; 2023).

In the realm of research participation expectations, the expressed interest of participants doesn't always guarantee seamless involvement, as a significant obstacle may emerge concerning time availability and the compatibility of researchers' schedules with the intended sample. This becomes particularly evident when examining the experiences of transgender prostitutes who, despite initial interest, declined participation, citing their recent arrival in Portugal and the ongoing adaptation phase to the new country. This nuanced scenario suggests a potential correlation between the challenges of forming a representative sample and the nomadic nature of their circumstances (da Silva & Justo, 2020).

Moreover, a substantial challenge arises from schedule incompatibility inherent to the nature of prostitution itself. Given that this activity primarily occurs during the night, a substantial portion of the day is dedicated to sleep or addressing personal matters that must be handled during conventional working hours (from 9 am to 5 pm). The prospect of conducting interviews with transgender prostitutes during their working hours raises ethical concerns about the appropriateness of questioning individuals amid their professional commitments. Delving into this ethical dilemma (Borges & Faria, 2023), it becomes imperative to carefully consider the potential necessity of interrupting interviews due to participants attending to clients.

Introducing another layer of complexity, there exists the possibility that such interruptions may lead to disengagement among interviewees, resulting in unfinished interviews (da Silva & Justo, 2020). This consideration, combined with the unpredictable nature of this population's life, significantly complicates their availability for research participation. The fluid circumstances emphasize the intricate balance researchers must navigate, seeking valuable insights while ensuring the ethical treatment of those contributing to the study. The multifaceted challenges underscore the need for a thoughtful and nuanced approach to addressing the complexities of research within this unique context.

Participant Compensation

The ethical implications of compensating participants for their involvement in the study were brought into question when confronted with challenges regarding potential participant engagement. On one hand, it was recognized that such compensation conflicted with fundamental principles guiding investigative conduct, notably the principle of voluntariness. Despite participants being thoroughly informed about the purpose and objectives of the compensation, uncertainty lingered regarding the voluntary nature of their participation, given the associated incentive (Head, 2009). In essence, the inquiry arises: would their engagement and interest remain unchanged if not financially rewarded, or would they participate solely for the sake of payment? This raises the concern of whether, through this method, there is a potential coercion of individuals to participate in studies.

According to Goodman et al. (2004) careful consideration of the individuals involved is crucial, as offering compensation to someone with a low socioeconomic status may induce a feeling of obligation due to the irresistible nature of the offered amount in their circumstances. Furthermore, there is the risk of biasing results, as recipients may, instead of providing honest responses, perceive the payment as a service and share information they believe aligns with the researcher's expectations, thereby introducing social desirability (Russell et al., 2000).

On the other hand, compensating participation does not necessarily imply a lack of voluntariness, as the decision to accept or decline involvement remains at the participant's discretion. Accordingly, it is viewed as a favorable practice to compensate for the time invested and potential losses, especially if it interferes with their work schedule (Head, 2009). In essence, it serves as a demonstration of respect not only for the time contributed but also for the challenges participants may face in addressing certain topics (Sullivan & Cain, 2004).

In navigating the complex terrain of participant compensation in research studies, an essential aspect to ponder is the delicate balance between the pursuit of knowledge and the preservation of individuals' values and dignity (Cain, 2004). While this issue elicits a diverse range of opinions, it prompts researchers to conduct a meticulous evaluation of the potential advantages and drawbacks associated with compensation in each unique context (Goodman et al., 2004).

It is imperative to underscore that this consideration extends beyond the mere provision of financial incentives. One must explore the ethical implications of compensation, especially in contexts where vulnerable or marginalized populations are involved (Berger, 2016). An intriguing example is the question of whether to pay transgender prostitutes for their participation in research. The decision not to pursue this avenue in the current study highlights the nuanced nature of these deliberations.

The decision not to compensate transgender prostitutes is grounded in the principle of avoiding potential exploitation and coercion (Pio & Singh, 2016). Offering financial incentives to individuals engaged in sex work, particularly those who may already face socio-economic challenges, carries the risk of creating a coercive environment. This could lead to a perception of obligation, potentially compromising the voluntariness and ethical integrity of their participation.

Furthermore, the sensitive nature of the study, which may involve discussions about stigmatized or taboo topics, necessitates a cautious approach to compensation. While compensating participants is recognized as a demonstration of respect for their time and potential losses, it is equally crucial to avoid inadvertently coercing participation or compromising the integrity of the research findings (Head, 2009).

In line with ethical guidelines, any decision to provide remuneration must be transparently communicated to participants through explicit inclusion in the informed consent process. This ensures that individuals are fully aware of the compensation structure and can make an informed decision about their involvement in the study (Borges & Faria, 2023).

The complexities surrounding participant compensation in research studies underscore the importance of thoughtful consideration and ethical scrutiny. While there is no universally correct answer, researchers must approach this issue with sensitivity, especially when dealing with vulnerable or marginalized populations. The decision not to compensate certain groups, as exemplified in the case of transgender prostitutes in this study, reflects a commitment to upholding ethical standards and respecting the autonomy and dignity of research participants (Berger, 2016).

DISCUSSION

Strategies to Address Challenges in Building a Representative Sample of Transgender Prostitutes

This section aims to provide a thorough exploration of solutions designed to effectively address and overcome the limitations and constraints encountered in the recruitment of transgender prostitutes participants for research. In our pursuit of inclusivity and meaningful engagement, it becomes imperative to delve into a nuanced set of strategies that not only tackle existing barriers but also anticipate and mitigate potential future challenges in this complex research landscape.

While the use of institutions has been identified as a limitation, it is still viewed as a viable means of reaching the target population (Borges, Guerreiro & Conde, 2022). Consequently, one effective strategy to bridge these gaps involves establishing connections with diverse institutions, carefully observing the necessary procedures, and soliciting their collaboration to enhance accessibility to this population. For example, Santos (2013) exemplifies this approach by turning to a non-governmental institution to access the desired sample, specifically males involved in prostitution. Similarly, researchers collaborating with healthcare institutions may prove advantageous in recruiting participants for scientific studies involving transgender prostitutes. This collaborative effort allows researchers to present their study to healthcare professionals who, in direct contact with the target population, can disseminate information and encourage active participation. Researchers may also consider distributing informative materials, such as brochures, to further engage and inform potential participants.

Furthermore, a strategic approach involves proactively exploring institutions that offer volunteer programs, even if their primary focus does not perfectly align with the study's subject matter. By engaging with these programs, researchers can propose short-term involvement, fostering a sense of trust and rapport with individuals within the transgender prostitutes community (Berger, 2016). When presenting the study, it becomes crucial to emphasize that participants are under no obligation to engage and that their involvement is entirely voluntary, with no imposition from the collaborating institution. This method not only provides an opportunity to establish connections but also ensures transparency and autonomy in participant recruitment (Borges & Faria, 2023).

Another impactful strategy in addressing the challenges of constructing a representative sample of transgender prostitutes involves the development of informative brochures that succinctly outline the study's purpose, objectives, and a compelling call for participation. This approach facilitates the distribution of these informative materials to local organizations that provide support to the target population, extending to healthcare institutions as well. Furthermore, researchers can directly engage with individuals in the identified areas, making the distribution of these brochures a tangible and personalized outreach effort. This multi-faceted dissemination approach enhances the visibility of the study, reaching both organizational hubs and the individuals themselves, thereby fostering a comprehensive and inclusive recruitment strategy.

An alternative strategy centers around pinpointing specific areas where prostitution, particularly transgender prostitution, is concentrated and directly interacting with individuals in those regions. While traditional sampling methods retain validity, this approach capitalizes on the potential for heightened awareness and a more explicit articulation of the study's objectives, thereby fostering increased participant engagement (Cho & Trent, 2006). Additionally, harnessing the power of online platforms, such as websites, proves instrumental in sample acquisition within this unique context (Vartabedian, 2019).

By referencing the initially designed study, this strategy allowed for a targeted subject search in Portugal, facilitating a refined approach that aligns with specific research criteria. Moreover, the utilization of websites offers a practical means of accessing potential participants, as most platforms conveniently provide readily available contact information (Vartabedian, 2019). This dual-pronged approach not only enhances the study's reach but also streamlines the process of participant recruitment, ensuring a more tailored and efficient engagement with the transgender prostitutes community.

The revisitation of the financial incentive issue prompts careful consideration. As mentioned earlier, the ethical appropriateness of providing financial incentives remains a topic without unanimous agreement among researchers; nevertheless, it is a consideration not easily disregarded (Castro, 2008). It is paramount to emphasize that, should remuneration be selected as an incentive for participation, all previously discussed implications must be meticulously weighed and evaluated. Furthermore, it is imperative to acknowledge the elevated risk of social desirability in this context (Castro, 2008).

Within the study framework, explicit mention should be made of the deliberate selection of financial incentives as a strategy for sample composition, accompanied by a transparent discussion of the potential consequences (Castro, 2008). This level of transparency is essential to uphold the study's integrity, ensuring that participants are fully informed and that ethical considerations are robustly addressed (Castro, 2008). In navigating the nuanced landscape of financial incentives, a judicious approach is required, one that meticulously balances the ethical dimensions of participant engagement and the potential impact on the study's outcomes.

Alternative approach involves positioning the study as a form of "advertisement" in collaboration with institutions dedicated to the phenomenon under investigation.

Many of these institutions maintain websites that offer comprehensive information about their identity, mission, objectives, and the support they provide. A proactive step would be to create a dedicated research section within these websites, where researchers can succinctly present the study's topic and purpose (Aquino et. al, 2013).

Following approval by the collaborating institution, a clear and concise message could be prominently displayed, announcing the study's timeframe and inviting interested individuals to contact the research team. This strategic message might read, for example, ""We're conducting a groundbreaking study and we want YOUR voice to be heard! If you're a member of the vibrant transgender community and have stories to share in relation to prostitution, we invite you to join our transformative research". To facilitate expressions of interest, a mechanism, such as the researcher's email contact or an online questionnaire, should be readily accessible.

This approach ensures that individuals visiting the institution's site for reasons unrelated to the study become aware of and comprehend the study's focus, thereby fostering an appreciation for the importance of their potential participation. By leveraging established platforms, this strategy not only maximizes outreach but also integrates the study seamlessly into the existing discourse of the institutions, enhancing visibility and encouraging active involvement from the target population.

Recruiting participants and promoting the study can be effectively achieved through tailor-made events designed for the target population. These events may include engaging lectures featuring diverse professionals and impactful testimonials from individuals who have firsthand experience with or are currently navigating similar conditions Smyth, 1998). The active involvement of researchers in disseminating information about the study is not just beneficial but crucial for building trust and rapport.

Event execution should prioritize robust security measures to guarantee the safety, protection, and overall well-being of all participants involved. This necessitates meticulous planning to ensure the required confidentiality and privacy standards are met. Researchers should consider utilizing secure venues, implementing potential security protocols to prevent any form of discrimination, and providing comprehensive training for all event collaborators and organizers who may find themselves in sensitive situations or unexpected incidents.

The overarching goal is to foster an environment that prioritizes respect, protection, and appreciation for participants, both during and after the event. This commitment not only contributes significantly to the successful advancement of the research cause but also plays a pivotal role in encouraging increased participation in subsequent studies or events. It is a holistic approach that underscores the ethical responsibility of researchers to create a secure and supportive space for participants, ultimately leading to a more meaningful and impactful research engagement.

Alternative adaptation to enhance participant recruitment involves modifying the research methodology itself. One effective adjustment is substituting individual interviews with focus groups, a method characterized by facilitated discussions among individuals who share common characteristics and a mutual interest in a specific topic (Galego & Gomes, 2005) This strategic shift has the potential to facilitate participant recruitment, creating an environment where individuals may feel more at ease sharing their experiences with others who are encountering similar conditions and comparable situations (Galego & Gomes, 2005).

For instance, the utilization of focus groups proved successful in the study conducted by Guimarães and Merchán-Hamann (2005) on the perceptions and social representations of the daily lives of female sex workers. This approach fosters a sense of community and shared understanding, allowing participants to draw strength and comfort from the collective experience. By adapting the research method to focus groups, researchers acknowledge the unique dynamics of the transgender sex worker community and tailor their approach to ensure a more inclusive and participant-friendly research environment (Galego & Gomes, 2005). This strategy not only facilitates recruitment but also enriches the depth and authenticity of the insights gathered during the research process.

In a more contentious approach, researchers may consider infiltrating the community, opting for observational research methods (Sussman, 2016). While this strategy offers the advantage of direct contact with the reality under investigation, it inevitably raises ethical concerns that demand careful consideration. Foremost among these concerns is the inherent risk that the researcher might be exposed as a "fraud", potentially jeopardizing the credibility of studies and, by extension, the reputation of researchers within this specific population.

This method prompts a critical question about its inherent nature — whether it can be perceived as inherently deceptive, thus posing a potential threat to the credibility of future investigations. Researchers find themselves grappling with a significant decision: whether to disclose their identity and purpose or withhold such information to prevent potential alterations in subjects' behavior due to awareness of being observed (Sussman, 2016).

Moreover, ethical quandaries extend to situations where a researcher witnesses a crime in areas prone to criminal activities. Should the researcher report the incident to authorities, thereby revealing their presence, or maintain silence, acknowledging that their awareness stems from the act of infiltration? These are intricate questions that necessitate meticulous consideration, among others, and the answers are far from straightforward.

In the pursuit of comprehending the social context of sex workers in Portugal, Csalog (2021) opted for ethnography as the preferred method, firmly grounded in participant observation. This methodological choice exemplifies a commitment to deeply understanding the lived experiences within the community while acknowledging and navigating the complex ethical terrain inherent in such research endeavors.

CONCLUSION

This comprehensive exploration has outlined a diverse set of strategies tailored to effectively address the challenges inherent in recruiting transgender prostitutes for research. By acknowledging the potential limitations and actively engaging with nuanced solutions, we strive for inclusivity and meaningful participation, ensuring a robust and ethical research framework.

Analyzing any social phenomenon invariably unveils its inherent complexity, and this study is no exception. Undoubtedly, the primary impediment, as iterated earlier, resides in the glaring lack of information encountered concerning the unique intricacies of transgender prostitution. Delving into the challenges of constructing the sample for our initially targeted study prompted the emergence of myriad questions and potential interpretations. Yet, in substantiating our conclusions for each limitation, the absence of empirical evidence compelled us to scrutinize these challenges in both phenomena individually, ultimately generalizing to the specific issue at hand.

Throughout this chapter, it becomes abundantly clear that gaining access to a sample of transgender sex workers poses an extraordinary challenge. However, upon retracing the origins of prostitution and transgender experiences to the present day, the noteworthy societal advancements pertaining to these phenomena demand an unequivocal response from the realms of science and research. Consequently, researchers are not merely encouraged but impelled to traverse unexplored avenues, steering clear of redundant inquiry and championing investigations in underexplored territories (Borges & Faria, 2023). In the face of anticipated difficulties, challenges must not serve as discouragement but rather as a clarion call to underscore the objectivity and sensitivity requisite for probing into these profound issues (Berger, 2016). Thus, science must align itself with the dynamic evolution of societies. With the advent of new phenomena or their increased visibility, the scientific community is duty-bound to unravel their intricacies across diverse dimensions (Borges, Guerreiro & Conde, 2022).

In this context, we vehemently stress that researchers must exhibit unwavering reliability, empathy, and multidisciplinary in their interactions with the transgender sex worker population. The latter quality promises to infuse broader and more holistic approaches into investigations, magnifying the spotlight on prevalent issues and comprehensively unraveling them (Borges & Faria, 2023).

Equally pivotal are the prospective approaches that researchers might adopt for recruiting these individuals, with an emphatic focus on incorporating methods that ardently respect participants' freedoms and guarantees, thus ensuring the sanctity of their safety and dignity. This imperative underscores the ethical responsibility and the pivotal role of researchers in unraveling the complexities of transgender prostitution and contributing meaningfully to the broader discourse on this crucial social phenomenon (Borges & Faria, 2023).

In essence, this chapter significantly advances future research on transgender prostitution by offering tailored strategies that effectively address recruitment challenges, promoting inclusivity and meaningful participation within a robust and ethical research framework.

REFERENCES

Andrade, C. (2021). The inconvenient truth about convenience and purposive samples. *Indian Journal of Psychological Medicine*, *43*(1), 86–88. doi:10.1177/0253717620977000 PMID:34349313

Aquino, E. M., Araujo, M. J., Almeida, M. D. C. C., Conceição, P., Andrade, C. R. D., Cade, N. V., Carvalho, M. S., Figueiredo, R. C., Fonseca, M. J. M., Giatti, L., Menezes, G. M. S., Nunes, M. A., Souza, A. G., Vasconcellos-Silva, P. R., & Vigo, A. (2013). Recrutamento de participantes no Estudo Longitudinal de Saúde do Adulto. *Revista de Saude Publica*, *47*(suppl 2), 10–18. doi:10.1590/S0034-8910.2013047003953 PMID:24346716

Berger, R. (2016). Now I see it, now I don't: Researcher's position and reflexivity in qualitative research. *Qualitative Research*, *15*(2), 1–16.

Borges, G., & Faria, R. (2023). Language, emotions, and access to refugee women: Ingredients for reflexivity. In A. M. Díaz Fernández, C. Del-Real, & L. Molnar (Eds.), *Fieldwork Experiences in Criminology and Security Studies: Methods, Ethics, and Emotions*. Springer Nature. doi:10.1007/978-3-031-41574-6_17

Borges, G. M., Guerreiro, A., Conde, L. (2022). Stroking reflexivity into practice: The pros and cons of resorting to gatekeepers to conduct qualitative criminological research. *The Journal of Qualitative Criminal Justice and Criminology*.

Borges, Z. N., Perurena, F. C., Passamani, G. R., & Bulsing, M. (2013). Patriarcado, heteronormatividade e misoginia em debate: pontos e contrapontos para o combate à homofobia nas escolas. *Latitude, 7*(1).

Borrillo, D. (2010). *História e crítica de um preconceito*. Autêntica.

Bucher, J., Manasse, M., & Milton, J. (2015). Soliciting strain: Examining both sides of street prostitution through general strain theory. *Journal of Crime and Justice*, *38*(4), 435–453. doi:10.1080/0735648X.2014.949823

Campbell, R., & Wasco, S. M. (2005). Understanding rape and sexual assault: 20 years of progress and future directions. *Journal of Interpersonal Violence*, *20*(1), 127–131. doi:10.1177/0886260504268604 PMID:15618569

Castro, L. D. D. (2008). *Pagamento a participantes de pesquisa*. Academic Press.

Ceccarelli, P. R. (2008). Prostituição–Corpo como mercadoria. *Mente & Cérebro–sexo, 4*(1), 1-14.

Chandra, Y., & Shag, L. (2017). An RQDA-based constructivist methodology for qualitative research. *Qualitative Market Research*, *20*(1), 90–122. doi:10.1108/QMR-02-2016-0014

Cho, J., & Trent, A. (2006). Validity in qualitative research revisited. *Qualitative Research*, *6*(3), 319–340. doi:10.1177/1468794106065006

Cohan, D., Lutnick, A., Davidson, P., Cloniger, C., Herlyn, A., Breyer, J., ... Klausner, J. (2006). Sex worker health: San Francisco style. *Sexually Transmitted Infections*, *82*(5), 418–422. doi:10.1136/sti.2006.020628 PMID:16854996

Costa, H. A. (2008). Lopes, Ana (2006), Trabalhadores do sexo uni-vos! Organização laboral na indústria do sexo. *Revista Critica de Ciencias Sociais*, (80), 213–217. doi:10.4000/rccs.706

Csalog, R. A. (2021). Mulheres (in) visíveis: prostituição, trabalho e migrações nas ruas de Lisboa. *e-Cadernos CES*, (35).

da Silva, L. C., & Justo, J. S. (2020). Errância Queer e Nomadismo Feminino: Trajetividades e Resistências de Mulheres no Trecho. *Revista Subjetividades*, *20*(2), 1–12. doi:10.5020/23590777.rs.v20i2.e9372

da Silva, R. A. (2011). A prostituição ontem e hoje: algumas reflexões em Georg Simmel. *Faculdade do Sudeste Goiano, 6*.

de Jesus, J. G. (2013). Transfobia e crimes de ódio: Assassinatos de pessoas pdgênero como genocídio. *História agora, 16*, 101-123.

Diário da República. (2021). Ordem dos Psicólogos Portugueses.

Duke, A., & Davidson, M. M. (2009). Same-sex intimate partner violence: Lesbian, gay, and bisexual affirmative outreach and advocacy. *Journal of Aggression, Maltreatment & Trauma*, *18*(8), 795–816. doi:10.1080/10926770903291787

Dwyer, A. (2014). Pleasures, Perversities, and Partnerships: The Historical Emergence of LGBT-Police Relationships. In D. Peterson & V. R. Panfil (Eds.), *The Handbook of LGBT Communities, Crime, and Justice*. Springer. doi:10.1007/978-1-4614-9188-0_8

Dwyer, A., Ball, M., & Crofts, T. (2016). Queering criminologies. In *Queering criminology* (pp. 1–11). Palgrave Macmillan UK.

Farley, M. (2004). "Bad for the body, bad for the heart": Prostitution harms women even if legalized or decriminalized. *Violence Against Women*, *10*(10), 1087–1125. doi:10.1177/1077801204268607

Farley, M., Baral, I., Kiremire, M., & Sezgin, U. (1998). Prostitution in five countries: Violence and post-traumatic stress disorder. *Feminism & Psychology*, *8*(4), 405–426. doi:10.1177/0959353598084002

Fehrenbacher, A. E., Park, J. N., Footer, K. H., Silberzahn, B. E., Allen, S. T., & Sherman, S. G. (2020). Exposure to police and client violence among incarcerated female sex workers in Baltimore City, Maryland. *American Journal of Public Health*, *110*(S1), S152–S159. doi:10.2105/AJPH.2019.305451 PMID:31967867

Freeman, J. (1996). The feminist debate over prostitution reform. Applications of Feminist Legal Theory to Women's Lives, Sex, Violence, Work and Reproduction, 241, 246.

Geist, F. M. (2017). Staging the trans sex worker. *Transgender Studies Quarterly*, *4*(1), 112–127. doi:10.1215/23289252-3711577

Goodman, L. A., Liang, B., Helms, J. E., Latta, R. E., Sparks, E., & Weintraub, S. R. (2004). Training counseling psychologists as social justice agents: Feminist and multicultural principles in action. *The Counseling Psychologist*, *32*(6), 793–836. doi:10.1177/0011000004268802

Grant, J. M., Mottet, L. A., Tanis, J. J., & Min, D. (2011). *Transgender discrimination survey*. National Center for Transgender Equality and National Gay and Lesbian Task Force.

Guazi, T. S. (2021). Diretrizes para o uso de entrevistas semiestruturadas em investigações científicas. *Revista Educação, Pesquisa eInclusão, 2*.

Guimarães, K., & Merchán-Hamann, E. (2005). Comercializando fantasias: A representação social da prostituição, dilemas da profissão e a construção da cidadania. *Estudos Feministas*, *13*(3), 525–544. doi:10.1590/S0104-026X2005000300004

Hayeck, C. M. (2009). Refletindo sobre a violência. *Revista Brasileira de História & Ciências Sociais, 1*(1).

Herbst, J. H., Jacobs, E. D., Finlayson, T. J., McKleroy, V. S., Neumann, M. S., & Crepaz, N. (2008). Estimating HIV prevalence and risk behaviors of transgender persons in the United States: A systematic review. *AIDS and Behavior*, *12*(1), 1–17. doi:10.1007/s10461-007-9299-3 PMID:17694429

Hill, D. B., & Willoughby, B. L. B. (2005). The development and validation of the Genderism and Transphobia Scale. *Sex Roles*, *53*(7-8), 531–544. doi:10.1007/s11199-005-7140-x

Imai, K. (2017). *Quantitative social science: An introduction*. Princeton University Press.

Johnson, J. R. (2013). Cisgender privilege, intersectionality, and the criminalization of CeCe McDonald: Why intercultural communication needs transgender studies. *Journal of International and Intercultural Communication*, *6*(2), 135–144. doi:10.1080/17513057.2013.776094

Jordan, J. (2005). *The Sex Industry in New Zealand: a literature review*. Ministry of Justice.

Katsulis, Y., Durfee, A., Lopez, V., & Robillard, A. (2014). Predictors of workplace violence among female sex workers in Tijuana, Mexico. *Violence Against Women*, 1–27. PMID:25091980

Korstjens, I., & Moser, A. (2018). Practical guidance to qualitative research: Trustworthiness and publishing. *The European Journal of General Practice*, *24*(1), 120–124. doi:10.1080/13814788.2017.1375092 PMID:29202616

Laidlaw, L. (2018). Challenging dominant portrayals of the trans sex worker: On gender, violence, and protection. *Man. LJ*, *41*, 351.

LeVay, S. (1996). *Queer Science: The Use and Abuse of Research into Homosexuality*. The MIT Press. doi:10.7551/mitpress/5726.001.0001

Lombardi, E. L., Wilchins, R. A., Priessing, D., & Malouf, D. (2001). Gender violence: Transgender experiences with violence and discrimination. *Journal of Homosexuality*, *42*(1), 89–101. doi:10.1300/J082v42n01_05 PMID:11991568

Lyons, T., Krüsi, A., Pierre, L., Kerr, T., Small, W., & Shannon, K. (2017). Negotiating violence in the context of transphobia and criminalization: The experiences of trans sex workers in Vancouver, Canada. *Qualitative Health Research*, *27*(2), 182–190. doi:10.1177/1049732315613311 PMID:26515922

Maria, S. G. D. S. (2001). *Mulheres sobreviventes de violação* (Doctoral dissertation). Universidade Aberta.

Monto, M. A. (2004). Female prostitution, customers, and violence. *Violence Against Women*, *10*(2), 160–188. doi:10.1177/1077801203260948

Moreira, V., Rolo, A., & Cardoso, J. (2016). Violence in the context of prostitution: psychological impact. *Psiquiatria, Psicologia & Justiça*, 62-72.

Mossman, E. (2007). *International approaches to decriminalising or legalising prostitution*. Ministry of Justice.

Nadal, K. L., Davidoff, K. C., & Fujii-Doe, W. (2014). Transgender women and the sex work industry: Roots in systemic, institutional, and interpersonal discrimination. *Journal of Trauma & Dissociation*, *15*(2), 169–183. doi:10.1080/15299732.2014. 867572 PMID:24313294

Nemoto, T., Bödeker, B., & Iwamoto, M. (2011). Social support, exposure to violence and transphobia, and correlates of depression among male-to-female transgender women with a history of sex work. *American Journal of Public Health*, *101*(10), 1980–1988. doi:10.2105/AJPH.2010.197285 PMID:21493940

Noy, C. (2008). Sampling knowledge: The hermeneutics of snowball sampling in qualitative research. *International Journal of Social Research Methodology*, *11*(4), 327–344. doi:10.1080/13645570701401305

Nussbaum, M. C. (2010). *From Disgust to Humanity: Sexual Orientation and Constitutional Law*. Oxford University Press.

Padilha, M. I. C. D. S., Ramos, F. R. S., Borenstein, M. S., & Martins, C. R. (2005). A responsabilidade do pesquisador ou sobre o que dizemos acerca da ética em pesquisa. *Texto & Contexto Enfermagem*, *14*(1), 96–105. doi:10.1590/S0104-07072005000100013

Panhwar, A. H., Ansari, S., & Shah, A. (2017). Post-positivism: An Effective Paradigm for Social and Educational Research. *International Research Journal of Arts & Humanities*, *45*(45), 253–260.

Pasko, L. (2002). Naked Power: The Practice of Stripping as a Confidence Game. *Sexualities*, *5*(1), 49–66. doi:10.1177/1363460702005001003

Pio, E., & Singh, S. (2016). Vulnerability and resilience: Critical reflexivity in gendered violence research. *Third World Quarterly*, *37*(2), 227–244. doi:10.1080/01436597.2015.1089166

Raphael, J., & Shapiro, D. L. (2004). Violence in indoor and outdoor prostitution venues. *Violence Against Women*, *10*(2), 126–139. doi:10.1177/1077801203260529

Ribeiro, L. P., Neves Riani, S. R., & Antunes-Rocha, M. I. (2019). Representaciones sociales de personas transgénero (travestis y transexuales) sobre la violencia. *Revista de Psicología, 37*(2), 496–527. doi:10.18800/psico.201902.006

Russell, M. L., Moralejo, D. G., & Burgess, E. D. (2000). Paying research subjects: Participants' perspectives. *Journal of Medical Ethics, 26*(2), 126–130. doi:10.1136/jme.26.2.126 PMID:10786324

Rydstrom, J., & Mustola, K. (2007). *Criminally Queer: Homosexuality and Criminal Law in Scandinavia, 1842-1999.* Aksant Academic Publishers. doi:10.26530/OAPEN_353810

Sacramento, O., & Ribeiro, M. (2014). Mulheres marcadas: prostituicao, ordem e exclusao. *Cuadernos de trabajo social, 27*(1).

Santiago, I. M. F. L., Braz, E. D. C., & do Nascimento, J. B. (2021). Violência e transfobia: vivências de travestis que exercem a prostituição-campina Grande-PB. *Revista Gênero, 22*(1).

Santos, J. V. T. D. (2002). Microfísica da violência, uma questão social mundial. *Ciência e cultura, 54*(1), 22–24.

Santos, M. L. D. (2013). *Da batalha na calçada ao circuito do prazer: um estudo sobre prostituição masculina no centro de Fortaleza.* Tese de Doutoramento, Universidade Federal do Ceará.

Sherman, S. G., Park, J. N., Galai, N., Allen, S. T., Huettner, S. S., Silberzahn, B. E., Decker, M. R., Poteat, T. C., & Footer, K. H. (2019). Drivers of HIV infection among cisgender and transgender female sex worker populations in Baltimore City: Results from the SAPPHIRE study. *Journal of Acquired Immune Deficiency Syndromes, 80*(5), 513–521. doi:10.1097/QAI.0000000000001959 PMID:30649029

Smyth, J. M. (1998). Written emotional expression: Effect sizes, outcome types, and moderating variables. *Journal of Consulting and Clinical Psychology, 66*(1), 174–184. doi:10.1037/0022-006X.66.1.174 PMID:9489272

Stenersen, M. R., Thomas, K., & McKee, S. (2022). Police harassment and violence against transgender & gender diverse sex workers in the United States. *Journal of Homosexuality*, 1–13. PMID:36228168

Stotzer, R. L. (2009). Violence against transgender people: A review of United States data. *Aggression and Violent Behavior, 14*(3), 170–179. doi:10.1016/j.avb.2009.01.006

Stutterheim, S. E., van Dijk, M., Wang, H., & Jonas, K. J. (2021). The worldwide burden of HIV in transgender individuals: An updated systematic review and meta-analysis. *PLoS One*, *16*(12), e0260063. doi:10.1371/journal.pone.0260063 PMID:34851961

Sullivan, C. M., & Cain, D. (2004). Ethical and safety considerations when obtaining information from or about battered women for research purposes. *Journal of Interpersonal Violence*, *19*(5), 603–618. doi:10.1177/0886260504263249 PMID:15104864

Teodoro, M. C. M., & Silva, T. C. (2015). A História de Exclusão Social e Condenaçào Moral da Prostituição. *Revista Brasileira de História do Direito*, *1*(1), 208–233. doi:10.26668/IndexLawJournals/2526-009X/2015.v1i1.676

Vartabedian, J. (2019). Bodies and desires on the internet: An approach to trans women sex workers' websites. *Sexualities*, *22*(1-2), 224–243. doi:10.1177/1363460717713381

Westbrook, L., & Saperstein, A. (2015). New categories are not enough: Rethinking the measurement of sex and gender in social surveys. *Gender & Society*, *29*(4), 534–560. doi:10.1177/0891243215584758

Williams, E. N., & Morrow, S. L. (2009). Achieving trustworthiness in qualitative research: A pan-paradigmatic perspective. *Psychotherapy Research*, *19*(4-5), 576–582. doi:10.1080/10503300802702113 PMID:19579089

Compilation of References

Aarons, G., Brown, S., Sticed, E., & Coe, M. (2001). Psychometric evaluation of the marijuana and stimulant effect expectancy questionnaires for adolescents. *Addictive Behaviors*, *26*(2), 219–236. doi:10.1016/S0306-4603(00)00103-9 PMID:11316378

Aarten, P. G., Mulder, E., & Pemberton, A. (2018). The Narrative of Victimization and deradicalization: An expert view. *Studies in Conflict and Terrorism*, *41*(7), 577–572. doi:10.10 80/1057610X.2017.1311111

Aas, K. (2011). 'Crimmigrant' bodies and the bona fide traveler: Surveillance, citizenship and global governance. *Theoretical Criminology*, *15*(3), 331–346. doi:10.1177/1362480610396643

Aas, K. F. (2013). *Globalization & crime: Key approaches to criminology*. Sage Publications.

Aas, K. F. (2019). *The crimmigrant other: Migration and Penal Power*. Routledge.

Aas, K. F., & Bosworth, M. (2013). *The borders of punishment: Migration, Citizenship, and Social Exclusion*. Oxford University Press. doi:10.1093/acprof:oso/9780199669394.001.0001

Aas, K. F., & Gundhus, H. O. I. (2015). Policing humanitarian borderlands: Frontex, human rights and the precariousness of life. *British Journal of Criminology*, *55*(1), 1–18. doi:10.1093/bjc/azu086

Ackerson, L. K., & Subramanian, S. V. (2016). State Gender Inequality, Socioeconomic Status and Intimate Partner Violence (IPV) in India : A Multilevel Analysis. *The Australian Journal of Social Issues*, 81–103.

Akmeşe, Z., & Deniz, K. (2017). Hate Speech in social media: LGBTI persons. *15th International Symposium Communication in the Millennium*.

Aliverti, A. (2020). Benevolent policing? Vulnerability and the moral pains of border controls. *British Journal of Criminology*, *60*(5), 1117–1135. doi:10.1093/bjc/azaa026

Allen, J., Leadbeater, B., & Aber, J. (1990). The relationship of adolescents' expectations and values to delinquency, hard drug use, and unprotected sexual intercourse. *Development and Psychopathology*, *2*(1), 85–98. doi:10.1017/S0954579400000614

Alston, P. P., & Knuckey, S. (Eds.). (2016). *The transformation of human rights fact-finding*. Oxford University Press. doi:10.1093/acprof:oso/9780190239480.001.0001

Álvarez Lara, M. C., & Castillo Mauricio, M. S. (2022). *Ciberbullying en niños y adolescentes desde la perspectiva de género: Una revisión sistemática.* https://hdl.handle.net/20.500.12692/86862

American Psychiatric Association. (2013). *Diagnostic and Statistical Manual of Mental Disorder* (5th ed.). APA.

Anderson, B. (2013). *Us and them: The dangerous politics of immigration control.* Oxford University Press. doi:10.1093/acprof:oso/9780199691593.001.0001

Andrade, C. (2021). The inconvenient truth about convenience and purposive samples. *Indian Journal of Psychological Medicine*, *43*(1), 86–88. doi:10.1177/0253717620977000 PMID:34349313

APAV (2023). *Estatísticas APAV - Relatório Anual 2022.* Associação Portuguesa de Apoio à Vítima.

Apsler, R., Cummins, M. R., & Carl, C. (2003). Perceptions of the police by female victims of domestic partner violence. *Violence Against Women*, *9*(11), 1318–1335. Advance online publication. doi:10.1177/1077801203255554

Aquino, E. M., Araujo, M. J., Almeida, M. D. C. C., Conceição, P., Andrade, C. R. D., Cade, N. V., Carvalho, M. S., Figueiredo, R. C., Fonseca, M. J. M., Giatti, L., Menezes, G. M. S., Nunes, M. A., Souza, A. G., Vasconcellos-Silva, P. R., & Vigo, A. (2013). Recrutamento de participantes no Estudo Longitudinal de Saúde do Adulto. *Revista de Saude Publica*, *47*(suppl 2), 10–18. doi:10.1590/S0034-8910.2013047003953 PMID:24346716

Asher, C., & Gask, L. (2010). Reasons for illicit drug use in people with schizophrenia: Qualitative study. *Psychiatry*, *10*, 94–109. doi:10.116/1471-244X-10-94 PMID:21092168

Aslan, A., & Karakus Yilmaz, T. (2021). Changes in Safer Internet Use of Children in Turkey between 2010-2015 and Impact of Contextual Issues. *Malaysian Online Journal of Educational Technology*, *9*(1), 1–18. doi:10.17220/mojet.2021.9.1.238

Åslund, O., & Engdahl, M. (2018). The value of earning for learning: Performance bonuses in immigrant language training. *Economics of Education Review*, *62*, 192–204. doi:10.1016/j.econedurev.2017.11.010

Athanasopoulos, A. (2017). Fortress Europe?: The Aegean Sea Frontier and the Strengthening of EU's External Borders. In G. Wahlers (Ed.), *Borders* (pp. 14–25). Konrad Adenauer Stiftung.

Atlani, L., & Rousseau, C. (2000). The politics of culture in humanitarian aid to women refugees who have experienced sexual violence. *Transcultural Psychiatry*, *37*(3), 435–449. doi:10.1177/136346150003700309

Azambuja, M., Nogueira, C., Neves, S., & Oliveira, J. (2013). Gender Violence in Portugal: Discourses, Knowledge, and Practices. *Indian Journal of Gender Studies*, *20*(1), 31–50. doi:10.1177/0971521512465935

Bacchus, L. J., Ranganathan, M., Watts, C., & Devries, K. (2018). Recent intimate partner violence against women and health: A systematic review and meta-analysis of cohort studies. *BMJ Open*, *8*(7), e019995. Advance online publication. doi:10.1136/bmjopen-2017-019995 PMID:30056376

Baczynska, G., & Ledwith, S. (2016). How Europe built fences to keep people out. *Reuters*. Retrieved from: https://www.reuters.com/article/us-europe-migrants-fences-in sight-idUSKCN0X10U7

Bakker, J. I. (2019). Grounded theory methodology and grounded theory method: introduction to the special issue. *Sociological Focus, 52*(2), 91-106. doi:10.1080/00380237.2019.1550592

Bandura, A. (1977). Self-efficacy: Toward a unifying theory of behavioral change. *Psychological Review, 84*(2), 191–215. doi:10.1037/0033-295X.84.2.191 PMID:847061

Bandura, A. (1986). *Social foundations of thought and action: A social cognitive theory.* Prentice Hall.

Bandura, A. (2001). Social cognitive theory: An agentic perspective. *Annual Review of Psychology, 52*(1), 1–26. doi:10.1146/annurev.psych.52.1.1 PMID:11148297

Bang-Ping, J. (2009). Sexual dysfunction in men who abuse illicit drugs: A preliminary report. *Journal of Sexual Medicine, 6*(4), 1072–1080. doi:10.1111/j.1743-6109.2007.00707.x PMID:18093094

Bardin, L. (2013). *Análise de Conteúdo* [Content analysis]. Edições 70.

Barker, V. (2018). *Nordic nationalism and penal order walling the welfare state.* Routledge. doi:10.1093/iclq/53.1.47

Barlow, D. (1986). Causes of sexual dysfunction: The role of anxiety and cognitive interference. *Journal of Consulting and Clinical Psychology, 54*(2), 140–157. doi:10.1037/0022-006X.54.2.140 PMID:3700800

Barnett, O. W., Miller-Perrin, C. L., & Perrin, R. D. (2010). *Family violence across the lifespan: an introduction.* SAGE Publications.

Bartholomew, N., Hiller, M., Knight, K., Nucatola, D., & Simpson, D. (2000). Effectiveness of communication and relationship skills training for men in substance abuse treatment. *Journal of Substance Abuse Treatment, 18*(3), 217–225. doi:10.1016/S0740-5472(99)00051-3 PMID:10742634

Bauman, Z. (1998). *Globalization: The human consequences.* Columbia University Press.

Bauman, Z. (2016). *Strangers at our door.* Cambridge Polity Press.

Becker, H. S. (1963). *Outsiders: Studies in the sociology of deviance.* Free Press Glencoe.

Bellis, M., & Hughes, K. (2004). Sex potions. Relationships between alcohol, drugs and sex. *Adicciones, 16*(4), 249–258. doi:10.20882/adicciones.390

Bellis, M., Hughes, K., Calafat, A., Juan, M., Ramon, A., Rodriguez, J., Mendes, F., Schnitzer, S., & Phillips-Howard, P. (2008). Sexual uses of alcohol and drugs and the associated health risks: A cross sectional study of young people in nine European cities. *BMC Public Health*, *8*(1), 155–165. doi:10.1186/1471-2458-8-155 PMID:18471281

Berg, B. L. (2001). *Qualitative research methods for the social sciences.* Allyn and Bacon.

Berger, R. (2016). Now I see it, now I don't: Researcher's position and reflexivity in qualitative research. *Qualitative Research*, *15*(2), 1–16. doi:10.1177/1468794112468475

Bermúdez, L., Araújo, L., Reyes, A., Hernández-Quero, J., & Teva, I. (2016). Analysis of cognitive variables and sexual risk behaviors among infected and HIV-uninfected people from Spain. *AIDS Care*, *28*(7), 890–897. doi:10.1080/09540121.2016.1161163 PMID:26981840

Berniell, I., & Facchini, G. (2021). COVID-19 lockdown and domestic violence: Evidence from internet-search behavior in 11 countries. *European Economic Review*, *136*, 103775. doi:10.1016/j.euroecorev.2021.103775 PMID:35721306

Berry, M., Garcia-Blanco, I., & Moore, K. (2015). *Press coverage of the refugee and migrant crisis in the EU: A content analysis of five european countries. report prepared for the United Nations High Commission for Refugees*. Cardiff School of Journalism, Media and Cultural Studies Press.

Blakemore, S. J., & Mills, K. L. (2014). Is adolescence a sensitive period for sociocultural processing? *Annual Review of Psychology*, *65*(1), 187–207. doi:10.1146/annurev-psych-010213-115202 PMID:24016274

Bodelón, E. G. (2014). Institutional violence and gender violence. *Anales de La Cátedra Francisco Suárez*, *48*, 131–155. doi:10.30827/acfs.v48i0.2783

Borges, G. M., Guerreiro, A., Conde, L. (2022). Stroking reflexivity into practice: The pros and cons of resorting to gatekeepers to conduct qualitative criminological research. *Journal of Qualitative Criminal Justice & Criminology*. doi:10.21428/88de04a1.31b36875

Borges, G. M., Guerreiro, A., Conde, L. (2022). Stroking reflexivity into practice: The pros and cons of resorting to gatekeepers to conduct qualitative criminological research. *The Journal of Qualitative Criminal Justice and Criminology*.

Borges, Z. N., Perurena, F. C., Passamani, G. R., & Bulsing, M. (2013). Patriarcado, heteronormatividade e misoginia em debate: pontos e contrapontos para o combate à homofobia nas escolas. *Latitude, 7*(1).

Borges, G. M. (2023). *Journey of Violence: Refugee Women's Experiences Across Three Stages and Places*. Int. Migration & Integration. doi:10.1007/s12134-023-01102-z

Borges, G. M., & Faria, R. (2022). Breathing Under Water: Gendering the Violence Against Refugee Women. In *Research Anthology on Child and Domestic Abuse and Its Prevention* (pp. 19–37). IGI Global. doi:10.4018/978-1-6684-5598-2.ch002

Borges, G., & Faria, R. (2023). Language, emotions, and access to refugee women: Ingredients for reflexivity. In A. M. Díaz Fernández, C. Del-Real, & L. Molnar (Eds.), *Fieldwork Experiences in Criminology and Security Studies: Methods, Ethics, and Emotions*. Springer Nature. doi:10.1007/978-3-031-41574-6_17

Borrajo, E., Gámez-Guadix, M., Pereda, N., & Calvete, E. (2015). The development and validation of the cyber dating abuse questionnaire among young couples. *Computers in Human Behavior*, *48*, 358–365. doi:10.1016/j.chb.2015.01.063

Borrillo, D. (2010). *História e crítica de um preconceito*. Autêntica.

Bosma, A., Mulder, E., & Pemberton, A. (2018). The Ideal Victim through other (s') eyes. In M. Duggan, M. (Ed.), Revisiting the "Ideal Victim": Developments in Critical Victimology (pp. 27-42). Bristol University Press.

Bosworth, M. (2011). Human rights and immigration detention. In Are Human Rights for Migrants? Critical Reflections on the Status of Irregular Migrants in Europe and the United States (pp. 165-183). Routledge.

Bosworth, M. (2008). Border control and the limits of the sovereign state. *Social & Legal Studies*, *17*(2), 199–215. doi:10.1177/0964663908089611

Bosworth, M., & Guild, M. (2008). Governing through migration control: Security and citizenship in Britain. *British Journal of Criminology*, *48*(6), 703–719. doi:10.1093/bjc/azn059

Boyd, M., & Grieco, E. (2003). Women and migration: Incorporating gender into international migration theory. *Migration Information Source*, 1-7. www.migrationinformation.org/feature/print.cfm?ID=106

Braun, V., & Clarke, V. (2006). Using thematic analysis in psychology. *Qualitative Research in Psychology*, *3*(2), 77–101. doi:10.1191/1478088706qp063oa

Brell, C., Dustmann, C., & Preston, I. (2020). The labor market integration of refugee migrants in high-income countries. *The Journal of Economic Perspectives*, *34*(1), 94–121. doi:10.1257/jep.34.1.94

Broll, R. (2014). "Criminals Are Inside of Our Homes": Intimate Partner Violence and Fear of Crime. *Canadian Journal of Criminology and Criminal Justice/La Revue Canadienne de Criminologie et de Justice Pénale, 56*, 1–22. doi:10.3138/cjccj.2011.E24

Bronfenbrenner, U. (1994). Ecological models of human development. In T. Husen & T. Postlethwaite (Eds.), *The International Encyclopedia of Education* (2nd ed., Vol. 3, pp. 1643–1647). Elsevier.

Brotto, L., Atallah, S., Johnson-Agbakwu, C., Rosenbaum, T., Abdo, C., Byers, E., Graham, C., Nobre, P., & Wylie, K. (2016). Psychological and interpersonal dimensions of sexual function and dysfunction. *Journal of Sexual Medicine*, *13*(4), 538–571. doi:10.1016/j.jsxm.2016.01.019 PMID:27045257

Brown, S., Goldman, M., Inn, A., & Anderson, L. (1980). Expectations of reinforcement from alcohol: Their domain and relation to drinking patterns. *Journal of Consulting and Clinical Psychology*, *48*(4), 419–426. doi:10.1037/0022-006X.48.4.419 PMID:7400427

Bucher, J., Manasse, M., & Milton, J. (2015). Soliciting strain: Examining both sides of street prostitution through general strain theory. *Journal of Crime and Justice*, *38*(4), 435–453. doi:10.1080/0735648X.2014.949823

Burrow, A. L., & Rainone, N. (2017). How many likes did I get?: Purpose moderates links between positive social media feedback and self-esteem. *Journal of Experimental Social Psychology*, *69*, 232–236. doi:10.1016/j.jesp.2016.09.005

Busch, N. B., & Valentine, D. (2000). Empowerment practice: A focus on battered women. *Affilia*, *15*(1), 82–95. doi:10.1177/08861090022093840

Butina, M. (2015). A narrative approach to qualitative inquiry. *Clinical Laboratory Science*, *18*(3), 190–196. doi:10.29074/ascls.28.3.190

Butler, J. (2016). *Frames of war: When is life grievable?* Verso Books.

Buxton, R. (2023). Justice in waiting: The harms and wrongs of temporary refugee protection. *European Journal of Political Theory*, *22*(1), 51–72. doi:10.1177/1474885120973578

Buzawa, E. S., & Austin, T. (1993). Determining police response to domestic violence victims: The role of victim preference. *The American Behavioral Scientist*, *36*(5), 610–623. doi:10.1177/0002764293036005006

Buzawa, E. S., & Buzawa, C. G. (1996). *Domestic violence: the criminal justice response.* SAGE Publications.

Cabral, P., & Rodríguez-Díaz, F. (2017). Violência conjugal: Crenças de atuais e futuros profissionais, implicados na sua reposta e prevenção - direito, saúde e educação [Marital violence: beliefs of current and future professionals, involved in its response and prevention - law, health and education]. *Saber & Educar*, *23*(23), 152–167. doi:10.17346/se.vol23.275

Calafat, A., Juan, M., Becoña, E., & Montecón, A. (2008). Qué drogas se prefieren para las relaciones sexuales en contextos recreativos. *Adicciones*, *20*(1), 37–48. doi:10.20882/adicciones.287 PMID:18299780

Campbell, J. C. (2002). Health consequences of intimate partner violence. *Lancet*, *359*(9314), 1331–1336. doi:10.1016/S0140-6736(02)08336-8 PMID:11965295

Campbell, J. C., Jones, A. S., Dienemann, J., Kub, J., Schollenberger, J., O'Campo, P. J., Gielen, A. C., & Wynne, C. (2002). Intimate partner violence and physical health consequences. *Archives of Internal Medicine*, *162*(10), 1157–1163. doi:10.1001/archinte.162.10.1157 PMID:12020187

Campbell, R., & Wasco, S. M. (2005). Understanding rape and sexual assault: 20 years of progress and future directions. *Journal of Interpersonal Violence*, *20*(1), 127–131. doi:10.1177/0886260504268604 PMID:15618569

Campion, E. D. (2018). The career adaptive refugee: Exploring the structural and personal barriers to refugee resettlement. *Journal of Vocational Behavior*, *105*(2), 6–16. doi:10.1016/j.jvb.2017.10.008

Canning, V. (2017). *Gendered harm and structural violence in the British asylum system*. Taylor & Francis eBooks.

Canning, V. (2020). Corrosive Control: State-Corporate and Gendered Harm in Bordered Britain. *Critical Criminology*, *28*(2), 259–275. doi:10.1007/s10612-020-09509-1

Carastathis, A. (2014). The concept of intersectionality in feminist theory. *Philosophy Compass*, *9*(5), 304–314. doi:10.1111/phc3.12129

Caridade, S., & Braga, T. (2019). Versão portuguesa do Cyber Dating Abuse Questionaire (CDAQ)–Questionário sobre Ciberabuso no Namoro (CibAN): Adaptação e propriedades psicométricas [Portuguese version of the Cyber Dating Abuse Questionnaire (CDAQ)–Cyber Abuse in Dating Questionnaire (CibAN): Adaptation and psychometric properties]. *Análise Psicológica*, *105*(1), 93–105. doi:10.14417/ap.1543

Caridade, S., Braga, T., & Borrajo, E. (2019). Cyber dating abuse (CDA): Evidence from a systematic review. *Aggression and Violent Behavior*, *48*, 152–168. doi:10.1016/j.avb.2019.08.018

Carman, M., Fairchild, J., Parsons, M., Farrugia, C., Power, J., & Bourne, A. (2021). *Pride in prevention: A guide to primary prevention of family violence experienced by LGBTIQ communities*. Academic Press.

Carmona-TorresJ.Carvalhal-SilvaR. M.Viera-MendesM. H.Recio-AndradeB.GoergenT. Rodríguez-BorregoM. A. (2017). Elder abuse within the family environment in the Azores Islands. *Revista Latino-Americana de Enfermagem*, *25*. https://doi.org/ doi:10.1590/1518-8345.1871.2932

Carqueja, H. (2000). Doença e toxicodependências. *Toxicodependências (Lisboa)*, *6*(3), 83–85.

Carroll, J., McGinley, J., & Macck, S. (2001). Exploring the self-reported sexual problems and concerns of drug-dependent males and females in modified, therapeutic community treatment. *Journal of Substance Abuse Treatment*, *20*, 245–250. doi:10.1016/S0740-5472(01)00164-7 PMID:11516595

Castells, M. (1996). *The Rise of the Network Society, The Information Age: Economy, Society and Culture*. Blackwell.

Castells, M. (2020). Space of Flows, Space of Places: Materials for a Theory of Urbanism in the Information Age. In T. Richard & F. S. LeGates (Eds.), *The city reader* (pp. 14–25). Routledge. doi:10.4324/9780429261732-30

Castro, L. D. D. (2008). *Pagamento a participantes de pesquisa*. Academic Press.

Cava, M. J., Martínez-Ferrer, B., Buelga, S., & Carrascosa, L. (2020). Sexist attitudes, romantic myths, and offline dating violence as predictors of cyber dating violence perpetration in adolescents. *Computers in Human Behavior*, *111*, 106449. doi:10.1016/j.chb.2020.106449

Ceccarelli, P. R. (2008). Prostituição–Corpo como mercadoria. *Mente & Cérebro–sexo, 4*(1), 1-14.

Chandra, Y., & Shag, L. (2017). An RQDA-based constructivist methodology for qualitative research. *Qualitative Market Research, 20*(1), 90–122. doi:10.1108/QMR-02-2016-0014

Charmaz, K. (2005). Grounded theory in the 21st century: applications for advancing social justice studies. In N. Denzin, & Y. Lincoln (Eds.), The sage handbook of qualitative research (pp. 507-535). SAGE Publications.

Charmaz, K., & Thornberg, R. (2021). The pursuit of quality in grounded theory. *Qualitative Research in Psychology, 18*(3), 305–327. doi:10.1080/14780887.2020.1780357

Charmaz, K., Thornberg, R., & Keane, E. (2017). Evolving grounded theory and social justice inquiry. In N. K. Denzin & Y. S. Lincoln (Eds.), *The SAGE handbook of qualitative research* (pp. 411–443). Sage Publications.

Chataway, M. L., & Hart, T. C. (2018). *A Social-Psychological Process of "Fear of Crime" for Men and Women: Revisiting Gender Differences from a New Perspective.* doi:10.1080/155648 86.2018.1552221

Chatzakou, D., Leontiadis, I., Blackburn, J., De Cristofaro, E., Stringhini, G., Vakali, A., & Kourtellis, N. (2019). Detecting cyberbullying and cyberaggression in social media. *ACM Transactions on the Web, 13*(3), 1–51. doi:10.1145/3343484

Chen, W., Hall, B. J., & Renzaho, A. M. N. (2017). Pre-migration and post-migration factors associated with mental health in humanitarian migrants in Australia and the moderation effect of post-migration stressors: Findings from the first wave data of the BNLA cohort study. *The Lancet. Psychiatry, 4*(3), 219–229. doi:10.1016/S2215-0366(17)30032-9 PMID:28161455

Chiarenza, A., Dauvrin, M., Chiesa, V., Baatout, S., & Verrept, H. (2019). Supporting access to healthcare for refugees and migrants in European countries under particular migratory pressure. *BMC Health Services Research, 19*(1), 513. doi:10.1186/s12913-019-4353-1 PMID:31337406

Ching Espinosa, E. G. P. (2021). *Cyberbullying en niños y adolescentes: una revisión sistemática.* https://hdl.handle.net/20.500.12692/66060

Chocarro, E., & Garaigordobil, M. (2019). Bullying and cyberbullying: Sex differences in victims, aggressors and observers. *Pensamiento Psicológico, 17*(2), 57–71. doi:10.11144/Javerianacali. PPSI17-2.bcds

Cho, J., & Trent, A. (2006). Validity in qualitative research revisited. *Qualitative Research, 6*(3), 319–340. doi:10.1177/1468794106065006

Chokova, M., Ward, D., & Teixeira, A. C. (2013). *The Female Condition During Mussolini's and Salazar's Regimes.* https://repository.wellesley.edu/object/ir409

Christie, N. (2018). The Ideal Victim. In M. Duggan (Ed.), Revisiting the "Ideal Victim": Developments in Critical Victimology (pp. 11-24). Bristol University Press.

Ciranka, S., & Van den Bos, W. (2019). Social influence in adolescent decision-making: A formal framework. *Frontiers in Psychology*, *10*, 1915. doi:10.3389/fpsyg.2019.01915 PMID:31555164

Clark, M. (2011). Conceptualizing addiction: How useful is the construct? *International Journal of Humanities and Social Science*, *1*(13), 55–64.

Cochrane, B. (2018). Harms at the crossroads of carework and irregular migration. *Journal of Refugee Studies*, *33*(3), 500–520. doi:10.1093/jrs/fey056

Coelho, A. (2010). *Beliefs and attitudes of police officers towards violence against women* [Master's thesis, University of Porto]. University of Porto Institutional Repository. https://repositorio-aberto.up.pt/bitstream/10216/55356/2/DissertaoCincias%20Forenses.pdf

Coelho, A. M. (2010). *Crenças e atitudes dos agentes policiais face à violência contra a mulher* [Beliefs and attitudes of police officers towards violence against women] [Dissertação de mestrado não publicada]. Universidade do Porto.

Coelho, R. P. P. S. (2019). *Violência doméstica e de género: crenças, atitudes e valores dos militares da GNR* [Domestic and gender-based violence: beliefs, attitudes and values of GNR soldiers] [Dissertação de mestrado não publicado]. Universidade Aberta.

Cohan, D., Lutnick, A., Davidson, P., Cloniger, C., Herlyn, A., Breyer, J., ... Klausner, J. (2006). Sex worker health: San Francisco style. *Sexually Transmitted Infections*, *82*(5), 418–422. doi:10.1136/sti.2006.020628 PMID:16854996

Cohen, S. (2011). *Folk Devils and Moral Panics: The Creation of the Mods and Rockers*. Routledge. doi:10.4324/9780203828250

Condry, R. (2010). Secondary Victims and Secondary Victimization. International Handbook of Victimology, 219-249. doi:10.1201/EBK1420085471-c8

Connelly, F. M., & Clandinin, D. J. (1990). Stories of experience and Narrative inquiry. *Educational Researcher*, *19*(5), 2–14. doi:10.2307/1176100

Constantino, M., Arnkoff, D., Glass, C., Ametrano, R., & Smith, J. (2011). Expectations. *Journal of Clinical Psychology*, *67*(2), 184–192. doi:10.1002/jclp.20754 PMID:21128304

Cook, E., & Walklate, S. (2019). Excavating Victim Stories: making sense of agency, suffering and redemption. In E. Cook, S. Walklate, J. Fleetwood, L. Presser, S. Sandberg, & T. Ugelvik (Eds.), *The Emerald Handbook of Narrative Criminology* (pp. 239–257). Emerald Publishing Limited. doi:10.1108/978-1-78769-005-920191023

Correia, A. L., & Sani, A. I. (2015). As casas de abrigo em Portugal: Caraterização estrutural e funcional destas respostas sociais [Shelters in Portugal: structural and functional characterization of these social responses]. *Análise Psicológica*, *33*(1), 89–96. doi:10.14417/ap.918

Correia, A., & Neves, S. (2021). Narrativas mediáticas sobre o femicídio na intimidade em Portugal - Implicações e desafios. *Media & Jornalismo*, *21*(39), 229–245. doi:10.14195/2183-5462_39_12

Correia, I., & Vala, J. (2003). When Will a Victim Be Secondarily Victimized? The Effect of Observer's Belief in a Just World, Victim's Innocence and Persistence of Suffering. *Social Justice Research*, *16*(4), 379–400. doi:10.1023/A:1026313716185

Costa, D. (2018). A evolução de políticas públicas em Portugal na área da Violência Doméstica. In I. Dias (Ed.), *Violência Doméstica e de Género: uma abordagem multidisciplinar* (pp. 123–156). Pactor.

Costa, H. A. (2008). Lopes, Ana (2006), Trabalhadores do sexo uni-vos! Organização laboral na indústria do sexo. *Revista Critica de Ciencias Sociais*, (80), 213–217. doi:10.4000/rccs.706

Council of Europe. (2011). *Council of Europe Convention on preventing and combating violence against women and domestic violence*. https://rm.coe.int/168008482e

Council of Europe. (2019). GREVIO baseline evaluation report: Portugal. Strasbourg: Secretariat of the monitoring mechanism of the Council of Europe Convention on Preventing and Combating Violence against Women and Domestic Violence, Council of Europe.

Council of Europe. (2020). *Cyberviolence*. https://www.coe.int/en/web/cyberviolence/home#%7B%2250020850%22:[0]%7D

Cowen, P., Harrison, P., & Burns, T. (2012). *Shorter Oxford textbook of psychiatry* (6th ed., Vol. 1 & 2). University Press. doi:10.1093/med/9780199605613.001.0001

CPR. (2022). Aida: Asylum Information Database. Country Report: Portugal.

Crenshaw, K. (1989). Demarginalizing the intersection of race and sex: a black feminist critique of antidiscrimination doctri, feminist theory and antiracist politics. *University of Chicago Legal Forum*, (1), 139-167. https://chicagounbound.uchicago.edu/uclf/vol1989/iss1/8

Crenshaw, K. (1991). Mapping the Margins: Intersectionality, Identity Politics, and Violence against Women of Color. *Stanford Law Review*, *43*(6), 1241–1299. doi:10.2307/1229039

Creswell, J. W. (2007). *Qualitative inquiry and research design: choosing among five approaches*. SAGE Publications.

Creswell, J. W. (2014). *Research design: qualitative, quantitative, and mixed methods approaches*. SAGE Publications.

Crone, E. A., & Konijn, E. A. (2018). Media use and brain development during adolescence. *Nature Communications*, *9*(1), 588. doi:10.1038/s41467-018-03126-x PMID:29467362

Csalog, R. A. (2021). Mulheres (in) visíveis: prostituição, trabalho e migrações nas ruas de Lisboa. *e-Cadernos CES*, (35).

da Silva, R. A. (2011). A prostituição ontem e hoje: algumas reflexões em Georg Simmel. *Faculdade do Sudeste Goiano, 6.*

da Silva, L. C., & Justo, J. S. (2020). Errância Queer e Nomadismo Feminino: Trajetividades e Resistências de Mulheres no Trecho. *Revista Subjetividades, 20*(2), 1–12. doi:10.5020/23590777. rs.v20i2.e9372

Davaki, K. (2021). *The traumas endured by refugee women and their consequences for integration and participation in the EU host country.* Policy Department for Citizens' Rights and Constitutional Affairs Directorate-General for Internal Policies.

Davis, R. C., & Erez, E. (1998). *Immigrant Population as Victims: Toward a Multicultural Criminal Justice System.* https://www.ojp.gov/pdffiles/167571.pdf

Davis, R. C., & Smith, B. (1995). Domestic violence reforms: Empty promises or fulfilled expectations? *Crime and Delinquency, 41*(4), 541–552. doi:10.1177/0011128795041004010

Day V. Telles L. Zoratto P. Azambuja M. Machado D. Silveira M. Debiaggi M. Reis M. Cardoso R. Blank P. (2003). Violência doméstica e suas diferentes manifestações. *Revista de Psiquiatria do Rio Grande do Sul, 25*(1). https://doi.org/ doi:10.1590/S0101-81082003000400003

de Jesus, J. G. (2013). Transfobia e crimes de ódio: Assassinatos de pessoas pdgênero como genocídio. *História agora, 16*, 101-123.

Degenhardt, L. (2005). Drug use and risk behaviour among regular ecstasy users: Does sexuality make a difference? *Culture, Health & Sexuality, 7*(6), 599–614. doi:10.1080/13691050500349875 PMID:16864225

DeJong, C., Burgess-Proctor, A., & Elis, L. (2008). Police officer perceptions of intimate partner violence: An analysis of observational data. *Violence and Victims, 23*(6), 683–696. doi:10.1891/0886-6708.23.6.683 PMID:19069561

Demarchi, G., & Lenehan, S. (2019). *Gender in waiting: Men and women asylum seekers in European reception facilities.* The World Bank. doi:10.1596/31209

Dhamoon, R. K. (2011). Considerations on Mainstreaming Intersectionality. *Political Research Quarterly, 64*(1), 230–243. doi:10.1177/1065912910379227

Diário da República. (2021). Ordem dos Psicólogos Portugueses.

Dias, I. (2005). *Violência na Família: Uma abordagem sociológica.* Edições Afrontamento.

Dionis, M. S., Timar, M., & Domscheit-Berg, A. (2016). *Protecting refugee Women and girls from violence: A collection of good practices.* World Future Council.

Direção Geral de Reinserção e Serviços Prisionais (DGRSP). (2022). *Programas específicos de reabilitação.* https://dgrsp.justica.gov.pt/Justi%C3%A7a-de-adultos/Penas-e-medidas-privativas-de-liberdade/Programas-e-projetos/Programas-espec%C3%ADficos-de-reabilita%C3%A7%C3%A3o#MedidasAlternativasPriso

Ditton, J., & Farrall, S. (2016). *The fear of crime.* Routledge.

Domínguez Ruiz, I. E. (2022). Between the city and the country: Heterogeneous victimization experiences among LGBTI individuals. *Cogent Social Sciences*, *8*(1), 2107281. doi:10.1080/2 3311886.2022.2107281

Donoso V. (2022). *Youth digital skills: Insights from the ySKILLS project.* Hamburg: Leibniz-Institut für Medienforschung | Hans-Bredow-Institut (HBI); CO:RE - Children Online: Research and Evidence. doi:10.21241/ssoar.78951

Douglas, H. (2008). The criminal law's response to domestic violence: What's going on? *The Sydney Law Review*, *30*(3), 439–469.

Dowd, R. (2011). Dissecting discrimination in refugee law: An analysis of its meaning and its cumulative effect. *International Journal of Refugee Law*, *23*(1), 28–53. doi:10.1093/ijrl/eeq043

Driskell, J., & Mullen, B. (1990). Status, expectations, and behavior: A meta-analytic review and test of the theory. *Personality and Social Psychology Bulletin*, *16*(3), 541–553. doi:10.1177/0146167290163012

Duarte, M., & Oliveira, A. (2012). Women on the margins: domestic violence and immigrant women. *Sociology: Journal of the Faculty of Letters of the University of Porto, 23*, 223-237. https://ojs.letras.up.pt/index.php/Sociologia/article/view/1428

Due, C., Green, E., & Ziersch, A. (2020). Psychological trauma and access to primary healthcare for people from refugee and asylum-seeker backgrounds: A mixed methods systematic review. *International Journal of Mental Health Systems*, *14*(71), 1–18. doi:10.1186/s13033-020-00404-4 PMID:32944067

Dueñas, J. M., Racionero-Plaza, S., Melgar, P., & Sanvicén-Torné, P. (2021). Identifying violence against the LGTBI+ community in Catalan universities. *Life Sciences, Society and Policy*, *17*(1), 1–10. doi:10.1186/s40504-021-00112-y PMID:33618762

Duke, A., & Davidson, M. M. (2009). Same-sex intimate partner violence: Lesbian, gay, and bisexual affirmative outreach and advocacy. *Journal of Aggression, Maltreatment & Trauma*, *18*(8), 795–816. doi:10.1080/10926770903291787

Dustmann, C., Fasani, F., Frattini, T., Minale, L., & Schönberg, U. (2017). On the economics and politics of refugee migration. *Economic Policy*, *32*(91), 497–550. doi:10.1093/epolic/eix008

Dwyer, A. (2014). Pleasures, Perversities, and Partnerships: The Historical Emergence of LGBT-Police Relationships. In D. Peterson & V. R. Panfil (Eds.), *The Handbook of LGBT Communities, Crime, and Justice*. Springer. doi:10.1007/978-1-4614-9188-0_8

Dwyer, A., Ball, M., & Crofts, T. (2016). Queering criminologies. In *Queering criminology* (pp. 1–11). Palgrave Macmillan UK.

Eaton, N., Thompson, R. Jr, Hu, M., Goldstein, R., Saha, T., & Hasin, D. (2015). Regularly drinking alcohol before sexual activity in a national representative sample: Prevalence, sociodemographics, and associations with psychiatric and substance use disorders. *American Journal of Public Health*, *105*(7), 1387–1393. doi:10.2105/AJPH.2015.302556 PMID:25973812

Edwards, A. (2005). Human rights, refugees and the right "to enjoy" asylum. *International Journal of Refugee Law*, *17*(2), 293–330. doi:10.1093/ijrl/eei011

Eggenhofer-Rehart, P. P. M., Latzke, M., Pernkopf, K., Zellhofer, D., Mayhofer, W., & Stevre, J. (2018). Refugees' career capital welcome? Afghan and Syrian eefugee job seekers in Austria. *Journal of Vocational Behavior*, *105*, 31–45. doi:10.1016/j.jvb.2018.01.004

El-Bassel, N., Fontdevila, J., Gilbert, L., Voisin, D., Richman, B., & Pitchell, P. (2001). HIV risks of men in methadone maintenance tretment programs who abuse their intimate partners: A forgotten issue. *Journal of Substance Abuse*, *13*(1-2), 1–15. doi:10.1016/S0899-3289(01)00068-2 PMID:11547622

El-Bassel, N., Gilbert, L., & Rajah, V. (2003). The relationship between drug abuse and sexual performance among women on methadone. Heightening the risk of sexual intimate violence and HIV. *Addictive Behaviors*, *28*(8), 1385–1403. doi:10.1016/S0306-4603(02)00266-6 PMID:14512062

Erez, E., Ammar, N., & Orloff, L. E. (2003). *Violence against Immigrant Women and Systemic Responses: An exploratory study*. Report submitted to National Institute of Justice in fulfillment of requirements for Grant. https://www.ojp.gov/pdffiles1/nij/grants/202561.pdf

Erez, E., & Belknap, J. (1998). In their own words: Battered women's assessment of the criminal processing system's responses. *Violence and Victims*, *13*(3), 251–268. doi:10.1891/0886-6708.13.3.251 PMID:9836413

European Institute for Gender Equality. (2020). *Violence at a glance*. https://eige.europa.eu/gender-equality-index/2020/domain/violence

European Institute for Gender Equality. (2022). *Pandemic and Care*. European Institute for Gender Equality.

European Union Agency for Fundamental Rights (FRA) (2014). *Violence against women: an EU-wide survey*. Luxemburg: Publication Office of the European Union.

EUROSTAT. (2014-2019). *Asylum and managed migration*. European Commission.

Faria, R. (2022). "Being" Ethical in Research. In R. Faria & M. Dodge (Eds.), *Qualitative Research in Criminology: Cutting-Edge Methods* (pp. 229–240). Springer International Publishing. doi:10.1007/978-3-031-18401-7_14

Farley, M. (2004). "Bad for the body, bad for the heart": Prostitution harms women even if legalized or decriminalized. *Violence Against Women*, *10*(10), 1087–1125. doi:10.1177/1077801204268607

Farley, M., Baral, I., Kiremire, M., & Sezgin, U. (1998). Prostitution in five countries: Violence and post-traumatic stress disorder. *Feminism & Psychology*, *8*(4), 405–426. doi:10.1177/0959353598084002

Farmer, P. (2005). *Pathologies of power: Health, human rights, and the new war on the poor*. University of California Press.

Fassin, D. (2018). *The will to punish.* Oxford University Press. doi:10.1093/oso/9780190888589.001.0001

Fathi, M. (2017). *Intersectionality, Class and Migration – narratives of iranian women migrants in the U.K.* Springer. doi:10.1057/978-1-137-52530-7

Fehrenbacher, A. E., Park, J. N., Footer, K. H., Silberzahn, B. E., Allen, S. T., & Sherman, S. G. (2020). Exposure to police and client violence among incarcerated female sex workers in Baltimore City, Maryland. *American Journal of Public Health*, *110*(S1), S152–S159. doi:10.2105/AJPH.2019.305451 PMID:31967867

Fekadu, Z., & Kraft, P. (2002). Expanding the theory of planned behavior: The role of social norms and group identification. *Journal of Health Psychology*, *7*(1), 33–43. doi:10.1177/1359105302007001650 PMID:22114225

Felson, R. B., Ackerman, J. M., & Gallagher, C. A. (2005). Police intervention and the repeat of domestic assault. *Criminology*, *43*(3), 563–588. doi:10.1111/j.0011-1348.2005.00017.x

Felson, R. B., Messner, S. F., Hoskin, A. W., & Deane, G. (2002). Reasons for reporting and not reporting domestic violence to the police. *Criminology*, *40*(3), 617–648. doi:10.1111/j.1745-9125.2002.tb00968.x

Ferraro, K. (1995). Fear of crime: Interpreting victimization risk. State University of New York Press.

Ferraro, K. (1996). Women's Fear of Victimization: Shadow of Sexual Assault?*. *Social Forces*, *75*(2), 667–690. doi:10.2307/2580418

Ferreira, E. (2020). Intimate Partner Violence - findings and lessons from a national deterrence policy. *European Law Enforcement Research Bulletin, 20.*

Ferreira-Borges, C., & Filho, H. (2004). *Uso, abusos e dependências: alcoolismo e toxicodependência.* Climepsi Editores.

Ferros, L. (2011). *Toxicodependência: afectos e psicopatologia.* Livpsic.

Fisher, B. S., & Sloan, J. J. (2003). Unraveling the fear of victimization among college women: Is the "shadow of sexual assault hypothesis" supported?. *Justice Quarterly, 20*(3), 633–659. https://doi.org/https://doi.org/10.1080/07418820300095641

Fitz-Gibbon, K., Walklate, S., McCulloch, J., & Maher, J. (2018). *Intimate Partner Violence, Risk and Security: Securing Women's Lives in a Global World* (1st ed.). Routledge. doi:10.4324/9781315204765

Fleury-Steiner, R. E., Bybee, D., Sullivan, C. M., Belknap, J., & Melton, H. C. (2006). Contextual factors impacting battered women's intentions to reuse the criminal legal system. *Journal of Community Psychology*, *34*(3), 327–342. doi:10.1002/jcop.20102

Flick, U. (2018). Triangulation. In N. Denzin, & Y. Lincoln (Eds.), The Sage handbook of qualitative research. SAGE Publications.

Fontana, A., & Frey, J. H. (2005). The interview: from neutral stance to political involvement. In N. K. Denzin & Y. S. Lincoln (Eds.), *The Sage handbook of qualitative research* (pp. 695–727). SAGE Publications.

Foreigners and Borders Service. (2023). *Immigration, Borders and Asylum Report 2022*. https://www.sef.pt/pt/Documents/RIFA2022%20vF2a.pdf

Foster, J. (2003). Police cultures. In T. Newburn (Ed.), *Handbook of policing* (pp. 196–227). Willan Publishing.

Fotaki, M. (2019). A crisis of humanitarianism: Refugees at the gates of Europe. *International Journal of Health Policy and Management*, 8(6), 321–324. doi:10.15171/ijhpm.2019.22 PMID:31256563

Fouad, N., & Guillen, A. (2006). Outcome expectations: Looking to the past and potential future. *Journal of Career Assessment*, 14(1), 130–142. doi:10.1177/1069072705281370

Fox, K. A., Nobles, M. R., & Piquero, A. R. (2009). Gender, crime victimization and fear of crime. *Security Journal*, 22(1), 24–39. doi:10.1057/sj.2008.13

Fox, V. (2002). Historical Perspectives on Violence Against Women. *Journal of International Women's Studies*, 4(November), 15–34. https://vc.bridgew.edu/jiws/vol4/iss1/2

Freedman, J. (2015). *Gendering the international asylum and refugee debate*. Palgrave Macmillan. doi:10.1057/9781137456236

Freedman, J. (2016a). Sexual and gender-based violence against refugee women: A hidden aspect of the refugee "crisis". *Reproductive Health Matters*, 4(47), 18–26. doi:10.1016/j.rhm.2016.05.003 PMID:27578335

Freedman, J. (2016b). Engendering security at the borders of Europe: Women migrants and the Mediterranean crisis. *Journal of Refugee Studies*, 29(4), 568–582. doi:10.1093/jrs/few019

Freedman, J. (2019). Grand challenges: Refugees and conflict. *Frontiers in Human Dynamics*, 3, 1–3. doi:10.3389/fhumd.2019.00001

Freedman, J., Crankshaw, T. L., & Mutambara, V. M. (2020). Sexual and reproductive health of asylum seeking and refugee women in South Africa: Understanding the determinants of vulnerability. *Sexual and Reproductive Health Matters*, 28(1), 323–334. doi:10.1080/26410397 .2020.1758440 PMID:32425112

Freeman, J. (1996). The feminist debate over prostitution reform. Applications of Feminist Legal Theory to Women's Lives, Sex, Violence, Work and Reproduction, 241, 246.

Freeman, G., & Wohn, D. Y. (2020). Streaming your identity: Navigating the presentation of gender and sexuality through live streaming. *Computer Supported Cooperative Work, 29*(6), 795–825. doi:10.1007/s10606-020-09386-w

Freire, P. (2009). *Pedagogy of the oppressed* (48th ed.). Paz e Terra.

Fricker, M. (2017). Evolving concepts of epistemic injustice. In Routledge Handbook of Epistemic Injustice. Routledge. doi:10.4324/9781315212043-5

Galende, N., Ozamiz-Etxebarria, N., Jaureguizar, J., & Redondo, I. (2020). Cyber dating violence prevention programs in universal populations: A systematic review. *Psychology Research and Behavior Management, 13*, 1089–1099. doi:10.2147/PRBM.S275414 PMID:33299362

Galtung, J. (1969). Violence, peace, and peace research. *Journal of Peace Research, 6*(3), 167–191. doi:10.1177/002234336900600301

Gama, A., Pedro, A. R., Carvalho, M. J., Guerreiro, A., Duarte, V., Quintas, J., Matias, A., Keygnaertg, I., & Dias, S. (2021). Domestic Violence during the COVID-19 Pandemic in Portugal. *Portuguese Journal of Public Health, 38*(1, Suppl. 1), 32–40. doi:10.1159/000514341

Garaigordobil, M., Mollo-Torrico, J. P., & Larrain, E. (2019). Prevalencia de Bullying y Cyberbullying en Latinoamérica: una revisión. *Revista Iberoamericana de psicología, 11*(3), 1–18. doi:10.33881/2027-1786.rip.11301

García-Carrión, R., Villarejo-Carballido, B., & Villardón-Gallego, L. (2019). Children and adolescents mental health: A systematic review of interaction-based interventions in schools and communities. *Frontiers in Psychology, 10*, 918. doi:10.3389/fpsyg.2019.00918 PMID:31068881

Gartley, T., & Due, C. (2017). The interpreter is not an invisible being: A thematic analysis of the impact of interpreters in mental health service provision with refugee clients. *Australian Psychologist, 52*(1), 31–40. doi:10.1111/ap.12181

Gauthier, S. (2010). The perceptions of judicial and psychosocial interveners of the consequences of dropped charges in domestic violence cases. *Violence Against Women, 16*(12), 1375–1395. doi:10.1177/1077801210389163 PMID:21164215

Geist, F. M. (2017). Staging the trans sex worker. *Transgender Studies Quarterly, 4*(1), 112–127. doi:10.1215/23289252-3711577

Gkiomisi, A., Gkrizioti, M., Gkiomisi, A., Anastasilakis, D. A., & Kardaras, P. (2017). Cyberbullying among Greek high school adolescents. *Indian Journal of Pediatrics, 84*(5), 364–368. doi:10.1007/s12098-016-2256-2 PMID:27957645

Goldsamt, L., Clatts, M., Le, G., & Yu, G. (2015). Injection and sexual risk practices among young heroin users in Hanoi, Vietnam. *Drugs: Education Prevention & Policy, 22*(2), 166–172. doi:10.3109/09687637.2014.979765 PMID:25995608

Gómez, C., & Cartón, M. (2006). Drogas y disfunción sexual. *Adicciones, 18*(1), 231–243.

Gonçalves, M., & Matos, M. (2020). Victimized immigrant women in Portugal: Factors associated with formal and informal help-seeking. *Revista de Psicología Social*, *35*(2), 370–412. doi:10.1 080/02134748.2020.1725360

Goodman, L. A., Liang, B., Helms, J. E., Latta, R. E., Sparks, E., & Weintraub, S. R. (2004). Training counseling psychologists as social justice agents: Feminist and multicultural principles in action. *The Counseling Psychologist*, *32*(6), 793–836. doi:10.1177/0011000004268802

Goodson, I. F., & Gill, S. R. (2011). The narrative turn in social research. *Counterpoints*, *386*, 17-33. https://www.jstor.org/stable/42981362

Goodwin-Gill, G. S. (2003). *Refugees and Responsibility in the Twenty-First Century: More Lessons Learned from the South Pacific.* Available at: https://digitalcommons.law.uw.edu/wilj/vol12/iss1/5

Goodwin-Gill, G. S. (2009). *Introduction to the 1951 Convention/1967 Protocol relating to the Status of Refugees.* UN Audio-Visual Library of International Law.

Goodwin-Gill, G. S. (2011). The right to seek asylum: Interception at sea and the principle of *non-refoulement. International Journal of Refugee Law*, *23*(3), 443–457. doi:10.1093/ijrl/eer018

Goodwin-Gill, G. S., & McAdam, J. (2007). *The refugee in international law* (3rd ed.). Oxford University Press.

Gover, A. R., Paul, D. P., & Dodge, M. (2011). Law enforcement officers' attitudes about domestic violence. *Violence Against Women*, *17*(5), 619–636. doi:10.1177/1077801211407477 PMID:21551213

Grant, J. M., Mottet, L. A., Tanis, J. J., & Min, D. (2011). *Transgender discrimination survey.* National Center for Transgender Equality and National Gay and Lesbian Task Force.

Grant, S., & Rowe, M. (2011). Running the risk: Police officer discretion and family violence in New Zealand. *Policing and Society*, *21*(1), 49–66. Advance online publication. doi:10.1080 /10439463.2010.540662

Graves, K., & Leight, B. (1995). The relationship of substance use to sexual activity among young adults in the United States. *Family Planning Perspectives*, *27*(1), 18–22. doi:10.2307/2135972 PMID:7720848

Gray, E., Jackson, J., & Farrall, S. (2011). Feelings and Functions in the Fear of Crime: Applying a New Approach to Victimisation Insecurity. *British Journal of Criminology*, *51*(1), 75–94. doi:10.1093/bjc/azq066

Green, S. (2012). Crime, victimisation and vulnerability. In S. Walklate (Ed.), *Handbook Of Victims and Victimology* (pp. 91–117). Willan.

Greenwood, J., & Bancroft, J. (1977). Notas de aconselhamento para problemas sexuais. *A Sexologia Clínica*, 363-364.

Griswold, K. S., Vest, B. M., Lynch-Jiles, A., Sawch, D., Kolesnikova, K., Byimana, L., & Kefi, P. (2021). "I just need to be with my family": Resettlement experiences of asylum seeker and refugee survivors of torture. *Globalization and Health*, *17*(27), 1–7. doi:10.1186/s12992-021-00681-9 PMID:33750402

Group of Experts on Action against Violence against Women and Domestic Violence. (2019). *Baseline evaluation report: Portugal.* Council of Europe. https://www.cig.gov.pt/wp- content/uploads/2019/01/Relat%C3%B3rio-GREVIO.pdf

Guazi, T. S. (2021). Diretrizes para o uso de entrevistas semiestruturadas em investigações científicas. *Revista Educação, Pesquisa eInclusão, 2.*

Guedes, I. M. E. de S. (2012). *Sentimento de Insegurança, Personalidade e Emoções Disposicionais: que relações?* Universidade do Porto.

Guia, M. J. (2015). *Imigração, 'Crimigração' e Crime Violento: Os Reclusos Condenados e as Representações sobre Imigração e Crime.* Tese de Doutoramento em Direito, Justiça e Cidadania no Séc. XXI, apresentada à Faculdade de Economia da Universidade de Coimbra.

Guia, M. J., & Pedroso, J. (2015). A insustentável resposta da "crimigração" Face à irregularidade dos migrantes: Uma perspetiva da União Europeia. *REMHU –. Revista Interdisciplinar da Mobilidade Humana*, *45*(45), 129–144. doi:10.1590/1980-8585250319880004507

Guimarães, K., & Merchán-Hamann, E. (2005). Comercializando fantasias: A representação social da prostituição, dilemas da profissão e a construção da cidadania. *Estudos Feministas*, *13*(3), 525–544. doi:10.1590/S0104-026X2005000300004

Hainmueller, J., Hangartner, D., & Lawrence, D. (2016). When lives are put on hold: Lengthy asylum processes decrease employment among refugees. *Science Advances*, *2*(8), 1–7. doi:10.1126/sciadv.1600432 PMID:27493995

Hale, C. (1996). Fear of Crime: A Review of the Literature. *International Review of Victimology*, *4*(2), 79–150. doi:10.1177/026975809600400201

Hamilton, I., Pringle, R., & Hemingway, S. (2015). Psychotropic induced sexual dysfunction for people with a dual diagnosis. *Advances in Dual Diagnosis*, *8*(4), 167–178. doi:10.1108/ADD-09-2015-0021

Harne, L., & Radford, J. (2008). *Tackling domestic violence: theories, policies and practice.* Open University Press.

Hathaway, J. C. (2005). *The rights of refugees under international law.* Cambridge University Press. doi:10.1017/CBO9780511614859

Hathaway, J. C., & Fosterm, M. (2014). *The law of refugee status* (2nd ed.). Cambridge University Press. doi:10.1017/CBO9780511998300

Hayeck, C. M. (2009). Refletindo sobre a violência. *Revista Brasileira de História & Ciências Sociais, 1*(1).

Heise, L. L. (1998). Violence against women: An integrated, ecological framework. *Violence Against Women*, *4*(3), 262–290. doi:10.1177/1077801298004003002 PMID:12296014

Hellfeldt, K., López-Romero, L., & Andershed, H. (2020). Cyberbullying and psychological well-being in young adolescence: The potential protective mediation effects of social support from family, friends, and teachers. *International Journal of Environmental Research and Public Health*, *17*(1), 45. doi:10.3390/ijerph17010045 PMID:31861641

Hendry, B. P., Hellsten, L.-A. M., McIntyre, L. J., & Smith, B. R. R. (2023). Recommendations for cyberbullying prevention and intervention: A Western Canadian perspective from key stakeholders. *Frontiers in Psychology*, *14*, 1067484. doi:10.3389/fpsyg.2023.1067484 PMID:36960003

Herbst, J. H., Jacobs, E. D., Finlayson, T. J., McKleroy, V. S., Neumann, M. S., & Crepaz, N. (2008). Estimating HIV prevalence and risk behaviors of transgender persons in the United States: A systematic review. *AIDS and Behavior*, *12*(1), 1–17. doi:10.1007/s10461-007-9299-3 PMID:17694429

Herman, J. (1990). Sex offenders: a feminist perspective. In W. Marshall, D. Laws, & H. Barbaree (Eds.), *Handbook of sexual assault: issues, theories, and treatment of the offender* (pp. 177–198). Plenum Press. doi:10.1007/978-1-4899-0915-2_11

Hermans, M. P. P. J., Kooistra, J., Cannegieter, S. C., Rosendaal, F. R., Mook-Kanamori, D. O., & Nemeth, B. (2017). Healthcare and disease burden among refugees in long-stay refugee camps at Lesbos, Greece. *European Journal of Epidemiology*, *32*(9), 851–854. doi:10.1007/s10654-017-0269-4 PMID:28597126

Herrera Moreno, M. (2014). ¿Quién Teme A La Victimidad? El Debate Identitario En Victimología. *Revista De Derecho Penal y Criminología*, (12), 343-404. https://revistas.uned.es/index.php/RDPC/article/view/24528

Hersh, M., & Obser, K. (2016). *Falling through the cracks: Refugee women and girls in Germany and Sweden*. Women's Refugee Commission.

Hill, D. B., & Willoughby, B. L. B. (2005). The development and validation of the Genderism and Transphobia Scale. *Sex Roles*, *53*(7-8), 531–544. doi:10.1007/s11199-005-7140-x

Hillmann, F., & Koca, B. T. (2021). By women, for women, and with women": On the integration of highly qualified female refugees into the labour Markets of Berlin and Brandenburg. *Comparative Migration Studies*, *9*(3), 1–12. doi:10.1186/s40878-020-00211-3

Hirtenlehner, H., Farrall, S., & Groß, E. (2023). Are women of all age groups equally affected by the shadow of sexual assault? *European Journal of Criminology*, *20*(3), 834–855. doi:10.1177/14773708231156330

Hogarth, L., Dickinson, A., Wright, A., Kouvaraki, M., & Duka, T. (2007). The role of drug expectancy in the control of human drug seeking. *Journal of Experimental Psychology. Animal Behavior Processes*, *33*(4), 484–496. doi:10.1037/0097-7403.33.4.484 PMID:17924795

Holtmaat, R., & Post, P. (2018). Enhancing LGBTI rights by changing the interpretation of the convention on the elimination of all forms of discrimination against women? In Human Rights, Sexual Orientation, and Gender Identity (pp. 53-70). Routledge.

Horn, R., Wachter, K., Friis-Healy, E. A., Ngugi, S. W., Creighton, J., & Puffer, E. S. (2021). Mapping complex systems: Responses to intimate partner violence against women in three refugee camps. *Frontiers in Human Dynamics*, *3*, 1–15. doi:10.3389/fhumd.2021.613792

Horwitz, S. H., Mitchell, D., LaRussa-Trott, M., Santiago, L., Pearson, J., Skiff, D. M., & Cerulli, C. (2011). An inside view of police officers' experience with domestic violence. *Journal of Family Violence*, *26*(8), 617–625. doi:10.1007/s10896-011-9396-y

Hvidtfeldt, C., Petersen, J. H., & Norredam, M. (2020). Prolonged periods of waiting for an asylum decision and the risk of psychiatric diagnoses: A 22-year longitudinal cohort study from Denmark. *International Journal of Epidemiology*, *49*(2), 400–409. doi:10.1093/ije/dyz091 PMID:31106354

Hynie, M. (2018). The social determinants of refugee mental health in the post-migration context: A critical review. *Canadian Journal of Psychiatry*, *63*(5), 297–303. doi:10.1177/0706743717746666 PMID:29202665

Iglesias, C., Cardoso, C., & Sousa, P. (2020). *Macrosystem and Women's Fear of Crime in Intimate Relations: An Integrated Model*. doi:10.1017/cri.2020.10

Imai, K. (2017). *Quantitative social science: An introduction*. Princeton University Press.

Internal Security System - ISS. (2014). *Violência doméstica: relatório anual de monitorização. Ministério da Administração Interna* [Domestic violence: annual monitoring report. Ministry of Internal Affairs]. https://www.cig.gov.pt/siic/2014/12/violencia-domestica-2013 -relatorio-anual-de- monitorizacao-mai-agosto-de-2014/

Internal Security System - ISS. (2022). *Violência Doméstica - 2021. Relatório anual de monitorização. Ministério da Administração Interna* [Domestic Violence - 2021. Annual monitoring report. Ministry of Internal Affairs]. https://www.sg.mai.gov.pt/Documents/Relat%C3%B3rio%20de%20Mo nitoriza%C3%A7%C3%A3o%20de%202021.pdf

James, R. (2007). Strategies for incorporating women-specific sexuality education into addiction treatment models. *American Journal of Sexuality Education*, *2*(3), 3–25. doi:10.1300/J455v02n03_02

Janssen, E., & Bancroft, J. (2007). The Dual Control Model: The role of sexual inhibition and excitation in sexual arousal and behavior. In E. Janssen (Ed.), *The psychophysiology of sex* (pp. 197–222). Indiana University Press.

Jensen, N. K., Norredam, M., Priebe, S., & Krasnik, A. (2013). How do general practitioners experience provide care to refugees with mental health problems? A qualitative study from Denmark. *BMC Family Practice*, *14*(17), 1–9. doi:10.1186/1471-2296-14-17 PMID:23356401

Jerónimo, P. (2019). *Gender Equality: Old and New Challenges*. University of Minho Law School. https://repositorium.sdum.uminho.pt/handle/1822/79497

Johnson, J. R. (2013). Cisgender privilege, intersectionality, and the criminalization of CeCe McDonald: Why intercultural communication needs transgender studies. *Journal of International and Intercultural Communication*, 6(2), 135–144. doi:10.1080/17513057.2013.776094

Johnson, L., & Stylianou, A. M. (2022). Coordinated community responses to domestic violence: A systematic review of the literature. *Trauma, Violence & Abuse*, 23(2), 506–522. doi:10.1177/1524838020957984 PMID:32954993

Jones, B., Corbin, W., & Fromme, K. (2001). A review of expectancy theory and alcohol consumption. *Addiction (Abingdon, England)*, 96(1), 57–72. doi:10.1046/j.1360-0443.2001.961575.x PMID:11177520

Jordan, J. (2004). *The word of a woman?: police, rape and belief*. Palgrave MacMillan. doi:10.1057/9780230511057

Jordan, J. (2005). *The Sex Industry in New Zealand: a literature review*. Ministry of Justice.

Jun, W. (2020). A study on the cause analysis of cyberbullying in Korean adolescents. *International Journal of Environmental Research and Public Health*, 17(13), 4648. doi:10.3390/ijerph17134648 PMID:32605227

Kallivayalil, D. (2004). Gender and cultural socialization in Indian immigrant families in the United States. *Feminism & Psychology*, 14(4), 535–559. doi:10.1177/0959353504046871

Kanal, M., & Rottmann, S. (2021). Everyday agency: Rethinking refugee women's agency in specific cultural contexts. *Frontiers in Psychology*, 12, 1–14. doi:10.3389/fpsyg.2021.726729 PMID:34867608

Katsulis, Y., Durfee, A., Lopez, V., & Robillard, A. (2014). Predictors of workplace violence among female sex workers in Tijuana, Mexico. *Violence Against Women*, 1–27. PMID:25091980

Katz, E., Fromme, K., & D'Amico, E. (2000). Effects of outcome expectancies and personality on young adults' illicit drug use, heavy drnking, and risky sexual behavior. *Cognitive Therapy and Research*, 24(1), 1–22. doi:10.1023/A:1005460107337

Keen, E., & Georgescu, M. (2016). *Referências. Manual para o combate do discurso de ódio online através da educação para os direitos humanos*. Conselho da Europa: Fundação Calouste Gulbenkian.

Kelly, L. (1988). *Surviving sexual violence*. Polity Press.

Kelly, L. (2005). Inside outsiders: Mainstreaming violence against women in human rights discourse and practice. *International Feminist Journal of Politics*, 7(4), 471–495. doi:10.1080/14616740500284391

Kennedy, B. L., & Thornberg, R. (2018). Deduction, induction, and abduction. In U. Flick (Ed.), *The sage handbook of qualitative data collection* (pp. 49–64). Sage Publications. doi:10.4135/9781526416070.n4

Killias, M. (1990). Vulnerability: Towards a better understanding of a key variable in the genesis of fear of crime. *Violence and Victims*, *5*(2), 97–108. doi:10.1891/0886-6708.5.2.97 PMID:2278956

Killias, M., & Clerici, C. (2000). Different Measures of Vulnerability in their Relation to Different Dimensions of Fear of Crime. *British Journal of Criminology*, *40*(3), 437–450. doi:10.1093/bjc/40.3.437

Klevens, J., Baker, C. K., Shelley, G. A., & Ingram, E. M. (2008). Exploring the links between components of coordinated community responses and their impact on contact with intimate partner violence services. *Violence Against Women*, *14*(3), 346–358. Advance online publication. doi:10.1177/1077801207313968 PMID:18292374

Kline, R. (1990). The relation of alcohol expectancies to drinking patterns among alcoholics: Generalization across gender and race. *Journal of Studies on Alcohol*, *51*(2), 175–182. doi:10.15288/jsa.1990.51.175 PMID:2308356

Knibbe, R. (1998). Measuring drinking context. *Alcohol, Clinical and Experimental Research*, *22*(2), 15s–20s. doi:10.1111/j.1530-0277.1998.tb04369.x PMID:9603302

Knudsen, S. (2006). Intersectionality – a theoretical inspiration in the analysis of minority cultures and identities in textbooks. In Caught in the web or lost in the textbook, 8th (pp. 61–76). Academic Press.

Kofman, E. (2020). Gender and the feminization of migration. In C. Inglis, W. Li, & B. Khadria (Eds.), The sage handbook of international migration (pp. 2016–2231). Sage Publications.

Konvalina-Simas, T. (2012). *Introdução à biopsicossociologia do comportamento desviante*. Maia: Reis dos Livros.

Kopetz, C., Reynolds, E., Hart, C., Kruglanski, A., & Lejuez, C. (2010). Social context and perceived effects of drugs on sexual behavior among individuals who use both heroin and cocaine. *Experimental and Clinical Psychopharmacology*, *18*(3), 214–220. doi:10.1037/a0019635 PMID:20545385

Korstjens, I., & Moser, A. (2018). Practical guidance to qualitative research: Trustworthiness and publishing. *The European Journal of General Practice*, *24*(1), 120–124. doi:10.1080/13814788.2017.1375092 PMID:29202616

Koskela, H., & Pain, R. (2000a). *Revisiting fear and place : women's fear of attack and the built environment*. Academic Press.

Koskela, H., & Pain, R. (2000b). Revisiting fear and place: Women's fear of attack and the built environment. *Geoforum*, *31*(2), 269–280. doi:10.1016/S0016-7185(99)00033-0

Kowalski, R. M., Limber, S. P., & McCord, A. (2019). A developmental approach to cyberbullying: Prevalence and protective factors. *Aggression and Violent Behavior*, *45*, 20–32. https://psycnet.apa.org/doi/10.1016/j.avb.2018.02.009. doi:10.1016/j.avb.2018.02.009

Kraus, E., Sauer, K. L., & Wenzel, L. (2019). Together or apart? Spousal migration and reunification practices of recent refugees to Germany. *ZtF. Zeitschrift für Familienforschung*, *31*(3), 303–332. doi:10.3224/zff.v31i3.04

Kuiper, L., Beloate, L., Dupuy, B., & Coolen, L. (2019). Drug-taking in a social-sexual context enhances vulnerability for addiction in male rats. *Neuropsychopharmacology*, *44*(3), 503–513. doi:10.1038/s41386-018-0235-1 PMID:30337639

Kula, M. E. (2022). Cyberbullying: A Literature Review on Cross-Cultural Research in the Last Quarter. In M. Kula (Ed.), *Handbook of Research on Digital Violence and Discrimination Studies* (pp. 610–630). IGI Global. doi:10.4018/978-1-7998-9187-1.ch027

La Pera, G., Carderi, A., Marianantoni, Z., Lentini, M., & Taggi, F. (2006). The role of sexual dysfunctions in inducing the use of drug in young males. *Archivio Italiano di Urologia, Andrologia*, *78*(3), 101–106. PMID:17137024

La Pera, G., Carderi, A., Marianantoni, Z., Peris, F., Lentini, M., & Taggi, F. (2008a). Sexual dysfunction prior to first drug use among former drug addicts and its possible causal meaning on drug addiction: Preliminary results. *Journal of Sexual Medicine*, *5*(1), 164–172. doi:10.1111/j.1743-6109.2007.00571.x PMID:17666038

La Pera, G., Carderi, A., Marianantoni, Z., Sette, D., Gallo, G., Livi, S., & Macchia, T. (2008b). Can sexual dysfunctions lead to substance abuse disorders? *Sexologies*, *17*(S1), 134–135. doi:10.1016/S1158-1360(08)72889-5

Labbe, A., & Maisto, S. (2011). Alcohol expectancy challenges for college students: A narrative review. *Clinical Psychology Review*, *31*(4), 673–683. doi:10.1016/j.cpr.2011.02.007 PMID:21482325

Labriola, M., Bradley, S., O'Sullivan, C. S., Rempel, M., & Moore, S. (2009). *A national portrait of domestic violence courts*. Center for Court Innovation. https://www.ncjrs.gov/pdffiles1/nij/grants/229659.pdf

Laidlaw, L. (2018). Challenging dominant portrayals of the trans sex worker: On gender, violence, and protection. *Man. LJ*, *41*, 351.

Lebano, A., Hamed, S., Bradby, H., Gil-Salmerón, A., Durá-Ferrandis, E., Garcés-Ferrer, J., Azzedine, F., Riza, E., Karnaki, P., Zota, D., & Linos, A. (2020). Migrants' and refugees' health status and healthcare in Europe: A scoping literature review. *BMC Public Health*, *20*(1039), 1–16. doi:10.1186/s12889-020-08749-8 PMID:32605605

Leisenring, A. (2012). Victims' perceptions of police response to intimate partner violence. *Journal of Police Crisis Negotiations*, *12*(2), 146–164. doi:10.1080/15332586.2012.728926

Leonard, R. (1997). Theorizing the relationship between agency and communion. *Theory & Psychology*, *7*(6), 823–835. doi:10.1177/0959354397076005

Leonhardt, M., & Overå, S. (2021). Are there differences in video gaming and use of social media among boys and girls?—A mixed methods approach. *International Journal of Environmental Research and Public Health*, *18*(11), 6085. doi:10.3390/ijerph18116085 PMID:34200039

Leppink, E., Chamberlain, S., Redden, S., & Grant, J. (2016). Problematic sexual behavior in young adults: Associations across clinical, behavioral, and neurocognitive variables. *Psychiatry Research, 246,* 230-235. doi: , 2016.09.044 doi:10.1016/j.psychres

Lerner, M. J. (1980). The Belief in a Just World. In *The Belief in a Just World. Perspectives in Social Psychology.* Springer. doi:10.1007/978-1-4899-0448-5_2

LeVay, S. (1996). *Queer Science: The Use and Abuse of Research into Homosexuality.* The MIT Press. doi:10.7551/mitpress/5726.001.0001

Lewis, R. (2004). Making justice work: Effective legal interventions for domestic violence. *British Journal of Criminology*, *44*(2), 204–224. doi:10.1093/bjc/44.2.204

Li, C., Wang, P., Martin-Moratinos, M., Bella-Fernández, M., & Blasco-Fontecilla, H. (2022). Traditional bullying and cyberbullying in the digital age and its associated mental health problems in children and adolescents: A meta-analysis. *European Child & Adolescent Psychiatry*, 1–15. doi:10.1007/s00787-021-01763-0 PMID:36585978

Lindsmith, A. (1980). A general theory of addiction to opiate-type drugs. *NIDA Research Monograph*, *30*, 34–37. PMID:6779192

Lisboa, M., Barroso, Z., Patrício, J., & Leandro, A. (2009a). *Violência e género – Inquérito nacional sobre a violência exercida contra mulheres e homens.* Comissão para a Cidadania e Igualdade de Género.

Lisboa, M., Barroso, Z., Patrício, J., Leandro, A. (2009b). *Inquérito Nacional sobre a Violência Exercida contra Mulheres e Homens.* Comissão para a Cidadania e Igualdade de Género.

Lisboa, M., Cerejo, D., & Brasil, E. (2020). De onde vimos e para onde vamos? Conhecimento e políticas públicas em Portugal sobre a violência doméstica, nas últimas três décadas. In S. Neves (Coord.), Violências de Género na Intimidade (pp. 13–39). Edições ISMAI.

Löbel, L. M., & Jacobsen, J. (2021). Waiting for kin: A longitudinal study of family reunification and refugee mental health in Germany. *Journal of Ethnic and Migration Studies*, *47*(13), 2916–2937. doi:10.1080/1369183X.2021.1884538

Lochmann, A., Rapoport, H., & Speciale, B. (2019). The effect of language training on immigrants' economic integration: Empirical evidence from France. *European Economic Review*, *113*, 265–296. doi:10.1016/j.euroecorev.2019.01.008

Loewenstein, G., Nagin, D., & Paternoster, R. (1997). The effect of sexual arousal on expectations of sexual forcefulness. *Journal of Research in Crime and Delinquency*, *34*(4), 443–473. doi:10.1177/0022427897034004003

Logan, T. K., & Walker, R. (2021). The Gender Safety Gap: Examining the Impact of Victimization History, Perceived Risk, and Personal Control. *Journal of Interpersonal Violence*, *36*(1–2), 603–631. doi:10.1177/0886260517729405 PMID:29294904

Loken, M., & Hagen, J. J. (2022). Queering gender-based violence scholarship: An integrated research agenda. *International Studies Review*, *24*(4), viac050. doi:10.1093/isr/viac050

Lombardi, E. L., Wilchins, R. A., Priessing, D., & Malouf, D. (2001). Gender violence: Transgender experiences with violence and discrimination. *Journal of Homosexuality*, *42*(1), 89–101. doi:10.1300/J082v42n01_05 PMID:11991568

Lorga, P. (2001). Toxicodependência e sexualidade: Revisão bibliográfica a propósito das suas possíveis interacções (ParteI). *Toxicodependências (Lisboa)*, *7*(3), 41–52.

Lorga, P. (2002). Toxicodependência e sexualidade: Revisão bibliográfica a propósito das suas possíveis interacções (ParteII). *Toxicodependências (Lisboa)*, *8*(1), 53–64.

Lourenço, N., Gama Lisboa, M., & Pais, E. (1997). *Violência contra as mulheres*. Comissão para a Igualdade e para os Direitos das Mulheres.

Lupton, D., & Tulloch, J. (2003). Theorizing fear of crime: Beyond the rational/irrational opposition. *The British Journal of Sociology*, *50*(3), 507–523. doi:10.1111/j.1468-4446.1999.00507.x PMID:15259198

Lynch, I., & Sanger, N. (2016). *I'm your maker: power, heteronormativity and violence in women's same-sex relationships*. Academic Press.

Lyons, T., Krüsi, A., Pierre, L., Kerr, T., Small, W., & Shannon, K. (2017). Negotiating violence in the context of transphobia and criminalization: The experiences of trans sex workers in Vancouver, Canada. *Qualitative Health Research*, *27*(2), 182–190. doi:10.1177/1049732315613311 PMID:26515922

Machado, P., Pais, L. G., Morgado, S., & Felgueiras, S. (2021). An inter-organisational response to domestic violence: The pivotal role of police in Porto, Portugal. *European Law Enforcement Research Bulletin, 21*.

Machado, B., Caridade, S., Araújo, I., & Faria, P. L. (2022). Mapping the cyber interpersonal violence among young populations: A scoping review. *Social Sciences (Basel, Switzerland)*, *11*(5), 207. doi:10.3390/socsci11050207

Machado, P., Pais, L. G., Felgueiras, S., & Quaresma, C. (2021). Frontline Response to High Impact Domestic Violence in Portugal. In B. Lobnikar, C. Vogt, & J. Kersten (Eds.), *Improving Frontline Responses to Domestic Violence in Europe* (pp. 215–238). University of Maribor. doi:10.18690/978-961-286-543-6.13

Madriz, E. (1997). Images of Criminals and Victims: a Study on Women's Fear and Social Control. *Sage Publications, 11*(3), 342–356.

Magić, B., & Selun, J. (2018). *Safe at school: Education sector responses to violence based on sexual orientation, gender identity/expression or sex characteristics in Europe.* Report Commissioned by the Council of Europe.

Mahlknecht, B., & Bork-Hüffer, T. (2023). 'She felt incredibly ashamed': Gendered (cyber-) bullying and the hypersexualized female body. *Gender, Place and Culture, 30*(7), 989–1011. doi:10.1080/0966369X.2022.2115981

Malheiros, J. M. (Org.). (2007). *Imigração brasileira em Portugal. Alto Comissariado para a Imigração e Diálogo Intercultural (ACIDI, I. P.).* https://www.om.acm.gov.pt/documents/58428/179693/1_ImigrBrasileira.pdf/7d926056-f322-427a-8393-73fb1848da37

Mangrio, E., & Forss, K. S. (2017). Refugees' experiences of healthcare in the host country: A scoping review. *BMC Health Services Research, 17*(814), 1–18. doi:10.1186/s12913-017-2731-0 PMID:29216876

Mangrio, E., Zdravkovic, S., & Carlson, E. (2019). Refugee women's experience of the resettlement process: A qualitative study. *BMC Women's Health, 19*(1), 147. doi:10.1186/s12905-019-0843-x PMID:31775733

Manita, C. (2007). *Dinâmicas e consequências da violência doméstica: o(s) valor(es) da liberdade e da vida.* Conferência Regional Parlamentos Unidos contra a Violência Doméstica contra as Mulheres.

Manita, C. (2008). Programas de intervenção em agressores de violência conjugal: Intervenção psicológica e prevenção da violência doméstica. *Ousar Integrar: Revista de Reinserção Social e Prova, 1*, 21–32.

Manzanares, R.C. (Dir.); Mayo, M. J. S., & Tarrío, C. T. (Coord.). (2014). *Justicia Restaurativa y violência de género: más allá de la Ley Orgánica 1/2004.* Universidade de Santiago de Compostela, Servizo de Publicacións e Intercambio Científico.

Maria, S. G. D. S. (2001). *Mulheres sobreviventes de violação* (Doctoral dissertation). Universidade Aberta.

Marques, J. (2021). A look at Domestic and Gender-based Violence in Portugal: from law to discourses. In NORDSCI (Orgs), *Conference Proceedings-International Conference on Social Sciences* (pp. 245–253). Bulgaria: SAIMA Consult. 10.32008/NORDSCI2021/B2/V4/21

Martins, N., Correia, P., & Pereira, S. (2021). Ciberjustiça em Portugal: A Vigilância Eletrónica como Estratégia da Política Criminal. *Lex Humana, 13*, 177–189.

Mason, J. (2002). *Qualitative researching.* SAGE Publications.

Masters, W., & Johnson, V. (1970). *Human sexual inadequacy.* Little, Brown and Co.

Matos, M. (2010). *Sexualidade, afectos e cultura. Gestão de problemas de saúde em meio escolar.* Coisas de Ler.

Mattison, A., Ross, M., Wolfson, T., & Franklin, D.HNRC Group. (2001). Circuit party attendance, club drug use, and unsafe sex in gay men. *Journal of Substance Abuse*, *13*(1-2), 119–126. doi:10.1016/S0899-3289(01)00060-8 PMID:11547613

Mavhandu-Mudzusi, A. H. (2017). Impact of stigma and discrimination on sexual well- being of LGBTI students in a South African rural university. *South African Journal of Higher Education*, *31*(4), 208–218.

May, D. C. (2001). The effect of fear of sexual victimization on adolescent fear of crime. *Sociological Spectrum*, *21*(2), 141–174. doi:10.1080/02732170119080

May, D. C., Rader, N. E., & Goodrum, S. (2010). A gendered assessment of the "'threat of victimization'": Examining gender differences in fear of crime, perceived risk, avoidance, and defensive behaviors. *Criminal Justice Review*, *35*(2), 159–182. doi:10.1177/0734016809349166

McAdams, D. P. (2013). The psychological self as actor, agent, and author. *Perspectives on Psychological Science*, *8*(3), 272–295. doi:10.1177/1745691612464657 PMID:26172971

McElrath, K. (2005). MDMA and sexual behavior: Ecstasy users' perceptions about sexuality and sexual risk. *Substance Use & Misuse*, *40*(9), 1461–1477. doi:10.1081/JA-200066814 PMID:16048828

McKee, S., Hinson, R., Wall, A., & Spriel, P. (1998). Alcohol outcome expectancies and coping styles as predictors of alcohol use in young adults. *Addictive Behaviors*, *23*(1), 17–22. doi:10.1016/S0306-4603(97)00008-7 PMID:9468737

Mellgren, C., & Ivert, A. K. (2019). Is Women's Fear of Crime Fear of Sexual Assault? A Test of the Shadow of Sexual Assault Hypothesis in a Sample of Swedish University Students. *Violence Against Women*, *25*(5), 511–527. doi:10.1177/1077801218793226 PMID:30156127

Melossi, D. (2003). 'In a Peaceful Life': Migration and the crime of modernity in Europe/Italy. *Punishment & Society*, *5*(4), 371–397. doi:10.1177/14624745030054001

Melossi, D. (2015). *Crime, punishment and migration.* Sage Publications. doi:10.4135/9781473920965

Meltzer, H., Doos, L., Vostanis, P. P., Ford, T., & Goodman, R. (2009). The mental health of children who witness domestic violence. *Child & Family Social Work*, *14*(4), 491–501. doi:10.1111/j.1365-2206.2009.00633.x

Miles-Johnson, T. (2013). LGBTI variations in crime reporting: How sexual identity influences decisions to call the cops. *SAGE Open*, *3*(2). doi:10.1177/2158244013490707

Miller, B. (1990). The interrelationships between alcohol and drugs and family violence. *NIDA Research Monograph*, *103*, 177–207. PMID:2096287

Minayo, M. C. S., & Sanches, O. (1993). Quantitative and Qualitative Methods: Opposition or Complementarity? *Cad. Saúde Pub., Rio de Janeiro*, *9*(3), 239-262. https://www.scielo.br/j/csp/a/Bgpmz7T7cNv8K9Hg4J9fJDb/?format=pdf&lang=pt

Mintz, J., O'Hare, K., O'Brien, C., & Goldschmidt, J. (1974). Sexual problems of heroin addicts. *Archives of General Psychiatry*, *31*(5), 700–703. doi:10.1001/archpsyc.1974.01760170088014 PMID:4474860

Mishna, F., Schwan, K. J., Birze, A., Van Wert, M., Lacombe-Duncan, A., McInroy, L., & Attar-Schwartz, S. (2020). Gendered and sexualized bullying and cyber bullying: Spotlighting girls and making boys invisible. *Youth & Society*, *52*(3), 403–426. doi:10.1177/0044118X18757150

Mishra, D., Le, A. N., & McDowell, Z. (2023). *Communication Technology and Gender Violence*. Springer Nature.

Montesanti, S. R., & Thurston, W. E. (2015). Mapping the role of structural and interpersonal violence in the lives of women: Implications for public health interventions and policy. *BMC Women's Health*, *15*(1), 100. doi:10.1186/s12905-015-0256-4 PMID:26554358

Monto, M. A. (2004). Female prostitution, customers, and violence. *Violence Against Women*, *10*(2), 160–188. doi:10.1177/1077801203260948

Morais-Gonçalves, D., Lopes-Borges, S., & Gaspar, H. (2018). Reincidência, Fatores de Risco e Avaliação de Risco em Vítimas de Violência Doméstica. *Trabajo Social Global –*. *Global Social Work*, *8*(15), 78–113. doi:10.30827/tsg-gsw.v8i15.7424

Moreira, V., Rolo, A., & Cardoso, J. (2016). Violence in the context of prostitution: psychological impact. *Psiquiatria, Psicologia & Justiça*, 62-72.

Morgan, D. (2008). Sampling. In L. Given (Ed.), *The sage encyclopedia of qualitative research method* (pp. 799–800). SAGE Publications.

Morrison, A., & Orlando, M. B. (2004). *The costs and impacts of gender-based violence in developing countries*. Academic Press.

Mossman, E. (2007). *International approaches to decriminalising or legalising prostitution*. Ministry of Justice.

Muñoz-Fernández, N., & Sánchez-Jiménez, V. (2020). Cyber-aggression and psychological aggression in adolescent couples: A short-term longitudinal study on prevalence and common and differential predictors. *Computers in Human Behavior*, *104*, 106191. doi:10.1016/j.chb.2019.106191

Nadal, K. L., Davidoff, K. C., & Fujii-Doe, W. (2014). Transgender women and the sex work industry: Roots in systemic, institutional, and interpersonal discrimination. *Journal of Trauma & Dissociation*, *15*(2), 169–183. doi:10.1080/15299732.2014.867572 PMID:24313294

Narrative Victimology: Speaker, audience, timing. (2019). In Hourigan, K. L. (Ed.), *The Emerald Handbook of Narrative Criminology* (pp. 259–277). Emerald Publishing Limited. doi:10.1108/978-1-78769-005-920191024

National Center on Addiction and Substance Abuse. (1999). *Dangerous Liaisons: substance abuse and sex*. NCASA.

Nemoto, T., Bödeker, B., & Iwamoto, M. (2011). Social support, exposure to violence and transphobia, and correlates of depression among male-to-female transgender women with a history of sex work. *American Journal of Public Health*, *101*(10), 1980–1988. doi:10.2105/AJPH.2010.197285 PMID:21493940

Neves, J. (2008). Violência doméstica – bem jurídico e boas práticas. *Revista do Centro de Estudos Judiciários*, *8*, 43–63.

Neves, S. (2016). Femicídio: O fim da linha da violência de género. *Ex Aequo (Oeiras)*, *34*(34). Advance online publication. doi:10.22355/exaequo.2016.34.01

Neves, S., & Brasil, E. (2018). A intervenção junto de mulheres vítimas de violência doméstica em Portugal: percursos, paradigmas, práticas e desafios. In I. Dias (Ed.), *Violência Doméstica e de Género: uma abordagem multidisciplinar* (pp. 175–188). Pactor.

Neves, S., & Correia, A. (2022). Intimate Partner Femicide in Portugal. The perception of intervention professionals with intimate partner violence. *Observatorio (OBS*)*, *16*(2), 117–137. doi:10.15847/obsOBS16220221916

Neves, S., & Nogueira, C. (2005). Metodologias Feministas: A reflexividade ao serviço da Investigação nas Ciências Sociais. *Psicologia: Reflexão e Crítica*, *18*(3), 408–412. doi:10.1590/S0102-79722005000300015

Neves, S., & Nogueira, C. (2010). Deconstructing gendered discourses of love, power and violence in intimate relationships. In D. Jack & A. Ali (Eds.), *Silencing the Self Across Cultures Depression and Gender in the Social World* (pp. 241–261). Oxford University Press. doi:10.1093/acprof:oso/9780195398090.003.0012

Neves, S., Santos, I., & Topa, J. (2023). The Implementation of Dating Violence Prevention Programmes in Portugal and Their Effectiveness: Perspectives of Professionals. *Social Sciences (Basel, Switzerland)*, *12*(9), 9. Advance online publication. doi:10.3390/socsci12010009

Newcomb, M., & Mustanski, B. (2014). Cognitive influences on sexual risk and risk appraisals in men who have sex with men. *Health Psychology*, *33*(7), 690–698. doi:10.1037/hea0000010 PMID:23977876

Nimbi, F., Tripodi, F., Rossi, R., & Simonelli, C. (2018). Expanding the analysis of psychosocial factors of sexual desire in men. *Journal of Sexual Medicine*, *15*(2), 230–244. doi:10.1016/j.jsxm.2017.11.227 PMID:29292060

Noaks, L., & Wincup, E. (2004). *Criminological research*. SAGE Publications Ltd., doi:10.4135/9781849208789

Nobre, P., Pinto-Gouveia, J., & Gomes, F. (2003). Sexual dysfunctional beliefs questionnaire: An instrument to assess sexual dysfunctional beliefs as vulnerability factors to sexual problems. *Sexual and Relationship Therapy*, *18*(2), 171–204. doi:10.1080/1468199031000061281

Nogueira, E., Simões, E., & Sani, A. (2020). A publicidade institucional e a sua repercussão mediática: uma análise de campanhas publicitárias no combate à violência doméstica. In M. Batista & A. Almeida (Eds). Performatividades de género na democracia ameaçada (pp.147–155). Grácio Editor.

Noy, C. (2008). Sampling knowledge: The hermeneutics of snowball sampling in qualitative research. *International Journal of Social Research Methodology*, *11*(4), 327–344. doi:10.1080/13645570701401305

Nussbaum, M. C. (2010). *From Disgust to Humanity: Sexual Orientation and Constitutional Law*. Oxford University Press.

Nyman, H., & Provozin, A. (2019). *The harmful effects of online and offline anti LGBTI hate speech*. Academic Press.

O'Hair, D., Allman, J., & Moore, S. (1996). A cognitive-affective model of relational expectations in the provider-patient context. *Journal of Health Psychology*, *1*(3), 307–322. doi:10.1177/135910539600100305 PMID:22011994

O'Halloran, K. (2015). Family violence in an LGBTIQ context. *DVRCV Advocate*, (2), 10–13.

O'Hare, T. (1998). Alcohol expectancies and excessive drinking contexts in young adults. *Social Work Research*, *22*(1), 44–50. doi:10.1093/swr/22.1.44

Observatório Europeu da Droga e da Toxicodependência. (2022). *Relatório Europeu sobre drogas. Tendências e evoluções*. Serviço das Publicações da União Europeia. doi:10.2810/21871

Oliveira, C. (2020). *Entry, reception and integration of applicants and beneficiaries of international protection in Portugal - 2020 asylum statistical report*. Academic Press.

Özascilar, M. (2013). Predicting fear of crime: A test of the shadow of sexual assault hypothesis. *International Review of Victimology*, *19*(3), 269–284. doi:10.1177/0269758013492754

Padilha, M. I. C. D. S., Ramos, F. R. S., Borenstein, M. S., & Martins, C. R. (2005). A responsabilidade do pesquisador ou sobre o que dizemos acerca da ética em pesquisa. *Texto & Contexto Enfermagem*, *14*(1), 96–105. doi:10.1590/S0104-07072005000100013

Pain, R. (1997). Whither women's fear? perceptions of sexual violence in public and private space. *International Review of Victimology*, *4*(4), 297–312. doi:10.1177/026975809700400404

Pain, R. (2001). Gender, Race, Age and Fear in the City. *Urban Studies (Edinburgh, Scotland)*, *38*(5–6), 899–913. doi:10.1080/00420980120046590

Pain, R. (2014). Everyday terrorism Connecting domestic violence and global terrorism. *Progress in Human Geography*, *38*(4), 531–550. doi:10.1177/0309132513512231

Palaganas, E., Sanchez, M. C., Molintas, M. V. P., & Caricativo, R. D. (2017). Reflexivity in Qualitative Research: A Journey of Learning. *The Qualitative Report*, *22*(2), 426–438. doi:10.46743/2160-3715/2017.2552

Palha, A., & Esteves, M. (2002). A study of the sexuality of opiate addicts. *Journal of Sex & Marital Therapy*, *28*(5), 427–437. doi:10.1080/00926230290001547 PMID:12378844

Pallmann, I., Ziegler, J., & Pfeffer-Hoffmann, C. (2019). *Refugee women as a target group of labour market policies*. Mensch & Buch.

Panhwar, A. H., Ansari, S., & Shah, A. (2017). Post-positivism: An Effective Paradigm for Social and Educational Research. *International Research Journal of Arts & Humanities*, *45*(45), 253–260.

Pasko, L. (2002). Naked Power: The Practice of Stripping as a Confidence Game. *Sexualities*, *5*(1), 49–66. doi:10.1177/1363460702005001003

Patanè, F., Bolhuis, M. P. P., van Wijk, J., & Kreiensiek, H. (2020). Asylum-seekers prosecuted for human smuggling: A case study of *Sacristy* in Italy. *Refugee Survey Quarterly*, *39*(2), 123–152. doi:10.1093/rsq/hdaa008

Patrício, L. (2014). *Políticas e dependências. Álcool e (de) mais drogas em Portugal 30 anos depois*. Vega.

Patrick, M., Wray-Lake, L., Finlay, A., & Maggs, J. (2010). Cognitive effects. The long arm of expectancies: Adolescent alcohol expectancies predict adult alcohol use. *Alcohol and Alcoholism (Oxford, Oxfordshire)*, *45*(1), 17–24. doi:10.1093/alcalc/agp066 PMID:19808940

Peixoto, A. (2012). *Propensity, experiences and consequences of Victimization: social representations* [Doctoral dissertation, New University of Lisbon]. New University of Lisbon Institutional Repository. http://hdl.handle.net/10362/7880

Peixoto, M., & Nobre, P. (2017). The activation of incompetence schemas in response to negative sexual events in heterosexual and lesbian women: The moderator role of personality traits and dysfunctional sexual beliefs. *Journal of Sex Research*, *54*(9), 1188–1196. doi:10.1080/0022449 9.2016.1267103 PMID:28059574

Pemberton, A. (2016). Empathy for victims in criminal justice: Revisiting Susan Bandes in Victimology. In H. Conway & J. Stannard (Eds.), *Emotional Dynamics of Law and Legal Discourse*. Hart Publishing.

Pemberton, A., Aarten, P. G., & Mulder, E. (2017). Beyond retribution, restoration and procedural justice: The Big Two of communion and agency in victims' perspectives on justice. *Psychology, Crime & Law*, *23*(7), 682–698. doi:10.1080/1068316X.2017.1298760

Pemberton, A., & Aarten, P. P. G. M. (2018). Narrative in the study of victimological processes in terrorism and political violence: An initial exploration. *Studies in Conflict and Terrorism*, *41*(7), 541–556. doi:10.1080/1057610X.2017.1311110

Pemberton, A., & Mulder, E. (2023). Bringing injustice back in: Secondary Victimization as epistemic injustice. *Criminology & Criminal Justice*. Advance online publication. doi:10.1177/17488958231181345

Pemberton, A., Mulder, E., & Aarten, P. G. (2019a). Stories of injustice: Towards a narrative victimology. *European Journal of Criminology*, *16*(4), 391–412. doi:10.1177/1477370818770843

Pemberton, A., Mulder, E., & Aarten, P. G. (2019b). Stories as property: Narrative ownership as a key concept in victims' experiences with criminal justice. *Criminology & Criminal Justice*, *19*(4), 404–420. doi:10.1177/1748895818778320

Peters, E., Khondkaryan, E., & Sullivan, T. (2012). Associations between expectancies of alcohol and drug use, severity of partner violence, and posttraumatic stress among women. *Journal of Interpersonal Violence*, *27*(11), 2108–2127. doi:10.1177/0886260511432151 PMID:22258078

Pham, S. (2017). Twitter tries new measures in crackdown on harassment. *CN-Ntech*.

Pinchevsky, G. M. (2017). Understanding decision-making in specialized domestic violence courts: Can contemporary theoretical frameworks help guide these decisions? *Violence Against Women*, *23*(6), 749–771. doi:10.1177/1077801216648792 PMID:27216474

Pio, E., & Singh, S. (2016). Vulnerability and resilience: Critical reflexivity in gendered violence research. *Third World Quarterly*, *37*(2), 227–244. doi:10.1080/01436597.2015.1089166

Poiares, N. (2020). Violência doméstica e redes sociais: a proteção jurídico-penal da vida privada na internet. In T. Castro (Ed.), Revista Científica Sobre Cyberlaw do Centro de Investigação Jurídica do Ciberespaço. Faculdade de Direito da Universidade de Lisboa.

Poiares, N. (2016). *A letra e os espíritos da lei: a violência doméstica em Portugal* [The letter and spirit of the law: domestic violence in Portugal]. Chiado.

Post, L. A., Klevens, J., Maxwell, C. D., Shelley, G. A., & Ingram, E. (2010). An examination of whether coordinated community responses affect intimate partner violence. *Journal of Interpersonal Violence*, *25*(1), 75–93. doi:10.1177/0886260508329125 PMID:19196879

Presser, L., & Sandberg, S. (2019). Narrative Criminology as Critical Criminology. *Critical Criminology*, *27*(1), 131–143. doi:10.1007/s10612-019-09437-9

Quintas, J., & Sousa, P. (2017). *Avaliação científica do programa 'UM PASSO MAIS': relatório*. Universidade do Porto.

Rader, N. (2017). *Fear of Crime*. Oxford University Press. doi:10.1093/acrefore/9780190264079.013.10

Rahman, M., Nakamura, K., Seino, K., & Kizuki, M. (2013). Does Gender Inequity Increase the Risk of Intimate Partner Violence among Women? Evidence from a National Bangladeshi Sample. *PLoS One*, *8*(12), e82423. doi:10.1371/journal.pone.0082423 PMID:24376536

Rajah, V., Frye, V., & Haviland, M. (2006). "Aren't I a victim?": Notes on identity challenges relating to police action in a mandatory arrest jurisdiction. *Violence Against Women*, *12*(10), 897–916. doi:10.1177/1077801206292872 PMID:16957172

Raphael, J., & Shapiro, D. L. (2004). Violence in indoor and outdoor prostitution venues. *Violence Against Women, 10*(2), 126–139. doi:10.1177/1077801203260529

Rawson, R., Washton, A., Domier, C., & Reiber, C. (2002). Drugs and sexual effects: Role of drug type and gender. *Journal of Substance Abuse Treatment, 22*(2), 103–108. doi:10.1016/S0740-5472(01)00215-X PMID:11932136

Rees, S., Horsley, P., Moussa, B., & Fisher, J. (2017). *Intimate partner violence and LGBTIQ people: Raising awareness in general practice.* Academic Press.

Reid, L. W., & Konrad, M. (2004). The gender gap in fear: Assessing the interactive effects of gender and perceived risk on fear of crime. *Sociological Spectrum, 24*(4), 399–425. doi:10.1080/02732170490431331

Reilly, N., Sahraoui, N., & McGarry, O. (2021). Exclusion, minimization, inaction: A critical review of Ireland's policy response to gender-based violence as it affects migrant women. *Frontiers in Human Dynamics, 3*, 1–17. doi:10.3389/fhumd.2021.642445

Ribeiro, S. (2019). *Droga e Exectativas Sexuais: Impacto das expectativas acerca do efeito do consume de opiáceos na sexualidade.* Dissertação de doutoramento. FPCE-Universidade do Porto.

Ribeiro, L. P., Neves Riani, S. R., & Antunes-Rocha, M. I. (2019). Representaciones sociales de personas transgénero (travestis y transexuales) sobre la violencia. *Revista de Psicología, 37*(2), 496–527. doi:10.18800/psico.201902.006

Ribeiro, S., Negreiros, J., Oliveira, J., & Teixeira, P. (2015). Substance Use and Sexual Behavior Survey: A validation study. *Psicologia, Saúde & Doenças, 16*(2), 207–216. doi:10.15309/15psd160207

Riessman, C. K. (2000). Analysis of personal narratives. *Inside interviewing: New lenses, new concerns*, 331-346. https://uel.ac.uk/sites/default/files/analysis-of-personal-narratives.pdf

Riessman, C. K. (1993). *Narrative analysis.* SAGE Publishings.

Rios-Gonzalez, O., Peña-Axt, J. C., Legorburo-Torres, G., Avgousti, A., & Sancho, L. N. (2023). Impact of an evidence-based training for educators on bystander intervention for the prevention of violence against LGBTI+ youth. *Humanities & Social Sciences Communications, 10*(1), 1–13. doi:10.1057/s41599-023-02117-8

Ritchie, J., Lewis, J., & Elam, G. (2003). Designing and Selecting Samples: Qualitative research in practice. In J. Ritchie, & J. Lewis (Eds.), Qualitative research practice: a guide for social science students and researchers (pp. 77-104). SAGE Publications.

Robertshaw, L., Dhesi, S., & Jones, L. L. (2017). Challenges and facilitators for health professionals providing primary healthcare for refugees and asylum seekers in high-income countries: A systematic review and thematic synthesis of qualitative research. *BMJ Open, 7*(8), 1–18. doi:10.1136/bmjopen-2017-015981 PMID:28780549

Robinson, A. L., & Stroshine Chandek, M. (2000). Philosophy into practice? Community policing units and domestic violence victim participation. *Policing*, *23*(3), 280–302. doi:10.1108/13639510010342985

Rodella Sapia, M. D., Wangmo, T., Dagron, S., & Elger, B. S. (2020). Understanding access to professional healthcare among asylum seekers facing gender-based violence: A qualitative study from a stakeholder perspective. *BMC International Health and Human Rights*, *20*(1), 25. doi:10.1186/s12914-020-00244-w PMID:32957996

Rodríguez-Blanes, G. M., Vives-Cases, C., Miralles-Bueno, J. J., San Sebastián, M., & Goicolea, I. (2017). Detección de violencia del compañero íntimo en atención primaria de salud y sus factores asociados. *Gaceta Sanitaria*, *31*(5), 410–415. doi:10.1016/j.gaceta.2016.11.008 PMID:28188013

Rohlof, H. G., Knipscheer, J. W., & Kleber, R. J. (2014). Somatization in refugees: A review. *Social Psychiatry and Psychiatric Epidemiology*, *49*(11), 1793–1804. doi:10.1007/s00127-014-0877-1 PMID:24816685

Rohsenow, D. (1983). Drinking habits and expectancies about alcohol's effects for self versus others. *Journal of Consulting and Clinical Psychology*, *51*(5), 752–756. doi:10.1037/0022-006X.51.5.752 PMID:6630690

Rola, R., & Oliveira, M. (2019). *O estatuto de vítima na violência doméstica. A atribuição do estatuto de vítima às crianças que vivem o crime*. Revista Electrónica de Estudios Penales y de la Seguridad.

Romo, N. (2004). *Género y uso de droga: la invisibilidade de las mujeres*. Fundación Medicina y Humanidades Médicas.

Romo, N., Marcos, J., Rodríguez, A., Cabrera, A., & Hernán, M. (2009). Girl power: Risky sexual behaviour and gender identity amongst young Spanish recreational drug users. *Sexualities*, *12*(3), 3355–3377. doi:10.1177/1363460709103895

Rosa, H., Pereira, N., Ribeiro, R., Ferreira, P. C., Carvalho, J. P., Oliveira, S., Coheur, L., Paulino, P., Simão, A. M. V., & Trancoso, I. (2019). Automatic cyberbullying detection: A systematic review. *Computers in Human Behavior*, *93*, 333–345. doi:10.1016/j.chb.2018.12.021

Rössler, P. (2017). *The international encyclopedia of media effects, 4 volume set*. John Wiley & Sons. doi:10.1002/9781118783764

Russell, D. (1976). *Crimes against women: international tribunal proceedings*. Les-Femmes Publishing.

Russell, M. L., Moralejo, D. G., & Burgess, E. D. (2000). Paying research subjects: Participants' perspectives. *Journal of Medical Ethics*, *26*(2), 126–130. doi:10.1136/jme.26.2.126 PMID:10786324

Russell, M., & Light, L. (2006). Police and victim perspectives on empowerment of domestic violence victims. *Police Quarterly*, *9*(4), 375–396. Advance online publication. doi:10.1177/1098611104264495

Rydstrom, J., & Mustola, K. (2007). *Criminally Queer: Homosexuality and Criminal Law in Scandinavia, 1842-1999*. Aksant Academic Publishers. doi:10.26530/OAPEN_353810

Sacramento, O., & Ribeiro, M. (2014). Mulheres marcadas: prostituicao, ordem e exclusao. *Cuadernos de trabajo social, 27*(1).

Safer Internet Center. (2022). *Estudo sobre competências digitais de adolescentes portugueses indica maior à-vontade em comunicação e interação* [Study on digital skills of Portuguese teenagers indicates greater ease in communication and interaction]. https://www.internetsegura.pt/noticias/estudo-sobre-competencias-digitais-de-adolescentes-portugueses-indica-maior-vontade-em

Salawu, S., He, Y., & Lumsden, J. (2017). Approaches to automated detection of cyberbullying: A survey. *IEEE Transactions on Affective Computing, 11*(1), 3–24. doi:10.1109/TAFFC.2017.2761757

Saldaña, J. (2011). *Fundamentals of qualitative research*. Oxford university press.

Saldaña, J. (2012). *The coding manual for qualitative researchers*. SAGE Publications.

Saleiro, S., Ramalho, N., Menezes, M., & Gato, J. (2022). Estudo nacional sobre as necessidades das pessoas LGBTI e sobre a discriminação em razão da orientação sexual, identidade e expressão de género e características sexuais. Lisboa: Commission for Citizenship and Gender Equality.

Sánchez-Fuentes, M., Santos-Iglesias, P., & Sierra, J. (2014). A systematic review of sexual satisfaction. *International Journal of Clinical and Health Psychology, 14*(1), 67–75. doi:10.1016/S1697-2600(14)70038-9

Sandelowski, M. (1995). Sample size in qualitative research. *Research in Nursing & Health, 18*(2), 179–183. doi:10.1002/nur.4770180211 PMID:7899572

Sándor, B. (2021). *Como Prevenir e Combater a Violência contra Crianças e Jovens LGBTI+ e de Género Diverso*. Academic Press.

Sani, A. I., Coelho, A., & Manita, C. (2018). Intervention in domestic violence situations: Police attitudes and beliefs. *Psychology, Community & Health, 7*(1), 72–86. doi:10.5964/pch.v7i1.247

Sani, A., & Carvalho, C. (2018). Violência Doméstica e Crianças em Risco: Estudo Empírico com Autos da Polícia Portuguesa. *Psicologia: Teoria e Pesquisa (Brasília), 34*(34). Advance online publication. doi:10.1590/0102.3772e34417

Sani, A., & Correia, A. (2019). A intervenção técnica junto de crianças em acolhimento residencial em casa de abrigo para vítimas de violência doméstica. *Revista de Ciências Sociais Configurações, 23*(23), 138–158. doi:10.4000/configuracoes.7214

Sani, A., & Morais, C. (2015). A polícia no apoio às vítimas de violência doméstica: Estudo exploratório com polícias e vítimas [The police in supporting victims of domestic violence: exploratory study with police and victims]. *Direito e Democracia, 16*(1), 5–18.

Sanna, L. (1992). Self-efficacy theory: Implications for social facilitation and social loafing. *Journal of Personality and Social Psychology, 62*(5), 774–786. doi:10.1037/0022-3514.62.5.774

Sansonetti, S. (2016). *Female refugees and asylum seekers: the issue of integration.* Women's Rights & Gender Equality.

Santiago, I. M. F. L., Braz, E. D. C., & do Nascimento, J. B. (2021). Violência e transfobia: vivências de travestis que exercem a prostituição-campina Grande-PB. *Revista Gênero, 22*(1).

Santos, A. C., Esteves, M., & Santos, A. (2020). National analysis on violence against LGBTI+ children: Portugal. Academic Press.

Santos, J. V. T. D. (2002). Microfísica da violência, uma questão social mundial. *Ciência e cultura, 54*(1), 22–24.

Santos, M. L. D. (2013). *Da batalha na calçada ao circuito do prazer: um estudo sobre prostituição masculina no centro de Fortaleza.* Tese de Doutoramento, Universidade Federal do Ceará.

Sapia, M. R. (2018). Refugee women, victims of GBV - which issues for the health care system? A qualitative study. *European Journal of Public Health, 27*(3), 411–419. doi:10.1093/eurpub/cky048.184

Sarah, R. (2013). The narrative turn: interdisciplinary methods and perspectives. *Student Anthropologist, 3*(3), 64-80). DOI: doi:10.1002/j.sda2.20130303.0005

Scarcelli, C. M., Krijnen, T., & Nixon, P. (2021). Sexuality, gender, media. Identity articulations in the contemporary media landscape. *Information Communication and Society, 24*(8), 1063–1072. doi:10.1080/1369118X.2020.1804603

Schafer, J., & Brown, S. (1991). Marijuana and cocaine effect expectancies and drug use patterns. *Journal of Consulting and Clinical Psychology, 59*(4), 558–565. doi:10.1037/0022-006X.59.4.558 PMID:1918560

Scott, J. W. (1995). Gender: A useful category for historical analysis. *Educação e Realidade, 20*(2), 71–99. https://seer.ufrgs.br/index.php/educacaoerealidade/article/download/71721/40667/297572

Sherman, S. G., Park, J. N., Galai, N., Allen, S. T., Huettner, S. S., Silberzahn, B. E., Decker, M. R., Poteat, T. C., & Footer, K. H. (2019). Drivers of HIV infection among cisgender and transgender female sex worker populations in Baltimore City: Results from the SAPPHIRE study. *Journal of Acquired Immune Deficiency Syndromes, 80*(5), 513–521. doi:10.1097/QAI.0000000000001959 PMID:30649029

Shishehgar, S., Gholizadeh, L., DiGiacomo, M., Green, A., & Davidson, P. M. (2017). Health and socio-cultural experiences of refugee women: An integrative review. *Journal of Immigrant and Minority Health, 19*(4), 959–973. doi:10.1007/s10903-016-0379-1 PMID:26976004

Signorelli, M., Taft, A., Gartland, D., Hooker, L., McKee, C., MacMillan, H., Brown, S., & Hegarty, K. (2022). How Valid is the Question of Fear of a Partner in Identifying Intimate Partner Abuse? A Cross-Sectional Analysis of Four Studies. *Journal of Interpersonal Violence, 37*(5–6), 2535–2556. doi:10.1177/0886260520934439 PMID:32646314

Sistema de Segurança Interna (SSI). (2023). *Relatório Anual de Segurança Interna 2022 – RASI.* Sistema de Segurança Interna.

Smith, D. (1982). Sexological aspects of substance use and abuse. *Journal of Psychoactive Drugs, 14*(1-2), 1–3. doi:10.1080/02791072.1982.10471906 PMID:7119933

Smith, W. R., & Torstensson, M. (1997). Gender differences in risk perception and neutralizing fear of crime: Toward resolving the paradoxes. *British Journal of Criminology, 37*(4), 608–634. doi:10.1093/oxfordjournals.bjc.a014201

Smith, W. R., Torstensson, M., & Johansson, K. (2001). Perceived Risk and Fear of Crime: Gender Differences in Contextual Sensitivity. *International Review of Victimology, 8*(2), 159–181. doi:10.1177/026975800100800204

Smyth, J. M. (1998). Written emotional expression: Effect sizes, outcome types, and moderating variables. *Journal of Consulting and Clinical Psychology, 66*(1), 174–184. doi:10.1037/0022-006X.66.1.174 PMID:9489272

Soriano-Moreno, D. R., Saldaña-Cabanillas, D., Vasquez-Yeng, L., Valencia-Huamani, J. A., Alave-Rosas, J. L., & Soriano, A. N. (2022). Discrimination and mental health in the minority sexual population: Cross-sectional analysis of the first peruvian virtual survey. *PLoS One, 17*(6), e0268755. doi:10.1371/journal.pone.0268755 PMID:35657953

Soulignac, R., Waber, L., & Khazaal, Y. (2011). Sexuality and addictions: Narrations for links and meanings. *Sexologies, 20*(2), 100–101. doi:10.1016/j.sexol.2010.06.003

Sousa, E., Neves, S., Ferreira, M., Topa, J., Vieira, C. P., Borges, J., Costa, R., & Lira, A. (2023). Domestic Violence against LGBTI People: Perspectives of Portuguese Education Professionals. *International Journal of Environmental Research and Public Health, 20*(13), 6196. doi:10.3390/ijerph20136196 PMID:37444044

Sousa, J. (2021). (In)Existência de Estereótipos de Gênero na Jurisprudência Portuguesa. *Revista de Gênero. Sexualidade e Direito, 7*(1), 130–150. doi:10.26668/2525-9849/Index_Law_Journals/2021.v7i1.7716

Špatenková, N., & Olecká, I. (2020). Invisible older people: LGBTI+. *Social Pathology & Prevention, 6*(2).

Stacy, A., Newcomb, M., & Bentler, P. (1991). Cognitive motivation and drug use: A 9-year longitudinal study. *Journal of Abnormal Psychology, 100*(4), 502–515. doi:10.1037/0021-843X.100.4.502 PMID:1757664

Stacy, A., Widaman, K., & Marlatt, G. (1990). Expectancy models of alcohol use. *Journal of Personality and Social Psychology, 58*(5), 918–928. doi:10.1037/0022-3514.58.5.918 PMID:2348377

Stalans, L. J., & Lurigio, A. J. (1995). Responding to domestic violence against women. *Crime and Delinquency, 41*(4), 387–398. doi:10.1177/0011128795041004001

Stanko, E. A. (1993). The case of fearful women: Gender, personal safety and fear of crime. *Women & Criminal Justice*, *4*(1), 117–135. doi:10.1300/J012v04n01_06

Stanko, E. A. (1995). Women, Crime, and Fear. *The Annals of the American Academy of Political and Social Science*, *539*(1), 46–58. doi:10.1177/0002716295539001004

Starks, T., Millar, B., Tuck, A., & Wells, B. (2015). The role of sexual expectancies of substance use as a mediator between adult attachment and drug use among gay and bisexual men. *Drug and Alcohol Dependence*, *153*, 187–193. doi:10.1016/j.drugalcdep.2015.05.028 PMID:26051159

Steibelt, E. (2009). The context of gender-based violence for Vietnamese women migrant factory workers in Southern Vietnam. *Gender Asia in*, 217-61. https://publications.iom.int/es/system/files/pdf/gender_and_labour_migration_asia.pdf#page=217

Stenersen, M. R., Thomas, K., & McKee, S. (2022). Police harassment and violence against transgender & gender diverse sex workers in the United States. *Journal of Homosexuality*, 1–13. PMID:36228168

Stephens, B. J., & Sinden, P. G. (2000). Victims' voices: Domestic assault victims' perceptions of police demeanor. *Journal of Interpersonal Violence*, *15*(5), 534–547. doi:10.1177/088626000015005006

Stephenson, V. L., Wickham, B. M., & Capezza, N. M. (2018). Psychological abuse in the context of social media. *Violence and Gender*, *5*(3), 129–134. doi:10.1089/vio.2017.0061

Stonard, K. E. (2020). "Technology was designed for this": Adolescents' perceptions of the role and impact of the use of technology in cyber dating violence. *Computers in Human Behavior*, *105*, 106211. doi:10.1016/j.chb.2019.106211

Stotzer, R. L. (2009). Violence against transgender people: A review of United States data. *Aggression and Violent Behavior*, *14*(3), 170–179. doi:10.1016/j.avb.2009.01.006

Strauss, A., & Corbin, J. (1998). *Basics of Qualitative Research: Techniques and Procedures for Developing Grounded Theory*. Sage Publications.

Strobl, R. (2010). Becoming a Victim. In G. S. Shlomo, P. Knepper, & M. Kett (Eds.), *Internation Handbook Of Victimology* (pp. 3–23). CRC Press Taylor & Francis Group. doi:10.1201/EBK1420085471-c1

Stumpf, J. (2006). The crimmigration crisis: Immigrants, crime, and sovereign power. *The American University Law Review*, *56*(2), 367–419.

Stutterheim, S. E., van Dijk, M., Wang, H., & Jonas, K. J. (2021). The worldwide burden of HIV in transgender individuals: An updated systematic review and meta-analysis. *PLoS One*, *16*(12), e0260063. doi:10.1371/journal.pone.0260063 PMID:34851961

Sulleyman, A. (2017). Twitter temporarily limiting users for abusive behaviour. *Independent*.

Sullivan, C. M., & Cain, D. (2004). Ethical and safety considerations when obtaining information from or about battered women for research purposes. *Journal of Interpersonal Violence*, *19*(5), 603–618. doi:10.1177/0886260504263249 PMID:15104864

Sumnall, H., Beynon, C., Conchie, S., Riley, S., & Cole, J. (2007). An investigation of subjective experiences of sex after alcohol or drug intoxication. *Journal of Psychopharmacology (Oxford, England)*, *21*(5), 525–537. doi:10.1177/0269881106075590 PMID:17446200

Surmiak, A. (2018). Confidentiality in qualitative research involving vulnerable participants: Researchers' perspectives. *FQS*, *19*(3), 1–26.

Symonds, M. (2010). The "Second Injury" to Victims of Violent Acts. *American Journal of Psychoanalysis*, *70*(1), 34–41. doi:10.1057/ajp.2009.38 PMID:20212437

Tavares, I., Laan, E., & Nobre, P. (2017). Cognitive-affective dimensions of female orgasm: The role of automatic thoughts and affect during sexual activity. *Journal of Sexual Medicine*, *14*(6), 818–828. doi:10.1016/j.jsxm.2017.04.004 PMID:28479134

Tavares, M. (2011). *Feminismos - Percursos e Desafios (1947-2007)*. Texto Editores.

Telzer, E. H., Van Hoorn, J., Rogers, C. R., & Do, K. T. (2018). Social influence on positive youth development: A developmental neuroscience perspective. *Advances in Child Development and Behavior*, *54*, 215–258. doi:10.1016/bs.acdb.2017.10.003 PMID:29455864

Teodoro, M. C. M., & Silva, T. C. (2015). A História de Exclusão Social e Condenaçào Moral da Prostituição. *Revista Brasileira de História do Direito*, *1*(1), 208–233. doi:10.26668/IndexLawJournals/2526-009X/2015.v1i1.676

Tewksbury, R. (2011). Qualitative Methodology. In C. D. Bryant (Ed.), *The Routledge Handbook of Deviant Behavior*. Routledge Handbooks Online. doi:10.4324/9780203880548.ch9

The European Parliament. (2016). *Action Plan on the integration of third country nationals*. Communication from the commission to the European Parliament, the Council, the European Economic and Social Committee and the Committee of the Regions.

Thompson, J., Kao, T., & Thomas, R. (2005). The relationship between alcohol use and risk-taking sexual behaviors in a large behavioral study. *Preventive Medicine*, *41*(1), 247–252. doi:10.1016/j.ypmed.2004.11.008 PMID:15917018

Tolman, E. (1932). *Purposive Behavior in Animal and Men*. Appleton – Century – Crofts.

Tomás, C. A., Fernandes, N., Sani, A. I., & Martins, P. C. (2018). A (in)visibilidade das crianças na violência doméstica em Portugal. *SER Social*, *20*(43), 387–410. doi:10.26512/ser_social.v20i43.18867

Tracy, S. J. (2019). *Qualitative research methods: Collecting evidence, crafting analysis, communicating impact*. John Wiley & Sons.

Trautwein, U., Marsh, H., Nagengast, B., Lüdtke, O., Nagy, G., & Jonkmann, K. (2012). Probing for multiplicative term in modern expectancy-value theory: A latent interaction modeling study. *Journal of Educational Psychology*, *104*(3), 763–777. doi:10.1037/a0027470

Triggs, G. (2015). *The forgotten children: National inquiry into children in immigration detention 2014*. Australian Human Rights Commission Sydney.

UMAR. (2019). *Observatório das Mulheres Assassinadas*. UMAR.

UMAR. (2021). *Relatório Anual 2020 (1 de janeiro de 2020 a 31 de dezembro de 2020)*. Observatório de Mulheres Assassinadas. UMAR.

UNESCO. (2016). *Cities welcoming refugees and migrants*. The United Nations Educational, Scientific and Cultural Organization.

UNFPA. (2023). *Violence against women and girls has invaded all spaces, including virtual ones, and this must end*. Retrieved from https://www.unfpa.org/press/violence-against-women-and-girls-has-invaded-all-spaces-including-virtual-ones-and-must-end

UNICEF. (2018). *Child protection from violence, exploitation and abuse*. UNICEF.

United Nations (UN). (2006). *Ending violence against women: from words to action Study of the Secretary-General*. Author.

United Nations Division for the Advancement of Women. (2003). *Sexual Violence and Armed Conflict: United Nations Response. Women 2000 and Beyond and UNDAW*. Author.

United Nations Office on Drugs and Crime (UNODC). (2019). *Global study on homicide: Gender-related killing of women and girls*. Division for Policy Analysis and Public Affairs.

United Nations Women. (2021). *Measuring the Shadow Pandemic: Violence Against Women During Covid-19*. United Nations Women.

United Nations. (1979). *Convenção sobre a Eliminação de todas as Formas de Discriminação Contra as Mulheres*. https://gddc.ministeriopublico.pt/sites/default/files/documentos/instrumentos/convencao_eliminacao_todas_formas_discriminacao_contra_mulheres.pdf

Valibhoy, M. C., Kaplan, I., & Szwarc, J. (2017). It comes down to just how human someone can be: A qualitative study with young people from refugee backgrounds about their experiences of Australian mental health services. *Transcultural Psychiatry*, *54*(1), 23–45. doi:10.1177/1363461516662810 PMID:27550374

Van Hee, C., Jacobs, G., Emmery, C., Desmet, B., Lefever, E., Verhoeven, B., De Pauw, G., Daelemans, W., & Hoste, V. (2018). Automatic detection of cyberbullying in social media text. *PLoS One*, *13*(10), e0203794. doi:10.1371/journal.pone.0203794 PMID:30296299

Van Hoorn, J., McCormick, E. M., & Telzer, E. H. (2018). Moderate social sensitivity in a risky context supports adaptive decision making in adolescence: Evidence from brain and behavior. *Social Cognitive and Affective Neuroscience*, *13*(5), 546–556. doi:10.1093/scan/nsy016 PMID:29529318

Vartabedian, J. (2019). Bodies and desires on the internet: An approach to trans women sex workers' websites. *Sexualities*, *22*(1-2), 224–243. doi:10.1177/1363460717713381

Vogels, E. A., Gelles-Watnick, R., & Massarat, N. (2022). *Teens, social media and technology*. Pew Research Center. https://www.pewresearch.org/internet/2018/05/31/teens-social-media-technology-2018/

Walklate, S. (2006). *Criminology: the basics*. Routledge. doi:10.4324/9780203448212

Walklate, S., Maher, J., McCulloch, J., Fitz-Gibbon, K., & Beavis, K. (2019). Victim stories and victim policy: Is there a case for a narrative Victimology? *Crime, Media, Culture*, *15*(2), 199–215. doi:10.1177/1741659018760105

Wang, C.-W., Musumari, P. M., Techasrivichien, T., Suguimoto, S. P., Chan, C.-C., Ono-Kihara, M., Kihara, M., & Nakayama, T. (2019). "I felt angry, but I couldn't do anything about it": A qualitative study of cyberbullying among Taiwanese high school students. *BMC Public Health*, *19*(1), 1–11. doi:10.1186/s12889-019-7005-9 PMID:31138175

Warr, M. (1984). Fear of Victimization: Why are Women and the Elderly More Affraid? *Social Science Quarterly*, 681–702.

Wemmers, J.-A. (2013). Victims' experiences in the criminal justice system and their recovery from crime. *International Review of Victimology*, *19*(3), 221–233. doi:10.1177/0269758013492755

Westbrook, L., & Saperstein, A. (2015). New categories are not enough: Rethinking the measurement of sex and gender in social surveys. *Gender & Society*, *29*(4), 534–560. doi:10.1177/0891243215584758

West, R. (2013). *EMCDDA Insights, 14. Models of addiction*. Publications Office of the European Union., doi:10.2810/99994

White, S. J., Sin, J., Sweeney, A., Salisbury, T., Wahlich, C., Margarita, C., ... Mantovani, N. (2024). Global Prevalence and Mental Health Outcomes of Intimate Partner Violence Among Women : A Systematic Review and Meta-Analysis. *Trauma, Violence & Abuse*, *25*(1), 494–511. doi:10.1177/15248380231155529 PMID:36825800

WHO. (2021). *Violence against women Prevalence Estimates, 2018. Global, regional and national prevalence estimates for intimate partner violence against women and global and regional prevalence estimates for non-partner sexual violence against women*. WHO.

Williams, E. N., & Morrow, S. L. (2009). Achieving trustworthiness in qualitative research: A pan-paradigmatic perspective. *Psychotherapy Research*, *19*(4-5), 576–582. doi:10.1080/10503300802702113 PMID:19579089

Willie, T. C., & Kershaw, T. S. (2019). An ecological analysis of gender inequality and intimate partner violence in the United States. *Preventive Medicine*, *118*, 257–263. doi:10.1016/j.ypmed.2018.10.019 PMID:30393017

Wilson, G., & Lawson, D. (1976). Expectancies, alcohol, and sexual arousal in male social drinkers. *Journal of Abnormal Psychology, 85*(6), 587–594. doi:10.1037/0021-843X.85.6.587 PMID:993455

Wilson, G., & Lawson, D. (1978). Expectancies, alcohol, and sexual arousal in women. *Journal of Abnormal Psychology, 87*(3), 358–367. doi:10.1037/0021-843X.87.8.358 PMID:681606

Winters, M., Rechel, B., de Jong, L., & Pavlova, M. (2018). A systematic review on the use of healthcare services by undocumented migrants in Europe. *BMC Health Services Research, 18*(1), 1–30. doi:10.1186/s12913-018-2838-y PMID:29347933

World Health Organization. (2019). *The International Classification of Diseases – 11ᵗʰ revision.* WHO.

Yıldız, U., & Sert, D. (2019). Dynamics of mobility-stasis in refugee journeys: Case of resettlement from Turkey to Canada. *Migration Studies*, 1–20. doi:10.1093/migration/mnz005

Yodanis, C. L., Woodhouse, B. B., Warr, M., Smith, W. R., Torstensson, M., Johansson, K., ... Britton, D. M. (2004). Dangerous Places and the Unpredictable Stranger: Constructions of Fear of Crime. *Social Science Quarterly, 33*(2), 209–226.

Yuval-Davis, N. (2006). Intersectionality and Feminist Politics. *European Journal of Women's Studies, 13*(3), 193–209. doi:10.1177/1350506806065752

Zedner, L. (2020). *Reading the crimmigrant other.* Border Criminologies.

Ziems, C., Vigfusson, Y., & Morstatter, F. (2020). Aggressive, repetitive, intentional, visible, and imbalanced: Refining representations for cyberbullying classification. *Proceedings of the International AAAI Conference on Web and Social Media, 14*, 808–819. https://github.com/cjziems/cyberbullying-representations808

About the Contributors

Gabriela Mesquita Borges, PhD in Criminology (2023) from the University of Porto, Portugal, is a dedicated researcher with a profound focus on exploring the intricate dimensions that grant insight into the experiences, inter-subjective narratives, and perspectives of refugee women throughout their life journeys within various geographical and symbolic contexts. Her research delves into three pivotal stages: their country of origin, their displacement journey, and their country of asylum. Her in-depth analysis encompasses an examination of the reception conditions and integration practices within the Portuguese asylum system, all from a gender-informed standpoint. Borges's work is inherently interdisciplinary, drawing from the realms of criminology, victimology, feminist studies, sociology, and law. Her research takes inspiration from the Middle Eastern, African, and European contexts, contributing to a global perspective on these critical issues. In 2023, Borges became a researcher at the Center for Legal, Economic and Environmental Studies (CEJEA) of the University of Lusiada. Also, since 2023, Borges has been a valued collaborating researcher at the Communication and Society Research Centre (CECS), University of Minho, Portugal. Her impressive publication record includes notable contributions, such as book chapters for Springer and IGI Global presses, as well as articles in esteemed journals like The Journal of Qualitative Criminal Justice and Criminology. Throughout her illustrious career, Borges has actively participated in numerous international and national scientific projects, collaborating in diverse capacities. Her research findings have been shared at prestigious conferences in her fields of expertise, where she has also been a sought-after guest speaker. Her exceptional work has fostered productive connections with leading research groups, notably joining COST ACTION CA16111 - International Ethnic and Migrant Minorities' Survey Data Network in 2018. In recognition of her expertise, Borges was invited to contribute to various academic working groups and committees. Her involvement in the European Society of Criminology Working Group on Qualitative Research Methodologies and Epistemologies, since 2018, led to her appointment as a co-chair of this influential working group in 2023. Furthermore, Borges's passion for education and knowledge dissemination shines through her role as a guest lecturer. From 2020 to 2023, she imparted her expertise at the Law Department of the University of Minho, teaching a range of courses at both the undergraduate and master's levels, covering topics such as criminology, sexual crimes, prison and correctional models, diversion and crime prevention, security and policing, sexual criminality, and qualitative research methods. In 2023, she expanded her academic reach by accepting an invitation to lecture at the University of Lusiada Norte, where she teaches subjects such as Introduction to Victimology, Current Victimology, Clinical Criminology, and The intersection of crime and gender discrimination.

Ana Guerreiro has a Ph.D. in Criminology with a FCT Fellowship (Ref.ª SFRH/BD/143202/2019) at FDUP - Faculty of Law of the University of Porto, through the Interdisciplinary Research Centre on Crime, Justice and Security (CJS). She is an Assistant Professor at UMaia - University of Maia and an Invited Assistant Professor at FDUP - School of Criminology, University of Porto. Ana is currently the Director of the Research Unit in Criminology and Behavioral Sciences of the UMaia (UICCC/UMaia), a Full Member at the Interdisciplinary Centre for Gender Studies of the Institute of Social and Political Sciences, University of Lisbon (CIEG-ISCSP, UL), and a Collaborator Researcher at the Centre for Interdisciplinary Research on Justice, University of Porto (CIJ, FDUP). Her main research areas are gender studies, female crime, gender violence, organized and violent crime, criminal networks, sentencing studies, and prevention policies.

Miriam Pina is an Invited Professor at the Faculty of Law of the University of Porto (FDUP) since 2008. She is also a Ph.D student at the École des Sciences Criminelles of the University of Lausanne with a FCT Fellowship (2020.06913.BD), holds a Master's Degree in Criminology and Security from the same University, with honorable mention Summa Cum Laude, and a degree in Psychology, with a specialization in Psychology of Deviant Behavior, from the Faculty of Psychology and Educational Sciences of the University of Porto. Currently, Miriam serves as a teacher and Internship Coordinator for the degree in Criminology at FDUP, Scientific Coordinator of the Advanced Post-University Specialization in Victimology at the Portuguese Institute of Psychology (INSPSIC), and, since 2020, a doctoral fellow at the Foundation for Science and Technology (FCT). In 2021, she published the work "ENTRE DROGUE ET CRIME: CONTIGENCE OR NÉCESSITÉ? Une étude empirique sur les trajectoires d'un groupe de tenus condamnés" and in February 2022, received the Pedagogical Innovation Award from the University of Porto. As a researcher, she has collaborated with the Universities of Porto, Lausanne, and Zurich on several national and international projects, including the Effects of Drug Substitution Programs on Offending among Drug-Addicts Project, which produced the Campbell Collaboration meta-analysis. Currently, she is a Collaborator Researcher of the Center for Interdisciplinary Research on Justice (CIJ, FDUP) and a member of the Council of the School of Criminology (FDUP).

* * *

Beatriz Andrade is a recent graduate in Criminology from the University of Lusiada (Porto, Portugal). With a solid academic background and a thirst for knowledge, she has completed her studies with enthusiasm and dedication. Throughout her undergraduate years, she has engaged in various research projects and coursework, exploring different facets of criminology. As she steps into the professional world, she is eager to apply her skills and contribute to addressing the complex challenges within the field of criminology. With a shared commitment to making a positive impact on society, she is ready to embark on her career journey and embrace the opportunities that lie ahead.

Catarina Capucho Conde is a recent graduate in Criminology from the University of Lusiada (Porto, Portugal). With a solid academic background and a thirst for knowledge, she has completed her studies with enthusiasm and dedication. Throughout her undergraduate years, she has engaged in various research projects and coursework, exploring different facets of criminology. As she steps into the professional world, she is eager to apply her skills and contribute to addressing the complex challenges within the field of criminology. With a shared commitment to making a positive impact on society, she is ready to embark on her career journey and embrace the opportunities that lie ahead.

Sónia Caridade is a Ph.D. in Psychology of Justice. Assistant professor at the School of Psychology at the University of Minho, Portugal, and a researcher at the Psychology Research Center (CIPsi) and Collaborator at the Interdisciplinary Center for Gender Studies (CIEG). Coordinator of the Tech-Violence research group within the Victims, Offenders and Justice System Laboratory of CIPsi-UM. She has a lot of experience in problem behavior and involvement with the justice system. ORCID ID: 0000-0003-0387-7900.

Nathália Castro da Silva holds a Master's degree in Criminology from the Faculty of Law of the University of Porto. She has a Postgraduate in Criminal Sciences and a Bachelor's Degree in Law. She is a Brazilian and Portuguese lawyer. She is a member of the International Association of Portuguese Language Criminology. She has carried out research with migrant women victims of crime and their processes of interaction with criminal police agencies. Her research interests include victimological research using qualitative methodologies, the study of victimised migrant women, the phenomenon of secondary victimisation, intersectional perspectives on data analysis and the development of Narrative Victimology.

Ariana Pinto Correia holds a PhD in Psychology by Porto University, with the thesis Intimate Partner Femicide: Practices, Social Discourses and Media Narratives. Since 2011, has been collaborating with several academical and field projects, under the spectrum of gender violence, focusing on intimate gender violence, domestic violence, intimate partner femicide and social construction of crime. Recognized specialist from Gender Equality and Citizenship Commission in Gender Equality, Domestic Violence and Violence against Women. She is an invited assistant professor in Maia University and coordinated UNi+ Programme, that aims to prevent and fight dating violence among university students. She is also part from the founder commission of Plano i Association, an NGO based in Porto, that promotes human right under an intersectional matrix.

Rita Faria is Assistant Professor of Criminology at the School of Criminology - Faculty of Law of the University of Porto and Head of the only PhD program in Criminology in Portugal. She holds a PhD in Criminology, an MA in Sociology and a Degree in Law. She has been actively researching and publishing on matters such as environmental crimes and Green Criminology, as well as white-collar crime, financial, corporate and occupational crimes. She has experience supervising research about gender in criminology and victimology. She is Editor in Chief of "Criminology in Europe", the European Society of Criminology newsletter, and a Board member of the same society. She is founder and member of the Working Group on Qualitative Research Methodologies and Epistemologies (WG-QRME) - of the European Society of Criminology. In 2023, her research profile was highlighted by Centro Ciência Viva as one of the 101 female Portuguese scientists.

Mafalda Gonçalves Ferreira is a criminologist, with a master's degree in Legal Medicine from the Abel Salazar Institute of Biomedical Sciences – University of Porto (ICBAS) and a PhD in Forensic Sciences from the Faculty of Medicine of the University of Porto (FMUP). She is also the vice-president of the Plano i Association, a collaborating member of the Interdisciplinary Center for Gender Studies (CIEG – ISCSP-ULisboa) and a member of the list of experts recognized by the CIG in the areas of equality between men and women, violence against women and domestic violence, sexual orientation, gender identity and expression and sexual characteristics at birth. She was the executive coordinator of the (INMATES) project – Intimacy(s) and emotions – awareness and intervention for the prevention of gender violence, promotion of gender equality and social diversity in a prison context and of the Gis Center – Center for Responses to LGBTI Populations, as well as a member of the research team of the international project UNI4EQUITY Strengthening Universities Response To Sexual Harassment and trainer in the areas of gender violence, gender equality and LGBTI issues.

Fabiana Gonçalves is a recent graduate in Criminology from the University of Lusiada (Porto, Portugal). With a solid academic background and a thirst for knowledge, she has completed her studies with enthusiasm and dedication. Throughout her undergraduate years, she has engaged in various research projects and coursework, exploring different facets of criminology. As she steps into the professional world, she is eager to apply her skills and contribute to addressing the complex challenges within the field of criminology. With a shared commitment to making a positive impact on society, she is ready to embark on her career journey and embrace the opportunities that lie ahead.

Jorge Garcia is professor at the School of Criminology of the University of Porto, Portugal, and professor at the San Jorge University (USJ), Spain. He is member of the Centro de Investigação Interdisciplinar em Justiça (CIIJ) (Portugal) and collaborates with the Laboratorio de Sociología Jurídica (Spain) .His publications include El maltrato familiar hacia las personas mayores. Un análisis sociojurídico (2012), or "Towards an Inclusive Victimology and a New Understanding of Public Compassion to Victims: From and Beyond Christie's Ideal Victim" (in M. Duggan ed., Revisiting the 'Ideal Victim': Developments in Critical Victimology, 2018).

Camila Iglesias is a dedicated PhD scholar in Criminology at the Faculty of Law of the University of Porto, where she pursues her academic endeavors with a fervent passion for understanding the complexities of crime and justice. Her scholarship is generously funded by the prestigious Foundation for Science and Technology (FCT), under the reference number 2021.06499.BD, reflecting her academic excellence and potential for groundbreaking research contributions. Additionally, Camila serves as a valued researcher at the Interdisciplinary Research Centre on Crime, Justice, and Security (CJS), where she collaborates with esteemed colleagues to explore multifaceted issues within the realm of criminology. With a relentless commitment to advancing knowledge and addressing pressing societal concerns, Camila endeavors to make meaningful contributions to the field of criminology through her scholarly pursuits and research endeavors.

Bárbara Machado is a Master in Forensic Medicine from the University of Porto, Institute of Biomedical Sciences Abel Salazar and a degree in Nursing from the Instituto Politécnico de Saude do Norte Escola Superior de Saúde do Vale do Ave. Attending the Integrated Masters in Integrated Masters in Medicine at) University of Porto Institute of Biomedical Sciences Abel Salazar and a PhD in Public Health from Universidade Nova de Lisboa National School of Public Health. She is a Principal Assistant at Centro Hospitalar do Médio Ave EPE, Guest Assistant at the Escola Superior de Enfermagem do Porto and Guest Assistant at the Instituto Politécnico de Saude do Norte Escola Superior de Saúde do Vale do Ave.

Sofia Neves has a PhD in Social Psychology from the University of Minho, and a Bachelor of Science in Psychology from the same institution. She is an Associate Professor at the University of Maia (UMaia), a researcher at the Interdisciplinary Centre for Gender Studies (CIEG-ISCSP/ULisboa), and President of the Directorate of the Plano i Association. Her research areas, in which she has been coordinating several scientific projects, are domestic and gender-based violence, and discrimination and violence based on sexual orientation and identity and/or gender expression.

Sílvia Maria Rocha Ribeiro completed her Ph.D. in Psychology on June 26, 2019, at the University of Porto Faculty of Psychology and Educational Sciences. She also holds a Master's degree in Clinical, Cognitive-behavioral, and Systemic Psychology, obtained in 2006 from the University of Coimbra Faculty of Psychology and Educational Sciences. Currently, she serves as an Assistant Professor at Universidade Lusíada Porto and holds positions in various institutions, including Administration Regional de Saúde do Norte IP, Instituto Português de Psicologia e Outras Ciências, Sociedade Portuguesa de Sexologia Clínica, and Direção Regional da Educação do Norte. Sílvia is a Clinical Psychologist Sexual Therapist at Clínica da Saúde and is involved in research at Universidade Lusíada Porto's Center for Research in Developmental Psychology. Her academic interests lie in the fields of Psychology and Law, with a focus on Criminology. Sílvia has published one article in specialized journals and her work often revolves around themes such as psychotherapy.

Cynthia Silva is a multifaceted professional with expertise as a criminologist, trainer, and project technician specializing in violence prevention. With a passion for making a difference, she is dedicated to creating safer communities through her work. Cynthia is also an accomplished author, having contributed to both research articles and children's literature, demonstrating her commitment to education and social impact.

Estefânia Gonçalves Silva completed PhD degree in Social Psychology by Universidade do Minho. She is Assistant Professor at ISMAI - Universidade da Maia (University of Maia), where she teaches in the course of Criminology, Psychology and the master's in clinical forensic psychology - Intervention with Aggressors and

Victims, and integrated member at the Interdisciplinary Centre for Gender Studies (CIEG) at the Institute of Social and Political Sciences of the University of Lisbon, Portugal (ISCSP-ULisboa). She is Psychologist, with a specialization in Social, Justice and Community Psychology according to the Portuguese Psychologists Association and specialist recognized in Gender Equality, Gender Violence and Migrations by the Commission for Citizenship and Gender Equality (CIG). She is a certified trainer for the Scientific Pedagogical Council for Continuing Education and author of several publications and oral communications in national and international courses and conferences. Her research is mainly focused on gender, migrations, gender violence, work-family-balance.Currently, she is the Principal Investigator of the project "Boomerang - Study on the perceptions of the economic impact of unequal sharing of unpaid work in the lives of immigrant women and men in Portugal", financed by EEA - European Economic Area grants. The aim of the project is to characterize the perceptions of the economic impact of unequal sharing of unpaid work and divorce in the lives of immigrant women and men in Portugal.

Joana Topa has a PhD in Social Psychology (2013) from the University of Minho, a Master's in Clinical and Health Psychology (2009) and a degree in Psychology (2004) from the University Institute of Maia. She has been an Assistant Professor at the University of Maia since 2010, where she teaches in Criminology Degree and Master's Degree, Psychology Degree and in Master's Degree in Forensic Clinical Psychology - Intervention with Aggressors and Victims. Furthermore, she is an integrated researcher at the Interdisciplinary Centre for Gender Studies (CIEG - Instituto Superior de Ciências Sociais e Políticas, University of Lisbon) and a collaborating researcher at the Psychology Centre of the University of Porto, and at the Criminology and Behavioural Sciences Research Unit of the University of Maia (UICCC/UMAIA). Her main areas of research are gender studies, migration, health, gender violence, diversity, social inequalities and multiple discrimination. More recently, she has focussed on issues such as criminal recidivism, racism and citizenship.

Joana Torres earned her PhD in Criminology from the Faculty of Law at the University of Porto, where she led research funded by the Foundation for Science and Technology. Her research, titled "Political and Institutional Analysis of the Implementation of the Istanbul Convention in Portugal: Focusing on Intimate Partner Violence," delved into critical societal issues. She holds a Bachelor's degree in Criminology (2012) and a Master's degree in Psychology of Justice (2014) from the University Institute of Maia, along with another Bachelor's degree in Psychology (2016). Additionally, she holds a postgraduate degree in Human Rights from the University of Coimbra and is currently pursuing a Master's degree in Public

Health at the National School of Public Health. As an esteemed educator, Joana serves as a lecturer in both undergraduate and graduate programs in Criminology at the University of Maia and Fernando Pessoa University. Her expertise extends across various disciplines, including Victimology, Juvenile Delinquency, Forensic Evaluation Concepts, Public Opinion and Criminal Justice, and Criminology and Comparative Culture. Over the years, she has contributed significantly to numerous research centers and groups, collaborating with institutions such as CJS-FDUP, UICCC/ISMAI, and the Dating Violence Observatory.

Index

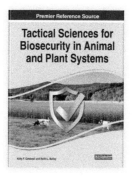

 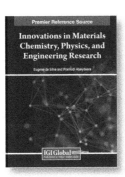 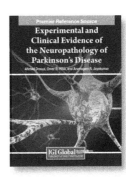 

Submit an Open Access Book Proposal

Have Your Work Fully & Freely Available Worldwide After Publication

Seeking the Following Book Classification Types:

Authored & Edited Monographs • Casebooks • Encyclopedias • Handbooks of Research

Gold, Platinum, & Retrospective OA Opportunities to Choose From

Easily Track Your Work in Our Advanced Manuscript Submission System With **Rapid Turnaround Times**

Double-Blind Peer Review by Notable Editorial Boards (*Committee on Publication Ethics* (COPE) Certified

Publications Adhere to All **Current OA Mandates & Compliances**

Affordable APCs *(Often 50% Lower Than the Industry Average)* Including Robust Editorial Service Provisions

Direct Connections with **Prominent Research Funders** & OA Regulatory Groups

Institution Level OA Agreements Available (Recommend or Contact Your Librarian for Details)

Join a **Diverse Community of 150,000+ Researchers Worldwide** Publishing With IGI Global

Content Spread Widely to Leading Repositories (AGOSR, ResearchGate, CORE, & More)

Premier Reference Source

Food Sustainability, Environmental Awareness, and Adaptation and Mitigation Strategies for Developing Countries

Premier Reference Source

New Models of Higher Education
Unbundled, Rebundled, Customized, and DIY

Handbook of Research on

The Global View of Open Access and Scholarly Communications

Retrospective Open Access Publishing

You Can Unlock Your Recently Published Work, Including Full Book & Individual Chapter Content to Enjoy All the Benefits of Open Access Publishing

Learn More

Milton Keynes UK
Ingram Content Group UK Ltd.
UKHW021107270324
440147UK00007B/191